Use and Abuse
of
America's Natural Resources

Use and Abuse
of
America's Natural Resources

Advisory Editor

STUART BRUCHEY
Allan Nevins Professor of American
Economic History, Columbia University

Associate Editor

ELEANOR BRUCHEY

ROMANCE
OF THE NATIONAL PARKS

BY

HARLEAN JAMES

ARNO PRESS
A NEW YORK TIMES COMPANY
New York • 1972

Use and Abuse of America's Natural Resources
ISBN for complete set: 0-405-04500-X
See last pages of this volume for titles.

Manufactured in the United States of America

————————————

Library of Congress Cataloging in Publication Data

James, Harlean, 1877–
    Romance of the national parks.

    (Use and abuse of America's natural resources)
    1. National parks and reserves––United States.
I. Title. II. Series.
E160.J25 1972   333.7'8'0973   72-2847
ISBN 0-405-04513-1

ROMANCE
OF THE NATIONAL PARKS

Photograph—Department of the Interior

Courtesy—Portfolio, American Planning and Civic Association

MARIPOSA GROVE OF REDWOODS IN YOSEMITE

ROMANCE
OF THE NATIONAL PARKS

BY

HARLEAN JAMES
EXECUTIVE SECRETARY, AMERICAN PLANNING AND CIVIC ASSOCIATION

NEW YORK
THE MACMILLAN COMPANY
1939

Mount Pleasant Press
HARRISBURG, PENNSYLVANIA

To

J. HORACE McFARLAND

WHO, AS PRESIDENT OF THE AMERICAN CIVIC ASSOCI-
ATION, ACTIVELY PROMOTED PUBLIC EDUCATION IN
NATIONAL PARK POSSIBILITIES, AND FIRST PROPOSED
A NATIONAL PARK SYSTEM

WHO FOR THIRTY YEARS HAS JOINED IN DEFENDING
THE NATIONAL PARKS AGAINST SELFISH AGGRESSION

AND

WHO HAS NEVER BEEN FOUND WANTING WHEN
THE NATIONAL PARKS NEEDED A FRIEND

FOREWORD

I HAVE had the good fortune to be intimately connected with national parks ever since I first went to Washington in 1913 as a member of the staff of Franklin K. Lane, Secretary of the Interior. I had the privilege of assisting at the birth of the National Park Service, which I served for seventeen years.

Only one who is thoroughly familiar with the inside history of the national parks can appreciate how faithfully Miss James has translated to the public the trend of Congressional legislation during the past sixty years, and the significance of the development of the National Park Service under the guidance and with the support of succeeding Secretaries of the Interior.

We have in national parks today a widely recognized form of land-use which includes recreation, inspiration and education, and which rules out certain conflicting uses appropriate in a multiple-use program applied to other lands. Miss James shows clearly that the National Park System is built upon this recognition.

When I resigned from the Directorship of the National Park Service to enter the business field, I was very glad to accept the invitation of the American Civic Association to become a member of its Executive Board, for I was thoroughly familiar with the active part that Dr. J. Horace McFarland, its President for twenty years, had played in the educational campaign leading to the establishment of the National Park Service. When I was invited in 1937 to become President of the American Planning and Civic Association, to succeed the Honorable Frederic A. Delano, who then became Chairman of the Board, I was proud thus to become the successor of Mr. Delano and Dr. McFarland, and to aid in giving continuing coöperation to the Department of the Interior for the protection of national park ideals and for the defense of national park areas from destructive adverse uses.

For eighteen years, in association with three presidents, Miss James has served the American Civic Association and its successor, the American Planning and Civic Association. During these years millions of American citizens have visited national parks and have become familiar with them. Miss James not only traces the past

FOREWORD

history and present service of national parks and monuments; she looks into the future and shows what may be accomplished to guarantee to this and future generations the effective preservation of adequate national parks which meet the high standards developed by Congress and the Department of the Interior.

Thus, the pages which follow do read as romance to me. I can bear testimony to the accuracy and spirit of what Miss James has written, and I commend to the reading public the perusal of this book on the "Romance of the National Parks."

HORACE M. ALBRIGHT

New York, April, 1939

PREFACE

THE purpose of this book has been to bring together in brief form the history of the movement which led to the creation of national parks and to outline the development of the system. The legislation of Congress and the administration of national parks by the Department of the Interior have contributed to a substantially consistent policy which recognizes national parks as a definite and separate form of land-use.

The space devoted to the different parks and monuments is in no wise a measure of their importance and interest. Certain parks have achieved significance because of the part they have played in the development of the national park idea.

No attempt has been made to present all of the functions of the National Park Service, or to outline all of the additional services rendered during the recent emergency years. Not all of the areas administered by the Service have been mentioned, as the mere catalogue of these is so long that it would make tedious reading. There is, however, on pages 234–5, a map which presents a comprehensive picture of the National Park Service Areas and Projects.

Acknowledgments are made to Dr. Harold C. Bryant, of the National Park Service, for aid in finding source material; to Horace M. Albright, former Director of the Service and now President of the American Planning and Civic Association; to Arno B. Cammerer, Director, Arthur E. Demaray, Associate Director, and George L. Collins, all of the Park Service; to Mrs. Edward R. Padgett, Editor of *Planning and Civic Comment* and to Mrs. Charles W. Williams, of the staff of the American Planning and Civic Association, who read the manuscript and made valuable suggestions; to the many park rangers who all unknowingly and anonymously contributed to the making of this book; to the American Forestry Association, Sierra Club, Appalachian Mountain Club, American Society of Landscape Architects, and the American Planning and Civic Association, all of which organizations furnished plates for the illustrations.

The author is grateful for the opportunity to consult and quote from the John Muir books, the bulletins issued by the National

PREFACE

Park Service, and the many other publications on which she drew heavily in order to bring together the heterogeneous types of material included in the narrative.

It is hoped that those who read the volume may be influenced to visit the parks, and find there inspiration and understanding of the great forces which created them. To become acquainted with the National Park Service field men in the gray-green uniforms is an experience worth remembering. These men are the interpreters of the parks to the public.

If those who visit the national parks and monuments find in this volume the impulse to penetrate beyond the paved highways, and to find in them something of the rest, recreation and knowledge which is there for the taking, the author will feel that in some small measure the book is justified.

But for Dr. J. Horace McFarland this book would never have been written. He suggested the preparation of the manuscript. He helped to make part of the history recorded in it.

HARLEAN JAMES

Washington, D. C., April, 1939

CONTENTS

BOOK I—HISTORY

CONTENTS

BOOK II—JOURNEYS

ILLUSTRATIONS

[xiii]

ILLUSTRATIONS

Romance of the National Parks

BOOK I—HISTORY

"NATIONAL PARK" LANGFORD

"There ought to be no private ownership in any portion of that region (the Yellowstone), but the whole of it ought to be set aside as a great National Park."

—Cornelius Hedges, quoted in Langford's Diary of the
Washburn-Doane-Langford Expedition, September 20, 1870.

FOR many centuries, although a comparatively new creation geologically speaking, the Yellowstone country existed unseen, unnamed, in the heart of a continent unknown to the civilized peoples of the world. Any prehistoric occupancy of the area which may have existed certainly left no scars of use and no tradition among the Indians. Jurisdiction to the great Northwest Territory came with the Louisiana Purchase, but there existed little knowledge of the vast domain on the part of either the seller or the buyer. The Lewis and Clark Expedition, authorized by President Jefferson to explore and hold for the young Republic the great country acquired from the French, passed within fifty miles of the present Yellowstone National Park, but from the Indians at Mandan, where they spent the winter, they heard nothing of the fabulous headwaters of the Yellowstone. Whether this was due to ignorance or to reticence in mentioning what may have seemed to them manifestations of the Evil Spirit is not known. The Blackfeet, Crow, and Shoshone Indians who hunted, trapped, and fished in what we now know as Montana, Idaho, and Wyoming, probably penetrated the park on occasion, but generally avoided the region, perhaps because of its inaccessibility and its short season free from snow and bitter weather, but possibly because the boiling cauldrons and the spurting jets of steam appeared to them, like the thunder and lightning, as exhibitions of the wrath and power of the gods. The early Indian guides who entered with various exploration parties seemed unfamiliar with the terrain, but their exclamations indicated that to them the geysers and springs and paint pots were thoroughly *bad*.

The only Indians known to live in the Yellowstone country were the Sheepeaters, a tribe of small, poor, and peaceful Indians who had little property in the way of horses, clothing or permanent abodes. For food they had the mountain sheep, and they fashioned primitive utensils and weapons from obsidian.

Today the Indians no longer roam the plains. They live stodgily in the reservations which have been grudgingly granted them by the white man. They eat food from the white man's tin cans. No longer are obsidian spearpoints and utensils of any use. The Indians adopted the white man's weapons, and with firearms they have united with the white man to exterminate to a pitiful protected remnant the bison which once furnished them meat and excitement. And so we inherit the beauty of Obsidian Cliff, seen by thousands of tourists every summer in Yellowstone National Park, and no doubt worth more in revenue as an object of natural art than it ever was as an obsidian quarry.

Though Lewis and Clark missed the Yellowstone and all of its wonders, John Colter, one of their party, turned back and came into the country in 1807, probably the first white man to enter its sacred precincts. But Colter's tales seemed so "tall" to those who heard them that the country came to be known as "Colter's Hell" —a mirage in reverse action, as it were. Discredited as were his "romances" about what he had seen, he did in 1810 furnish important information for the map of the Lewis and Clark Expedition, then in course of preparation. His route of 1807, which revealed the Teton Mountains, Jackson's Hole, the source of the Snake River, the Yellowstone Lake and River, proved of much more importance to posterity than the more spectacular escape from the Indians once depicted so commonly in the geography and history books.

Except for a few trappers during the heyday of the half century which saw the exploitation of the wild fur-bearing animals in America, the Yellowstone remained uncontaminated by man. Serenely its craggy mountains lifted their peaks skyward, covered with soft blankets of snow for most of the year, their slopes strewn with bright blossoms during the short, mild summers. High on the Great Divide the headwaters of the Snake and Yellowstone trickled in little nearby rills, one toward the Gulf of Mexico and the Atlantic, the other to the Colorado and the Pacific. And nestling on the east side of the Divide were the blue waters of Lake Yellowstone, with its irregular forested shores, less than five miles from Shoshone, Lewis, and Heart Lakes, yet unnamed, on the other side of the

Divide. The brightly colored yellow stone canyon and falls, though unknown to the great American public, had an Indian name which was first translated into French and then into English, Yellow Rock or Yellow Stone. The hot springs boiled, the paint-pots bubbled, and the geysers spouted steam with none to observe. The lovely colors of the pools and the intricately fragile deposits formed and reformed, their secret beauty unseen and unheralded.

The land of enchantment seemed to hold its own protection. Its marvels were shunned by the belligerent tribes of the surrounding country; the lowly Sheepeaters seemed hardly conscious of the marvels which were near them. They left the country as they found it. The trappers caught abundant beaver and other fur-bearing animals on the plains at lower altitudes where they could set their traps in winter, when the fur was at its best. Even the gold rush to California in '49 brought no travelers into the high Yellowstone country. The wagon routes lay north or south of this seemingly impenetrable mass of mountains. In time, mining developed in Montana and other nearby States, but there was little prospecting in these snow-mantled mountains at the crest of the continent.

About the time that persistent rumors concerning the marvels of the Yellowstone might have stimulated exploration, the Civil War, which almost rent the Union in twain, came along and utilized on one side or the other all the bold spirits who might otherwise have organized expeditions into this strange country.

Although Captain Raynolds, of the Corps of Topographical Engineers, U. S. A., had, in the company of Bridger, skirted the high Yellowstone country in 1859, his report was not issued until after the close of the Civil War. In September of 1869, Messrs. Folsom, Cook and Peterson, although they failed to secure a military escort, set out to discover what actually did lie in the upper Yellowstone country. They threaded the Missouri River to Three Forks, then went by way of Bozeman and Fort Ellis to the Yellowstone, and along that river to the falls and to the lake. They crossed the mountains to Shoshone Lake and finally reached the Lower Geyser Basin. They saw the Fountain Geyser, traveled along the Firehole River to Excelsior Geyser and Prismatic Lake. Mr. Folsom wrote an account of the trip which was published in July, 1871, in the *Western Monthly* of Chicago.

The most famous and significant expedition into the Yellowstone was the Washburn-Doane-Langford party, which made the pack-train trip in 1870. Not only did the members of this expedition see the principal features of the Yellowstone high country, but they left ample records of what they saw, and they came home with a new idea, an idea which was to create a new form of land-use in the United States.

There were nine civilian members of the party, including General Henry D. Washburn, surveyor general of Montana, who had served in the Civil War; Judge Cornelius Hedges, a distinguished member of the Montana bar; Samuel T. Hauser, a civil engineer and president of the First National Bank of Helena, afterwards Governor of Montana; Walter Trumbull, assistant assessor of internal revenue, and a son of United States Senator Lyman Trumbull of Illinois; Truman Everts, assessor of internal revenue for Montana, and Nathaniel P. Langford, who was collector of internal revenue for Montana, and who was designated as the official diarist of the trip. General Washburn was chosen captain of the party. A military escort from Fort Ellis was furnished on the order of Major General Hancock. General Chittenden, in his book published in 1895, stated that General Sheridan, who passed through Helena prior to his departure for the scene of the Franco-Prussian War, "spent some time in arranging for a military escort to accompany the party." In spite of the fact that nearly all of the men under Major Baker were in the field fighting Indians, Langford recorded that five men under the command of Lieutenant Gustavus C. Doane of the Second U. S. Cavalry were detailed, and "we are satisfied." As finally organized, there were nine civilians, six soldiers, two packers, two cooks, and thirty-five horses and mules.

Langford has given us an intensely human account of the day-by-day doings of the party, but the official report of Lieutenant Doane, which was transmitted by Secretary of War Belknap to the Committee of Territories of the United States Senate and published as Senate Document No. 51, 41st Congress, third session, contains the most complete, detailed, and penetrating descriptions to be found.

On the sixth day out, the party came to Tower Fall, where, Lieutenant Doane wrote: "A view from the summit of one of (the rock) spires is exceedingly beautiful; the clear icy stream plunges from a brink 100 feet beneath to the bottom of the chasm, over

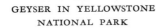

GEYSER IN YELLOWSTONE NATIONAL PARK

Photograph—J. E. Haynes
Courtesy—Portfolio, American Planning
and Civic Association

A WAYSIDE EXHIBIT IN YELLOW-STONE, SHOWING HOW OBSIDIAN CLIFF WAS FORMED

Photograph—Department of the Interior

[5]

TWO VIEWS OF OLD FAITHFUL, YELLOWSTONE NATIONAL PARK

Photographs—Department of the Interior   Courtesy—Portfolio, American Planning and Civic Association

200 feet below, and thence rushes through the narrow gorge, tumbling over boulders and tree trunks fallen in the channel. The sides of the chasm are worn away into caverns lined with variously tinted mosses, nourished by clouds of spray which rise from the cataract; while above, and to the left, a spur from the great plateau rises above all, with a perpendicular front of 400 feet. . . . Nothing can be more chastely beautiful than this lovely cascade, hidden away in the dim light of overshadowing rocks and woods, its very voice hushed to a low murmur, unheard at the distance of a few hundred yards."

On the eighth day they came in sight of the Grand Canyon of the Yellowstone, "its perpendicular sides, wherever visible, of . . . yellow sulphuric tint . . . and its crest on either side of the river, mantled with heavy timber, extending beyond in an unbroken forest as far as the eye could reach." From here they saw their first column of steam, "rising from a dense woods to the height of several hundred feet."

At this point Lieutenant Doane confessed surprise and amazement. "We had all heard fabulous stories of this region, and were somewhat skeptical of appearances." After the trip was over Cornelius Hedges remarked, "I think a more confirmed set of skeptics never went out into the wilderness than those who composed our party, and never was a party more completely surprised and captivated with the wonders of nature."

But in the next few days of exploration when they saw so many remarkable sights, they were awed by the Falls and the Canyon of the Yellowstone as a superb spectacle. Said Lieutenant Doane: "Both of these cataracts (Upper and Lower Falls) deserve to be ranked among the great waterfalls of the continent. . . . Every cascade has a language and an idea peculiarly its own, embodied, as it were, in the flow of the waters. Thus the impression on the mind conveyed by Niagara may be summed up as 'Overwhelming power'; of the Yosemite, as 'Altitude'; of the Shoshone Fall, in the midst of the desert, as 'Going to waste.' (Alas! No longer going to waste since the power development displaced its beauty.) So the upper fall of the Yellowstone may be said to embody the idea of 'Momentum,' and the lower fall 'Gravitation.' In scenic beauty, the upper cataract fall excels the lower. It has life, animation, while the lower one simply follows its channel; both, how-

[7]

ever, are eclipsed, as it were, by the singular wonders of the mighty canyon below. This deepens rapidly; the stream flowing over rapids continually."

The ground on the brink rises also to the foot of Mt. Washburn, an eminence named for General Washburn, as, according to Cornelius Hedges, "he was the first to climb its bare, bald summit, and thence reported to us the welcome news that he saw the beautiful lake that had been the proposed object of our journey."

From then on, the expedition saw and perforce had to believe the unbelievable. Day after day, the climax of the marvels seen the day before reached new heights of beauty and of incomprehensibility. They were all practical men, living under practical frontier conditions. They had to accept the evidences of their senses. Fortunately, too, more than one of the number proved to be apperceptive to natural beauty and to possess the soul of a poet.

Curiously enough, even from these distinguished gentlemen of undoubted standing, the facts seemed too fabulous for the American public to accept. Dr. Holland, the editor of *Scribner's* (later *Century*) *Magazine*, sent to Mr. Langford a number of uncomplimentary criticisms of his articles in the May and June issues of 1871.

One reviewer said: "This Langford must be the champion liar of the Northwest." Langford confessed to a feeling of satisfaction when a letter was published later in the summer, written by a member of the U. S. Geological Survey, containing the words: "Langford did not dare tell one-half of what he saw."

Langford paid his respects to the falls and the canyon. The stupendous scene had on him a profound emotional effect. He wrote in his Diary: "The scenery surrounding the canyon and falls on both banks of the Yellowstone is enlivened by all the hues of abundant vegetation. The foothills approach the river, crowned with a vesture of evergreen pines. Meadows verdant with grasses and shrubbery stretch away to the base of the distant mountains, which, rolling into ridges, rising into peaks, and breaking into chains, are defined in the deepest blue upon the horizon. To render the scene still more imposing, remarkable volcanic deposits, wonderful boiling springs, jets of heated vapor, large collections of sulphur, immense rocks and petrifications abound in great profusion in this immediate vicinity. The river is filled with trout, and bear, elk, deer, mountain lions and lesser game roam the plains, forests and mountain fastnesses.

"The two grand falls of the Yellowstone form a fitting completion to this stupendous climax of wonders. They impart life, power, light and majesty to an assemblage of elements, which without them would be the most gloomy and horrible solitude in nature. Their eternal anthem, echoing from canyon, mountain, rock and woodland, thrills you with delight, and you gaze with rapture at the iris-crowned curtains of fleecy foam as they plunge into gulfs enveloped in mist and spray. The stillness which held your senses spellbound, as you peered into the dismal depths of the canyon below, is now broken by the uproar of waters; the terror it inspired is superseded by admiration and astonishment, and the scene, late so painful from its silence and gloom, is now animate with joy and revelry."

The descriptions of the springs, geysers and other marvels were given in great detail. Lieutenant Doane presented workmanlike word pictures of all that they saw. Langford must have written late each night after the day's explorations. According to Langford's entry on September 1: "Six miles above the upper fall we entered upon a region remarkable for the number and variety of its hot springs and craters. The principal spring, and the one that first meets the eye as you approach from the north, is a hot sulphur spring, of oval shape, the water of which is constantly boiling and is thrown up to a height of from three to seven feet. . . . Farther along the base of this mountain is a sulphurous cavern about twenty feet deep, and seven or eight feet in diameter at its mouth, out of which the steam is thrown in jets with a sound resembling the puffing of a steamboat when laboring over a sandbar, and with as much uniformity and intonation as if emitted by a high-pressure engine. From hundreds of fissures in the adjoining mountain from base to summit, issue hot sulphur vapors, the apertures through which they escape being encased in thick incrustations of sulphur. . . . . There are nearby a number of small sulphur springs. . . . .

"About one hundred yards from these springs is a large hot spring of irregular shape, but averaging forty feet long by twenty-five wide, the water of which is a dark muddy color. Still farther on are twenty or thirty springs of boiling mud of different degrees of consistency and color. . . . The mud in these springs is in most cases a little thinner than mortar prepared for plastering, and, as it is thrown up from one to two feet, I can liken its appearance to nothing so much as Indian meal hasty pudding when the process of boiling is nearly completed, except that the puffing, bloated bubbles are greatly magnified, being from a few inches to two feet in diameter. In some of the springs the mud is of a dark brown color, in others nearly pink, and in one it was almost yellow. . . .

"All of these springs are embraced within a circle the radius of which is from a thousand to twelve hundred feet, and the whole of this surface seems to be a smothered crater covered over with an incrustation of sufficient strength and thickness to bear usually a very heavy weight, but which in several instances yielded and even broke through under the weight of our horses as we rode over it. . . . Under the whole of this incrustation the hottest fire seemed to be raging, and the heat issuing from the vents or from the crevices caused from the breaking in of the surface is too intense to be borne by the gloved hand for an instant."

Even in the midst of the incredible performances in the basins, Langford found words of admiration for Yellowstone Lake. Said he: "Yellowstone Lake, as seen from our camp tonight (September 3, 1870), seems to me to be the most beautiful body of water in the world. In front of our camp it has a wide sandy beach like that of the ocean, which extends for miles and as far as the eye can reach, save that occasionally there is to be found a sharp projection of rocks. The overlooking bench rises from the water's edge about eight feet, forming a bank of sand or natural levee, which serves to prevent the overflow of the land adjoining, which, when the lake is receiving the water from the mountain streams that empty into it while the snows are melting, is several feet below the surface of the lake. . . . From our camp we can see several islands from five to ten miles distant in a direct line. Two of the three 'Tetons,' which are so plainly visible to travelers going to Montana from Eagle Rock bridge on Snake River, and which are such well known and prominent landmarks on that stage route, we notice tonight."

Along the Yellowstone River the party had followed Indian and game trails for the most part, but when they struck out to follow the borders of the lake around the south side they were obliged to find their way through forests where the down timber had never been cleared—and never is a long time! On the 7th of September

Langford and Doane went on a scouting tour to determine the best line of travel to follow in passing around the lake. Langford remarked in his Diary: "There is just enough excitement attending these scouting expeditions to make them a real pleasure, overbalancing the labor attendant upon them. There is very little probability that any large band of Indians will be met with on this side of the lake, owing to the superstitions which originate in the volcanic forces here found."

He climbed a mountain where he thought "the view from the summit of this mountain, for wild and rugged grandeur, is surpassed by none I ever before saw. The Yellowstone basin and the Wind River mountains were spread out before us like a map. On the south the eye followed the source of the Yellowstone above the lake, until, twenty-five miles away, it was lost in an immense canyon, beyond which two immense jets of vapor rose to a height of probably three hundred feet, indicating that there were other and perhaps greater wonders than those embraced in our prescribed limit of exploration. On the north the outlet of the lake and the steam from the mud geyser and mud volcano were distinctly visible, while on the southeast the view followed to the horizon a succession of lofty peaks and ridges at least thirty miles in width, whose jagged slopes were filled with yawning caverns, pine-embowered recesses and beetling precipices, some hundreds and some thousands of feet in height. This is the range which Captain Raynolds, approaching from the east, found impassable while on his exploring tour to the Yellowstone in the year 1860. . . .

"The valley at the base of this range was dotted with small lakes. Lakes abound everywhere—in the valleys, on the mountains and further down on their slopes at all elevations. . . .

"This range of mountains has a marvelous history. As it is the loftiest, so it is probably the most remarkable lateral ridge of the Rocky range. In the expedition sent across the continent by Mr. Astor, in 1811, under command of Captain Wilson P. Hunt, that gentleman met with the first serious obstacle to his progress at the eastern base of this range. After numerous efforts to scale it, he turned away and followed the valley of Snake River, encountering the most discouraging disasters until he arrived at Astoria. . . . I have read somewhere . . . that the Indians regard this ridge of mountains as the crest of the world, and that among the Blackfeet there is a fable that he who attains its summit catches a view of the 'Land of Souls' and beholds the 'Happy Hunting Grounds' spread out below him, brightening with the abodes of the free and generous spirits.''

The next day the party zigzagged over fallen timber—''a terrible day for both men and horses.'' It was while traversing this trackless forest, with the attendant difficulties of urging on the pack train and extricating the horses when wedged between trees, requiring re-adjustment of the packs, that Mr. Everts became separated from the party for thirty-seven days of peril until he was rescued by a scouting party some time after the return of the expedition. After vain searching and delay until provisions began to run short, the expedition pushed on around the thumb of the lake to the Upper and Lower Geyser Basins on the Firehole River. They came upon and named Old Faithful, then, as now, erupting steam and hot water at regular intervals. In announcing the start on the 16th of September for the search of the Firehole basin, Mr. Langford remarked: ''Our journey around Yellowstone Lake in close proximity to the beach is doubtless the first ever attempted; and, although it has been attended with difficulty and distress, these have been to me as nothing compared with the enjoyment the journey has afforded, and it is with the greatest regret that I turn my face from it home-wards.''

But the form of the future was not yet quite cast. Langford re-marked on the evening of the 16th in his Diary, concerning the lake: ''It is dotted with islands of great beauty, as yet unvisited by man, but which at no remote period will be adorned with villas and the ornaments of civilized life. The winds from the mountain gorges roll its placid waters into a furious sea, and crest its billows with foam. Forests of pine, deep, dark and almost impenetrable, are scattered at random along its banks, and its beautiful margin pre-sents every variety of sand and pebbly beach, glittering with crystals, carnelians and chalcedony. . . . . It possesses adaptabilities for the highest display of artificial culture, amid the greatest wonders of Nature that the world affords, and is beautified by the grandeur of the most extensive mountain scenery, and not many years can elapse before the march of civil improvement will reclaim this delightful solitude, and garnish it with all the attractions of cultivated taste and refinement.''

Twice they crossed the main divide and encountered snow, and what with the loss of one of their number, short rations and the accumulated fatigue of the journey, the members of the expedition were low in their minds. Imagine their revivification when they came upon Old Faithful and the many other geysers and springs which they named. Many of these names survive to the present day. Langford commented: "The water in some of the springs presents to the eye the colors of all the precious gems known to commerce. In one spring the hue is like that of an emerald, in another like that of a turquoise, another has the ultramarine hue of the sapphire, another has the color of the topaz; and the suggestion has been made that the names of these jewels may very properly be given to many of these springs."

But now the form of the future was to be cast. On Tuesday, September 20, Langford recorded in his Diary: "Last night, and also this morning in camp, the entire party had a rather unusual discussion. The proposition was made by some member that we utilize the result of our exploration by taking up quarter sections of land at the most prominent points of interest, and a general discussion followed. One member of our party suggested that if there could be secured by pre-emption a good title to two or three quarter sections of land opposite the lower fall of the Yellowstone and extending down the river along the canyon, they would eventually become a source of great profit to the owners. Another member of the party thought that it would be more desirable to take up a quarter section of land at the Upper Geyser Basin, for the reason that that locality could be more easily reached by tourists and pleasure seekers. A third suggestion was that each member of the party pre-empt a claim, and in order that no one should have an advantage over the others, the whole should be thrown into a common pool for the benefit of the entire party.

"Mr. Hedges then said that he did not approve of any of these plans—that there ought to be no private ownership of any portion of that region, but that the whole of it ought to be set apart as a great National Park, and that each one of us ought to make an effort to have this accomplished. His suggestion met with an instantaneous and favorable response from all—except one—of the members of our party, and each hour since the matter was first broached, our enthusiasm has increased. It has been the main theme of our conversation today as we journeyed. I lay awake half of last night thinking about it;—and if my wakefulness deprived my bedfellow (Hedges) of any sleep, he has only himself and his disturbing national-park proposition to answer for it.

"Our purpose to create a park can only be accomplished by untiring work and concerted action in a warfare against the incredulity and unbelief of our national legislators when our proposal shall be presented for their approval. Nevertheless, I believe we can win the battle.

"I do not know of any portion of our country where a national park can be established furnishing to visitors more wonderful attractions than here. These wonders are so different from anything we have ever seen—they are so various, so extensive—that the feeling in my mind from the moment they began to appear until we left them has been one of intense surprise and of incredulity. Every day spent in surveying them has revealed to me some new beauty, and now that I have left them, I begin to feel a skepticism which clothes them in a memory clouded by doubt."

Langford closed his Diary with an entry on September 27 at Helena, Montana: "My narrations have excited great wonder, and I cannot resist the conviction that many of my auditors believe that I have 'drawn a long bow' in my descriptions. I am perfectly free to acknowledge that this does not surprise me. It seems a most natural thing for them to do so; for, in the midst of my narrations, I find myself almost as ready to doubt the reality of the scenes I have attempted to describe as the most skeptical of my listeners. They pass along my memory like the faintly defined outlines of a dream. And when I dwell upon their strange peculiarities, their vastness, their variety, and the distinctive features of novelty which mark them all, so entirely out of the range of all objects that compose the natural scenery and wonders of this continent, I who have seen them can scarcely realize that in those far-off recesses of the mountains they have existed so long in impenetrable seclusion, and that hereafter they will stand foremost among the natural attractions of the world. Astonishment and wonder become so firmly impressed upon the mind in the presence of these objects, that belief stands appalled, and incredulity is dumb. You can see Niagara, comprehend its beauties, and carry from it a memory ever ready to summon before you all its grandeur. You can stand in the valley of the

Yosemite, and look up its mile of vertical granite, and distinctly recall its minutest feature; but amid the canyon and falls, the boiling springs and sulphur mountain, and, above all, the mud volcano and and the geysers of the Yellowstone, your memory becomes filled and clogged with objects new in experience, wonderful in extent, and possessing unlimited grandeur and beauty. It is a new phase in the natural world; a fresh exhibition of the handiwork of the Great Architect; and, while you see and wonder, you seem to need an additional sense, fully to comprehend and believe."

The Washburn-Doane-Langford expedition laid before the reading world a description of a little known and seldom explored region, as it penetrated, probably, beyond any former explorations. But its historical significance lies in the birth of a new idea—an idea closely connected with democracy—the idea of the common ownership of land and resources, dedicated to the use and enjoyment of the people. This idea is the more remarkable that it overlaps the era of individual enterprise on the part of the American people—an era in which the Federal Government was still making persistent efforts to push public lands into private ownership. The idea, too, of recognizing enjoyment as of importance was novel, for the people of the United States were, for the most part, still strongly in thrall to the Puritan objective of hard work. It was distinctly a new thing to recognize communion with Nature as desirable.

Since the expedition of 1870, many scientific parties have conducted research in the Yellowstone and have published their findings. There were the famous expeditions under Hayden, Powell, King, and Wheeler. There was the expedition of the Engineer Corps of the Army, with Captains Barlow and Heap in charge. This expedition was accompanied by Thomas Moran, whose pictures made the Yellowstone famous, and by W. H. Jackson, who brought back many authentic photographs. Jackson at 96 is still hale and hearty, and visits the Yellowstone and Tetons annually. Dr. Hayden visited the region again in 1872 and again in 1878, which resulted in the publication in 1883 of a comprehensive report by Dr. Hayden and his associates.

In an introduction, written to precede a reprint of his Diary in 1905, Mr. Langford stated that the question has frequently been asked him, "Who originated the plan of setting apart this region as a National Park?" Mr. Langford's statement follows: "I answer that Judge Cornelius Hedges of Helena wrote the first articles ever published by the press urging the dedication of this region as a park. The *Helena Herald* of November 9, 1870, contains a letter of Mr. Hedges, in which he advocated the scheme, and in my lectures delivered in Washington and New York in January of 1871, I directed attention to Mr. Hedges' suggestion and urged the passage by Congress of an act setting apart that region as a public park. All this was several months prior to the first exploration by the U. S. Geological Survey, in charge of Dr. Hayden. The suggestion that the region should be made into a National Park was first broached to the members of our party on September 19, 1870, by Mr. Hedges, while we were in camp at the confluence of the Firehole and Gibbon Rivers, as related in this Diary. After the return home of our party, I was informed by General Washburn that on the eve of the departure of our expedition from Helena, David E. Folsom had suggested to him the desirability of creating a park at the grand canyon and falls of the Yellowstone. This fact was unknown to Mr. Hedges— and the boundary lines of the proposed park were extended by him so as to be commensurate with the wider range of our explorations.''

The evidence would indicate that Cornelius Hedges was the first to make known the concept of a great national park for all the people. Probably, as in the case of many inventions, the idea may have been in the air and caught up by different persons, almost simultaneously. Whether Dr. Hayden heard of the project from some of the Washburn expedition or whether some such idea was forming in his own mind, we may never know.

Once the idea was conceived, the next step was to bring about its realization. There were two great obstacles to this. Legislative bodies are prone to be conservative. They hesitate to try new plans, except in time of revolution when educational campaigns have assumed an emotional appeal. The idea of a national park provided by the Federal Government was new indeed; but the description of the region, however faithful, could hardly be expected to carry conviction to a Congress composed then, as now, of many town lawyers and few who had participated in pioneering explorations.

Every bit of help which could be mustered was needed. Langford went to Washington in the winter of 1871–72. He delivered lectures there and in New York. Before he left Montana for the East, he, Cornelius Hedges, and the newly elected delegate to Congress from the Territory of Montana adopted a tentative plan of action. Langford and Delegate Clagett apparently drew the act of dedication, except for the boundary descriptions which they secured from Dr. Hayden. Mr. Clagett introduced the bill into the House on December 18, 1871. Senator Pomeroy introduced it into the Senate. As is usual, after the bill was referred to the Committee on Public Lands in each house, the chairman of the sub-committee in the House having the bill in charge, addressed a letter to the Secretary of the Interior, who, on January 29, 1872, endorsed the measure. With the letter came a brief report by Dr. Hayden, who was in a strategic position. A scientist of note who had, on behalf of the Federal Government, visited the area in person, secured convincing scientific data, specimens, and numerous photographs, could hardly be disbelieved. Dr. Hayden was enthusiastic. He and Langford visited personally practically every member of Congress. Four hundred copies of Langford's articles in the May and June *Scribner's Magazine* were placed on the desks of members of Congress at the psychological date when the bill was to be voted on. The result was that the Senate passed the bill on January 30, the House on February 27, and on March 1, 1872, President Grant signed the bill.

The wording of the act is little short of a masterpiece. The described area is by the act "reserved and withdrawn from settlement, occupancy or sale under the laws of the United States, and dedicated and set apart as a public park or pleasuring ground for the benefit and enjoyment of the people." The park was to be under the exclusive control of the Secretary of the Interior, who was directed to make regulations which "shall provide for the preservation from injury or spoliation of all timber, mineral deposits, natural curiosities or wonders within said park, and their retention in their natural condition." Thus was a policy declared at the outset—a policy of conservation applied to a new kind of area. The act included guidance for the sort of administration which should be set up and for the sort of facilities which it was thought would be required. The Secretary was authorized, in his discretion, to "grant leases for building purposes, for terms not exceeding ten years, of small parcels of ground, at such places in said park as shall require the erection of buildings for the accommodation of visitors," and "all of the proceeds of said leases, and all other revenues that may be derived from any source connected with the park" were "to be expended

[17]

under his direction in the management of the same, and the construction of roads and bridle-paths," and "shall provide against the wanton destruction of the fish and game found within the park, and against their capture or destruction for the purposes of merchandise or profit." Though it has been necessary to amend the act in order to develop a responsible administration and settle many troublesome problems, today the original act is still the guiding star for the administration of Yellowstone National Park.

Neither Delegate Clagett nor Mr. Langford seems to have known of it, but it transpired that Dr. Hayden, in order to muster votes for the bill, must have made promises that Congress would not be called on for some time for funds for the park. Such promises are not unknown, even in recent legislation! At any rate, no money was forthcoming from Congress. Mr. Langford served as superintendent of the park for five years without pay and with no money for protection or development. His assistant superintendents also served without pay. In the 1905 introduction to his Diary, Mr. Langford stated that in the second year of his services as superintendent, some of his friends in Congress proposed to give him a salary sufficiently large to pay actual expenses. But, he declared, "I requested them to make no effort in this behalf, saying that I feared that some successful applicant for such a salaried position, giving little thought to the matter, would approve the applications for leases; and that as long as I could prevent the granting of any exclusive concessions I would be willing to serve as superintendent without compensation." It was, perhaps, during this period that Langford's friends suggested that his initials N. P. stood for "National Park," and he sometimes wrote in the Spencerian script of the day, "National Park" Langford.

As soon as the park was created, applications began to pour in on the Secretary of the Interior for leases and concessions of all sorts. Apparently, many people thought that they could still "take up" land within the park. As soon as the region became known, all sorts of merchants, ranchers, and inn-keepers from far and near applied for licenses to operate concessions. It mattered not that many of them knew nothing of mountain or pioneer conditions.

Hunters also gave much trouble. Even today it is most difficult to withdraw areas from hunting. Hunters seem to believe that they have a vested right to stalk game on publicly owned lands. In the interests of conservation and in the face of the rapid disappearance of game, the States now enforce rigorous laws for open and closed seasons and for licensing hunters and fishermen. Today Yellowstone and all other national parks are game sanctuaries. Commercial fishing is barred and no hunting is allowed, but visitors to the national parks may enjoy the age-old Waltonian fishing pastime under ideally protected conditions. In the seventies, however, the wagon roads which opened up the park brought in many hunters from the vicinity. It was physically impossible to protect an area of over 3,000 square miles of the most rugged character in the country. Were it not for the protection given wildlife in national parks and established refuges, there would be no hunting anywhere!

Mr. Langford, who had been fired by a fine conception and a high sense of service, was frustrated at every turn. He was criticized by the local papers. He was given no help and no funds from Washington. Uncle Sam, having good-naturedly granted, through Congress, the petition of the little band of enthusiasts, apparently had no realization that he had taken on any responsibilities. The act still read well, but the practice was disappointing. Langford's disillusionment was, at the end of five years, almost complete. It seems a miracle that the park project was not abandoned. Only in after years could Langford look back on the service which he and his friends had rendered as leading to the establishment of an enduring national park—the first of its kind in the United States.

In 1877, P. W. Norris of Michigan came into the park as superintendent. His reports to the Secretary of the Interior are most illuminating. He sought appropriations for roads. He was obliged to complain about the depredations of the American tourist. He was succeeded by incompetent and unwise superintendents, most of whom entered upon their duties with no knowledge of the country or climate, and several of whom were involved in scandals concerning concessions and private gain. In 1855, when Congress declined to appropriate money for the administration of the park, the Secretary of the Interior called upon the Secretary of War for troops to patrol the park, as he was authorized to do by an Act of Congress passed in 1883. For more than thirty years soldiers manned the park.

General Hiram M. Chittenden, who served in his early military days as Assistant Officer in charge for the two years, 1891-2, published a book on "The Yellowstone National Park" in 1895. Be-

[19]

ginning in 1899, General Chittenden began a second tour of duty in the park, in charge of road-building. His name, therefore, is closely associated with all that is best in the park. His book, which has gone through many editions, remains one of the standard works on Yellowstone. He was responsible for valuable research, was sympathetic with park aims, and believed in preserving the park as nearly as possible in its natural condition.

In 1918, the year after the National Park Service was created, the War Department was relieved of its responsibilities in the park, and on June 28, 1919, Horace M. Albright became superintendent of Yellowstone National Park. During the ten years that Mr. Albright served as superintendent, a new system of administration was developed, the services of park rangers perfected, and the principles of park protection crystallized. A number of serious assaults on the integrity of the park were launched by politicians during this period, but, with the aid of public opinion and conservation organizations, the National Park Service was enabled to withstand all raids on the Yellowstone. When Mr. Albright became Director of the National Park Service early in 1929, he was succeeded by Roger Toll, of Colorado, who served until his tragic death in 1936. He was succeeded by Edmund Rogers, also of Colorado, who is now in charge of the park.

In spite of early difficulties and discouragements, in spite of initial mistakes and neglects, Yellowstone is now firmly established as an outstanding national park in a system of national parks which are created and administered along lines set forth in the act of dedication in 1872. A new and special form of land-use has been inaugurated which meets with favor in the eyes of the American people. They are both landlords and tenants in common of lands administered for their benefit and enjoyment. It was this phrase from the act of dedication that was carved into the entrance gate at Gardiner, where, on April 24, 1903, President Theodore Roosevelt laid the corner-stone:

For the benefit and enjoyment of the people.

Photograph—Joseph S. Dixon   Courtesy—Portfolio, American Planning and Civic Association

HALF DOME, AT THE HEAD OF YOSEMITE VALLEY

YOSEMITE VALLEY

TEN-EI-YA AND YOSEMITE

"I will not leave my home, but be with the spirits among the rocks, the water-falls, in the rivers and in the winds; wheresoever you go I will be with you. You will not see me, but you will fear the spirit of the old chief, and grow cold. The great spirits have spoken!"
—Quoted from Chief Ten-ei-ya by Dr. L. H. Bunnell
in "Discovery of the Yosemite," 1880.

WHEN Yosemite Valley became known to the white settlers of California, some twenty years before the famous Washburn expedition advertised Yellowstone to the American public, it was the well-beloved home of a band of Indians closely related to the Monos whose hunting-grounds were on the east side of the Sierra Nevada Mountains. Curiously inaccessible, in the heart of the high Sierra peaks, snow-bound in the winter months, the valley was unknown to the *padres* and Spanish *dons*. A small band of warlike Indians—Yosemites by name—occupied the valley as their stronghold. They built encampments—*rancherias*, as the Spanish called them—and stored acorns on the floor of the valley. Their trails led to natural caverns and recesses in the granite rocks, to which they could retire in case of attack.

Within Indian memory or tradition no white man had ever entered or seen the valley before 1851, though some of the early American settlers had heard of the "deep valley" of the Yosemites from their Indian friends. Few Indians unrelated to the Yosemites had ever been allowed to penetrate into the valley. In winter the trails over the crests to the land of the Monos were impassable. The lofty granite walls and high peaks and ridges gave the home of the Yosemites a protection which few man-built fortresses could command.

For centuries after the Great Artist, using colossal glaciers for etching tools, had carved the magic picture, the valley may have existed alone, unseen and unknown even to the Indians. In the 1850's, the Yosemites, numbering about two hundred, lived in this enchanted valley. When the American settlers came into the Mariposa country, south of the valley, the Yosemites resented and feared them. The old chief sent out raiding parties to murder and rob the settlers and burn their settlements. It was a military expedition in 1851, to bring the defiant Yosemites into proposed peace pacts with the United States Government—the Great White Father—that introduced the first white men into the enchanted valley.

[23]

The scant contact with the Sierra Nevada Mountains before 1851 may be told in a few words. California was in communication with the eastern seaboard by boat via Cape Horn before the hardy pioneers crossed the high crests of the stubborn Sierra. To Jedediah Smith, a fur trader, is given the credit for the first transcontinental journey to California. In 1826 he led an exploring party from the Great Salt Lake. In California he was met with the opposition of the Spanish Governor, who saw no good to his domain from the exploiting trade of the American trappers. After long and laborious mountain travel into regions unpenetrated by the Spanish, Smith and his followers worked their way from the region of the Cajon Pass to the San Joaquin Valley. They saw "few beaver and elk, deer and antelope in abundance," and so they started back to the Great Salt Lake across the Sierra Nevada, where the peaks pierce the clouds and the valleys are deep between steep granite walls. They found the route, probably north of Yosemite Valley, beset with hardships and difficulties, but lived to return another day.

A good many fur trappers and traders, in the next few years, traveled into California over the mountains. They brought back fabulous and alluring stories of the pleasant land of sunshine which lay beyond the snow-capped granite guardian walls. One division of Captain Bonneville's exploring party, under Joseph Walker, reached California through the Humboldt Valley, south of Carson Lake. They probably threaded the ridge between the Tuolumne and Merced Rivers into the high Yosemite country, but the Indian guides later reported that they purposely led the explorers by a route which would avoid the valley.

Washington Irving, in 1837, wrote an account of Bonneville's expedition, and Zeno Leonard, who accompanied the Walker party, published in 1839 a narrative of the trip. They must have seen some of the finest views in the high Sierra. According to the Leonard account: "We traveled for miles every day, still on top of the mountains, and our course continually obstructed with snow hills and rocks. Here we began to encounter in our path many small streams which would shoot out from under these high snow-banks, and after running a short distance in deep chasms which they have through the ages cut in the rocks, precipitate themselves from one lofty precipice to another, until they are exhausted in rain below. Some of these precipices appeared to us to be more than a mile high."

[24]

Also Leonard mentioned "some trees of the redwood species, incredibly large—some of which would measure from 16 to 18 fathoms round the trunk at the height of a man's head from the ground."

Other curious travelers penetrated the region. Then came the settlers—that motley procession of the adventurous, the dissatisfied and the optimistic. They came into the promised land on foot, on horseback and later in wagons, following to their sources the rivers from the Gila to the Truckee.

The Spanish did not welcome the Americans. They were contemptuous of American money-grubbing enterprise. And the easygoing, luxury-loving Spanish-Californians feared the self-sacrificing, energetic pioneers of the wilderness. Dr. Carl Russell, in his book, "100 Years in Yosemite," quoted the Mexican, Castro, as having stated before the Assembly in Monterey: "Those Americans are so contriving that some day they will build ladders to touch the sky, and once in the heavens they will change the whole face of the Universe and even the color of the stars."

In 1848 the "contriving" Americans had taken over California, for better or for worse, and the process of change soon began, for the discovery of gold a few months after California became a part of the United States brought the "forty-niners," the greatest army of "diggers" ever assembled. If gold could have been secured at the cost of destroying the fair surface of the entire range of colorful mountains, no doubt the Sierra Nevada today would be desecrated by deserts of desolate piles and pits of waste and slag. Fortunately, the scars of picks and shovels in the hands of pigmy prospectors could do little damage to the gigantic Sierra. And the big, machine-worked mines were, in comparison to the size and extent of the mountain range, few and far between. But the height of the gold rush was over before that momentous day on which white men first saw the incomparable Yosemite Valley. The Sierra barrier between the East and the West had been conquered, though the flinty-hearted cliffs and the marauding Indians claimed tolls in death and disaster, and hardship was exacted from all who crossed these mighty mountains.

It was not until 1851, after the Sierra slopes had become infested with prospectors and some sizable mines put into operation, that the Americans actually saw the Yosemite Valley. James Savage, who probably had participated in at least one of Fremont's famous expeditions, had established in 1849–50 a trading post not more than fifteen miles below the Yosemite Valley. He knew and understood the Indians. He was adopted into many of the friendly foothill tribes. It is recorded that the five wives he took from different tribes gave him direct access to Indian gossip. The Indians had confidence in him. The squaws dug gold for him. Indeed the Indians brought gold dust into his trading post in exchange for trinkets of little value in American markets, though it must be remembered that gold had no value in inter-Indian markets. Savage was a born leader, generally esteemed by the settlers and revered by the Indians, though his profits at his trading posts were a bit on the profiteering side, unless the risk of doing business at all be taken into due consideration.

And all during these years of settlement, in a supposedly impregnable stronghold in the high Sierra, was this band of warlike Yosemites who stole horses and stock from the settlers and raided their posts with fire and pillage. Late in 1850, raids on Savage's Fresno and Mariposa stores resulted in the death of those in charge, and aroused an indignant resistance which led to an Indian war. Many of the hitherto friendly Indians were induced to join in the war against "the white gold diggers," to drive the white men from their mountains. The Indians were told by the belligerent chiefs that the white men would run from them, and that those who joined in the war would be the first to secure the property of the gold diggers. Particularly, they coveted horses, live-stock, clothing.

After other raids and cruel murders, a punitive party of settlers marched "among the densely wooded mountains in pursuit of the savages," but the Indians were able to repulse the settlers, and escape. The hastily brought together defense company had few supplies, lacked organization and collective training. Savage had joined the expedition, which, with about 100 men, tried to capture some 500 fighting Indians from the Yosemite, Chow-chilla, Kah-we-ah and other tribes. In a surprise attack by the settlers, an instigating Indian chief was killed, and the Indians retired to the mountains.

The Indian war was on. The famous Mariposa Battalion was organized, under a proclamation by Governor McDougal calling for volunteers to prevent further outrages and to punish the marauders. On January 24, 1851, the volunteers were mustered into the service. They provided their own horses and equipment. The

State furnished camp supplies and baggage trains, and the Federal Government paid the expense of maintenance, but the battalion was under the direction of the Indian Commissioners. Savage was chosen leader and commissioned as Major. While the battalion was waiting for the Commissioners to act, the depredations of the Indians continued. Part of the battalion was assigned to the Kings and Kah-we-ah Rivers and part to the San Joaquin and Merced. These volunteer soldiers went out to wage a strange war. Their instructions were to capture the Indians in their strongholds and escort them safely into the Commissioners' camp on the Fresno.

With the northern party rode a young doctor, L. H. Bunnell by name, who had come to California from New York by way of Detroit and western wilds, and who had learned something of Indian languages and psychology. Thirty years after, he wrote an excellent and interesting account of the first brief foray and the later sojourn in the Yosemite Valley in 1851.

Major Savage with his men rode toward the "deep valley" over the Black Ridge to the South Fork of the Merced. They encountered deep, damp snow which impeded their progress. But finally they surprised a Noot-chu village on the banks of the Merced. They persuaded Chief Pon-wat-chee to send his people in to the Commissioners and to aid the soldiers in bringing in the Yosemites.

Ten-ei-ya, the old chief of the Yosemites, was induced to come to the battalion camp. Major Savage, according to Dr. Bunnell, told the chief that "if he would go to the Commissioners and make a treaty of peace with them, as the other Indians were going to do, there would be no more war." But Dr. Bunnell has reported that Ten-ei-ya declared with dignity: "My people do not want anything from the 'Great Father' you tell me about. The Great Spirit is our father, and he has always supplied us with all we need. We do not want anything from white men. Our women are able to do our work. Go, then; let us remain in the mountains where we were born; where the ashes of our fathers have been given to the winds. . . . My people do not want to go to the plains."

Major Savage gave the old chief an ultimatum. "Your people must go to the Commissioners and make terms with them. If they do not, your young men will again steal our horses, your people will again kill and plunder the whites. It was your people who robbed my stores, burned my houses, and murdered my men. If they do not make a treaty, your whole tribe will be destroyed. Not one of them will be left alive." Sadly Chief Ten-ei-ya promised to send runners to bring his people in. But they did not come, and so it was decided to go to the village of the Yosemites.

Leaving a camp guard, Major Savage and his men, accompanied by Ten-ei-ya, proceeded over the ridge between the South Fork and the main Merced River. After they crossed the divide they encountered deep snow. Before they reached the valley they met seventy-two Yosemites coming in, all, explained Ten-ei-ya, who were willing to go to the plains. In the belief that the others were in hiding, as it was impossible at this time of year even for Indians to cross the high snow-enshrouded pass to reach the friendly Mono Indians on the east side of the mountains, Major Savage decided to go to the Indian village in the "deep valley."

It was as the party traveled that they suddenly came in full view of the valley of the Yosemites. Dr. Bunnell, who had once caught a glimpse of the "stupendous rocky peaks of the Sierra Nevada" while ascending the old Bear Valley trail from Ridley's ferry, on the Merced River, realized that what he had almost thought a dream was indeed a reality. "The face of the immense cliff," as the marching company saw it, "was shadowed by the declining sun." These were the first white men to behold El Capitan from the place we now call Inspiration Point.

Young Dr. Bunnell was greatly moved. "The grandeur of the scene was but softened by the haze that hung over the valley—light as gossamer—and by the clouds which partially dimmed the higher cliffs and mountains. This obscurity of vision but increased the awe with which I beheld it, and as I looked, a peculiar exalted sensation seemed to fill my whole being, and I found my eyes in tears with emotion." Dr. Bunnell had left the trail and his horse and wallowed alone to a projecting rock to examine the view. But he found scant sympathy from Major Savage or the other intrepid volunteers who were there on business bent—bringing in the Indians who were stealing their property and threatening lives.

That night the party camped on the floor of the valley around blazing fires, a memorable occasion and forerunner of many a later-day campfire. But these were soldiers—pro tem. at least—and there was no Hedges to think of "saving the valley for others." As a

[28]

matter of hard fact, it is probable that most of those hardy pioneers on that March winter night could not conceive that *anybody* would be in the least bit interested in a place so hard to reach and so gloomy in the early lengthening shadows. Indeed, young Dr. Bunnell remarked that it might appear sentimental, but that "the coarse jokes of the careless, and the indifference of the practical, sensibly jarred my more devout feelings . . . as if a sacred subject had been ruthlessly profaned, or the visible power of Deity disregarded." The campers did take seriously, however, the suggestion made by Dr. Bunnell that the valley should have a name, and they voted to adopt the name "Yosemity," the name of the Indians they had come to capture. Major Savage explained to them that the name "Yo-sem-i-ty" as pronounced by Ten-ei-ya, or "O-soom-i-ty" as pronounced by some other bands, signified a full-grown grizzly bear—given to Ten-ei-ya's band "because of their lawless and predatory character." Dr. Bunnell explained in his book that it was not until 1852 that Lieutenant Moore, of the U. S. Army, in his report first adopted the spelling "Yosemite," without, however, changing the pronunciation.

Ten-ei-ya, who was present at this first campfire of those who came to invade the homes of his people, explained that he was the descendant of an Ah-wah-ne-chee chief, and that the valley was called Ah-wah-nee. But Yosemite it is today and has been ever since that March campfire in 1851. Thus was the Yosemite discovered and named.

Ten-ei-ya gave assurance that no white man had ever before visited the valley. One reason he had consented to go to the Commissioners' camp and make peace was that he hoped to prevent an expedition into the valley and that he and his people might be allowed to return to their homes. He explained that the entrance to the valley had always been carefully guarded. The valley was theirs and they had put a spell on it that, they thought, would hold it sacred for themselves alone. No other Indians, declared Ten-ei-ya, ventured to enter the valley, except by his permission; "all feared the witches" and his displeasure. He had "made war upon the white gold diggers to drive them from the mountains, and prevent their entrance into Ah-wah-nee."

After that first soldiers' campfire, the party next day crossed the Merced by ford, and marched toward El Capitan. They found recently deserted Indian huts near its base. Later, near the Royal Arches, then unnamed, they found an encampment, and another near the base of Half Dome, also deserted. Finally, the search for the Yosemites hidden in the rocky fastnesses was abandoned.

The men were more concerned with their mission than with the aspect of the valley they had discovered. As Dr. Bunnell remarked, anent the solemn grandeur of the valley and the hardships of travel which involved the frequent crossing of torrential streams of cold water: "We were not a party of tourists seeking recreation, nor philosophers investigating the operations of nature. Our business there was to find Indians who were endeavoring to escape our *charitable* intentions toward them. But very few of the volunteers seemed to have any appreciation of the wonderful proportions of the enclosing granite rocks; their curiosity had been to see the stronghold of the enemy, and the general verdict was that it was gloomy enough."

Dr. Bunnell described to Major Savage the "side trips" he had made around Mirror Lake, and the views from the cliff up North Canyon and the fall of the South Canyon. He remarked: "Yosemite must be beautifully grand a few weeks later when the foliage and flowers are at their prime, and the rush of waters has somewhat subsided. Such cliffs and water-falls I never saw before, and I doubt if they exist in any other place."

But the Major declared: "The annoyances and disappointments of a fruitless search, together with the certainty of a snow storm approaching, makes all this beautiful scenery appear to me gloomy enough. In a word, it is what we supposed it to be before seeing it, a hell of a place."

The benevolence of the battalion was not appreciated by the Yosemites and they escaped before they reached the Commissioners' camp. Major Savage started out at the head of a second "round-up" expedition, but was recalled by the Commissioners, and the command proceeded under Captain Boling. Again young Dr. Bunnell accompanied the party, at times serving as interpreter and occasionally as surgeon. The volunteer soldiers went after the Chow-chillas, who had induced the Yosemites to slip away. Their route led them into the Upper San Joaquin. They burned the lodges and acorn stores of a deserted village where the embers of a funeral pyre still glowed. The Indians themselves retired before the raiding party, offering to fight only when they had the advantage. The destruction of their lodges and stores seemed to Captain Boling the only way to force them to come in to the Commissioners. Left alone in the mountains, they were sure to continue to murder the settlers. The men in the battalion, under severe provocation and in face of shouted taunts from little bands of Indians safely sheltered in rocky coves, did quite consistently refrain from shooting Indians on sight. Even when the Indians rolled down huge stones from above in order to annihilate the pursuing men, they contented themselves with trying to preserve their own safety, and followed, so far as they could, the orders of the Commissioners. If it had not been for the responsible leadership in the battalion, the story might have been a far less creditable one.

Following the return of the battalion to the Commissioners' camp, Major Savage met with the Chow-chillas and Kah-we-ahs at a feast provided by him, and treaties of peace were signed. Dr. Bunnell reported that the Chow-chillas, who had often joined with the Yosemites in raiding parties and in the Indian war, became the most tractable of the mountain Indians. This left the Yosemites as the only important mountain tribe still at war with the settlers. Chief Ten-ei-ya had resisted all the bribes and blandishments of the Commissioners. He and his braves wanted the freedom of their mountain home.

A division of the battalion, under Captain Boling, therefore, went after the Yosemites. During this second stay in the valley the soldiers played a catch-as-catch-can game with scattered parties of Indians occupying the high places, always ready and willing to roll stones down on the adventurous who scrambled too far up the rocky trails. Finally, from a perch on a high ledge above Mirror Lake, where his retreat had been cut off from above, the old Chief Ten-ei-ya descended on a trail through an oak-tree-top, and was captured again. When he was brought into camp he found that his favorite son had been killed, in violation of orders, while being held in camp. It was a bitter pill for the old chief to swallow.

For many nights Ten-ei-ya would lift his voice and call, believing that those of his people who were still in the mountains would hear him and come in. But there were no answers to his calls. Once he attempted to escape, and when he was brought before Captain Boling, he expected to be killed. His usual taciturn reserve was

[31]

broken, and he uttered a pathetic lamentation and a defiant threat, using Indian language interspersed with Spanish words.

"Kill me, Sir Captain! Yes, kill me, as you killed my son; as you would kill my people if they were to come to you! You would kill all my race if you had the power. Yes, Sir American, you can now tell your warriors to kill the old chief; you have made me sorrowful, my life dark; you killed the child of my heart; why not kill the father? But wait a little; when I am dead I will call to my people to come to you, I will call louder than you have had me call; that they shall hear me in their sleep, and come to avenge the death of their chief and his son. Yes, Sir American, my spirit will make trouble for you and your people, as you have caused trouble to me and my people. With the wizards, I will follow the white men and make them fear me. You may kill me, Sir Captain, but you shall not live in peace. I will follow in your footsteps, I will not leave my home, but be with the spirits among the rocks, the water-falls, in the rivers and in the winds; wheresoever you go I will be with you. You will not see me, but you will fear the spirit of the old chief, and grow cold. The great spirits have spoken! I am done."

Captain Boling's answer was to see that the old chief was fed. Dr. Bunnell, who had reported that he was moved to sympathy and respect for the lordly Ten-ei-ya while he was speaking, remarked that at his food he was "simply a dirty old Indian."

After a second attempt to escape, the proud old chief was tethered by a rope fastened around his waist. With Ten-ei-ya tied to him, Dr. Bunnell explored the high trails in search of Ten-ei-ya's un-caught people. Finally a detachment, taking Ten-ei-ya with them, left the valley on the north cliff trail above Mirror Lake. After reaching the summit, they followed the ridges just below the snow line, to the shores of a lake, now called Tenaya, where they surprised and captured without resistance the remnant of the Yosemites, thirty-five in number, including Ten-ei-ya's four squaws. The young chief of the village, which had so long evaded the pur-suing soldiers, declared that he was "not only willing, but anxious" to go to the Commissioners and join in a treaty of peace, for, said he, "Where can we now go that the Americans will not follow us?" and turning to the Captain, "Where can we make our homes that you will not find us?"

On the trip back to the valley, Dr. Bunnell had ample opportunity to see this marvelous high country not far from the present Tioga Road which leads from the valley through Tuolumne Meadows to Mono Lake. He maintained that the "sublime mountain scenery" exceeded any he had ever seen either in Mexico or in the Rocky Mountains. It was he who suggested that the lake where the last of the Yosemites had been found be called after Ten-ei-ya. And so it is called to this day. When Dr. Bunnell told the old chief of the honor bestowed upon him, Ten-ei-ya protested and said: "It already has a name; we call it Py-we-ack." It was Dr. Bunnell's opinion that "the whole mountain region of the water-sheds of the Merced and Tuolumne Rivers afford the most delightful views to be seen anywhere of mountain cliffs, cascades and water-falls, grand forests and mountain meadows." The old chief, Ten-ei-ya, looking back as they traveled from the lake along the high ridges, must have felt a similar emotion.

Thus were the Yosemites brought to the camp on the Fresno. Thus was the Indian war ended.

Major Savage and his friendly Indians re-established their close relations; but he "never re-visited the valley, and died without having seen the Vernal and Nevada Falls, or any of the views belonging to the region of the Yosemite, except those seen from the valley and from the old Indian trail on our first entrance." In 1852 Major Savage was killed in a controversy with a rival trader in the Kings, and so, no more of him.

Having accomplished their purpose, the members of the Mariposa Battalion were mustered out of the service, to return to their various pioneer occupations.

But old Ten-ei-ya, living in the reservation, suffered from the loss of his dignity and power, claimed that "he could not endure the heat at the agency, and said that he preferred acorns to the rations furnished him by the Government." He was granted leave, and joyfully with his family "took the trail to Yosemite once more." Later he was joined by other nostalgic members of his band.

After the murder of two prospectors who strayed into the valley in 1852, a detachment of regular soldiers, under Lieutenant Moore, captured a party of five of Ten-ei-ya's men who said they had killed the white men to prevent them from coming into their valley. The Indians were shot, but, though Lieutenant Moore crossed the Sierra over the Mono Pass, he failed to find Ten-ei-ya, for the friendly Monos had received and secreted Ten-ei-ya and his followers. It was said that Ten-ei-ya had been born and had lived among the Monos until his ambition made him a leader and founder of the Pai-ute colony in Ah-wah-nee. Dr. Bunnell has recorded that Ten-ei-ya's "history and warlike exploits formed part of the traditionary lore of the Monos," that "they were proud of his successes and boasted of his descent from their tribe, although Ten-ei-ya, himself, claimed that his father was the chief of an independent people, whose ancestors were of a different race." Dr. Bunnell, in analyzing his character, declared: "Ten-ei-ya had business cunning and sagacity in managing deserters from other tribes, who had sought his protection. He maintained a reputation as a chief whose leadership was never disputed by his followers, and he was the envy of the leaders of other tribes. After his subjection by the whites, he was deserted by his followers, and his supremacy was no longer acknowledged by the neighboring tribes, who had feared rather than respected him or the people of his band."

Ten-ei-ya and his refugee band stayed many moons with the Monos, but finally, according to Dr. Bunnell's account, in the summer of 1853 he and his people returned to their beloved Yosemite Valley, with the intention of remaining there unless they were driven out by the whites. The squaws constructed permanent wigwams near the head of the valley, among the rocks, where they could not easily be seen by visitors. But times may have been hard. At any rate, they made a raid on their friendly relatives, the Monos, and brought back some of the Mono ponies. They were followed into the valley by the indignant Monos, and when sleeping after a feast on horse meat, they were surprised, and sadly enough, Ten-ei-ya was stoned to death. Some of Ten-ei-ya's older men and women were permitted to escape down the valley, but the young men and women were made captives and held as slaves for their captors.

So Ten-ei-ya died, and the valley home he loved so well, after various vicissitudes, is now the famous Yosemite National Park. But that, as Mr. Kipling so often remarked, is another story—a story which will be told in the following pages.

JOHN MUIR AND THE SIERRA NEVADA

"Well may the Sierra be called the Range of Light, not the Snowy Range; for only in winter is it white, while all the year it is bright."
—John Muir, in "Our National Parks," 1901.

ON MARCH 27, 1868, a young Scotch-American, John Muir by name, arrived in San Francisco on the steamer "Nebraska" which had sailed around the Horn, but which he had boarded on the Pacific side of the Isthmus of Panama. With a young Englishman he made straight for the Oakland ferry without giving so much as a glance to the straight rows of buildings on San Francisco's gridiron streets. From Oakland the two young men started on a walking trip which took them down the Santa Clara Valley, across the Pacheco Pass, into the San Joaquin Valley. The scene, as he saw it from the pass, Muir has recorded in his journal:

"Looking down from a height of 1,500 feet, there, extending north and south as far as I could see, lay a vast level flower garden, smooth and level like a lake of gold—the floweriest part of the world I had yet seen. From the eastern margin of the golden plain arose the white Sierra. At the base ran a belt of gently sloping purplish foothills lightly dotted with oaks, above that a broad dark zone of coniferous forests, and above this forest zone arose the lofty mountain peaks, clad in snow. The atmosphere was so clear that although the nearest of the mountain peaks on the axis of the range were at a distance of more than 150 miles, they seemed to be at just the right distance to be seen broadly in their relationship to one another, marshaled in glorious ranks and groups, their snowy robes so smooth and bright that it seemed impossible for a man to walk across the open folds without being seen, even at this distance. Perhaps more than 300 miles of the range was comprehended in this one view."

They crossed the San Joaquin at Hill's Ferry and then followed the Merced toward the Yosemite, which they approached by way of Deer Flat, where the wagon road ended.

The Yosemite was calling to John Muir as a magnet to highly tempered steel. He did not even wait to earn money first, though his pockets had little enough in them. He must see the valley. In this there seems to be something of Fate, for this poor farm boy, born so many miles away in Scotland, had traveled far and incurred much physical discomfort to reach these "mountains of Light," where he spent so many fruitful years of his life, leaving the world richer for his love and learning of the Sierra Nevada Mountains, until his day little known and less understood.

He and his companion spent eight or ten days in the valley, visiting the walls, making sketches, and collecting flowers and ferns. The return trip was made by way of Wawona, where Galen Clark, a Yosemite pioneer, had located. The month in the Yosemite cost John Muir and his friend only three dollars each! Ferns and boughs or the springy forest floor furnished their beds; their shelter, a tree, a cave or the star-lit sky; their food, the scanty provisions they carried in their knapsacks. When they came out of the valley they put their strong young muscles to work in the harvest fields and so earned a small income which more than paid for their Spartan living.

In one of his early journals, Muir recorded: "This Yosemite trip only made me hungry for another far longer and further reaching, and I determined to set out again as soon as I had earned a little money to get near views of the mountains in all their snowy grandeur, and to study the wonderful forests, the noblest of their kind I had ever seen—sugar-pines eight and nine feet in diameter, with cones nearly two feet long, silver firs more than 200 feet in height, Douglas spruce and libocedrus, and the kingly Sequoias."

After spending some time in breaking mustangs, running a ferry, and shearing sheep, he became a sheep-herder in the employ of an Irishman, "Smoky Jack" Connel. On November 1, 1868, he wrote to his friend, Mrs. Carr, whom he had first come to know at the University of Wisconsin before her husband, Professor Carr, came to the University of California: "I am engaged at present in the very important and patriarchal business of sheep. I am a gentle shepherd. The gray box in which I reside is distant about seven miles northwest from Hopeton, two miles north of Snelling's. The Merced pours past me on the south, from the Yosemite; smooth domy hills and the tree fringe of the Tuolumne bound me on the north; the lordly Sierras join sky and plain on the east; and the far coast mountains on the west. My mutton family of 1,800 range over about ten square miles, and I have abundant opportunities for reading and botanizing."

In that charming book, "John of the Mountains," it was recorded by the editor, Mrs. Linnie Marsh Wolfe: "Early in June, 1869, the tall auburn-haired young shepherd John Muir took charge of the sheep of another Irishman, Pat Delaney, and went with them in quest of high green pastures. Assisting him were two dogs and the sub-shepherd Billy, so he had leisure to explore much of the Divide between the Tuolumne and Merced Basins, climb Mount Hoffman and Mount Dana, and penetrate Bloody Canyon to Mono Lake, which lay on the ashen plain 'like a burnished disk.' "

Muir never loved the sheep. He saw the devastation which the "hoofed locusts" were bringing to these enchanted valleys and precious meadows. In the end he fought bitterly to save the best of the high Sierra from destructive grazing.

When Muir returned from this shepherd's expedition, he took up his abode in Yosemite "as a convenient and grand vestibule to the Sierra." He sold the labor of a friend and himself to J. M. Hutchings, a pioneer in the valley, who, through the *California Magazine*, had done much to bring the charms of Yosemite to the public. Hutchings was operating a hotel, and wished to work up some of the down timber into buildings. Muir had had experience in a sawmill in Wisconsin, and so undertook to construct the sawmill. But this work was merely a means to an end. Muir spent as much time as he could on his "observatory," Sentinel Dome. From this and other points of vantage he sought to read the markings on the rocks. He was already developing his theories of glacial action. He wandered into the heights whenever he could. When the summer was over and he was down in the foothills, he determined to spend a winter in the mountains, and so on November 16, 1869, he set out "for Yosemite in particular, and the Sierra in general." He had a companion with him, and in his journal recorded: "I had long lived in bright flowery summer, and I wished to see the snow and ice, the divine jewelry of winter, once more, and to hear the storm-winds among the trees and rocks, and behold the thin azure of the mountains, and their clouds."

On December 6, 1869, Muir wrote to Mrs. Carr: "I am feasting in the Lord's mountain house, and what pen may write my blessings! I am going to dwell here all winter, magnificently 'snow-bound.' Just think of the grandeur of a mountain winter in Yosemite!" Muir remained in the Yosemite through 1870 and into 1871. In

September of 1871 he left the employment of Mr. Hutchings. He had in these years saved enough money to last him, he thought, for years to come, for he dressed in "tough old clothes, gray like the rocks," and could live for months on scanty rations.

Now began in earnest his "glorious toil" with "unmeasured time, and independent of companions and scientific association." Ever since he had arrived at Yosemite in 1868 he had reveled in the beauty of the High Sierra whenever he could make expeditions into the mountains. Now he spent long days and nights in studying the Book of Nature. He evolved and elaborated his theory concerning the creation of Yosemite and other granite valleys in the Sierra. His glacial theory was more daring than it seems today, for he was then a young, unknown man who appeared to many as a vagabond wanderer, only working at anything recognized to be work when he was forced to earn his scanty bread and tea. His theory contradicted the views of some of the most eminent geologists of his day.

John Muir has written many descriptions of Yosemite, at first detailed and fragmentary and later more comprehensive. Long after his life in Yosemite, he gathered together articles he had written for the *Atlantic Monthly* and in 1901 issued a book on "Our National Parks." The descriptions in this book have combined perspective with the first-hand impressions contained in his journals, wherefore a few of his pen pictures are copied here:

"Of all the mountain ranges I have climbed, I like the Sierra Nevada the best. Though extremely rugged, with its main features on the grandest scale in height and depth, it is nevertheless easy of access and hospitable; and its marvelous beauty, displayed in striking and alluring forms, woos the admiring wanderer on and on, higher and higher, charmed and enchanted. Benevolent, solemn, fateful, pervaded with divine light, every landscape glows like a countenance hallowed in eternal repose; and every one of its living creatures, clad in flesh and leaves, and every crystal of its rocks, whether on the surface shining in the sun or buried miles deep in what we call darkness, is throbbing and pulsing with the heartbeats of God. All the world lies warm in one heart, yet the Sierra seems to get more light than other mountains. The weather is mostly sunshine embellished with magnificent storms, and nearly everything shines from base to summit—the rocks, streams, lakes, glaciers, irised falls, and the forests of silver fir and silver pine.

IN YOSEMITE NATIONAL PARK

ECHO RIDGE ABOVE

Photograph—Marjory Bridge Farquhar

SAWTOOTH RIDGE

Photograph—Ansel Adams
Courtesy—Sierra Club Bulletin

CATHEDRAL CREEK FALL,
YOSEMITE NATIONAL PARK

Photograph—Marjory Bridge Farquhar

SAWTOOTH RIDGE, MINARETS, OUTSIDE YOSEMITE NATIONAL PARK

Photograph—Walter A. Starr

Courtesy—Sierra Club Bulletin

And how bright is the shining after summer showers and dewy nights, and after frosty nights in spring and autumn, when the morning sunbeams are pouring through the crystals on the bushes and grass, and in winter through the snow-laden trees!

"The average cloudiness for the whole year is perhaps less than ten-hundredths. Scarcely a day of all the summer is dark, though there is no lack of magnificent thundering cumuli. They rise in the warm midday hours, mostly over the middle region, in June and July, like new mountain ranges, higher Sierras, mightily augmenting the grandeur of the scenery while giving rain to the forests and gardens and bringing forth their fragrance. The wonderful weather and beauty inspire everybody to be up and doing. Every summer day is a workday to be confidently counted on, the short dashes of rain forming, not interruptions, but rests. The big blessed storm days of winter, when the whole range stands white, are not a whit less inspiring and kind. Well may the Sierra be called the Range of Light, not the Snowy Range; for only in winter is it white, while all the year it is bright.

"Of this glorious range the Yosemite National Park is a central section, thirty-six miles in length and forty-eight miles in breadth. The famous Yosemite Valley lies in the heart of it, and it includes the head waters of the Tuolumne and Merced Rivers, two of the most songful streams in the world; innumerable lakes and waterfalls and smooth silky lawns; the noblest forests, the loftiest granite domes, the deepest ice-sculptured canyons, the brightest crystalline pavements, and snowy mountains soaring into the sky twelve and thirteen thousand feet, arrayed in open ranks and spiry pinnacled groups partially separated by tremendous canyons and amphitheatres; gardens on their sunny brows, avalanches thundering down their long white slopes, cataracts roaring gray and foaming in the crooked rugged gorges, and glaciers in their shadowy recesses working in silence, slowly completing their sculpture; newborn lakes at their feet, blue and green, free or encumbered with drifting icebergs like miniature Arctic Oceans, shining, sparkling, calm as stars."

Four years before John Muir first saw Yosemite, Congress had in 1864 passed a bill, introduced by Senator Conness, to grant to the State of California "the 'cleft' or 'gorge' in the Granite Peak of the Sierra Nevada Mountains . . . known as the Yo-Semite

Valley, with its branches or spurs" but it was stipulated that the State of California "shall accept this grant upon the express conditions that the premises shall be held for public use, resort, and recreation" and "shall be inalienable for all time." To the State of California also was granted "the tracts embracing what is known as the 'Mariposa Big Tree Grove.'" Here is an Act of Congress, passed eight years before the Yellowstone Act became a law, in which there is a recognition of a public land-use for recreation! Though the act was passed only thirteen years after the first discovery of Yosemite, a number of counter private interests had already grown up.

After the visit of the first tourist party, organized by J. M. Hutchings, accompanied by Thomas Ayres, an artist, in 1855, many people desired to see this wonderland. It was only natural that some sort of accommodation for the public should be undertaken. The land was in the public domain and subject to entry. One homesteader and three who owned hotels or lodges, including Mr. Hutchings, were involved. The Act of Congress made no provision for caring for these private holdings. After prolonged litigation, the courts decided against recognizing the claims, but finally the California State Legislature appropriated $60,000 to recompense the four claimants, and it should be recorded that $5,000 of this appropriation was returned to the State treasury. Thus it was not until 1875 that the Commissioners secured full control of the valley.

The Board of Commissioners appointed by the Governor in 1866 had appointed Galen Clark as guardian of the park, but there were many vicissitudes in the administration of Yosemite, and there was very little money made available to meet the necessary expenses of protecting and administering the park. In 1880 the legislature provided for a new commission. But the criticisms continued.

In the meantime John Muir had begun to publish accounts of Yosemite. On February 5, 1876, he had an article in the Sacramento *Record-Union*, and after that a long line of publications came from his gifted pen. In 1880 Muir married Louie Strenzel, daughter of a pioneer orchardist and horticulturist, and during the succeeding years became an expert orchardist and leading citizen in California.

Through the encouragement of Robert Underwood Johnson, then

Above: THE RITTER RANGE, FROM IRON MOUNTAIN.

Photograph—Walter A. Starr

Right: AT THE HEAD OF SHADOW CREEK, MT. RITTER AND BANNER PEAK.

Photograph—Ansel Adams

Below: MINARETS, FROM THE AIR.

Photograph—Francis P. Farquhar
Courtesy—Sierra Club Bulletin

SUGAR PINES OF YOSEMITE:
SOME WERE SAVED AND
SOME WERE NOT

Photographs—Asahel Curtis and the
Department of the Interior

Courtesy—Portfolio, American Planning
and Civic Association

the editor of the *Century*, Muir began in 1889 to contribute to the magazine. Because Muir saw what was happening to his beloved Sierra country surrounding the Yosemite State Park, he advocated a national park. On October 1, 1890, Congress passed an act withdrawing from settlement all unappropriated lands in the designated public domain, and creating an extensive reservation to be under the exclusive control of the Secretary of the Interior. The act stipulated that the regulations should "provide for the preservation from injury of all timber, mineral deposits, natural curiosities or wonders within said reservation and their retention in their natural condition."

By this time Muir had become convinced that California needed an organization to watch the High Sierra country and help fight the battles which he foresaw would continue to arise. So in 1892, he brought together a group of public-spirited men—William E. Colby, Warren Olney, Sr., Dr. Willis Linn Jepson, and Dr. Joseph LeConte, and they organized the Sierra Club, "to explore, enjoy, and render accessible the mountain regions of the Pacific Coast," "to publish authentic information concerning them," and "to enlist the support and coöperation of the people and government in preserving the forests and other natural features of the Sierra Nevada Mountains." The Club was thus composed of mountain lovers and believers in conservation. The organization has grown in members and power. Through its annual outings, leading to detailed knowledge of the mountains, and the eminence of many of its members, the Club has been in a position to exercise a potent influence in legislative and administrative policies concerning the Sierra.

One of the first beneficial undertakings of the Club was to seek to bring about the recession to the Federal Government of the Yosemite State Park. Even under favorable circumstances it was an anomaly that the Federal Government should administer a rim of land around a core, set aside for the very same purpose, under the administration of the State. Then, as now, when the proposal was made to return to the Federal Government land which it had given to the State, there was bitter local opposition, especially in the county seats of the four nearby counties.

After the creation of the national park in 1890, Congress was slow in providing funds for administration. So the Department of the Interior called upon the War Department, as it had done in Yellowstone, and for twenty-three years the park was patrolled and protected by the Army.

While the four claimants in the floor of the valley had been compensated by the State, there were in the national park many private holdings which the Federal Government did not buy. This necessitated boundary changes, and the pressure was very great to take out of the park any land in which there might be potential mining values. In 1904 General Hiram Chittenden, known through his Yellowstone book, published in 1895 (see page 19), became chairman of a boundary commission, which agreed to eliminate from the national park large areas on the east and west. In 1906 a tract on the southwest was cut out of the park. Today many believe that some areas, not yet restored through the purchases of recent years, should be added to Yosemite, notably the lofty Minarets and stately Mt. Ritter, with their surrounding frame of high mountain peaks. Muir's journals of the seventies contained fascinating and detailed descriptions of this region.

From the South Fork of the San Joaquin Canyon he once recorded: "View very grand and universal. Ritter the noblest and most ornate of all." On a trip to the Minarets, he remarked: "The Minarets were now fairly within my grasp. I had been crossing canyons for five days. . . . Their appearance from here was impressively sublime because of their great height, narrow bases, linear arrangement and dark color. They are the most elaborately carved on the edges of any slate summits I have seen. Four lakes lie like open eyes below the ample clouds of névé that send them water. These névé slopes are large, and wonderfully adapted in form and situation for picturesque effects among the black angular slate slabs and peaks."

And again: "At the foot of a former moraine of this west glacier is a small lake not one hundred yards long, but grandly framed with a sheer wall of névé twenty feet high. . . . Beautiful caves reached back from the water's edge; in some places granite walls overleaned and big blocks broke off from the main névé wall, and, with angles sharp as those of ice, leaned into the lake. Undermined by the water, the fissures filled with blue light, and water dripped and trickled all along the white walls. The sun was shining. I never saw so grand a setting for a glacier lake. The

sharp peaks of Ritter seen over the snow shone with splendid effect."
Who can doubt that the highest use of this spectacular mountain
region is that of a national park?

So long as he lived, John Muir did much to direct public interest
to, and provide guardianship for, the High Sierra country. In
many instances he succeeded, though it is well recognized today
that some of the compromises forced upon the friends of the national
parks should be remedied so far as this is yet possible.

The closing years of John Muir's life were darkened by the
unsuccessful fight he and the Sierra Club made to save Hetch
Hetchy from being turned into a reservoir. In this fight he was
ably seconded by Dr. J. Horace McFarland, then President of the
American Civic Association.

But in spite of all that the friends of Yosemite National Park could
do, Congress in 1913 passed an act to permit the City of San Francisco to build a reservoir in Hetch Hetchy—a yosemite second in
beauty only to the big Yosemite. No one dreamed at that time that
within twenty-five years the Yosemite Valley would be so crowded
with summer visitors that its very charm and beauty are threatened
and that Hetch Hetchy would be sorely needed by its joint owners,
the people of the United States, for the purpose to which it was
dedicated when Yosemite National Park was created: "public
use, resort, and recreation." But even then it was realized that
the water flowed out of the park and that it was not a *waste* of
water to permit the park waters to ripple down the floor of the
valley to places where they could be impounded at possibly greater
expense. It was not essentially a question of apportionment of
waters. It was a question of money. The sacrifice of this exquisite
valley was exacted, not to provide water for the people of San
Francisco, but to save them money. John Muir and his associates
knew then that the valley should have been held inviolate, and we
recognize today as never before, the importance of protecting our
national parks. Hetch Hetchy remains a horrible example of a
disastrous mistake, which failed to save money.

The military regime in Yosemite came to an end in connection
with the creation of the National Park Service by Act of Congress
in 1916, following the initial proposal by Dr. J. Horace McFarland.
The Sierra Club supported the movement. Mr. Muir died in 1914,
soon after Congress authorized the Hetch Hetchy desecration.

In the years since then, Yosemite has been served well by three superintendents—W. B. Lewis and Colonel C. G. Thomson, now deceased, and the present incumbent, Lawrence Merriam.

During all this time, the park administrators have been harassed by private land holdings within the park and by too closely drawn boundaries. The most menacing holdings were tracts of timber within the park and on its border held by companies ready to begin cutting or actually harvesting their tree crop. In 1930, the park was put in a position to purchase over 10,000 acres of land at a cost in excess of $3,000,000, half of which was met by John D. Rockefeller, Jr. Following legislation and appropriation of funds by Congress in 1937, nearly 8,000 acres of sugar pines near the Big Oak Flat Road were acquired, at a cost in excess of a million and a half, though the summer before the purchase was actually made, the lumber companies put as many men as they could work into the area and wrought a terrible devastation.

Much as Muir loved Yosemite, no one can read his voluminous writings, many of them published through the devoted service of Dr. William F. Badé, his literary executor, and not be impressed with his love and knowledge of the entire Sierra Nevada.

Muir first visited the Big Trees in 1875. He was not the discoverer of these trees. They were first seen by white man in 1858 when Hale Tharp, a pioneer who had settled on a ranch about two and a half miles below Three Rivers in 1856, made a trip to what we now know as Giant Forest. Tharp reported that there were about 2,000 Indians then living along the Kaweah Rivers.

It will be remembered that the famous Mariposa Battalion divided its forces—that while two companies were scouring the Yosemite, another company under Captain Kuykendall went south to bring in the Indians on the Kaweah. Captain Kuykendall, according to Dr. Bunnell's account, "vigorously operated in the valleys, hills and mountains of the Kings and Kaweah Rivers and those of the smaller streams south. The Indians of the Kern River, owing to the influence of a Mission chief, 'Don Vicente,' who had a plantation at the Tejon Pass, remained peaceable, and were not disturbed. The success of Captain Kuykendall's campaigns enabled the Commissioners to make treaties with all the tribes within the Tulare Valley, and those that occupied the region south of the

Above: CREST OF THE SIERRA, MT. SILL
AND RIDGE NEAR MIDDLE PALISADE

Photograph—Ansel Adams

Right: JOHN MUIR SHELTER AT
MUIR PASS

Photograph—Marjory Bridge Farquhar
Courtesy—Sierra Club Bulletin

Below: MT. CLARENCE KING

Photograph—Ansel Adams
Courtesy—American Planning and Civic Annual

LITTLE PETE MEADOW AND
LANGILLE PEAK

Photograph—Herbert P. Rankin

ON THE JOHN MUIR TRAIL

EVOLUTION CREEK

Photograph—Ansel Adams
Courtesy—Sierra Club Bulletin

San Joaquin River." After an encounter on the Kings River, the Indians in alarm fled into the canyons. It was while pursuing the fugitives that Captain Kuykendall saw some of the country which he said "was simply indescribable." The stories of the South Sierra brought back by the Captain and his men "were received with doubts or as exaggerations." They declared that they had seen deeper valleys and higher cliffs than were described by those who visited Yosemite. One of the soldiers who afterwards visited Yosemite declared: "The Kings River country, and the territory southeast of it, beats the Yosemite in terrific grandeur, but in sublime beauty you have got us."

The Kings River had been discovered by an early Spanish explorer who crossed the river on Epiphany Sunday, 1805, and named it "Rio de los Sanctos Reyes"—River of the Holy Kings.

Apparently none of the Mariposa Battalion caught a glimpse of the Big Trees of the South Sierra. That discovery was reserved for Hale Tharp some eight years after the military visit to the Canyons of the Kaweahs. That story has been told in the book on the "Big Trees," written by Walter Fry, United States Commissioner, and John R. White, then Superintendent of Sequoia National Park. Mr. Tharp was quoted: "During the summer of 1858, accompanied by two Indians, I made my first trip into the Giant Forest. We went in by way of the Middle Fork River and Moro Rock, and camped a few days at Log Meadow, and came out by the same route. . . . I had two objects in making the trip. One was for the purpose of locating a high summer range for my stock, and the other was due to the fact that stories the Indians had told me of the 'big tree' forest caused me to wonder, so I decided to go and see." Said Mr. Tharp: "I made my second exploration trip into the Giant Forest during the summer of 1860. . . . I took with me John Swanson. We camped one night at Log Meadow, then went on over into the Kings River Canyon, returning again to Log Meadow after a period of about two weeks. . . . So far as I am aware, I am the first white man who ever visited either the Sequoia National Park or the Three Rivers region."

In the spring of 1861 Mr. Tharp began to occupy the Giant Forest as a summer range for stock. He reported that "We saw hundreds of deer, grouse, quail, and a few bear on our trip. We also saw six of the mountain gray wolves." Mr. Tharp recalled that "from 1861 to 1890, when the park was created, I held the Giant Forest country as my range, and some of my family went there every year with the stock. When the land up there was thrown on the market, with other men we bought large holdings." Hale Tharp's summer home at Giant Forest consisted of a huge hollow sequoia log fitted with door, window, and stone fireplace. Messrs. Fry and White have described this fallen tree as 24 feet in diameter at the butt and have estimated its height to have been 311 feet when it fell. This house-in-a-log is now carefully preserved by the National Park Service as one of the antiquities of the park.

It was in 1879 that John Muir was reported to have visited Hale Tharp at Log Meadow, though Muir made his first trip to the Kings and the Big Trees in 1875. It was in 1873 that Muir's Journals carried entries of his climb up Mt. Whitney from the east.

Muir's 1875 trip, as recorded in his book on "Our National Parks," must have been a real adventure. He took with him a "little Brownie mule," but reported that "many a time in the course of our journey when he was jaded and hungry, wedged fast in rocks or struggling in chaparral like a fly in a spiderweb, his troubles were sad to see, and I wished he would leave me and find his way home." Muir told in his book, "I struck out into the majestic trackless forest to the southeastward (from Mariposa Grove), hoping to find new groves or traces of old ones in the dense silver fir and pine woods about the head of Big Creek, where soil and climate seemed most favorable to their growth, but not a single tree or old monument of any sort came to light until I climbed the high rock called Wamellow by the Indians. Here I obtained telling views of the fertile forest-filled basin of the Upper Fresno. Innumerable spires of the noble yellow pine were displayed rising above one another on the braided slopes, and yet nobler sugar pines with superb arms outstretched in the rich autumn light, while away toward the southwest, on the verge of the glowing horizon, I discovered the majestic dome-like crowns of Big Trees towering high over all, singly and in close grove congregations. There is something wonderfully attractive in this king tree, even when beheld from afar, that draws us to it with indescribable enthusiasm; its superior height and massive smoothly rounded outlines proclaiming its character in any company; and when one of the oldest attains full stature on some commanding ridge it seems the very god of the woods."

While Muir declared that "no description can give any adequate idea of their singular majesty, much less of their beauty," yet he has left us some of the best descriptions anywhere to be found. He wrote: "Excepting the sugar pine, most of their neighbors with pointed tops seem to be forever shouting Excelsior, while the Big Tree, though soaring above them all, seems satisfied, its rounded head, poised lightly as a cloud, giving no impression of trying to go higher. Only in youth does it show like other conifers a heaven-ward yearning, keenly aspiring with a long quick-growing top. Indeed the whole tree for the first century or two, or until a hundred to a hundred and fifty feet high, is arrowhead in form, and, compared with the solemn rigidity of age, is as sensitive to the wind as a squirrel tail. The lower branches are gradually dropped as it grows older, and the upper ones thinned out until comparatively few are left. These, however, are developed to great size, divide again and again, and terminate in bossy rounded masses of leafy branchlets, while the head becomes dome-shaped. . . .

"Perfect specimens, unhurt by running fires or lightning, are singularly regular and symmetrical in general form, though not at all conventional, showing infinite variety in sure unity and harmony of plan. The immensely strong, stately shafts, with rich purplish brown bark, are free of limbs for a hundred and fifty feet or so, though dense tufts of sprays occur here and there, producing an ornamental effect, while long parallel furrows give a fluted columnar appearance. . . . A particularly knotty, angular, ungovernable-looking branch, five to eight feet in diameter and perhaps a thousand years old, may occasionally be seen pushing out from the trunk as if determined to break across the bounds of the regular curve, but like all the others, as soon as the general outline is approached the huge limb dissolves into massy bosses of branchlets and sprays, as if the tree were growing beneath an invisible bell glass against the sides of which the branches were moulded, while many small, varied departures from the ideal form give the impression of freedom to grow as they like.

"Except in picturesque old age, after being struck by lightning and broken by a thousand snowstorms, this regularity of form is one of the Big Tree's most distinguishing characteristics. Another

[53]

is the simple sculptural beauty of the trunk and its great thickness as compared with its height and the width of the branches, many of them being from eight to ten feet in diameter at a height of two hundred feet from the ground, and seeming more like finely modeled and sculptured architectural columns than the stems of trees, while the great strong limbs are like rafters supporting the magnificent dome head. . . .

"The bark of full grown trees is from one to two feet thick, rich cinnamon brown, purplish on young trees and shady parts of the old, forming magnificent masses of color with the underbrush and beds of flowers. . . .

"The cones are bright grass-green in color, about two and a half inches long, one and a half wide, and are made up of thirty or forty strong, closely packed, rhomboidal scales with four to eight seeds at the base of each. The seeds are extremely small and light. . . .

"The faint lisp of snowflakes as they alight is one of the smallest sounds mortal can hear. The sound of falling sequoia seeds, even when they happen to strike on flat leaves or flakes of bark, is about as faint. Very different is the bumping and thudding of the falling cones. . . .

"The Big Tree keeps its youth far longer than any of its neighbors. Most silver firs are old in their second or third century, pines in their fourth or fifth, while the Big Tree growing beside them is still in the bloom of its youth, juvenile in every feature at the age of old pines, and cannot be said to attain anything like prime size and beauty before its fifteen hundredth year, or under favorable circumstances become old before its three thousandth. . . .

"It is a curious fact that all the very old sequoias have lost their heads by lightning. . . . But of all living things sequoia is perhaps the only one able to wait long enough to make sure of being struck by lightning. Thousands of years it stands ready and waiting, offering its head to every passing cloud as if inviting its fate, praying for heaven's fire as a blessing; and when at last the old head is off, another of the same shape immediately begins to grow on. Every bud and branch seems excited, like bees that have lost their queen, and tries hard to repair the damage. Branches that for many centuries have been growing out horizontally at

FALLS IN UPPER PALISADE
CANYON

ON THE JOHN MUIR TRAIL

DEVILS CRAGS FROM PALISADE CREEK

Photographs—Ansel Adams   Courtesy—Sierra Club Bulletin

KINGS RIVER CANYON

Left: NORTH TOWER, FROM TALUS SLOPE OF GLACIER MONUMENT

Right: PARADISE PEAK, LOOKING EAST FROM SLOPES AT FOOT OF HELMET

Reproduced from Century Magazine plates made from drawings by Charles D. Robinson, by permission of D. Appleton-Century Co.

Courtesy—Planning and Civic Comment

once turn upward, and all their branchlets arrange themselves with reference to a new top of the same peculiar curve as the old one. Even the small subordinate branches halfway down the trunk do their best to push up to the top and help in this curious head-making."

Like all of Muir's descriptions these words reveal not only what he saw in a single contemplation but what he had observed over a long period of years. He knew the inner life of the sequoias as well as the face they turned toward the world.

Muir's writings, which began to appear in the late seventies, carried news of these impressive giant trees to the reading world, but it was as a result of local effort that the first legislation was proposed to protect these helpless giants which could be hacked down, even with the crude tools then in use, though many of the huge trees which were cut have never been removed from their graves and no one was the gainer. As in the case of many other fine movements there were several sources of information and action. Articles began to appear in the Visalia *Delta* in 1879. The first sawmills, according to Messrs. Fry and White, were about fifty miles east of Visalia, near what is now General Grant National Park. At the same time the California Academy of Sciences was already working for the creation of a liberal Sequoia National Park to embrace a great area in the Sierra between Sequoia and Yosemite. But in a letter to Colonel John R. White, dated June 8, 1929, Colonel George W. Stewart of Visalia, who was largely responsible for the long-continued effort to save the Sequoia country, told of the beginnings of the movement in Visalia. It seems that in 1879, Tipton Lindsey, Receiver of the United States Land Office at Visalia, suggested to J. D. Hyde, Register of the Land Office, that they make an attempt to have the General Grant Grove, then known as the Fresno-Tulare Grove, suspended from entry. As a result, the United States Surveyor-General at San Francisco, Theodore Wagner, formerly a resident of Visalia, issued an order suspending the four sections in which it was thought these trees were located. Later the order of suspension was amended to include the land now in General Grant National Park.

In December of 1881, Senator John F. Miller, who was familiar with the articles in the *Delta*, and had kept in sympathetic touch with the movement, introduced a bill into Congress to create a "national park of the whole west flank of the Sierra Nevada from Tehipite to a point southeast of Porterville and from the higher foothills eastward to the summit of the range." The bill was never reported out of committee because of the objections of the local residents.

Colonel Stewart, who had been absent in Hawaii for three years, again joined the *Delta* when he returned to Visalia. In his 1929 letter to Colonel White, he told of the case of three men who attempted to get possession of Giant Forest and surrounding timber by having a number of men from the Bay region apply for a quarter section of land each under the Timber and Stone Law, but the applications were suspended by the Land Office and the suspension was never revoked. Otherwise, no doubt, the Giant Forest would have fallen as other fine Big Trees fell before the crude cutting tools of the lumbermen, though, due to damages in felling, difficulties in "working" the lumber into useful shape and transporting it, there was always a high percentage of waste and often total loss.

The story recounted by Colonel Stewart in his letter to Colonel White cleared up a number of obscure points, and has given us an authentic record of what happened nearly fifty years ago to save the Big Trees for this and future generations. It is inconceivable that civilized America should now ever withdraw its solemn dedication of the Sequoia country to the enjoyment of the people. Colonel Stewart's account is that of an actor in the play. He wrote:

"At that time we had many editorials and special articles on forest fires, timber trespasses, the saving of the big trees, and kindred topics and were in the habit of sending marked copies of the *Delta* or clippings from its columns to the Secretary of the Interior. Later in 1885, in November, I believe, the Secretary suspended eighteen townships of mountain land from entry because of alleged incorrect surveys. The suspended area covered all, or practically all, of the sequoia groves on the public lands in Fresno and Tulare counties.

"In 1889 a meeting of Tulare County citizens held at Visalia adopted a resolution favoring the creation of a forest reserve to embrace a territory to be named later, and the meeting adjourned to meet later in Fresno. We went to that meeting with the suggested boundaries prepared, the same taking in the entire forest region from Yosemite (State) Park to some point in Kern County. The

Fresno meeting approved the idea, and the first petition naming a large and definite area for a forest reserve was sent to Washington before there was any law therefor.

"Some time that year or early in 1890 . . . the Secretary of the Interior revoked the suspension of 1885 as to the township in which the Atwell mill is situated. . . . Four of us wired a protest to Washington and followed this with a numerously signed petition, and the Secretary rescinded his order revoking the suspension.

"A few weeks later there were current rumors that the Giant Forest region was to be opened to entry. We then began to realize that a mere suspension of lands from entry was not a very efficient protection with a man like Noble at the head of the Department.

"It was then that we thought of the Yellowstone National Park, and read the act creating it and decided that only a national park would insure the permanent preservation of the Giant Forest and other big tree groves.

"I was editor and publisher of the *Delta* at that time. Mr. F. J. Walker, who had been an employee and later a publisher of the paper, was then not otherwise engaged and devoted about three months of his time to helping me on the *Delta*, and especially for the purpose of making this fight for the Forest. We took the matter up with General Vandever, member of Congress from our District, who at once became interested and introduced the bill.

"We wrote letters to every person in the United States, in and out of Congress, whom we knew to . . . favor the idea. Their name was not legion in those days. The response, with few exceptions, was cordial. The one in the East who was head and shoulders above all others in the good work was the editor of *Forest and Stream*, and he interested a number of influential persons and organizations there. . . . We desired to have a large park, embracing Mount Whitney, the Kings and Kern rivers, and the big tree areas, but under the circumstances thought it inadvisable to attempt so much. We had some difficulty in convincing others that it was not an opportune time to ask for so much, and we deemed the proper course to be to confine our efforts to saving the big trees, then in immediate danger. The river canyons we thought could be added if we once had a park in existence. We didn't think then the enlargement of the park would be so long deferred. . . .

"The creation of General Grant National Park was due to the timely suggestion of D. K. Zumwalt of Visalia at the psychological moment. Several people had been interested in the preservation of that area, but Mr. Zumwalt happened to be in Washington at the time the enlargement of Sequoia and the creation of Yosemite Park was up for passage, and his recommendation that the General Grant Grove be also made a park was acted upon favorably by General Vandever and by Congress."

But the hopes of Colonel Stewart and his friends who persuaded their enthusiastic supporters to accept half a loaf were to be long deferred. After the Acts of Congress of 1890, John Muir immediately set himself to work for the enlargement of Sequoia National Park to include Mt. Whitney, the Kern and Kings country. In an article in the *Century Magazine* in November, 1891, entitled, "A Rival to the Yosemite, the Canyon of the South Fork of the King's River, California," Muir presented to the American public the most remarkable descriptions of the Kings country which are extant. He wrote:

"The bottom of the valley is about 5,000 feet above the sea, and its level or gently sloping surface is diversified with flowery meadows and groves and open sunny flats, through the midst of which the crystal river, ever changing, ever beautiful, makes its way; now gliding softly with scarce a ripple over beds of brown pebbles, now rushing and leaping in wild exultation across avalanche rock-dams or terminal moraines, swaying from side to side, beaten with sunshine, or embowered with leaning pines and firs, alders, willows, and tall balsam poplars, which with the bushes and grass at their feet make charming banks. Gnarled snags and stumps here and there reach out from the banks, making cover for trout which seem to have caught their colors from rainbow spray, though hiding mostly in shadows, where the current swirls slowly and protecting sedges and willows dip their leaves.

"From this long, flowery, forested, well-watered park the walls rise abruptly in plain precipices or richly sculptured masses partly separated by side canyons, displaying wonderful wealth and variety of architectural forms, which are as wonderful in beauty of color and fineness of finish as in colossal height and mass. The so-called war of the elements has done them no harm. There is no unsightly defacement as yet; deep in the sky, inviting the onset of

KINGS RIVER CANYON.
PART OF SOUTH WALL OF
TEHIPITE VALLEY

Original drawing by Charles D. Robinson, who accompanied John Muir on his trip in 1891. Reproduced from plates in Century Magazine by permission of D. Appleton-Century Co.

Courtesy—Planning and Civic Comment

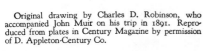

THE SPHINX,
OVERLOOKING THE KINGS CANYON

Photograph—Anse' Adams
Courtesy—Sierra Club Bulletin

[61]

Photograph—Ansel Adams

THE ROARING CASCADES OF THE KINGS RIVER

storms through unnumbered centuries, they will stand firm and seemingly as fresh and unworn as new-born flowers. . . .

"When from some commanding summit we view the mighty wilderness about this central valley, and, after tracing its tributary streams, note how every converging canyon shows in its sculpture, moraines and shining surfaces that it was once the channel of a glacier, contemplating this dark period of grinding ice, it would seem that here was a center of storm and stress to which no life would come. But it is just where the ancient glaciers bore down on the mountain flank with crushing and destructive and most concentrated energy that the most impressive displays of divine beauty are offered to our admiration. Even now the snow falls every winter about the valley to a depth of ten to twenty feet, and the booming of avalanches is a common sound. Nevertheless the frailest flowers, blue and gold and purple, bloom on the brows of the great canyon rocks, and on the frosty peaks, up to a height of 13,000 feet, as well as in sheltered hollows and on level meadows and lake borders and banks of streams."

Muir described the charming Paradise Valley and the "spacious and enchantingly beautiful" Tehipite Valley. He crossed the divide to the Middle Fork of the Kings by way of Copper Creek to this valley, about three miles long and half a mile wide, with walls from 2,500 to nearly 4,000 feet in height. He found the famous Tehipite Dome "sublimely simple and massive in structure," "one of the most striking and wonderful rocks in the Sierra." There were detailed descriptions of scores of marvelous peaks, the Sphinx, "one of the most remarkable in the Sierra," Cathedral Rocks, "most elaborately sculptured, and the most beautiful series of rocks . . . seen in any yosemite in the range," Glacier Monument, "the broadest, loftiest, and most sublimely beautiful of all these wonderful rocks," the North Tower, "a square, boldly sculptured mass 2,000 feet in height," the Dome arches, "heavily glaciated, and offering telling sections of domed and folded structure," and many others.

Muir made a number of trips to the Mt. Whitney-Kings-Kern country. He must many times have traversed the Sierra crests south of Yosemite. His name today is attached to a grove of Big Trees on the Kaweah River in Sequoia National Park, to the Muir Woods of *Sequoia sempervirens* in the shadow of Mt.

Tamalpais, to a mountain in the High Sierra, to an incomparable Pass, and to the John Muir Trail of nearly 200 miles, as measured in the guide book of Walter A. Starr, Jr., published posthumously in 1934. But though there are these memorials to John Muir, much of the superlatively fine region he passionately desired to see in the National Park System still remains outside, some of it injured beyond repair, some of it capable of being restored to its wilderness state, some of it threatened with future destruction, but much of it, mercifully, still waiting for its crown of kingdom which would be bestowed by declaring it forever immune to commercial exploitation and for all time preserved for the people.

It was twelve years after the death of John Muir before the Mt. Whitney and the Kern regions were added to Sequoia National Park, and that addition was the result of an unwilling, but seemingly inevitable, compromise on the part of those who were fighting for a larger area, including the Kings country. Twenty-five years ago, John Muir died, confidently expecting that the Kings canyons, about which he wrote so eloquently in 1891, twenty-two years before, would be given national-park status.

The fine service which John Muir rendered to the American people in acquainting them with the intimate life of the Sierra Nevada through unrivaled descriptions and first-hand information, can never be measured. For John Muir not only *saw* and *felt* his scenery, but he spent days and years studying the Book of Nature in the Sierra so that he could *read* and *interpret* its story to the world. It was he who discovered the traces of the great glaciers which carved the yosemites of the Sierra. He knew its trees, its flowers and shrubs. He knew the animals which roamed its mountain fastnesses. He knew its weather and its habits of flood and storm. He knew its sunshine.

It seems incredible that this act to place the Kings canyons and high surrounding Sierra in the national-park category of land-use should have been so long delayed.

DR. McFARLAND AND THE NATIONAL PARK SYSTEM

"Nowhere in official Washington can an inquirer find an office of the National Parks, or a desk devoted solely to their management."
—Dr. J. Horace McFarland, Annual Convention,
American Civic Association, Washington, December, 1911

IN 1890 the United States had four national parks, created through the unselfish devotion of a few public-spirited citizens who had the vision to see into the future and try to avert the disastrous results of excessive commercial exploitation of our lands and waters. So far no one had promulgated the idea of a National Park System. There were signs, however, that sporadic thinking and acting would bring into being enough of these new land-use areas to create a new category or class.

In 1890 visitors to Yellowstone or Yosemite traveled to certain railheads—the outposts of civilization—and then were transported by stage into the parks. If they penetrated beyond the rather rough wagon roads, they were obliged to walk or ride horseback. Who could have dreamed that a day would arrive when nearly thirty million automobiles would be distributed at the rate of one for every four people in the United States? What would our hard-working New England ancestors have thought of the vacation trips of the twenties, of the thousands of miles of hard pavements which were to follow 1916?

In 1893 a bill was introduced into Congress by Senator Watson C. Squire to create the Washington National Park, to include the spectacularly majestic Mt. Rainier, but it was not until March 2, 1899, in President McKinley's administration, that Mt. Rainier, with its ancient glaciers lying deep and its pristine snowy robe renewed each year, with its trailing glory of forests and streams, was created a national park. The four national parks which had been created up to this time were taken from the public domain. Mt. Rainier National Park was set aside from the "Pacific Forest Reserve." That is, it had already been removed from the public domain and placed in the forest-reserve class. These forest reserves, later to become "national forests," were an evidence that the conservation idea was beginning to take hold. Today the far-flung national forests bear eloquent testimony to the vision of those who have, through the years, promoted this form of land-use. But, with Yellowstone,

Yosemite, Sequoia, and General Grant leading the way, it was already becoming apparent that there were these two separate and distinct forms of public land-use, besides others which were coming to be recognized. At first Rainier was not adequately protected against mineral claims but in 1908 an amendment prohibited the location of new mining claims in the park, although the old ones were protected. In Mt. Rainier National Park, as in most of the other national parks, except Yellowstone, private rights had already been established, but the act of dedication provided that settler- and railroad-owned lands could be exchanged for lieu lands in order to clear the title to the park. The American people gave land away with a free hand, and then, when it was discovered that they had been mistaken, the lands were often bought back, sometimes with the grant of other lands and sometimes for cash from the public treasury. This process, however unprofitable, worked little harm where the lands themselves were not damaged. Unfortunately, the granted lands which bore some of the finest forests of the New World came back to the ownership of the people shorn of their glory and without much economic value. The extent of erosion-control of this era is one indication that lands which once were assets have become actual liabilities.

And so Mt. Rainier, with an all too scanty rim of protection, became a national park. It could hardly be said that even yet we were consciously working for a National Park System. When the twentieth century dawned, twenty-eight years after the establishment of Yellowstone National Park, we had but five national parks in three States. But in 1902 Crater Lake, with its icy waters of sapphire blue, became a national park. It was reserved from the public lands in the State of Oregon, "set apart forever as a public park or pleasure ground for the benefit of the people of the United States," and assigned to the Secretary of the Interior for control and custody. The act expressly forbade "all residence and settlement and the engaging in business or speculative enterprises," but the park was to be open to "scientists, excursionists and pleasure seekers," *and* to the locating and working of mining claims, a menace which has been removed from many of the existing parks but which still hangs like a dark cloud over projects for parks-to-be. We are a metal-hungry people, and in spite of over-production of certain metals and the uneconomic expense of operation for the mining of others, we still think that the impecunious should be permitted to "prospect" for wealth. Apparently we still have faith in Aladdin's lamp, rather than a sound economic system which will permit our people to become and remain joint owners of inspiring natural-scenic areas, safe from economic exploitation.

The Crater Lake Act mentioned specifically what was perhaps implicit in the original Yellowstone Act, and that is the invitation to scientists to come to the park. It was a good many years before we were to undertake seriously a program of education and science in the national parks, but it was coming, and here, thirty-five years ago, in the Crater Lake Act, was a recognition of its desirability.

We then had six national parks, all areas of indisputable beauty and national interest; all of them, except Yellowstone, spotted with private rights and easements which were long to trouble their administrators and limit their service to the public. The promoters of these national parks had vision, but they were obliged to make concessions to the commercial demands of the times. Public opinion was not yet sufficiently informed or possessed of that firm conviction which is needed to resist the pressure of local business interests. But the idea of national parks was growing, and as visitors increased year by year, the education of the American people was being carried on. The time was coming when the people would unite to protect their joint property from harmful encroachments—at first not always successfully, but who can doubt the ultimate outcome?

In 1903 Wind Cave National Park was created in South Dakota. Wind Cave is an interesting phenomenon, but in the light of later discoveries of larger and more impressive caves, it may be that its correct classification would bring it into the State Park System, to be administered in connection with the highly scenic Custer State Park, only a few miles north of it. Possibly it should have been a national monument, a land status which at the time of the Wind Cave Act had not yet been defined.

In 1902 the Secretary of the Interior was charged with the administration of mineral springs in the Chickasaw Indian territory. In 1906, when Oklahoma became a State, the sulphur springs were designated as Platt National Park. This was reminis-

cent of the Hot Springs, in Arkansas, much visited for their cura-
tive waters, which had been a public reservation since 1832. It was
awarded to the National Park Service in the Act of 1916, and
finally became a national park in 1921. (There is some question,
perhaps, as to whether a better classification and a more appropriate agency to administer these springs might be found.)

In 1906 Congress passed an Act for the Preservation of American
Antiquities, which authorized the President by proclamation to
set aside lands owned or controlled by the United States, containing "historic landmarks, historic or prehistoric structures
and other objects of historic or prehistoric interest," as national
monuments. Some fault has been found with the term "monument." To some critics it has unpleasant connotations. But so
far no one has been able to think of any more descriptive or appropriate title. It has now been in common use in the United States,
recognized by the law, for more than thirty years, and has come
to have a meaning of its own.

Honorable John F. Lacey, Congressman from Iowa, who had
taken the lead in securing passage of the Antiquities Act, also
sponsored the bill to create Mesa Verde National Park which
became a law three weeks after the approval of the Antiquities
Act. Except for the fact that the reservation was created by stat-
ute instead of by Executive Order, there seems no reason why Mesa
Verde, one of the most extensive and alluring archeological areas
in the United States, should not be a national monument, for its
scenery, though impressive, would hardly entitle it to become a
national park. Perhaps the difficulty has been that many have
thought of national monuments as less important than national
parks. This is not the case. From an archeological or scientific
point of view, they may be much more important.

In this little chronological account of how the national parks
and monuments came into existence, piecemeal, without comprehensive plan, it is clear, for the most part, that the period was
characterized by *laissez-faire*—"let it alone," or "let it happen"
as it may. Then in 1908 came an event of great significance.
President Theodore Roosevelt called a Conservation Conference
of Governors in Washington, and to this he invited public officials,
university presidents, and officers of the leading conservation
organizations. The Conference was called to give direction and

impetus to the then comparatively new conservation of our forests, which many realized were fast disappearing from the surface of our land. President Roosevelt also had in mind a broader program of conservation to include lands, waters, and minerals. The proceedings of that Conference, three inches thick, stand on the library shelves today. One may look through these five hundred odd pages and find many useful suggestions for the conservation of our natural resources and our economic assets. Speakers from California, Washington, Colorado, and Wyoming, where there were scenic assets recognized by the entire Nation, made no mention of conservation as applied to these precious possessions. In over 200,000 words not over 2,000 were devoted to conservation of natural scenery. Dr. McFarland shared with Governor Charles Evans Hughes of New York the honor of directing the attention of the Conference to this important subject.

Dr. McFarland urged consideration of "one of America's greatest resources—her unmatched natural scenery." Said he: "The National Parks, all too few in number and extent, ought to be held absolutely inviolate as intended by Congress. . . . The scenic value of all the national domain yet remaining should be jealously guarded as a distinctly important national resource, and not as a mere incidental increment. . . . We have for a century, Mr. Chairman, stood actually, if not ostensibly, for an uglier America; let us here and now resolve, for every patriotic and economic reason, to stand openly and solidly for a more beautiful, and therefore a more prosperous America!"

The high note of Governor Hughes' address was a sentence which indicated his sentiments: "The conservation of our resources means not merely their physical preservation but their safeguarding of the common interest in the beauties of nature and their protection both from the ruthless hand of the destroyer and from the grasp of selfish interest." Governor Hughes recounted as an important part of the achievements of the great State of New York the setting aside of the Adirondack Forest Park.

These fine sentiments earned in the thousand-word resolutions adopted by the Governors exactly one word, which indicated that among the desirable effects of conservation of natural resources "the *beauty*, healthfulness, and habitability of our country should be preserved and increased."

But the words of Dr. McFarland, though they may have fallen on ears attuned only to the conservation and utilization of material resources, acted as a spur to himself. From the time of the Conference, he put the force of his dynamic personality behind the movement to secure a single agency in the United States Government which should be responsible for protecting and administering the national parks. He began to envision a system. The first step was to secure the agency. In the eight years during which there were pending measures before Congress to establish such an agency, Glacier, Rocky Mountain, Hawaii, and Lassen National Parks were created, and a number of national monuments were set aside by Executive Order of the President.

Glacier National Park, embracing some of the finest of the northern Rocky Mountains, streaked with living glaciers and spotted with glacial lakes, comprising a long section of the Continental Divide, covered 1,500 square miles, directly adjoining the Waterton Lakes Park of Canada. The Act sounded a caution for the "preservation of the park in a state of nature, so far as consistent with the purpose of the Act," and "for the care and protection of the fish and game" within the park. Unfortunately, there were a great many private holdings within the boundaries. Many difficulties have attended the efforts to clear the park of private property, and the end is not yet.

Rocky Mountain National Park was established in 1915. The park came in with the usual wording that it should be set aside "for the benefit and enjoyment of the people of the United States," but most unfortunately it also provided "that the United States Reclamation Service may enter upon and utilize for flowage or other purposes any area within said park which may be necessary for the development and maintenance of a Government Reclamation project." This provision, as will be seen later, has risen to confound the park administrators, and to curtail the enjoyment of the people in the national park which they have dedicated to the pleasure of the people.

In August of 1916 Kilauea and Haleakala Volcanoes, with protective rims, on the Islands of Hawaii and Maui, were constituted Hawaii National Park by Act of Congress and it was provided that perpetual easements and rights-of-way should be acquired and transferred to the United States.

DR. McFARLAND AND THE NATIONAL PARK SYSTEM

In August of the same year, Lassen Volcanic National Park was created by Congress to protect Lassen Volcano in northern California. As Lassen has been active in recent years, this area has provided a laboratory of research, but the park is also much visited by those who love to camp and fish and so provides a by-product of interesting outdoor life.

Following the Conservation Congress of 1908, Dr. McFarland inaugurated a campaign of education to place the national parks in the hands of a single Federal administrator. In 1910, at his behest, Secretary Ballinger recommended such a bureau in his Annual Report. He stated, "The volume and importance of the work of the supervision of the national parks and reserves under the Secretary of the Interior has passed beyond the stage of satisfactory control by operations carried on with the small force available in the Secretary's office."

At the 1911 Annual Convention of the American Civic Association, President Taft, Secretary of the Interior Fisher, and Dr. McFarland made notable addresses. President Taft made the situation clear when he said: "Now we have in the United States a great many natural wonders, and in that lazy way we have in our Government of first taking up one thing and then another, we have set aside a number of National Parks, of forest reservations covering what ought to be National Parks, and what are called 'national monuments.' We have said to ourselves, 'Those cannot get away. We have surrounded them by a law which makes them necessarily Government property forever, and we will wait in our own good time to make them useful as parks to the people of this country. Since the Interior Department is the "lumber room" of the Government, into which we put everything that we don't know how to classify, and don't know what to do with, we will just put them under the Secretary of the Interior.' That is the condition of the National Parks today."

Secretary Fisher told of the first conference on national parks, held in Yellowstone National Park, under the auspices of the Department of the Interior, with Dr. McFarland as an honored guest and participant. Concerning the proposed Federal agency, he said: "I have talked this matter over with the President, and I know that he is favorably interested in it, and that he gladly accepted the suggestion that he come over here this evening to meet this audience and express his own views in favor of this movement in which the American Civic Association is taking so prominent and leading a part."

Dr. McFarland made a plea, first for the national parks themselves. Said he: "The national playgrounds . . . can, if they are held inviolable, preserve for us, as no minor possessions can, our unique scenic wonders, our great natural mysteries. The spouting geyser basins and marvelous hot springs of the Yellowstone, the atmospheric splendors of the Grand Canyon of the Colorado, the silver threads of the Falls of the Yosemite, the ancient homes of the cliff-dwellers on the Mesa Verde, the ice marvels of the Montana glaciers, the blue marvel of Crater Lake, the towering temples among the big trees of the Sierra—how long would they last unharmed and free to all the people if the hand of the Federal Government were withdrawn from them?"

Speaking of the need for a Federal bureau, Dr. McFarland declared: "Nowhere in official Washington can an inquirer find an office of the National Parks, or a desk devoted solely to their management. By passing around through three departments, and consulting clerks who have taken on the extra work of doing what they can for the Nation's playgrounds, it is possible to come at a little information.

"This is no one's fault. Uncle Sam has simply not waked up about his precious parks. He has not thrown over them the mantle of any complete legal protection—only the Yellowstone has any adequate legal status, and the Yosemite is technically a forest reserve. Selfish and greedy assaults have been made upon the parks, and it is under a legal 'joker' that San Francisco is now seeking to take to herself without having in ten years shown any adequate engineering reason for the assault, nearly half of Yosemite. . . . Now there is light and a determination to do as well for the Nation as any little city does for itself. The Great Father of the Nation, who honors us tonight by his presence, has been the unswerving friend of the Nation's scenic possessions."

Following this memorable meeting in Washington, President Taft sent to Congress on February 2, 1912, a special message: "I earnestly recommend the establishment of a Bureau of National Parks. Such legislation is essential to the proper management of those wondrous manifestations of nature, so startling and so beautiful that everyone recognizes the obligations of the Government to preserve them for the edification and recreation of the people.

"The Yellowstone Park, the Yosemite, the Grand Canyon of the Colorado, the Glacier National Park and the Mount Rainier National Park and others furnish appropriate instances. In only one case have we made anything like adequate preparation for the use of a park by the public. That case is the Yellowstone National Park. Every consideration of patriotism and the love of nature and of beauty and of art requires us to expend money enough to bring all these natural wonders within easy reach of our people. The first step in that direction is the establishment of a responsible bureau, which shall take upon itself the burden of supervising the parks and of making recommendations as to the best method of improving their accessibility and usefulness."

The *Outlook*, in its issue of September 30, 1911, commented upon the Yellowstone National Park Conference and upon the coöperation of the American Civic Association with the Department of the Interior: "It is in point to note that, at the instance and with the approval of the American Civic Association, Secretary Fisher's predecessor, Mr. Ballinger, had offered during the last session of the Sixtieth Congress a carefully drawn bill creating such a (bureau)." In the issue of February 3, 1912, the *Outlook* suggested that the new bureau be called the National Park Service, in conformity with the custom already established in naming the Forest Service. The bill considered by the Sixty-second Congress did in fact adopt that suggestion.

But when the American Civic Association held its 1912 Convention in Baltimore on November 20, the bill had not passed Congress. Again Secretary Fisher spoke. He said: "We did draw up and present to Congress a bill for the creation of a Bureau of National Parks, and this Association was one of the chief agencies that interested itself in pushing that bill. We had the bill considered in committee, and I think the general result was quite favorable, but our lawmakers—to indulge in a public confidence— were so engaged in preparing for the presidential election that they made little progress for us, and today we confront precisely the same situation; and though I am here to report progress, there is not very much progress to report. But I ask this Association to continue to use all the influence in its power to see that some effective means is provided to improve these conditions, and to apply sound principles of administration to our National Parks System."

On that occasion, too, the Right Honorable James Bryce, British Ambassador to the United States, made a memorable address. Ambassador Bryce displayed an intimate knowledge of the subject and of United States geography. Said he: "You have prodigious and magnificent forests; there are no others comparable for extent and splendor with those you possess. These forests, especially those on the Cascade range and the Sierra Nevada, are being allowed to be cut down ruthlessly by the lumbermen. I do not blame them; timber is wanted and they want to drive their trade, but the process goes on too fast and much of the charm of nature is lost while the interests of the future are forgotten. The same thing is happening in the Appalachian ranges in New England and the Alleghanies southward from Pennsylvania, a superbly beautiful country, where the forests made to be the delight of those who wish to ramble among them and enjoy the primitive charm of hills and woodland glades, have been despoiled. Sometimes the trees have been cut down and the land left bare. Sometimes an inextricable tangle of small boughs and twigs remains, so that when a dry year comes a fire rages among them and the land is so scorched that for many long years no great trees will rise to replace those that were destroyed." He continued: "You fortunately have a great supply of splendid water power. I am far from saying that a great deal of it, perhaps most of it, may not be very properly used for industrial purposes, but I do say that it has been used in some places to the detriment, and even to the ruin, of scenery."

Ambassador Bryce had visited four of the national parks. After praising their unique beauty, he paid tribute "to the taste and judgment with which, as it seemed to me three years ago, the hotels in the Yosemite were being managed. There were no offensive signs, no advertisements of medicines, no other external disfigurements to excite horror, and the inns were all of moderate size and not more than two stories high. I earnestly hope that the administration will always be continued on these lines, with this same regard for landscape beauty."

The summation of the address seems incontrovertible:

"The world seems likely to last a long, long time, and we ought to make provision for the future.

"The population of the world goes on constantly increasing and nowhere increasing so fast as in North America.

"A taste for natural beauty is increasing, and, as we hope, will go on increasing.

"The places of scenic beauty do not increase, but, on the contrary, are in danger of being reduced in number and diminished in quantity, and the danger is always increasing with the accumulation of wealth, owing to the desire of private persons to appropriate these places. There is no better service we can render to the masses of the people than to set about and preserve for them wide spaces of fine scenery for their delight."

By 1913 there was a new Secretary of the Interior, Franklin K. Lane. Soon after he was inducted into office, Dr. McFarland and Richard Watrous, Secretary of the American Civic Association, called upon him. They laid before him the great need for a National Park Service. Secretary Lane, who came from California and knew the national parks of the West, gave his callers most sympathetic attention. In April of 1914 hearings were held on the Raker bill. Adolph C. Miller, Assistant to the Secretary of the Interior, spoke for Mr. Lane. The bill was approved by the Secretaries of Interior and Agriculture. But the bill was not to pass the Sixty-third session of Congress.

In April of 1916, hearings were again held on two pending bills, one introduced by Judge Raker and one by William Kent. Stephen T. Mather had now become one of the principal actors in the national-park scene, and was taking the initiative for the Department of the Interior. In addition to the officials, Dr. McFarland and Mr. Watrous, of the American Civic Association, were the principal citizen witnesses. Dr. McFarland called attention to the fact that he and his associates had believed that there should be in the bill "whenever it might seem wise for Congress to pass it, a statement of what parks are for." "It was," he said, "Mr. Frederick Law Olmsted who framed the sentence . . . which is now a part of Mr. Kent's bill: 'The fundamental object of these aforesaid parks, monuments, and reservations is to conserve the scenery and the natural and historical objects therein and to provide for the enjoyment of said scenery and objects by the

[75]

public in any manner and by any means that will leave them unimpaired for the enjoyment of future generations.' "

It was at this hearing that Dr. McFarland produced a letter from Chief Forester Henry S. Graves, written in response to Dr. McFarland's letter, stating that he had heard rumors that the Forester was not in sympathy with the development of national parks under a separate and distinctive administration. Colonel Graves stated bluntly: "Most certainly I am in favor of establishing a national park service, with adequate authority to organize and administer effectively the national parks. . . . I have consistently expressed myself in this way in public and in private. A few weeks ago when you were at my office with the draft of a bill providing for a national park service I again expressed myself as favorable to the idea. At the same time I called your special attention to two points. One was to make certain that the officers in the new park service would all be in the classified civil service. The second matter related to the national monuments. The proposed bill transferred the monuments now under the jurisdiction of the Department of Agriculture to the Department of the Interior. I explained to you the difficulties of administration which would arise from this arrangement and suggested a modification of that part of the bill. . . .

"Your second question is whether 'there is proceeding with my knowledge and consent, within the Forest Service, or through its influence without the Forest Service, any opposition to this bill.' My reply is categorically, no."

And so, with the concurrence of the Departments of Interior and Agriculture, and with the support of the American Civic Association, the American Society of Landscape Architects and the American Scenic and Historic Preservation Society of New York, and with the editorial approval of the *Saturday Evening Post*, the *Outlook* and other journals, the Act of August 25, 1916, was adopted by Congress and approved by President Wilson. For eight years Dr. McFarland had worked in season and out of season, to bring about this result. He had interviewed, in turn, Secretaries Ballinger, Fisher, and Lane, had told his story and converted each one of them. It was not, however, until a deficiency appropriation was made available at the next session of Congress that the Service was organized, with Stephen T. Mather as Director.

STEPHEN T. MATHER AND HIS ASSOCIATES

"Dear Steve: If you don't like the way the parks are being run, come down and run them yourself."
—Franklin K. Lane to Stephen T. Mather in 1914, quoted in address of Horace M. Albright before the American Civic Association, printed in American Civic Annual, 1929.

HORACE M. ALBRIGHT, in an address before the American Civic Association, in 1929, after paying tribute to Dr. McFarland as "the one man who eloquently pleaded for preservation of the scenic resources of our country," who at the conferences in Yellowstone and Yosemite "had helped formulate important protective policies," and who "had been the trusted adviser of two Secretaries of the Interior," told the story of Mr. Mather's connection with the National Park Service: "That (1914) autumn, Secretary Lane got some letters of complaint about conditions in the western parks, especially Sequoia. The letters came from a Chicago businessman who had been spending his summers in the western mountains and parks since 1905, when he climbed Mount Rainier with the Sierra Club, and who had been in the University of California with the Secretary some thirty years before.

"The complaints were fair but firm, and there was an insistent demand that park conditions be improved. The complainant was Stephen T. Mather, borax manufacturer and Sierra Club man. Finally, Secretary Lane wrote him substantially as follows: 'Dear Steve: If you don't like the way the parks are being run, come down and run them yourself.' The letter also contained a serious request to visit him in Washington. Mr. Mather came one cold December day in 1914, and after several days' consideration of the offer made by Mr. Lane, accepted the position of Assistant to the Secretary. . . . After appointing him and getting him settled in an office, he said: 'By the way, Steve, I forgot to ask you your politics.' There was not then and never has been any politics in the National Park Service. . . .

"Mr. Mather's enthusiasm, public spirit, and generosity quickly won him friends in every direction, and especially in Congress. The stage was set for action and results. . . . Both Representatives John E. Raker and William Kent of California introduced the National Park Service bills in the House in the Sixty-fourth Congress, and Senator Smoot introduced the measure in the Senate.

"After an exciting series of hearings and the surmounting of many unexpected delays and difficulties, on August 25, 1916, the Kent Bill became a law, and the National Park Service was created as the ninth bureau of the Department of the Interior."

Honorable Louis C. Cramton, for many years chairman of the appropriations sub-committee in charge of funds for the Interior Department, in a speech delivered on the floor of the House of Representatives, outlined the early days of the Park Service: "When funds became available for actually establishing the National Park Bureau, Mr. Mather was appointed its first director. In the days of struggle before the creation of the bureau, and for many war years afterwards when funds for civilian bureaus were necessarily limited, Mr. Mather gave freely of his personal funds for the benefit of the National Park System.

"By no means the least factor in Mr. Mather's success in coördinating, administering, and developing the National Park System has been his uncanny ability to pick the right man for a particular job; and the loyalty to the cause, as represented by the chief, has caused many a park superintendent and other officer to give up opportunities for larger financial returns to stick to the 'park game,' as they call it. Working under Mr. Mather has been a game in the truest sense of the word.

"I have, in my service of many years on the Committee on Appropriations, come into rather close contact with many branches of the Government service in Washington and in the field, and nowhere have I seen such uniform devotion to the highest ideals of service to the country, such unselfish team-work, such an *esprit de corps* as in the National Park Service as organized and built up under Stephen T. Mather."

Never did a harassed executive inherit a more chaotic situation. Former Secretaries of the Interior, with little financial support from Congress, had called in the Army to patrol and guard Yellowstone. In some of the parks the Army Engineers built the roads; in others, toll roads had been built and were operated for fees. There was no clear line of demarcation between the responsibility of the Interior and War Departments. Secretary Garrison in 1914 had called to Secretary Lane's attention that appropriations charged to the War Department were really expended for the benefit of the Interior Department, and suggested that the time had come to take over the complete handling of the parks. Provision for caring for the public in hotels and lodges in the national parks was through the system of inviting private capital to erect the necessary buildings and operate them as concessions.

In the early years of his service, as Assistant to the Secretary of the Interior and as Director of the National Park Service, Mr. Mather drew around him a remarkable group of men. Horace M. Albright became Mr. Mather's right-hand man in working out the policies which were to guide the newly created National Park Service. In 1919, Mr. Albright succeeded the military officers in command at Yellowstone, becoming the first civilian superintendent in thirty-two years, and Field Assistant to the Director. In 1927, Mr. Albright, in addition to being Superintendent of Yellowstone, was made Assistant Director (field). When Mr. Mather resigned in 1929 because of ill health, Mr. Albright succeeded him as Director, and served five years in that capacity.

When Mr. Albright went to Yellowstone, Arno B. Cammerer, who had been Secretary of the Commission of Fine Arts, became the Assistant Director of the National Park Service. When Mr. Albright was appointed Director, Mr. Cammerer became Associate Director, and when Mr. Albright resigned in 1933, he was succeeded by Mr. Cammerer. Another man who has been continually with the National Park Service almost from the beginning is Arthur E. Demaray, who served successively as Editor, Administrative Assistant, and Assistant Director, and is now Associate Director of the Service.

After twenty-two years, the administration of the National Park Service is still in the hands of those who worked with Mr. Mather, absorbed his ideas and ideals, and who are striving to carry on the work as they believe Mr. Mather would have desired in the face of changing conditions and increasing responsibilities.

Superintendents called early into the Service who became well-known hosts for Uncle Sam in the parks and are still connected with the Service include George B. Dorr of Acadia National Park, Judge Walter Fry and Colonel John R. White of Sequoia National Park, Jesse Nusbaum of Mesa Verde, Edmund B. Rogers of Rocky Mountain and Yellowstone, Major O. A. Tomlinson of Mt. Rainier, M. R. Tillotson of Grand Canyon, J. Ross Eakin of Glacier, Grand Canyon, and Great Smoky Mountains, Thomas J.

Allen who served in various parks and is now a Regional Director, Eivind Scoyen of Zion, Glacier, and Sequoia, Major Thomas Boles of Hawaii and Carlsbad Caverns, Frank Pinkley in charge of the Southwest Monuments, and many others, too numerous to mention, who have dedicated their best efforts toward serving their trustees, the American people, the owners of the national parks. Three superintendents who died in office and who have left indelible marks on the parks they administered and will long be remembered by park visitors, are W. B. Lewis of Yosemite, Roger W. Toll of Mt. Rainier, Rocky Mountain, and Yellowstone, and Colonel C. G. Thomson of Crater Lake and Yosemite. At the time of the tragic death of Roger Toll, the Park Service also lost another member of the staff, a young man who had done much to develop park ideals and strengthen the service to the public, George M. Wright of California.

The phrase "Stephen T. Mather and his Associates" is, therefore, used advisedly, for the National Park Service today is being administered by the men who helped to develop standards and ideals with him and who have dedicated themselves to carrying on the work which Mr. Mather so nobly began.

Along with many complications and troubles, Mr. Mather inherited certain traditions. The act creating Yellowstone National Park carried three general directions: (1) that the area was being set aside "as a public park or pleasuring ground for the benefit and enjoyment of the people," (2) that all timber, mineral deposits, natural curiosities or wonders within the park should be preserved from injury or spoliation and retained in their natural condition, and (3) that provision should be made against the "wanton destruction of fish and game found within the park, and against their capture or destruction for the purposes of merchandise or profit."

After many earnest discussions with the staff of the National Park Service, on May 13, 1918, Secretary Lane wrote a letter to Mr. Mather setting forth for the information of the public an announcement of the policy of the Park Service. This policy, the Secretary stated, was based on three broad principles: "First, that the national parks must be maintained in absolutely unimpaired form for the use of future generations as well as those of our own time; second, that they are set apart for the use, observation, health, and pleasure of the people; and third, that the national interest must dictate all decisions affecting public or private enterprise in the parks." Stated obversely, the Secretary declared: "The commercial use of these reservations except as specially authorized by law, or such as may be incidental to the accommodation and entertainment of visitors, will not be permitted under any circumstances."

Since many of the national parks had been taken from national forests, and others created from the public domain adjoined existing national forests, it was natural that Mr. Lane should have laid down for the parks a policy on uses commonly permitted and encouraged in national forests. Concerning grazing he indicated to the Director of the National Park Service that in all national parks except Yellowstone he might permit grazing of cattle "in isolated regions not frequented by visitors and where no injury to the natural features of the parks may result from such use." But he banned utterly the grazing of sheep in national parks.

Secretary Lane gave specific instructions to the Director that he "should not permit the leasing of park lands for summer homes," and the reason he gave was this: "It is conceivable, and even exceedingly probable, that within a few years under a policy of permitting the establishment of summer homes in national parks, these reservations might become so generally settled as to exclude the public from convenient access to their streams, lakes, and other natural features, and thus destroy the very basis upon which this national playground system is being constructed." Since the building of summer homes is quite a common practice within the national forests, here was a distinct difference of policy in the national parks. Another difference of policy was announced in the prohibition of the cutting of trees except where absolutely necessary for buildings and other improvements for the accommodation of the public and the administration of the parks, and then the trees were to be removed without injury to the forests or disfigurement of the landscape.

The Secretary pointed out that roads, trails, and buildings should be built to harmonize with the landscape; he directed that all improvements should be carried out "in accordance with a preconceived plan developed with special reference to the preservation of the landscape," and that comprehensive plans for the future development of the national parks should be prepared.

The many private holdings in the parks, so long to harass the Service, were recognized as a menace to the public character of the parks, and a determination to eliminate them as rapidly as possible was recorded. Automobiles and motorcycles, newer then than now, were to be permitted in all of the national parks, but "mountain climbing, horseback riding, walking, . . . swimming, boating and fishing" were commended along with motoring.

The Secretary encouraged the educational use of the national parks, suggesting special facilities for classes in science and the establishment of museums in the parks.

For the future, the Secretary directed that, in studying new park projects, the Director should seek to find "Scenery of supreme and distinctive quality or some natural feature so extraordinary or unique as to be of national interest and importance."

It may be said in comment that as time has gone on, the tendency has been to stiffen rather than to relax these principles and standards of practice. Hunting never has been permitted in the national parks. Fishing for pleasure is encouraged. Grazing has been eliminated in many places and it is the hope of those now responsible for the administration of the parks that the time may come when there will be no grazing of cattle, as there is now no grazing of sheep in any national park or monument. Except in the rare instances when Congress has directed the introduction of extraneous and undesirable intrusions, and for the non-conforming uses which have sometimes been permitted for a period of years, the national parks have been protected from uses not compatible with their primary purpose. That is why they offer to the public today unrivaled opportunities to see the most beautiful and the most interesting regions in the United States and its possessions.

When Mr. Mather took over the directorship of the national parks, there were seventeen national parks and twenty-one national monuments. Except for the Sieur de Monts National Monument, now Acadia National Park, in Maine, all of the parks and monuments lay west of the Mississippi River. The system then included the national park in Alaska and the two volcanoes in Hawaii.

It will be recalled that the year in which the National Park Service was authorized by Congress saw also the first of the large Federal-aid grants to the States for the building of public highways, and that the month in which the Service was actually organized saw also the entrance of the United States into the World War. These two events exercised a very real influence on the national parks. The war caused an almost complete cessation in pleasure travel, to the extent that it was necessary to make repeated announcements that the national parks were open, as usual, to the public. But perhaps the movement which was to provide hard-surfaced highways for this country has left a more lasting and deeper impression on the parks. Motor travel, at first small in most of the national parks, with the improvement of highways has increased enormously, so that now, in most parks, it exceeds the substantial volume of visitors who come by rail and use buses in the parks. Those who come by rail generally are on "all-expense tours" and stay in the hotels or lodges. Those who come by automobile may patronize the hotels or lodges, but they frequently stay in the cabins or set up their Lares and Penates in the public camps provided for their comfort and convenience.

By some the great increase in visitors to the national parks is deplored. This is a valid criticism, no doubt, in those parks where the crowds are so great that they do actual damage to the park itself and limit the enjoyment of visitors. But it should be realized that the national parks do belong to the American people as a whole, and are open for their enjoyment and edification. When a pitcher of water is full, it will hold no more, and it is now recognized that there is such a thing as a park or a valley *full* of people, and that places of overflow must be provided. In Yosemite Valley, where the greatest congestion is reported, the high Sierra country around the park and the groves of Big Trees have been provided with facilities for caring for guests; these have good roads and trails, so that there is at least the invitation for valley visitors to go into other parts of the park. Probably other methods will need to be used to bring about a dispersal of large crowds at congested centers in the parks.

In Secretary Lane's letter of 1918, there was a direction to the effect that the buildings and other facilities for accommodating visitors be confined to as small an area as feasible. This principle has been followed in providing new facilities in old parks and in planning new parks. Hand in hand with this policy has been the definite aim of the National Park Service to hold great regions in each of the larger parks in as near a natural condition as possible,

[83]

so that visitors on foot and on horseback might enjoy the wilderness features. It is now clear that if there is to be anything like an adequate supply of wilderness regions in the national parks, these areas must be increased by incorporating into the National Park System those remaining untouched areas which meet the standards set by Yellowstone, Yosemite, and other superlative national parks. Already the inroads on the wilderness have been so great that there are comparatively few unspoiled areas left, just as Ambassador Bryce predicted in 1912. And as the wilderness has been vanishing, the demand for "back country" into which hikers and horseback riders may go is increasing. The trends are unmistakable.

The wisdom of Secretary Lane, Mr. Mather and his associates is increasingly apparent, as time demonstrates the need for the safeguards they set up. The Department of the Interior and the National Park Service have been obliged to accept from the hands of Congress national parks with undesirable easements and rights in them. Congress has even directed the desecration of certain national parks, as in the case of the Hetch Hetchy; but the Department and the Service have striven steadily to decrease and eliminate all adverse uses and practices in the national parks, and to foster restoration to natural conditions wherever possible. It has been found that in meadows which have been grazed for years, the wild flowers will come back in areas protected from grazing.

When Mr. Mather assumed office, there was little understanding of the national parks as a well-defined type of land-use. The public knew about Yellowstone as a land of wonders, and Yosemite as a valley incomparable, but few dreamed that the foundation was being laid for a new and entrancing type of reservation which would bring to young and old much enjoyment and many cultural opportunities.

Mr. Mather put himself and his private fortune at the service of the national parks. He purchased the Tioga Road entrance into Yosemite when he could not secure public appropriations to buy it. He interested his friends in aiding the parks. He lectured on national parks in all parts of the country, and gave to his audiences a new conception of national parks and their service to the public. He explained the difference between national parks and national forests. Even today there is much confused thinking about national parks and national forests.

STEPHEN T. MATHER AND HIS ASSOCIATES

Definitions sometimes seem tedious, but perhaps it is just as well to present a simple description of each which has been used by the American Civic Association as a measuring rod. According to the Park Primer, issued in four editions, beginning in 1922, "A NATIONAL PARK is an area, usually of some magnitude, distinguished by scenic, scientific, historic, or archeologic attractions and natural wonders and beauties which are distinctly *national* in importance and interest, selected as eminent examples of scenic, scientific or historic America, and preserved with characteristic natural scenery, wildlife and historic or archeologic heritage, in an unimpaired state, as a part of a National Park System for the use and enjoyment of this and future generations."

In this same Park Primer it is recognized that "Recreational uses of the National Forests are valuable to the public and may be broadly and beneficently extended and encouraged, always, however, in the knowledge that the primary purposes of national forests are the provision of timber and the conservation of water-sources, and that dependence for recreational uses of such areas must not lose sight of these primary purposes and other secondary commercial uses of National Forests. In National Forests, grazing and other commercial uses are permitted, hunting and fishing under state laws are allowed, private individuals may erect and occupy summer cottages. There are many beautiful and inspiring views in the National Forests. Especially fine stands of trees are frequently given protection. Forest cover along streams is sometimes left uncut. Study areas of characteristic timber are being set aside to be kept in their primitive state. Many wildlife sanctuaries are contained within National Forests. Generally speaking, the U. S. Forest Service pursues a policy of providing for selective cutting of timber as it becomes ripe for market, as authorized by law; supervises the grazing of herds owned by private individuals, permits fencing of pasture, and meets the economic demands made upon the forests."

Since this was written, the Forest Service has set aside a large number of Primitive Areas by Executive Order of the Secretary of Agriculture. These are generally roadless, but grazing and cutting of timber are not necessarily entirely excluded. The Forest Service is now developing recreation plans for certain areas in which conflicting commercial uses are being excluded or reduced. It so happens that some of the Primitive and Recreation Areas meet all of the national-park standards. These areas were in the forests when they were transferred, often by Executive Order of the President, from the public domain, long before there was a National Park Service. Now that the national-park land-use is recognized, the areas which meet all the national-park standards will undoubtedly, in the course of the next few years, be transferred to the National Park System.

The national parks and monuments have been added to the system carefully. Probably no Federal agency ever existed which has reported adversely on as many proposals for additional lands as has the National Park Service. When the public first became aware of the drawing power of national parks, every community, every State, and every promotion organization wanted to create a national park in its vicinity. One of the most famous fights to keep an area out of the National Park System was made when it was proposed that the Ouachita National Forest be transferred to the National Park Service. It was easily demonstrated that the Ouachita National Forest was being administered under a policy fully adapted to its best possibilities. It was an economic asset in a State which very much needed economic assets. Its scenery, while pleasant, was not outstanding and, in the opinion of land-planning students, would never have drawn a national patronage. Congress refused to consider a change of status, and the Forest Service was permitted to continue its already well-established policy of making the land pay its way.

If the Federal Government were the only agency dealing in parks it might not be possible to apply so strict an entrance examination; but, fortunately, the States are now building creditable State Park Systems to preserve in their natural condition the best examples of State scenery and to provide recreational and educational opportunities for the people of the State. There are also the county and regional parks and parkways in addition to the town and municipal park systems. It is, therefore, possible and practicable to limit national parks to national service.

For the most part, national parks have been added one by one. Mt. McKinley, Alaska, was created in 1917. At the time that the National Park Service was created, Grand Canyon was a national monument administered by the Forest Service. In 1919 it was made a national park by Congress. In the same year Acadia National Park was created to include a national monument and additional land purchased and given to the Government. This same year, Zion, that colorful canyon in Utah, became a national park, and in 1928, Bryce Canyon, which had been a national monument, was transformed into a national park.

Up to this time there had been only one national park in the East, where the public lands had long since passed into private ownership, and yet, almost miraculously there were some areas comparatively free from the scars of civilization. In the twenties, therefore, Secretary Work set up the Southern Appalachian National Park Commission, consisting of Representative Henry W. Temple of Pennsylvania, William C. Gregg of New Jersey, Major William A. Welch of New York, Harlan P. Kelsey then of Massachusetts, but formerly of North Carolina, and Colonel Glenn S. Smith of the Department of the Interior. The Commission was charged with the duty of recommending a national park in the Southern Appalachians. After careful survey of the ground, the Committee reported, recommending the Great Smoky Mountains and a long strip of the Blue Ridge in Virginia. The resulting Temple-Swanson Act authorized the Secretary of the Interior to accept lands for these parks and for Mammoth Cave National Park, in Kentucky. The problem was how to bring these areas, mostly privately owned, back into public ownership. The States of Tennessee and North Carolina appropriated money and raised private subscriptions to purchase the land, but when it seemed that the project was about to fail, Mr. John D. Rockefeller, Jr., made five million dollars available. The Great Smoky Mountains National Park was established for protection in 1930. Mr. Rockefeller helped to the extent of half a million dollars in the purchase of the Blue Ridge area, and the Shenandoah National Park was established in 1935. The Grand Tetons came into the system in 1929. In 1931 Isle Royale in Lake Superior, in 1934 the Everglades in Florida, and in 1935 Big Bend in Texas were authorized. But purchase of the necessary lands has dragged. The areas are not yet national parks.

In the Report of Director Albright, dated October 12, 1932, it was stated that the National Park Service administered twenty-two national parks, totaling some 13,000 square miles, and thirty-six national monuments, totaling some 6,500 square miles. Then on July 28, 1933, President Franklin D. Roosevelt by Executive Order transferred a long list of monuments to the Park Service. This brought under a single central jurisdiction all of the monuments created by Executive Order under the National Antiquities Act, and other miscellaneous areas, some of which have been re-transferred.

Today the National Park Service administers twenty-seven national parks and seventy-three national monuments, covering some seventeen and a half million acres of land and water, of which nearly six million acres lie in Alaska.

It must not be supposed that the national parks, even as they are today, have been easily defended against selfish and unwarranted encroachments. The Hetch Hetchy fight which resulted in turning the Hetch Hetchy yosemite without recompense over to the City and County of San Francisco was one of the most tragic and disastrous experiences in all national-park history. The people of San Francisco did, indeed, invest a vast sum of money in the making of the reservoir and in construction of the necessary accompanying works—something like a hundred million dollars, it is reported; but many engineers now think that a much smaller expenditure would have brought to the city all that was needed. There never was any claim that there were not alternative physical schemes, only that this proposal could be carried out more cheaply. And now even this claim seems disproved. It may take hundreds of years; but perhaps some day this great continent will be inhabited by a race of people who value their heritage of natural scenery so highly that they will redeem the Hetch Hetchy, and allow Nature to go to work with her age-taking remedies to restore the beauty that has been unthinkingly given away!

The Grand Canyon National Park, one of the most marvelous spectacles in the entire world, has been subject to repeated attacks. Its first protection came when, aroused by a reported project to encircle the rim by a sight-seeing electric trolley line, Gifford Pinchot, stirred up by Dr. McFarland, persuaded "Teddy" Roosevelt to make it a national monument by Executive Order. Thirty-two years were required to establish it as a national park, and when Congress did act in 1919, mining and grazing were permitted under the act. Since then, the mining provision has been revoked, but not until after a long fight, in which mining claims, outrageously enough, were staked along the Bright Angel Trail in a way to give a monopoly to the holders to conduct trips along this trail from the rim into the floor of the canyon far below! At last it was proved that these claims were not filed or maintained in good faith. The park is now safe from new filings, and old claims have been abrogated.

By Act of Congress in 1891, the Secretary of the Interior was authorized to grant, under certain conditions, rights-of-way in Yosemite, Sequoia, and General Grant parks for the construction of electrical plants and all their paraphernalia—reservoirs, mining, quarrying, and cutting of timber. In 1911 this authority was slightly amended to limit easements to fifty years, and in 1921 such installations were made by law subject to specific action of Congress.

Another menacing threat to three national parks was included in the acts of dedication—all before the creation of the National Park Service. In Glacier, Rocky Mountain, and Lassen National Parks, there was an identical provision that "the U. S. Reclamation Service may enter upon and utilize for flowage or other purposes any area within said park which may be necessary for the development and maintenance of a Government reclamation project." In the Grand Canyon Act, passed in 1919, the wording varies slightly, but does permit reclamation projects.

It just happened that at the time these parks were created, this country had been stirred by the new possibilities opened up through the reclamation of arid lands in the West. There were not only great engineers who installed the systems, but there were minor prophets who heralded reclamation as a deliverance which would give happy homes and pleasant living to many independent farmers. No one at that date knew, or apparently cared, whether the projects were economically sound, and certainly there were few who foresaw the era of over-production and stabilized population into which we were heading.

Perhaps it was not unnatural, therefore, that Secretary Lane, in whose Department the Reclamation Service was an established bureau, who was himself an ardent believer in the rosy promise of reclamation for the West, and who had only recently been introduced to his responsibilities concerning national parks, should not at once have realized that reclamation was incompatible with national parks. Indeed, Robert B. Marshall, whose training had been as a geographer, during the time when he was serving as Superintendent of National Parks, prior to the appointment of

Mr. Mather as Director, consistently advised the Secretary to look out for the interests of reclamation in all pending measures to create new national parks.

It was not until Judge John Barton Payne became Secretary of the Interior in 1920 that the National Park Service found a complete advocate. With his keen brain and his training in legal practice and on the bench, Judge Payne at once saw that if national parks were to survive at all, they must be held inviolate from adverse uses. In recent years public opinion has come to support the platform laid down by Judge Payne. Succeeding Secretaries of the Interior have generally supported the policies of the Park Service. Secretaries Wilbur and Ickes came in as known conservationists. In 1931 Congress wiped out many special privileges. In Rainier, Glacier, and Rocky Mountain parks authority for railway franchises was repealed; in Mesa Verde and Grand Canyon authorization for prospecting was abrogated; in Mt. McKinley prospecting was sharply restricted.

The one national park which came to us without strings of any kind is the first—Yellowstone. And yet predatory interests in Montana and Idaho have tried again and again to set up profitable enterprises in this park—profitable, it may be explained, because of the *free* storage they hoped to secure on the top of Yellowstone Lake, or from free franchises for railroads. From 1884 to 1893, private interests sought unsuccessfully to secure from Congress the authority for a right-of-way for a railroad through Yellowstone National Park, and when the proposal met resistance, an effort was made to eliminate the desired lands from the park. Louis Cramton, a member of Congress for eighteen years, in his "Early History of Yellowstone National Park and Its Relation to National Park Policies," issued in 1932, told of the years in which the House of Representatives seemed "amenable to the desire of these private interests, and the Senate was the stronghold of opposition under the leadership of Senator Vest, but," declared Mr. Cramton, "finally the time came that any railroad right-of-way proposal or park segregation scheme brought definite adverse report from Congressional committees."

One of the great menaces to national parks came with the passage of the Federal Water Power Act of 1920, which would have opened all national parks to power installations. Secretary Payne opposed the signing of the measure by President Wilson. It was only when a "gentleman's agreement" was reached between the leaders in Congress and the President that at the next session they would give active support to an amendment which would exclude national parks from the provisions of the act, that President Wilson finally signed the measure. In the next session of Congress, it appeared that, though the Congressional leaders were not disposed to recede from their promise, they personally would not have been disappointed if their efforts had met with failure. In other words, they apparently did not feel that they had guaranteed success. Dr. McFarland, representing the American Civic Association, was active, in coöperation with other conservation organizations, in making it impossible for the proposed amendment to fail. Finally the amendment was passed in the closing days of the session and all existing national parks were definitely excluded from the provisions of the Federal Water Power Act

In the meantime, both Montana and Idaho were pushing their claims for the waters of Lake Yellowstone. Montana desired a dam at the outlet of the lake, which lies high on the crest of the Rocky Mountains, in order to control the flow of flood waters into Montana. At the hearings there was ample testimony to the effect that the proposal, which was advanced by politicians to win political favor, was not even a sound engineering enterprise. Fortunately, Judge Payne made it clear at this hearing that Yellowstone Lake should not be tampered with. He saw clearly that such a commercial invasion in the hitherto inviolate Yellowstone Park would not only grievously injure the park but would ultimately set a precedent which would wreck other parks. In Judge Payne, the proposers of commercial works in national parks met their Waterloo.

At the same time that these Montana proposals were pending in the early twenties, Idaho proposed to build a reservoir in the southwest corner of Yellowstone, and finally, when it appeared that Congress was unwilling to grant such permission, a movement was set on foot to remove the area bodily from the park. This measure was fought bitterly by the National Park Service and the conservation organizations. Idaho at that time also proposed to divert water from Lake Yellowstone through a tunnel across the Divide. This proposal was revived in the last Congress and will undoubtedly appear again, though it does not seem probable that Congress will depart from the policy of nearly sixty years which has given Yellowstone National Park absolute protection from commercial projects.

The action of Congress in authorizing the Colorado-Big Thompson water diversion project was fought by all the conservation organizations, insofar as it affected Rocky Mountain National Park. Unfortunately, the provision in the act creating the park was still in effect. Moreover, the Reclamation Service made definite representations that there would be no need to enter on the park land in the construction of the tunnel underneath. The damage would fall principally on Grand Lake, the rim of which had already suffered from private occupation, and upon the Big Thompson approach highway. The time will come when national park approach roads will receive legal protection, but at the present time these roads are under various state and local jurisdictions. When they pass through national forests they have received some protection, and the tendency is to exercise increased care in nearby cutting operations.

Perhaps this account of the service which Mr. Mather and his associates have rendered to the American people in giving responsible custodianship to lands hitherto open to many misuses, in their efforts to free the parks from legal handicaps and threatened invasions, and in developing and adopting standards for qualifications and uses of the national parks, can best be closed by presenting a "Who's Who" in the National Park Service of today:

Arno B. Cammerer, Director; Arthur E. Demaray, Associate Director; John R. White, Acting Chief of Operations; George A. Moskey, Chief Counsel; Carl P. Russell, Supervisor of Research and Information; Conrad L. Wirth, Supervisor of Recreation and Land Planning; Ronald F. Lee, Supervisor of Historic Sites; Oliver G. Taylor, Chief of Engineering; Thomas C. Vint, Chief of Planning; John D. Coffman, Chief of Forestry; Isabelle F. Story, Editor-in-Chief; Miner R. Tillotson, Director, Region I, Richmond, Virginia; Thomas J. Allen, Jr., Director, Region II, Omaha, Nebraska; Hillory A. Tolson, Acting Director, Region III, Santa Fé, New Mexico; and Frank A. Kittredge, Director, Region IV, San Francisco, California.

BOOK II—JOURNEYS

PROSPECT: PHILOSOPHY OF PARKS AND PEOPLE

MAN, himself a product of Nature, has in the years since he emerged into the species *Homo sapiens*, spent considerable time—eons, in fact—in creating a man-made environment. This is superimposed upon or takes the place of Nature's Garden of Eden. In the process, Man has destroyed, or marred beyond recognition, much beautiful landscape. Thus, today a great part of the civilized world lives in the close ranks of city dwellings, surrounded by concrete-covered ground, in buildings of brick, stone, and steel which more or less effectively cut off the free sun and air provided by Nature. These human beings are often completely divorced from contact with the Earth. Indeed, today, were it not for city and regional parks and playgrounds, many children would not know at first hand anything about the trees, the streams, and the growing plant life which played such an important part, economically and emotionally, in the lives of the pioneers in America. The park zoo for many millions is the only place where children and adults actually see animals other than domestic cats and dogs or caged birds.

But, it may be said, the civilization which produced cities and city life has brought with it refinements of living and culture in art, music, literature, and learning unknown to aboriginal man. Without deprecating what the Arts and Sciences have done to lift Man from primitive living conditions (in which danger to life and limb no doubt counterbalanced the healthful advantages of living in the open) and to enlarge his opportunities for acquiring "knowledge of information," it is pertinent to inquire whether his narrowed contact with Nature has taken away from Man something of value which it is desirable to recapture.

Perhaps the false sense of importance which comes to many large money-makers in the marts of trade, to successful politicians, to the producers of lucrative jazz in art and music, and to all who gain power not based on human service, is one of the regrettable losses visited upon Man by man-made civilization. The great men of the past—teachers, scientists, statesmen, artists, musical com-

[93]

posers, creators of living literature—have nearly always possessed a quality of humility. They studied the history of men, institutions, and ideas which transcends the history of single individuals. Or they studied Science, which yields knowledge reluctantly, bit by bit, as a reward for persistent search and questioning, and invariably leaves the student with the realization that there is a vast reservoir of knowledge and laws which limited intelligence and mental powers have yet failed to penetrate. Or they listened to an inner voice or followed an inner light, and so came to be called inspired. These "great" discovered in various ways some inkling of the laws of life and living beyond their making. Their humility came from a realization that they were but an infinitesimal part of a Universe so great that it beggars human comprehension. They learned that they were subject to laws which, however little understood, moved inexorably; that, without choice, they came into the world and faced or sought to escape its problems.

Primitive peoples read the laws of Nature dimly, perhaps, and personified in their gods and superstitions the little knowledge that they sensed. But the "gods" kept them disciplined and humble. Today, many of the peoples who have cast off the formalized religions and superstitions of the past have also lost contact with the manifestations of Nature and the laws of the Universe. They have lost their sense of proportion, and their perspective has become distorted.

Moreover, the city habits of living indoors and of intense application to mundane problems, wear men out before their time. At best, the span of human life is short. Consider how many businessmen, who now live in an age when Science has contributed to the lengthening of human life, find themselves at fifty or sixty with wrecked digestions, worn-out hearts, hardened arteries or victims of some of the hundred-and-one diseases due to slothful indoor physical habits and continuous mental strain. It is a paradox that, with the possible prolongation of life, there are so many who cannot enjoy the later years saved to them by Science.

John Muir, who became in his middle years a successful orchardist, always referred to his earlier years in the Sierra, when he earned little money, ate sparingly, and wandered much, as the "free" years of his life. He might have called them the "rich" years of his life, when he was not encumbered with possessions and their care. This is no argument for avoiding responsibility or for escaping duties. But it is an argument for the rejuvenation and the restoration of equilibrium which comes from outdoor recreation.

One of the proverbial joys of youth comes from pleasure in physical movement and muscular well-being. Outdoor recreation can continue to give equal pleasure to the middle-aged and elderly, if they are able to ward off the painful diseases which attack the muscles and nerves of over-fed and under-exercised bodies.

But far beyond the pleasure of walking or riding horseback in the ordinary open country, indulging the eyes in pleasant prospects, feeling the welcome warmth of the sun and the revivifying breezes of the air, is the spiritual uplift which comes from the contemplation of superlative scenery. Man is indeed "in tune with the Infinite" when he scales high mountains and looks upon stupendous scenes.

Conrad Gesner, writing in 1555, as quoted in translation in the *Sierra Club Bulletin* of April, 1938, expressed something of this exaltation when he said: "For how great the pleasure, how great think you, are the joys of the spirit, touched as is fit it should be, in wondering at the mighty mass of mountains while gazing upon their immensity and, as it were, in lifting one's head among the clouds. In some way or other the mind is overturned by their dizzying height and is caught up in contemplation of the Supreme Architect."

Writing in the present period, Professor G. M. Trevelyan has not only traced the influence of natural beauty on human beings but has declared that sensitivity to fine scenery is indeed an index of the plane on which men and women are living. His words carry conviction: "The appeal of natural beauty is more commonly or at least more consciously felt today than ever before, just because it is no new argument, no new dogma, no doctrine, no change of fashion, but something far older yet far more fresh, fresh as when the shepherd on the plains of Shinar first noted the stern beauty of the patient stars. Through the loveliness of nature, through the touch of sun or rain, or the sight of the shining restlessness, we feel 'Unworded things and old to our pained heart appeal.' And to the young who have no pain, who have not yet kept watch on man's mortality, nature is a joy responding to their own, haunting them like a passion.

"This flag of beauty, hung out by the mysterious Universe, to claim the worship of the heart of man—what is it, and what does its signal mean to us? There is no clear interpretation. But that does not lessen its value. Like the Universe, like Life, natural beauty also is a mystery. But whatever it may be, whether casual in its origin as some hold who love it well, or whether as others hold, such splendor can be nothing less than the purposeful message of God—whatever its interpretation may be, natural beauty is the ultimate spiritual appeal of the Universe, of Nature, or of the God of Nature, to their nursling, man. It and it alone makes a common appeal to the sectaries of all our religious and scientific creeds, to the lovers of all our different schools of poetry and art, ancient and modern, and to many more beside these. It is the highest common denominator in the spiritual life of today."

Scenery breaks down into countless appeals—the air itself, the clouds, the mountain masses having form, texture, and color; water, restless and seething or smooth and quiet; all the plant cover from the tiny little ferns and fungi to the Big Trees. It is even inseparably linked to the birds and the beasts, large and small, living in their native habitats.

John Muir, in his Journal of 1868, spoke of the air. A young man on adventure bent, he was tramping down the Santa Clara Valley: "It was now springtime and the weather was the best we ever enjoyed. Larks and streams sang everywhere; the sky was cloudless, and the whole valley was a lake of light. The atmosphere was spicy and exhilarating. . . . This San José sky was not simply pure and bright, and mixed with plenty of well-tempered sunshine, but it possessed a positive flavor, a *taste* that thrilled throughout every tissue of the body. Every inspiration yielded a well-defined piece of pleasure that awakened thousands of new palates everywhere. Both my companion and myself had lived on common air for nearly thirty years, and never before this discovered that our bodies contained such multitudes of palates, or that this mortal flesh, so little valued by philosophers and teachers, was possessed of so vast a capacity for happiness.

"We were new creatures, born again, and truly not until this time were we fairly conscious that we were born at all. Never more, thought I as we strode forward at faster speed, never more shall I sentimentalize about getting free from the flesh, for it is steeped like a sponge in immortal pleasure."

[96]

PROSPECT: PHILOSOPHY OF PARKS AND PEOPLE

John C. Van Dyke, writing thirty-three years later, in 1901, commented on the air of the New World. Said he: "We have often heard of sunny Italy or the 'clear light' of Egypt, but believe me there is no sunlight there compared with that which falls upon the upper peaks of the Sierra Madre or the uninhabitable wastes of the Colorado Desert. Pure sunlight requires for its existence pure air, and the Old World has little of it left. . . . The same thick air is all over Europe, all around the Mediterranean, even over in Mesopotamia and by the banks of the Ganges. It has been breathed and burned and battle-smoked for ten thousand years. Ride up and over the high table lands of Montana—and one can still ride for days without seeing a trace of humanity—and how clear and scentless, how absolutely intangible that sky-blown sun-shot atmosphere! You breathe it without feeling it, you see through it a hundred miles and the picture is not blurred by it."

This ethereal air, then, is one of the first characteristics of national parks—one that is rapidly destroyed when, in the dry season, too many human beings are introduced into spaces which lose their clear air as they are too densely occupied.

Both John Muir and John Van Dyke deplored the damage to the wilderness character of the beautiful places of the earth. In 1897 Muir wrote: "The axe and saw are insanely busy, chips are flying thick as snowflakes, and every summer thousands of acres of priceless forests, with their underbrush, soil, springs, climate, and religion, are vanishing away in clouds of smoke."

Four years later, Van Dyke wrote: "With the coming of civilization the grasses and the wild flowers perish, the forest falls and its place is taken by brambles, the mountains are blasted in the search for minerals, the plains are broken by the plow and the soil is gradually washed into the rivers. Last of all, when the forests have gone the rains cease falling, the streams dry up, the ground parches and yields no life, and the artificial desert—the desert made by the tramp of human feet—begins to show itself. Yes; everyone must have cast a backward glance and seen Nature's beauties beaten to ashes under the successive marches of civilization."

Perhaps we must condone, or at least accept as inevitable, a certain amount of destruction and spoliation through the occupation of the land by the increasing horde of human beings, though it does seem strange that, as Van Dyke remarked: "Today, after

[97]

centuries of association, every bird and beast and creeping thing
—the wolf in the forest, the antelope on the plain, and wild fowl
in the sedge—fly from his (man's) approach. They know his
civilization means their destruction. Even the grizzly, secure in
the chaparral of his mountain home, flinches as he crosses the
white man's trail. The boot mark in the dust smells of blood and
iron. The great annihilator has come, and fear travels with him."

And where Man and his buildings, his roads and his great waste
piles do not penetrate, where even the sawmills have spared the
trees, the cattle and sheep have spread over the forest undergrowth
and in the mountain meadows and swept away from the surface
of the earth the beauty and safety of the covering blanket furnished
by Nature. Muir, in "My First Summer in the Sierra," following
his flock, told of the high Yosemite country near Crane Flat:
"We passed a number of charming garden-like meadows lying on
top of the divide or hanging like ribbons down its sides, imbedded
in the glorious forest. Some are taken up chiefly with . . . a
robust, hearty, liliaceous plant, fond of water and determined to
be seen. Columbine and larkspur grow on the dryer edges of the
meadows, with a tall handsome lupine standing waist-deep in long
grasses and sedges. Castilleias, too, of several species make a bright
show with beds of violets at their feet. But the glory of these
forest meadows is a lily. . . . The tallest are from seven to eight
feet high with magnificent racemes of ten to twenty or more small
orange-colored flowers; they stand out free in open ground, with
just enough grass and other companion plants about them to fringe
their feet, and show them off to best advantage. This . . . lily
. . . is a true mountaineer, reaching prime vigor and beauty at
a height of seven thousand feet. . . . And to think that the sheep
should be allowed in these lily meadows! after how many centuries
of Nature's care planting and watering them, tucking the bulbs
in snugly below winter frost, shading the tender roots with clouds
drawn above them like curtains, pouring refreshing rain, making
them perfect in beauty, and keeping them safe by a thousand
miracles; yet, strange to say, allowing the trampling of devastating
sheep. One might reasonably look for a wall of fire to fence such
gardens. . . . And so the beauty of lilies falls on angels and
men, bears and squirrels, wolves and sheep, birds and bees, but as
far as I have seen, man alone, and the animals he tames, destroy

these gardens. Awkward, lumbering bears . . . love to wallow in them in hot weather, and deer with their sharp feet cross them again and again, sauntering and feeding, yet never a lily have I seen spoiled by them. Rather, like gardeners, they seem to cultivate them, pressing and dibbling as required. Anyhow not a leaf or petal seems misplaced."

This New World, which came fresh from Nature into our hands less than three hundred years ago, has suffered incredibly from the scars of our occupation. Great forests have gone and left sad cut-over lands, as in Michigan. The grassy plains where the buffalo roamed have become the "dust bowl." All game has been depleted and many species exterminated.

National parks cannot indeed bring to life extinct species, but they can and do offer sanctuary to the wildlife which still exists, and in the national parks the visitor may, if he strays from the motor roads, find friendly game, for the birds and the beasts seem to know when they are protected. In the national parks man need not be feared by the animals. He may have the priceless experience of making friends with the trustful deer and the gentle moose, though perhaps he should not meet the predatory bear too carelessly!

About the only views which cannot be harmed by man are the skies and clouds. John Muir wrote frequently in appreciation of the clouds. Wordsworth in his "Guide to the Lake District" referred to the "skiey influences" which brought such pleasure.

The emotional and spiritual enjoyment of unspoiled scenery, especially when it is on the "ten-league canvas" scale, may indeed bring a new religion and play an important part in the continuance of our particular civilization, for it is as sure as that Babylon and Nineveh are no more that New York and San Francisco will one day be deserted or eclipsed by a new occupation, unless we are able to command a spiritual stamina not developed by close-pressed humanity devoted solely to trade and material welfare.

Many words have been written in prose and poetry about the forms, colors, lights, and shades of the mountains. Wordsworth cautioned his readers that walks in the early morning ought to be taken on the eastern side of the vales, otherwise they will "lose the morning light, first touching the tops and thence creeping down the sides of the opposite hills, as the sun ascends," but he sagely remarked: "It is upon the *mind* which a traveler brings along with him that his acquisitions, whether of pleasure or profit, must principally depend."

Both Wordsworth and John Muir loved storms. At Muir Inlet, Glacier Bay, Alaska, Muir wrote in June of 1890: "Orchestral harmony of the storm, the wind in fine tune, the whole sky one waterfall. . . . How hazy and trivial all selfish pursuits seem at such times, when the whole brave world is in a rush and roar and ecstasy of motion—air and ice and water and the mighty mountains rejoicing in their strength and singing in harmony! . . . Storms are never counted among the resources of a country, yet how far they go towards making brave people. No rush, no corrupting sloth among people who are called to cope with storms with faces set, whether this ministry of beauty be seen or no. . . . The storm was a grand festival." Nearly twenty years before, in the Yosemite, Muir had written: "The storms of winter which so exalt and glorify mountains strike terror into the souls of those who are unacquainted with them, or who have only seen the lights of cities, but to anyone who is in actual contact with the wilderness, these storms are only emphatic words of Nature's love."

The variety of Nature is infinite. It is only in the monotony of city streets and conventional patterns of living that boredom becomes oppressive.

It may seem that the importance of walking and horseback riding and of actual contact with the Earth is over-emphasized. Certainly the acme of enjoyment involves more than being borne in a smooth-running car and *seeing* color, form, light, and shade, and *hearing* the more obvious sounds of Nature. The liquid notes of water slipping over smooth stones, the roar of the frothing cascades, the rustling of the leaves on the trees, the songs of the undisturbed birds, the calls of the wild animals can be heard only in comparative peace and quiet. Only faintly, if at all, can this finer music be heard by those who ride in automobiles, especially when they are part of a fast-moving procession in the midst of noises and smells from the exhausts of hundreds or thousands of motors. It must be recognized that the full aesthetic and emotional effect of delicate scenic pictures cannot be experienced when in rapid motion. To see the national parks adequately, if one is bound to an automobile, one must frequently stop to make use of the many "lookouts" provided by a thoughtful Government and one must, if one is able to walk on shopping expeditions or on golf links, *walk* on the inviting trails which radiate from every camp, inn, or museum group.

But the automobile is not to be despised. It carries the most ardent of walkers and horseback riders to the portals of the wilderness. It makes it possible for everyone to reach the high places on the face of the earth. Sometimes only a few hundred yards from the highway, one may find lonesome-looking places and may sense in some degree the excitement of standing alone to gaze on far-distant views. But, as one who stands high on a "peak in Darien," it is the lover of Nature who strays from the beaten path and the man-made trails who may reach the most sublime heights of emotional and spiritual climax. These are super experiences, to be treasured and remembered as long as one lives.

It is well known that a knowledge of music, its principles, its themes, its harmonies, and its repertory of fine compositions, adds greatly to the *capacity* to enjoy it. A musically ignorant person may be much moved emotionally by a great piece of music, but an educated listener will be more discriminating and understanding without necessarily sacrificing the elemental emotions set astir by great music.

So it is with the work of Nature. What we are accustomed to call a fine scene is always much more than that. An eye sensitive to beauty might see only the contours and colors which exert in themselves a highly emotional influence on the beholder. But the Scientist has made it possible for even the casual travelers to learn something of the age-old forces which have created the scene. The informed beholder may become discriminatingly appreciative.

In the national parks, the museum exhibits and the nature trails offer incomparable opportunities for visitors to penetrate the mysteries of creation which have been in process for a long, long time. They may make the acquaintance of the mighty glaciers on the ground and see how they have worked and are working. They may become friendly with the flowers and the trees and learn to greet them by name. They may see the birds and the beasts living their accustomed lives. All this and more can be the reward of those who visit the national parks by train or automobile, with only a moderate amount of walking.

[101]

In 1928, Secretary of the Interior Ray Lyman Wilbur appointed a Committee on the Study of Educational Problems in the National Parks. On the committee were Harold C. Bryant, Hermon C. Bumpus, Vernon Kellogg, John C. Merriam, and Frank R. Oastler. These scientists stressed the inspirational and educational values existing in national parks and recommended a program of interpretation which would enrich the experience of every park visitor. The result was a stimulation of the park museums, park observation stations, the development of guided trips on nature trails and throughout the parks, the increased use of the auto caravans, the enlivening of the campfire talks and the encouragement of college and school trips into the parks for purposes of study. The large number of tourists who join in all of these activities in the national parks, where there is no compulsory school law, has proved that education of this sort can be made alluring.

All this and more is described in an illustrated seventy-page pamphlet on "Research and Education in the National Parks" by Harold Bryant and Wallace W. Atwood, Jr.

That there is much to learn from cosmic forces cannot be denied. Archibald Rutledge, writing in *American Forests*, told of a summer visit to Virginia Beach, where "either to the northward or to the southward of the resort proper, one may walk for lonely miles the magnificent beach." Here on a starry August night, in the light of a "white-winger moon," with the Atlantic rolling in "indolent power and placid triumph," Mr. Rutledge heard "above the muffled music of the surf," a low humming, and overhead, a thousand feet up, he saw the lights of a mail plane. Then he looked at the forest, the ocean, the moon, and the stars. He saw "Capella dipping below the verge on mighty wings of light; Vega . . . steadfast in her destined place, yet holding a speed no mind could reckon; and where the Known and Unknown dimly merged," he watched "how Aldebaran kept his tremendous course." The comparison of man-made miracles of speed with the infinitely greater speed of the stars in their courses is obvious. Mr. Rutledge was right when he said: "About us everywhere is the hush of mystery, the pregnant silence of the undivulged. Over the land and over the sea, brooding on imperial mountains, gleaming in the shy wildflower's little brimming eyes is this sense of promise, of the coming fulfilment of even more than our dreams. In the natural world we have been lovingly preceded. Nature is tremendous with the music of rhythmic laws, the full discovery of which will serve to emancipate our hearts, making us full masters of our destiny."

Dr. John C. Merriam, in his book on "The Living Past," has given an entrancing account of the discovery of a cave in California which revealed past history far back of anything known to man, and which also proved the accuracy of an Indian legend. Dr. Merriam explained: "Though the story came to us repeatedly, it was always in the same form: of a cave with a magic pool called in the Indian language, 'Samwel,' and that it was visited on account of the potency of its water in bringing good fortune. Always it concluded with an account of three maidens who failed to obtain good luck at the pool, and were told by a very aged woman of other water with stronger magic. A second pool was said to lie in a remote chamber, and to escape discovery excepting for the most adventurous. In the course of a long search for this more powerful charm the three maidens came to a pit with sloping borders. As they approached the entrance, one slipped on the moist rock. The others tried to save her, but she fell screaming into the darkness. They heard her 'strike and strike again, and all was still.' A rescue party was unable to reach the bottom of the well and efforts to find the maiden were abandoned." To prove the story true, the well was discovered, and there was the skeleton of the maiden. Dr. Merriam declared: "The body had not moved from the spot where the girl crashed against the solid stone immediately under the opening. Only the bones and a film of black mould remained. Here and there a beginning crystal of stalagmite gleamed in the dark covering, but the lapse of time had not been great enough to allow the lime deposited from dripping water to form a complete shroud. . . . Scattered about, wherever we looked, were the skulls and parts of skeletons of many animals, some so deeply covered with lime as almost to merge with the floor. The mountain lion at the foot of the ladder was heavily encased and cemented in the rock. Near the skeleton of the maiden was a large skull with gracefully curving horns. No head like it had been known to man before. Close by lay another creature with wide-sweeping, oxlike horns—a type of animal then seen for the first time. Across the cave was the perfect skull of a bear, incrusted and cemented to the floor. No human had known this type alive or dead. Spread before us was a veritable museum of ancient life, including also deer, squirrel, porcupine, raccoon, fox, rabbit, and many others. . . . The remains we saw . . . represented a stage in ancient life of America long antedating the fauna now ranging over mountains and valleys of northern California. . . . The scant traces of original material covering the skeleton of the Indian maiden, and the incomplete lime incrustation upon the bones, indicated that entrance of the girl into the cave had been at a very recent period compared with that of the strange creatures among whose heavily incrusted skeletons she had come to rest."

This miracle book of the past may be a bit unusual. But in the national parks and many other untouched areas in the United States are to be found records of past life which excite the imagination and lift the mists which have enshrouded the long-past ages of life upon this Earth. These signs of comparatively recent human and animal tragedies were read just as John Muir read the signs of the far-more-ancient glaciers carving the walls of Yosemite and other Sierra valleys.

Sigurd Olson, writing in a recent issue of *American Forests*, has made a plea for the wilderness. Drawing on his personal experiences, he has told us: "As a guide in the primitive lake regions of the Hudson's Bay watershed, I have lived with men from every walk of life, have learned to know them more intimately than their closest friends at home, their dreams, their hopes, their aspirations. I have seen them come from the cities down below, worried and sick at heart, and have watched them change under the stimulus of wilderness living into happy, carefree, joyous men, to whom the successful taking of a trout or the running of a rapids meant far more than the rise and fall in stocks and bonds. Ask these men what it is they have found and it would be difficult for them to say. This they do know, that hidden back there in the country beyond the steel and the traffic of towns is something real, something as definite as life itself, that for some reason or other is an answer and a challenge to civilization.

"At first, I accepted the change that was wrought with the matter of factness of any woodsman, but as the years went by I began to marvel at the infallibility of the wilderness formula. I came to see that here was a way of life as necessary and as deeply

OLYMPIC MOUNTAINS:
CLAD IN GREEN LUXURIANT
FORESTS

Photograph—Clive
Courtesy—American Forests

[105]

Photograph—Asahel Curtis Courtesy—American Forests

DOUGLAS FIR AND HEMLOCK IN THE HOH VALLEY, WHICH EXTENDS DEEP INTO
THE OLYMPICS, AT A LOW ALTITUDE, TO THE NORTH WALL OF MT. OLYMPUS

SEVEN LAKES BASIN, NEAR THE HEAD OF SOLEDUCK RIVER

OLYMPIC NATIONAL PARK

GLACIER LILIES, OLYMPIC NATIONAL PARK

Photographs—Asahel Curtis MT. SEATTLE ABOVE—MT. OLYMPUS BELOW Courtesy—American Forests

rooted in some men as the love of home and family, a vital cultural aspect of life which brought happiness and lasting content."

Continuing, Mr. Olson has remarked: "It is surprising how quickly a man sheds the habiliments of civilization and how soon he feels at home in the wilds."

The philosophy of the wilderness is one of sturdy self-reliance and not one of dependence, according to Mr. Olson. "Men have found at last that there is a penalty for too much comfort and ease, a penalty of lassitude and inertia and the frustrated feeling that goes with unreality." Mr. Olson would not disturb the peace of those who are content with life as they find it—"the picnickers and the strollers, and for them are highways and gravelled trails and country clubs. For them scenic vistas of the wild from the shelter of broad and cool verandas." But for those who "hunger and thirst" for the wilderness as a means of "escape from the perplexing problems of everyday life and freedom from the tyranny of wires, bells, schedules and pressing responsibilities," there is a reward in "peace of mind and relaxation," and "with this escape comes perspective. Far from the towns and all they denote, engrossed in their return to the old habits of wilderness living, men begin to wonder if the speed and pressure they have left are not a little senseless. . . . I believe that here is a sensation born of perspective that most men know in any wilderness. Whenever it comes, men are conscious of a unity with the primal forces of creation and all life that swiftly annihilates the feeling of futility, frustration and unreality. When men realize that they are on their own, that if they are to be sheltered and fed, and, what is more, returned to civilization, they must depend entirely on their own ingenuity, everything they do assumes a tremendous importance. . . . Life soon develops a new and fascinating angle and days which to the uninitiated may seem humdrum or commonplace are filled with the adventure of living for its own sake."

Mr. Olson realizes that the whole world cannot come back to primitive living, but he advocates for a short time each year that city dwellers repair "not necessarily to the great wildernesses of the Arctic or the Canadian lakes, but to some wild part of the country which has not yet been entirely caught up in some scheme of exploitation or development."

We must realize, with Mr. Olson, that the greater part of the

[109]

wilderness is gone, but in North America we do yet possess a rich estate in wilderness if we are only wise enough to salvage it.

In the national parks are many "oddities" of Nature, such as are found in Yellowstone, many spectacular scenes, such as the Grand Canyon of the Colorado, which draw to them great crowds of sightseers and which will remain popular until the end of time, but there are also in the national parks great unspoiled areas penetrated only by trail or completely free from the scars of man. These are precious possessions. But they are all too limited. There are many more wilderness areas useful principally for their inspirational and stabilizing effect on mankind, which should be brought into the parks, where they will be safe from the pressure of commercial exploitation.

In the past we have had far too modest ideas of the areas which should be set aside and protected for national parks. The existing parks are often too circumscribed to protect the native wildlife. For wilderness consists of far more than an area in which trees are not cut and roads are not built. It comprises the entire plant and animal life in what our scientists now call a *biotic* unit. That is no true wilderness which is so small that the animals may stray carelessly across the border where they may be shot down by the predatory hunter. The true wilderness must be large enough to protect its game as well as its forests and streams and ground cover. It must be large enough to serve a considerable number of people and yet give them a sense of distance from the inhabited places of the earth and from each other.

We have thought in too limited terms. Before it is too late we should see that the national parks which belong to all the people, not only take care of their owners and stockholders who travel along the paved highway to see what can be seen from a car window, but also meet the need of the urge for the primitive which many of our people inherit from their recent ancestors and long to indulge. Perhaps if these areas are numerous enough and large enough to serve our people without crowding, they may offer a promise of uplifting and prolonging our civilization and culture.

MAGNIFICENT MOUNTAINS OF THE NORTHWEST

PROBABLY a drive on a circuit which would take in all the national parks, not to mention the monuments, would easily equal the distance around the world. To the marathon motorist anything is possible, and no doubt it would be possible to "tag" each park and monument, drive over its roads and then take to the highway again—all within a few months. But the kaleidoscopic memories would be blurred and no one could hope, in so hurried a trip, to reach anything like a true understanding of the national parks or to receive the poignant aesthetic enjoyment and high inspirational uplift which are inherent in the parks.

It is possible, however, to visit a number of national parks on a single summer trip without mental and spiritual indigestion. Indeed, one of the best ways of becoming familiar with the national parks is to visit them in convenient regions.

At Mt. Rainier in 1938, the writer met a businessman and his wife, crowding fifty, who had been spending their vacations for twenty-five years in the national parks—only one or two in a season. When their children were young they brought them along. Now that all were married or settled in their own pursuits, this happy, vigorous couple were having a sort of silver wedding trip. They drove in their car and stopped in the camps where they felt that they could stay as long as they desired. They joined in all the scheduled trips and activities. They knew the flowers and the trees of the western mountains and could compare the qualifications of the ranger naturalists with others they had heard. They were good walkers, and in addition to the guided automobile caravans and hiking trips, they struck out for themselves with the convenient trail maps supplied in the parks. They evidently felt that they were visiting each summer one or two of their fine summer estates, in which their collective ownership made possible excellent facilities for their pleasure and profit. They not only enjoyed the parks they visited; they were discriminatingly appreciative of all they saw on these truly American journeys.

The first region selected for our imaginary journey lies in the extreme northwest corner of the continental United States, where magnificent mountains are as common as blackberries.

OLYMPIC NATIONAL PARK

Our first visit will be made to the Olympic Peninsula, where a national park was created by Congress in June of 1938. The Olympic Peninsula roughly has a hundred-mile frontage on the Pacific Ocean. From the extreme northwest point of Cape Flattery to Port Townsend on the north almost another hundred miles of waterfront lies on Juan de Fuca Strait. The Peninsula is separated from Everett, Seattle, and Tacoma by Puget Sound and the Hood Canal. Projecting eastward from the Pacific Ocean is Grays Harbor, which cuts the Peninsula from the mainland on the South. The Peninsula may be reached by motor road and ferry from Seattle and other western Washington towns. It may be reached from Olympia, the capital of the State, and from Oregon and California by the Olympic Highway which encircles the mountains.

Within this modern highway lies one of the most interesting and alluring wilderness mountain-and-valley areas remaining in this country. Ben Thompson, writing in *Planning and Civic Comment*, described this enchanted land: "Almost rimmed with the mills and smoke and noise of Puget Sound's industrial communities, it is still a wild land. Dark and jungle-like forests cover the lowlands and extend far up the narrow river bottoms. Successions of steep ridges under shaggy forest robes reach up to the central mass of tossed and jumbled peaks. On clear days its snowy crests stand out white and silent.

"Each summer, meadows of wild flowers creep up the slopes after the receding snow, while down in the lowlands a cougar stalks the river trail, leaving the tracks of his soft pads in the mud. In autumn, elk bugle through the woods, while the mountain beavers, high on the hillside, survey the coming of winter. Then snow settles down on the mountains, rain drenches the lowlands, and it is again an island of solitude."

John Muir first saw Mt. Olympus from the deck of a boat some fifteen miles south en route to Alaska in 1879. Again in 1890, from the same vantage point, he remarked: "The sail to Port Townsend is very interesting on account of the beauty and grandeur of the scenery, especially of the Olympic Mountains, which rise to eight thousand feet above the blue waters, with picturesquely sculptured summits and long withdrawing slopes heavily clad with spruce

[112]

and fir." These mountains do, indeed, present to the eye from certain high lookouts a dramatic skyline, but one traveling on the Olympic Highway would have no idea of the beauty hidden within the charmed circle of the interior of the ring road, for this highway passes through many sad cut-over regions, patches of second growth, and occasionally into virgin forests; it is so located that the interior mountains can seldom be seen.

The Peninsula was almost entirely covered with dense forests at one time, except where the high craggy peaks emerged above the timber line. Once it was a veritable lumberman's paradise. Muir remarked in one of his journal entries that many of the Sierra forests had remained intact because it was easier to bring timber a thousand miles by water from the Northwest than fifty miles from the California mountains. At any rate, 130 years after the Lewis and Clark Expedition into the Northwest, such vast areas of forest have been cut that the remaining stands in the heart of the Olympic Peninsula have achieved a scarcity value and become so unique as to qualify for national-park status.

It is now thirty-five years since a bill almost passed Congress to create the Elk National Park on the Olympic Peninsula "for the purpose of preserving the elk, game, fish, birds, animals, timber and curiosities therein." The bill, introduced in 1904, passed the House and failed in the Senate during the last hours of the session. Bills to create a game preserve failed in 1906 and 1908. Finally, in the closing days of his administration, President Theodore Roosevelt set aside the Mt. Olympus National Monument of something over 600,000 acres. In the meantime, the forest reserves were transferred from the Department of the Interior to the Department of Agriculture; in 1907 the name was changed to national forests. The elk were protected by state law, according to an account by Dr. Theodore Palmer in *Civic Comment:* "For a quarter of a century the dual arrangement continued under which the elk were protected by the state law, while the range was protected by the National Monument act as administered by the Forest Service."

In 1916, President Wilson, on the recommendation of the Forest Service, in an effort to provide timber for ship-building to win the war, by Executive Order reduced the Monument to less than half its original size. Then in 1933 came two more changes. Under a new state game law, the Game Commission of Washington authorized an open season on elk for six days and killing was permitted for the first time since 1905. It was in this year, too, that President Franklin D. Roosevelt by Executive Order transferred the Mt. Olympus National Monument, along with other national monuments, from the jurisdiction of the U. S. Forest Service to that of the National Park Service. No hunting is permitted in national monuments, but the protection of the high winter range for the elk was not enough. The movement to create a national park was revived. In the meantime each year more people were hiking or packing into the interior wilderness, and they wanted to see the area made into a national park. As might have been expected, perhaps, there was bitter opposition to enlarging the national monument to national-park proportions, and thus taking land from the economic uses permitted in national forests.

In *American Forests* for June, 1936, John B. Yeon presented the case for the park. The plan of the Forest Service, Mr. Yeon declared, "in accordance with the basic provisions of national forest legislation, has given prior consideration to the economic utilization of the timber. Preservation has been designated only where it does not materially interfere with the conversion of the forest into lumber. The areas reserved are for the most part economically worthless." On the other hand, "the plan for the Olympics advocated by the Park Service aims to add a solid block of forest to the solid reservation of the existing monument and incorporate both in the national park." This in contrast to the fingers of forest open for harvesting proposed by the Forest Service. Mr. Yeon continued: "This plan (of the Park Service) in accordance with the basic provisions of national park legislation gives prior consideration to the preservation of the area's natural geographic and biotic features. The scenic, recreational, educational and inspirational resources of the region, and the requirements for their use and protection without depletion, are the factors which have shaped the program. The application of this plan would result in the permanent survival of an unmodified forest on a scale commensurate with the mountains it covers and with the giant individual specimens it contains. It would save a forest landscape and not merely samples of trees. The natural aspect of the area would remain intact—the original horizons as well as foregrounds and the infinite details which compose the whole."

Mr. Yeon warned us that "The forests of the Olympics will not be commonplace again. No other large area in this zone will probably ever be held undisturbed for the five centuries required for such a forest to mature. If this were done, however, and every trace of modification eventually eroded or rotted away, this future forest would still be different in historic and scientific category from the one still flourishing in the Olympics today. Here is the culmination of an incalculably old growth process, far older, perhaps, than the combined age of all its living trees. The present forest has an ancient lineage; it is in the line of direct descent from the first plant forms growing in the earliest Olympic soils. The 'thrilling succession from the infinite which cannot be returned once continuity has been severed' is a real but intangible attribute which will be effaced from this area once it is disturbed and absent forever from subsequent forests of modern origins."

Fortunately, the fight was won for scenic and inspirational values when the Wallgren Bill of 1938 became a law establishing a defined national park of 634,000 acres, with authority to the President to add lands until the national park may include 892,292 acres. In this Olympic National Park, we find then, as described by John Yeon in 1936: "The forested valleys and canyons, in conjunction with the adjacent Alpine regions, result in a combination which enhances the interest of all features beyond what the component parts would, if isolated, possess in themselves. The area is surrounded on three sides . . . by salt water. It is almost an island—a miniature continent in itself. Within this area, rivers have their source and major being before their confluence with the ocean. The circuit of moisture, lifting from the sea, detained in glaciers, and flowing through streams and rivers back to the sea, is complete, like a diagrammatic functioning model of the workings of earth forces, and almost within the range of observation from a single vantage point."

Secretary Ickes has publicly pledged the Department of the Interior to the preservation of this wilderness area. There will be no roads into the interior. But that does not mean that visitors may not see the mountains and the forested valleys to advantage. The headquarters of the National Park Service, instead of being in the park, will be built on forty acres of land, adjoining Port Angeles, given to the Park Service by Clallam County. From Port Angeles travelers may drive out to some of the idyllic inns on the shores of Crescent Lake, or they may stay at the settlements at Sol Duc or Olympic Springs, from where the northern valleys may be explored. The rather rough road along Hurricane Ridge will undoubtedly be improved, and perhaps extended. From the ridge may be seen Mt. Olympus, with its blue glacier and the galaxy of snowy peaks around it. From the Olympic Highway on the East a road leads up the Hoh Valley to Jackson. From here one may walk as far up the valley as strength and inclination permit, remembering always that the very essence of the Hoh forests is their isolation from highways and motor traffic. In the Hoh are some of the largest Douglas firs in existence. One named for Colonel Graves will some day be a fitting monument to a former Chief Forester who has rendered to the country a fine service in vision and educational leadership.

Visitors may stop at the hotel at Lake Quinault at the southeastern corner of the park. They may drive up to Graves Creek Inn in the southern part of the park, though their hearts may be saddened by the cut-over lands which border the road and by the constant stream of trucks bearing giant firs to market. From Graves Creek Inn visitors may drive a short distance to the Quinault River where the road now ends, and let us hope, where it will always end. There is a high-hung foot and horse bridge across the Quinault at this point, and visitors should by all means walk across it. The banks of the river are almost perpendicular and the rocks are padded and tufted with delicate maidenhair ferns. A lovelier fern exhibit could not be imagined. As the trail traverses the stream up the valley, many of the misshapen trees are seen to be covered with green moss, which gives the region an unearthly aspect and justifies the name "Enchanted Valley." Just north of the old Monument line, about eleven miles from Graves Creek Inn, is an inn to which all food and supplies must be brought by pack train. From the Enchanted Valley one may ride horseback (or walk) across Anderson Pass and out along the Dosewallips to reach a highway which intersects the Olympic Highway on the east side of the park. Or the trip may be made in reverse action.

At the southeast corner the access road will probably be extended to the head of Lake Cushman.

One especially interesting pack trip may be made from Sol Duc

Photograph—C. Frank Brockman   Courtesy—American Forests

MT. RAINIER WINTER SPORTS

MAJESTIC MOUNT RAINIER

Springs, and along the Bogachiel ridge to the ranger station on the top of Bogachiel by way of Seven-lake Basin. Often on the snow-banks elk may be seen resting in the lazy summer afternoons. A trail from Bogachiel leads to the Blue Glacier on Mt. Olympus. There is also a trail down the south side of the mountain into the Hoh Valley far below. For this ride down the switchbacks from the ranger station to the floor of the valley more than a mile lower in altitude, one needs good knees, for the steady pressure to hold the saddle for two or three hours, with never a step up, but always down, is a little trying on the "tenderfoot." Once in the upper Hoh Valley, no matter how tired, the traveler is so consumed with admiration for the lofty and aged Douglas firs and other forest masterpieces that weariness is soon forgotten.

There are many trails and trips over the High Divide, the Low Divide, and up the Queets. Of course there is much rain on the Peninsula, particularly on the west side, and many of the pack-train parties are overtaken by rain, but the mountain clubs of the Northwest continue to hike and ride into these delectable mountains, and the American Forestry Association has annually, in recent years, scheduled popular pack-train trips into the Olympics.

Without roads which will cross the heart of this fine national park, but with half a dozen or more access roads which will bring visitors to points where they may find comfortable accommodations and with comparatively short walks see some part of the forested valleys, with one high ride on Hurricane Ridge from which the whole range may be seen, there will be ample facilities for the motorist to see and enjoy the park without ruining its wilderness character. And the park will be increasingly popular for the sturdy hiker and the untiring horseback rider. Riding along in an automobile or walking along the trails in the valleys, be-sides all the small, scampering animals, one may frequently see coveys of grouse, with their quail-like waddle, glide away into the forest, and occasionally, as a special treat, one may watch the stately iridescent pheasants, with their brilliant hues, walk in solemn procession across the stage with its dark evergreen drops.

Now that the long-standing controversies about the future of the heart of the Olympics are settled and the shouting and the tumult have died, we, the people, may well picture to ourselves the kingdom which we have inherited. William Harrison Peters, in April, 1936, *American Forests* gave us some unforgettable word sketches: "Beginning at the salt water where the Pacific roars against the rugged coast, and at the sparkling blue of the Strait of Juan de Fuca and Hood Canal, these wonderful forests climb to an elevation of 4,000 feet above the sea. They completely encircle the Olympic Mountains, a green unbroken belt fifty miles wide and more than 200 miles in circumference. Inside, and above the inner circumference of this sloping belt of rugged, timber-covered foothills, Mt. Olympus rears its peak of basalt and ice 8,000 feet above the surrounding seas.

"Between the belt of dense forest growth and the snow and ice of the high peaks, lies an area of delectable open meadows, grass covered, dotted with alpine lakes and spotted with clumps of mountain hemlock, alpine fir and an occasional Alaska cedar.

"From the glacier-covered peaks of the Olympics pour scores of streams. Born in clear mountain springs or tiny glacial lakes, they join to form brawling creeks which unite to send wide rivers flowing quietly through forest-covered valleys to the sea. These streams abound in fish, and the river valleys, broad and flat, shelter great herds of Roosevelt elk. The mountain ridges furnish sanctuary and browse for many deer; bears are plentiful. Grouse and pheasant occur in all parts of the region.

"During the summer months, the area at timberline is a carpet of alpine flowers. There are asters, violets, gentians, phlox, bluebell, hellebore, avalanche lily, *Erythronium parviflorum*, a sturdy flower that in early spring pushes through the receding snow drifts to bloom, a dozen varieties of the sedum, the 'hen and chicks' and 'stonecrop' of the natives, vermilion Indian paintbrush, and dozens of others of equal beauty and interest."

Major Owen A. Tomlinson in 1937, in the *American Planning and Civic Annual* gave a fine description of the Olympics: "Burdened with glistening and still active glaciers, never completely explored, the snowy white of the taller peaks contrasts with the luxuriant verdure of their evergreen slopes. The region surpasses in massive grandeur many more famous but less beautiful tourist territories. . . . Moulded by glaciation in a period approximated at some 20,000 years ago, the resultant spectacular topography is a marvel of distinctive, rugged and isolated domain, with many peaks unnamed and unclimbed."

APPROACH TO MT. RAINIER

AVALANCHE LILIES AT MT. RAINIER

PARADISE INN IS OPEN
THE YEAR ROUND

Courtesy—American Civic Annual

PARADISE VALLEY,
MT. RAINIER

COMMUNITY HOUSE IN PARADISE VALLEY

Photographs—Department of the Interior

Courtesy—Portfolio, American Planning and Civic Association

MAGNIFICENT MOUNTAINS OF THE NORTHWEST

The Sitka spruce, one of the great tree species, is preserved in the Olympic National Park; also Douglas fir, Western red cedar, and the smaller white fir and hemlock, "with age-old coatings of moss, hanging heavily to soften the solid contours of the branches." "Heavy tropic-like vegetation—the forest within a forest—disappears miraculously, leaving only huge trunked forest monarchs, then as suddenly reappears. Elsewhere, ferns carpet the trail and forest floor. Heavy-reeded waterways break suddenly into broad, pebbled expanses."

Surely future generations will rise up and call blesséd this generation which acted before it was too late to save these pedigreed forests of Douglas fir, Sitka spruce, Alaska cedar and hemlock!

MT. RAINIER

From the Olympic Peninsula visitors may easily go to Mt. Rainier, which has been a national park since 1899. It required considerable foresight to set aside Mt. Rainier as a national park forty years ago, looking forward from that year; but looking back from this year, we now know that so stupendous a mountain required a larger rim of protection. In 1931 the eastern boundary was extended to the summit of the Cascade Range and fifty odd square miles were added to the 325 square miles already in the park. The park is roughly in the form of a square with the mountain peak, 14,408 feet high, a little to the left of the center, and its glaciers radiating out in some places to points only three or four miles within the boundaries.

One may enter the park by highway from the southwest corner by the Nisqually River entrance, and drive by way of Longmire Springs, where the National Park Service has its headquarters office, to Paradise Valley, high on the slopes of the mountain. At Longmire there is quite a settlement, including a museum, an inn, a public camp, store, cafeteria, gasoline station, and post office.

It is here that Major Tomlinson has presided for enough years to make his name synonymous with Rainier. The Major is a quiet, retiring ex-army officer. He is thoroughly imbued with the Mather national-park ideals, and he knows the Washington mountains like a book.

The road to Paradise Valley passes close to the Nisqually Glacier. For many years this road was a single, one-way controlled highway on which travel was permitted only at certain hours; but now it is possible to use the widened improved highway at pleasure. At Paradise there is also a settlement, including an inn, a lodge, cabins, public camps beautifully situated, store, gasoline station, post office and community house where nightly lectures are given.

One may enter the northwest corner of the park by the Carbon River Road and find a ranger station and public campgrounds. On the east side of the park there is a very beautiful highway, called the Mather Memorial Parkway, which gives access to the Yakima Park section of the park both from the north and from the southeast. As this parkway comes through the gate, at a lookout within the park, there is an unforgettable view of Rainier which is more breath-taking than any to be seen from other vantage points. The afternoon sun on the icy mantle of Rainier gives the effect of a crystal-studded garment, faceted to catch every ray of light. At Yakima Park there are to be found cabins, cafeteria, camp (especially well located), and other facilities, including a picturesque campfire and amphitheatre which is well patronized when the park rangers give illustrated talks each evening during the summer months.

There is an entrance at the southeast corner to the Ohana-pecosh Ranger Station, where there are a lodge, cabins, camp, and hot baths.

The ascent of Mt. Rainier is only for the hardy. Though the mountain was first seen and named by Captain George Vancouver, of the British Royal Navy, in 1792, it was not until 1870 that its summit was reached. In that year two successful ascents were made, but it was not until 1883 that the summit was reached for the third time. Today, of course, ascents are quite common, but except for experienced mountaineers, would-be climbers must take guides with them. The National Park Service, in its pamphlet on the park, has stated plainly that "Mount Rainier is a difficult peak to climb. The route to the summit is not a definitely marked path. Dangerously crevassed ice covers a large proportion of the mountain's flanks, and the steep ridges between glaciers are composed of treacherous crumbling lava and pumice. Weather on the mountain is fickle. Midsummer snow storms, always accompanied by fierce gales, rise with unexpected suddenness." All these obstacles, of course, make the ascent all the more exciting and desirable to those who do take the trip, and one of the special lures of the park is the climbing of Mt. Rainier.

The park offers many interesting trips for those who do not attempt to scale the summit. There are five access highways through four main entrances, with less than sixty miles of highway in the entire park. But there are 240 miles of trails leading through and to some of the most charming high country in the park system. From the Nisqually entrance there is an excellent highway, within the boundaries of the park, leading north some fifteen miles to Klapatche Park. From this highway trails lead to Indian Henry's Hunting Ground, where there is a gorgeous display of wild flowers in the summer months. A trail skirts the Tahoma Glacier, and another leads to the Payallup Glacier.

There are innumerable walking and riding trips from Paradise Valley. It is an easy walk up to the Muir Shelter Cabin, where the mountaineers who expect to scale the summit spend the early hours of the night, before they start on their chilly, early-morning climb hoping to see the sunrise from the top. Muir Shelter, which is at the 10,000-foot elevation, is some 4,500 feet above Paradise, but the climb requires no special skill, although those who have not the "wind and the limb" may secure horses, and ride. There are excellent views all along the trail, and a feeling of having reached the snowy heights at Camp Muir. Leading out from Paradise there is a regular network of trails on which may be seen any summer day literally hundreds of people, young and old, climbing vigorously or sauntering along at their free will, enjoying the fine views and the exercise in the high, clear air.

On the guided trips, the glaciers are explained, the flowers and trees identified. Anyone who takes all the guided trips and who travels all the mapped trails on foot or horseback will certainly become well informed about the geology, flora and fauna of the park and have excellent opportunities for aesthetic enjoyment, to be found in few places in the world.

Running entirely around the mountain is the Wonderland Trail, which, with its various ramifications, is from a hundred to a hundred and forty miles in the circuit. Hikers, by carrying sleeping bag and food, can make a shelter each night, and so in a week or ten days the mountain can be seen from the highlands from every angle and the lower end of every glacier can be examined. The trail from Sunrise (Yakima Park) to Paradise is full of surprises. It runs along Frying Pan Creek to Summerland, where the wild flowers flourish, cutting across the Frying Pan Glacier and skirting the Ohanapecosh Glacier, past Indian Bar Shelter to the Nickel Creek Ranger Station and across the spectacular Canyon Bridge where, because of the great depth below and the roar of the falling water, riders are asked to dismount; up Stevens Creek past Louise Lake and Nerada Falls to the Paradise Highway. In July there is usually heavy snow on the passes and covering the Frying Pan Glacier, which lies far below. When the writer made the journey, the ranger at Nickel Creek had placed little red flags over the several miles of snow to indicate the safe places for the horses' feet. While one is not as near the summit of Rainier in crossing the Frying Pan Glacier as at Muir Shelter Cabin on the Paradise side, one feels nearer the mountain tops of everlasting snow, because as far as the eye can reach there is nothing but the shining whiteness of the snow and ice in sight. For the "wilderness feeling," this two-day hiking or riding trip cannot easily be matched.

Rainier National Park gives adequate access roads to the motorists, who, with a moderate amount of walking, may see and enjoy the mountain. But its real glory is seen from the trails, short and long, provided for hikers and riders. The number that annually take advantage of the trail facilities is an evidence that the American public is becoming "trail minded" and relearning the use of the human body for walking purposes!

Time was when Rainier closed up shop in winter. Not so today. Since skiing has taken this country by a storm as unaccountable as the black tulip craze in Holland, no snow field is complete without its amateur skiers, no fiction magazine without its ski story, no outdoor periodical without its article on skiing and skiing equipment. The sports shops of the United States which a few years ago were barren of any sort of ski equipment are now well stocked and apparently selling their stock. Rainier is one of the famous skiing places in the United States. Even in the dead of winter when cars can only be driven to a point a mile and a half below Paradise Inn, the Inn is kept open and the ski enthusiasts cheerfully pad up the mountain to claim their accommodations.

Photograph—Department of the Interior   Courtesy—Portfolio, American Planning and Civic Association

THE BLUE WATERS OF CRATER LAKE

[127]

CROSSING A CREVASSE IN
THE CASCADE RANGE

Photograph—John W. Murray
Courtesy—Appalachia

MT. BAKER IN THE
WASHINGTON CASCADES

Photographs—Aubrey R. Watzek
Courtesy—American Planning and Civic Annual

MT. MAGIC
IN THE CASCADES
NEAR LAKE CHELAN

Fortunately for those who love scenery, skiing does no damage to the summer scenery and provides an exciting and absorbing winter sport. Conservationists generally, however, discourage any sort of paraphernalia to haul the happy skiers up the mountain, as a permanent scar on natural scenery.

Mt. Rainier is unique. It has, according to Frank Brockman, writing in *American Forests*, "upon its broad flanks the largest glacial system in the continental United States, exclusive of Alaska. Twenty-eight glaciers comprise this great system, forming an ice mantle nearly fifty square miles in area and covering thirteen per cent of the total area of Mount Rainier National Park." For scientific research, for summit-scaling, for skiing, for aesthetic enjoyment, for trail-tripping, and for inspirational contemplation, Mt. Rainier is a first-rate mountain.

CRATER LAKE

One may easily travel from Mt. Rainier to Crater Lake by way of Portland, then south to Medford and 80 miles along the Rogue River road into the park, or from Portland to Bend, Oregon, and 106 miles south to the park, with perhaps a detour to Diamond Lake. From the south one may enter from Klamath, either by the Klamath Highway or the Pinnacles Road. Rail and stage travel offer direct and convenient arrangements and, as there is a landing field at Medford, it is possible to hop from New York or Los Angeles with time-annihilating speed.

To state that the lake is six miles wide, 2,000 feet deep, with a circular shore line of 26 miles, that this vast volume of water depends upon precipitation into the giant bowl left from an exploding volcano, which is now preserved in a park covering 250 square miles, can give no faint suggestion of the beauty of Crater Lake. With all the lakes there are in the world and all the poetic phrases which have been used to describe them, it would seem that one little six-mile lake in the Cascades might not deserve much in the way of superlatives. There are different kinds of lake beauty and surroundings, and one would not want to miss the lovely mountain beauty of the Sierra lakes and meadows, nor the broad expanse of tree-fringed Tahoe, nor the severely chaste glacial lakes of Glacier National Park, nor the rugged isolation of Yellowstone Lake, lying high on the top of the continent, nor the shining necklace of glacial lakes at the foot of the Tetons. They all have beauties of their own. But the deep opalescent blue of Crater Lake is like some ethereal light borrowed from the skies. The ancients would have called it a creation of the gods. No one can look upon it and not be moved emotionally and spiritually. The setting of the highly painted lava cliffs gives it the appearance of some new gem more lovely than the sapphire set in some new combination of metals never before seen. The changing hues give it different aspects during the passing hours of the day from dawn to sunset. On rainy, cloudy days, the color is wiped out of the lake as though a palette knife had scraped off every bit of pigment and the secret of its beauty lost forever. Then the sunlight returns and the painting is again a work of rare genius, not to be understood but to be worshipped as an unduplicatable masterpiece of Nature.

From the rim drive one is led from one ecstasy to another. There is the view across the little lake of pure cerulean blue, with glimpses of Wizard Island casting its reflections in the mirror of the lake and of the Phantom Ship, sometimes appearing in full sail and sometimes suddenly disappearing with the change of lights. Early in the summer, when the snowplows have left high walls of snow and ice at the side of the road, the rim drive gives a nice feeling of remoteness.

The Indians had legends about the lake. One concerns Llao Rock, which rises nearly 2,000 feet above the lake level. As related in the national park bulletin on Crater Lake, according to the legends of the Klamath and Modoc Indians, "the mystic land of the Gaywas was the home of the great god Llao. His throne in the infinite depths of the blue waters was surrounded by giant crawfish, his warriors, who were able to lift great claws out of the water and seize too venturesome enemies on the cliff tops. War broke out with Skell, the god of the neighboring Klamath marshes. Skell was captured and his heart used for a ball by Llao's monsters. But an eagle, one of Skell's servants, captured it in flight, and a coyote, another of Skell's servants, escaped with it; and Skell's body grew again around his living heart. Once more he was powerful and once more he waged war against the god of the lake. Then Llao was captured; but he was not so fortunate.

Upon the highest cliff his body was quartered and cast into the lake and eaten by his own monsters under the belief that it was Skell's body. But when Llao's head was thrown in, the monsters recognized it and would not eat it. Llao's head still lies in the lake, and white men call it Wizard Island. The cliff where Llao was quartered is named Llao Rock."

Crater Lake was discovered at least three times in the fifties and sixties before it received its present name in 1869. Following a trip to Crater Lake in 1885 by William Gladstone Steel, Professor Joseph Le Conte, and others, President Cleveland in 1886 issued a proclamation withdrawing ten townships, including Crater Lake, from settlement. Crater Lake National Park was created by Congress and approved by President Theodore Roosevelt in 1902.

In this national park, which contains one of the most beautiful single objects in the whole system and one which depends for its appreciation on its emotional and spiritual appeal, it is curious that the scientific information is the most complete. The Sinnott Memorial, which was constructed of native stone on Victor Rock, just inside the rim of the crater, offers a fine balcony from which to examine the lake and its surroundings. Through the means of high-powered field glasses, visitors are enabled to see "close-ups" of the walls of the lake and read in the legends at the glass of the geological history and present composition of each feature of the landscape. The large relief map of the Crater Lake Region receives a great deal of interested attention from visitors. Carefully prepared displays are on view in the exhibit room. The interpretation of science here has been managed with a great deal of skill and has been kept simple enough not to leave the visitors with scientific indigestion.

Crater Lake has, in common with the rest of the Southern Cascades, a wide variety of wild flowers. Over 500 flowering plants and ferns are listed. Many of these may be found in the Castle Crest Wild Flower Garden, near the National Park Headquarters, three miles from the rim. One of the attractions of the park is found in the brilliantly hued flowers. In the open sunny spaces the flaming fireweed, which flourishes in most of the western parks, reaches a climax of burning glory. The principal trees are ponderosa pines, mountain hemlock, a variety of pines, Shasta red fir, Engelmann spruce, and Douglas fir. Oaks, cottonwoods, and aspens give fresh young green to the spring and brilliant foliage to the autumn.

In spite of the highways and crowds of people coming into the park, many regions are wild enough to give cover to the smaller wild animals—deer, elk, bear, marmots, conies, minks, weasels, martens, beavers, badgers, porcupines, flying squirrels, and many others. In addition to the smaller birds there are to be found falcons, ospreys, golden and bald eagles, and horned owls.

Fish were planted in Crater Lake fifty years ago, and today the lake teems with rainbow and steelhead trout.

There are many interesting activities at Crater Lake. There is the camera hike for camera fans. There is the boat trip to Wizard Island, made by most visitors, and many like to go out in rowboats both by daylight and in the moonlight, when the mysterious lake, with its floating islands and its darkly shadowed cliffs, presents a scene of unutterable beauty.

It was at Crater Lake that the first annual ski races were held, and there is a permanent Crater Lake Ski Club. Since 1935 the roads have been kept clear of snow and the park has been open throughout the winter.

According to David Canfield, "the beauty of the park in winter . . . is in many respects, unequalled. The crowning spectacle, of course, is Crater Lake with its indescribable blue, nestling in a circle of high white-robed cliffs. The heavily burdened conifers with their magnificent mantles of snow are a never-ending delight; the fantastic curves and snow masses of the smaller trees cause one to marvel at the artistry of nature. The drifts offer mute testimony to the force and vagaries of the wind."

Either entering or departing, or as a loop trip, every park visitor should drive along the Pinnacles Road and see the peculiar formations in Wheeler Creek Canyon.

One should at least see the clock round at Crater Lake, and a longer stay would allow for interesting explorations and, even more important, for seeing the changing colors of the lake and its surroundings.

THE WILDERNESS WAY IN THE CASCADES

A project which has appealed to the imagination of the lovers of wilderness and mountain climbing has been fostered by Clinton

MEADOW LAKE AND
MT. SHUKSAN

IN THE NORTHERN
CASCADES

GLEAMING "PAH-TO"—
INDIAN NAME FOR MT. ADAMS
SECOND HIGHEST PEAK
IN WASHINGTON

Photograph—U. S. Forest Service
Courtesy—American Forests

[133]

Courtesy—American Forests

MT. BAKER, THE SILENT SENTINEL

Churchill Clarke, of Pasadena, California, in the Pacific Crest Trail, which, by linking together many existing trails, now runs from the Canadian line to Mexico, a total distance of 2,300 miles, of which all but 175 miles is within the borders of twenty national forests and five national parks. Eight hundred and fifty miles of the Pacific Crest Trail lie within the mountains of the Northwest. Robert Foote, writing in *American Forests*, has explained that the first 450 miles comprise the Cascade Crest Trail which "runs south through the most primitive and unexplored region in the United States. The Cascade Range, of Washington, is broken into heavily timbered gorges and ice-streaked ridges, above which rise mighty glacier peaks. To cover this trail requires forty or more days of hard tramping, over twenty-two mountain passes and around five glacier peaks and Mt. Rainier National Park. The Cascade Crest runs entirely through wilderness except for small recreation centers near Mt. Baker, Keechelus Lake and Mt. Rainier Park.

"In Oregon the Cascades are more gentle than in Washington, and the Oregon Skyline is not so difficult, is generally in better condition and well marked, crossing only four passes. Nevertheless, this 410 miles requires thirty-eight days of foot travel. The three outstanding peaks to be passed, Mt. Hood, Mt. Jefferson, and the Three Sisters, are strongly glacial though not entirely blanketed as is the case farther north. But in Oregon, the trail keeps to a higher average elevation than in Washington. Crater Lake National Park is an outstanding scenic area on this trail."

Considering that there still remains a most spectacular wilderness area in the United States in the Northern Cascades, and that the national parks as yet can claim only a little over 500 square miles in Rainier and Crater Lake, it is the opinion of many that a substantial Cascades National Park should be set aside for the pleasure and inspiration of the people of the United States. No mountain could be more impressive, perhaps, than Mt. Rainier, but Baker and Shuksan are not only stupendous in their scenic aspects, but they have a special personality.

Across the Skagit River lies a larger and even more remote region of glacial peaks, crests, and sharp cut valleys with turbulent streams and waterfalls, which will undoubtedly one day be brought into the national parks—not for development, but for preservation, and to provide more of that climax wilderness country which we are coming to demand for our civilization. No one who has ever walked or packed into this region could forget Lake Hart and Lake Lyman, lying in the shadow of the glacier-streaked peaks which are reflected in the glistening glass of their quiet waters, or the milky glacial waters of the Stehekin River, the heavenly blue of the gentians on Cloudy Pass, the marvelous views from Cascade Pass toward the Pacific, with the rugged crests of Mt. Magic like a fairy picture within a scene to the left, and endless crests on either side running toward the horizon beyond which are hidden Baker and Shuksan in a new climax. The roar of avalanches from the hanging glaciers, the calm of the capping glaciers, the quiet of the air where few birds sing, the rushing waters of the many streams, the rustling of the pines and spruces and cedars, the pungent scents of the virgin woods, the small filmy ferns, the tall coarse devil's walking canes, the fine ground cover of Oregon grape and mountain boxwood, with innumerable little flowers—all this and infinitely more will be the reward of those who travel by the trails of the Northern Cascades.

Hermann Ulrichs, writing in the February, 1937, *Sierra Club Bulletin*, has referred to the Northern Cascade section as the "last great stronghold of almost completely untouched primeval wilderness in the United States." He there maintained that "it will be regarded as the most spectacular, varied and truly Alpine of all our mountains." In amplification, Mr. Ulrichs drew an entrancing picture: "Wherever the climber goes, he is sure to see in some direction, one, if not several, of these solitary sentinels, often floating like a vision or mirage above the lower mists, strangely unreal and ethereal, and by their loftiness dwarfing the surrounding country. . . .

"It would be hard to imagine a more striking and felicitous contrast than that between this idyllic, really Arcadian country, of intimate beauty and delicacy, and the almost savage ruggedness and grandeur of the big peaks, the deep valleys far below, and the magnificent panoramas of distant snowy ranges glowing in the soft light."

THE PIONEER WESTERN PARKS

CALIFORNIA

A VISIT to the four California parks would make a very full summer. Indeed, there are those who go again and again to Yosemite or Sequoia and still feel that there are unknown places to explore and much to observe and learn. There must be, in the Coast Range, the Southern Cascades and the Sierra Nevada, within the State of California, at least 2,500 lineal miles of main mountain crests, of which 1,425 miles are in the Pacific Crest Trail. Less than 100 miles of these crests lie in national parks, passing through Lassen, Yosemite, and Sequoia National Parks.

LASSEN

Lassen Volcanic National Park, created by Congress in 1916, ten years after the land was withdrawn from settlement and declared a national monument by President Theodore Roosevelt, has been widely advertised because of the eruptions of 1914–15 and the sporadic outpourings of volcanic ash.

From the Northwest, Lassen may be reached from the highway running south from Crater Lake by way of Shasta and through Burney to the Manzanita Lake section. From the South, coming up through the rather hot Sacramento Valley, one may leave the main highway at Red Bluff for the road up the mountains to Mineral, a town outside the park boundaries, where the superintendent's headquarters are established. A good many visitors also come from the eastern California and Nevada towns by way of Susanville to Mineral, and then on to Lassen Volcanic Highway which connects with the Lassen Peak Loop Highway, a most spectacular drive during the summer months when the road is open for travel. The park highway leads by many springs and lakes around White Mountain and Summit Lake, over the devastated regions close by Lassen Peak, past Reflection Lake to Manzanita Lake, a distance of some fifty miles from Mineral. Every summer the road must be repaired from the snow and earth slides of the long winter before it is really safe for general use;

but those who are privileged to make the trip are very well repaid.

The park is an irregular rectangle ten by seventeen miles, containing 163 square miles. According to Collins and Lind in "Lassen Glimpses," published in 1929: "The area surrounding Lassen Peak and extending from it roughly for fifty miles east, south and west, and for some hundred miles north, was, back in geologic history during a period of strenuous volcanism, covered by lavas several thousands of feet in depth. These lavas issued principally from a main volcanic cone. By this action the terrain was wrought into the general shape of an immense dome, with the cone near the center and marking the highest point. Thus it may be seen that the Lassen Edifice, as this district is called, comprises a rather large section of country, owing its formation to the activities of a once tremendous volcano of which the present Lassen Peak is remaining evidence.

"Time, and Nature in her further processes of creation, caused decomposition of the lavas by which soil was formed. Forest growth commenced—to hold in storage moisture from the rains. Gradually in outward appearance this barren lava field was softened by the beauty of lake and forest, pleasant brooks and lovely flowers. The work of the old volcano was done, yet it has continued from time to time in less significant bursts of present-day activity, as though, like some old gentleman impelled by vanity, to voice in later generations the importance of past accomplishment.

"At the summit of the great dome, fringing the volcano and in reality part of it, though of secondary nature, were other lesser cones and lava vents whose discharge amplified the huge lava flows from their parent. As the main volcano went into decadence so did these others; and as glaciation, weathering and erosion followed, they were in part ground away. The result of this was the appearance of a unique area—a mass of remnant volcanoes interspersed with meadows, valleys, lakes, and streams. In part a fertile land of Nature's agriculture, contrasted by bits of present-day volcanics; all combined to make more interesting the magnificent spectacle of the old volcano rising in the midst. Perhaps nowhere in the world is the work of Nature in relation to physical geography evidenced more clearly or more interestingly. Here is a museum—a rather special treasure chest of Nature's varied handiwork."

Photograph—Department of the Interior   Courtesy—Portfolio, American Planning and Civic Association

LASSEN VOLCANIC NATIONAL PARK

IN JULY AND AUGUST
THE HOUSEKEEPING CABINS AT LASSEN NATIONAL PARK
ARE ALWAYS OCCUPIED

Of Lassen Peak itself, Collins and Lind have declared: "Lassen Peak is important in the geology of North America as a landmark denoting the fusion of lava Cascades with granite Sierra." It was Lassen Peak, formerly known as St. Joseph's Mountain, which served Peter Lassen as a guiding landmark when he piloted emigrants from Humboldt, Nevada, into the Sacramento Valley in California.

Lassen National Park offers not only a research area of great scientific importance but also an arena where interpretation of the processes of creation may be graphically illustrated for laymen. The climb up the mountain is not difficult and is undertaken by most of the able-bodied visitors. There are many other interesting phenomena in the park; the Cinder Cone and Lava Bed, which lie near Prospect Peak, and the blue waters of Butte Lake, in the northeast corner of the park, where there is a ranger station and a campground, attract many sightseers.

Again quoting from Collins and Lind: "The Cinder Cone country is a small district so startling and beautiful in an unusual way as to seem freakish. Almost a complete circle of ridges from six to eight thousand feet in height above sea level enclose a basin. . . . Evidence has been found to show that an ice pack over one thousand feet thick filled this basin during glacial times. Later it was the site of a rather large mountain lake." Several lava flows resulted in filling in most of the lake, leaving Snag and Butte Lakes.

The devastated area which resulted from the lava overflow from Lassen Crater in 1915 left a trail of destruction which will remain for many years, but reproduction is gradually being accomplished, and along the edges may be seen "young timber extending timidly into the barren flow."

Entirely apart from the marvels and wonders of Lassen National Park which draw visitors from all parts of the world, there is a very strong lure to the residents of a large area in the several adjoining States, which brings in camping and fishing parties who also make a point of climbing Lassen Peak and other mountains, who go on the various excursions around the park, and who also attend the nightly campfire programs conducted by the National Park Service. Lassen National Park renders an important educational and recreational service to the public.

YOSEMITE

From Lassen one may travel by way of the San Francisco Bay region, which in itself comprises many charming residence neighborhoods clustered around the Bay and its tributaries. Not far from Mt. Tamalpais, which overlooks the Golden Gate, is the charming Muir Woods—a national monument—which draws thousands of visitors annually to walk under its ancient coast redwoods (*Sequoia sempervirens*) and to sit in contemplation by the side of its crystal streams.

From the Bay region, or traveling directly south through Stockton, one may approach the El Portal entrance to Yosemite, either by train or by automobile. From El Portal one drives by the guarding rampart of El Capitan directly up the floor of the valley between the famous headlands on either side and within sight of the Bridalveil, Yosemite, and Ribbon Falls.

Many of those who visited the valley during the eighties and nineties, or even twenty-five or thirty years ago, resent the influx of people. Particularly on holidays during the summer are there great crowds to be found on the floor of the valley. At one time in the history of the park these crowds were more in evidence, though not larger, than they are today. Following carefully made plans the automobilists have been confined by inconspicuous barriers to the roads and to designated parking and camping places. The Yosemite is such a choice place on the earth's surface that it is natural for those who would like to enjoy it in solitude to resent the presence of so many of their fellow human beings in the valley. However, anyone who will look at the picture of Yosemite Valley (on page 22) will realize that great skill has been used to hide from view the hotels, inns, cabins, administration buildings, and living quarters of the park and hotel staffs, as well as twenty-three miles of highway. Indeed, it may be truthfully asserted that one may easily avoid the crowds in Yosemite Valley with a little care.

One of the pleasant experiences in Yosemite Valley is to drift around on the more secluded roads, including the road up to Mirror Lake at the head of the valley, in a car without a top, on a moonlight night. The span of starlit sky above the deep shadows of

Photograph—Department of the Interior   Courtesy—Portfolio, American Planning and Civic Association

AHWAHNEE HOTEL, YOSEMITE VALLEY

Photograph—Department of the Interior   Courtesy—Portfolio, American Planning and Civic Association

REAL SPORT ON SKIS IN YOSEMITE NATIONAL PARK

the cliffs, the sound of the rippling Merced River and the sight and sound of the falls, the reflection of sky and cliff in Mirror Lake, together with the cool, pure air of the Sierra, conspire to make such a night one to be remembered and treasured as long as one lives. While there are many beautiful places in the world, the Yosemite washed in moonlight seems to take on an ethereal quality which removes it from the Planet Earth.

One of the impressive ceremonies in Yosemite grew out of a chance revival of a rite, supposed to have been originated by James McCauley of the Mountain House. D. A. Curry, one of the pioneers in offering hospitality in the Yosemite, occasionally arranged, according to Dr. Carl Russell, to send some of the employees of Camp Curry to Glacier Point, over 3,000 feet above the floor of the valley, to build a fire and push it off. This came to be repeated until it was a nightly occurrence. Mr. Curry would call, "Hello," "All's well," and "Farewell," and the echo would be sent back from above. As the glowing embers of the fire are pushed over the cliff to float in the air until they turn to ash, there is always appropriate music. Visitors at the various campfires on the floor of the valley listen with rapt attention for the calls, the song, and the falling embers. No one who has witnessed it could ever forget Fire Fall!

Practically everyone who goes to Yosemite Valley drives or walks up to Glacier Point, where there are a Hotel and Mountain House, and from which one of the very best views in the park may be had. While Fire Fall is not as impressive at Glacier Point as from the floor of the valley, it is yet an experience to attend the campfire at the Point and to see the glowing embers pushed off the cliff while the calls come from below.

There are so many things to do and so many places to go in Yosemite that those who can, visit the park again and again. The valley, so beautiful and interesting in itself, is but a small part of the park. There are the drives to the three fine groves of Big Trees (*Sequoia gigantea*), the Tuolumne on the Big Oak Flat Road, the Merced Grove nearby, north of the valley, and the stately Wawona Grove south of the valley. There is the trip by way of the Tioga Road to Tuolumne Meadows and out over the Tioga Pass to Lake Tahoe, revealing some of the most spectacular Sierra country in Yosemite. Within the 1,176 square miles of the park there are 276 miles of roads and 688 miles of trails.

Hiking is very popular in California, due no doubt to the successful Sierra Club and other mountain groups. During the last fifteen years a series of High Sierra Camps has been developed which provide food and shelter for hikers in the form of a dormitory for men and one for women, and a mess and cook tent. With two exceptions, all food and supplies must be packed in by mules; but those who take the seven-day hiking trip need carry only a light pack with lunch and change of clothing. This makes it possible for many to take the swing around the back country who could not possibly pack bedding and food for seven days. But everyone gets up the trail to see Vernal and Nevada Falls.

Besides the wide range of accommodations in the valley, which run all the way from the de luxe service of the Ahwahnee, through the cottages, the tent cabins, and the dining-rooms at Camp Curry and other locations, to the public campgrounds, there are places to stay at Wawona Hotel, Big Trees Lodge, Glacier Point, Hotel and Mountain House, and Tuolumne Meadows Lodge.

It may be remembered that many of the mountains which John Muir loved to climb lie within the present Yosemite National Park—Hoffman and Lyell, not far from the valley, and a great galaxy of peaks and saw-tooth crests, wearing crystal gems of mountain lakes, which glorify the northern section of the park. On the southeastern boundary are Isber Pass, Triple Divide Peak, Fernandez and Chiquito Passes from which the Ritter-Minarets region, unfortunately outside the park, may be reached.

In addition to all the freedom of the park, to be claimed by those who ride or hike alone, there are many organized activities in Yosemite. Twice a day in summer there is an auto caravan led by a ranger naturalist who explains and interprets the interesting features in the park. There is a daily tour of the valley in open stages. A fine view of the valley is to be seen from the opening of the tunnel on the Wawona Road, just west of Bridalveil Fall. A ranger naturalist leads the seven-day hiking trips.

The Yosemite Museum was one of the first to be established, and furnishes interesting exhibits of the "geology, Indians, early history, trees, flowers, birds, and mammals" of Yosemite. The little group of native Yosemite Indians who demonstrate many

MOUNTAIN CAMP, MT. WHITNEY

From a sketch by T. Moran; from a lithograph in
Langley's "Researches on Solar Heat," 1884

Courtesy—Sierra Club Bulletin

SEQUOIA NATIONAL PARK

**AERIAL VIEW OF MT. WHITNEY AND
UPPER KERN BASIN
TABLE MOUNTAIN IN THE DISTANCE**

Photograph—Roy Curtis, Reno, Nevada
Courtesy—Sierra Club Bulletin

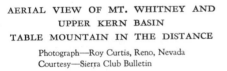

SEQUOIA GIGANTEA, WITH ITS DOMED CROWN,
DESCRIBED BY JOHN MUIR

Courtesy—American Forests

GENERAL SHERMAN TREE AT THE RIGHT, IN SEQUOIA
NATIONAL PARK. PROBABLY 4,000 YEARS OLD, THIS
GIANT IS 35 FEET IN DIAMETER AT ITS BASE
AND REACHES A HEIGHT OF 274 FEET

[148]

of the old customs back of the Museum, draw and hold the attention of all who visit them. There are campfire entertainments at various places in the park, but perhaps the most unique performance (outside of Fire Fall) is the nightly feeding of the bears, which may be observed across a stream. A ranger tells about the habits of the bears while the vast multitude watches their antics from a vantage point of safety.

Yosemite has become one of the most popular scenes of winter sports in the United States. Under its mantle of snow the valley is quite entrancing—no less so than it was when John Muir spent his first winter in the Sierra sixty years ago, for snow glorifies even the inevitable buildings and scars of occupation. The ice cone at the base of Upper Yosemite Fall which results from the frozen mist sometimes reaches a height of 300 feet and always adds to the winter beauty of the park. There are many skiing grounds in the park. According to the Yosemite bulletin, issued by the Park Service: "A new ski lodge, where ski equipment may be rented and light lunches and refreshments are served, is located at Badger Pass Meadow; elevation 7,300 feet, in the center of some of the finest skiing slopes in the West." Instructors are on hand to add to the skiing recruits. In the valley, which is protected from the winter winds, there are all kinds of skating events throughout the winter. There is a popular snowslide called "Ash Can Alley" down which merry boys and girls, yes, and men and women, slide in heavy tin pans which look exactly like the missing cover to the home ash-can.

Easter has come to be quite a day in Yosemite. A vast but breathlessly silent multitude assembles at Mirror Lake for the Sunrise Services. The first rays of the Sun as he touches with his magic golden wand the dusky ramparts of the valley and illumines the lake below, strike upon the eyes of the beholders with the dramatic force of a great annunciation. The high clear voices of the vested choir transform the valley into a great cathedral with flying buttresses and vaulted dome, transcending any mystic marvel of church architecture described by Henry Adams.

Yosemite is crowded on Easter, not only for the Sunrise Service, but also for the winter sports. Many of the visitors drive up to see the skiing and find it an exhilarating sight—the snowy mountain background, the bright costumes, the gay skiers.

Geologically, Yosemite Valley has a most dramatic history. To quote the national park bulletin: "The Yosemite Valley was cut to great depth in the first place by the Merced River, which flows through it and the Merced Canyon below. That river was repeatedly accelerated to torrential speed by the uplifts which in the course of many million years have given the Sierra Nevada its great height. Each time the river was accelerated it cut its channel deeper, and so at last it fashioned a narrow V-shaped canyon over 2,000 feet in depth. The lesser side streams, meanwhile, were unable to cut so fast, and as a consequence their valleys were left hanging high above the bottom of the canyon. The original Yosemite Canyon thus became adorned by many cascades of great height and beauty.

"Then came the Ice Age, and the Yosemite Canyon was invaded by a mighty glacier that descended slowly but irresistibly from the crest of the range. During the climax of the Ice Age this glacier filled the canyon literally to the brinks, and extended down to the site of El Portal. It reached within 700 feet of the crown of Half Dome, and overrode Glacier Point to a depth of 700 feet. Forcing its way with tremendous power, it gradually widened the narrow V-shaped canyon to a broad U-shaped trough. It cut back the sloping sides to sheer cliffs and transformed the cascades to leaping water-falls. It also added to the depth of the valley, excavating a lake basin in its rock floor. When at last the glacier melted away it left a lake 5½ miles long. But that lake did not endure, for the Merced River brought down vast quantities of sand and gravel, and in the course of time filled the lake completely, and produced the level parklike floor which adds so much to the visitor's enjoyment of the Valley." In comparison with such mighty public works, Boulder Dam and Grand Coulee seem ineffective and ephemeral!

From a motor-car window, from the back of a horse, or afoot, the Yosemite offers deep interest and intense pleasure for those who love the Sierra. The great variety of wild flowers always excites admiration. The actual tramping of feet and the processes of occupation have indeed destroyed the brilliant flower gardens of John Muir's day, but with management many of these have been restored, and in the mountains and valleys of the park, where there is little traffic, the flowers of Yosemite are still among the loveliest in the Sierra. With the variations of elevation there are zones of plant types. Definitely, the national park bulletin has directed attention to the fact that "Five life zones are represented characterized by a brush belt (chaparral) with its manzanita and wild lilac (*Ceanothus* sp.) interspersed with live oaks and the Digger pine forest at the lowest altitudes and grading into yellow mountain pine, and then to a timber line forest of mountain hemlock and white-barked pine. Lichens, mosses, and a few alpine flowering plants characterize the alpine-arctic zone. . . .

"Flowering plants in great profusion add new beauty with the advancing season. Early spring marks the flowering of the tree dogwood, followed by such shrubs as the Philadelphus (wild syringa), western azalea, and pink spiraea. Whole mountainsides blaze with ocean spray (*Holodiscus discolor*). Meadows at lower elevations start white with death camas and mariposa lilies (*Calochortus* sp.); turn to yellow with evening primroses (*Oenothera* sp.), buttercups, and goldenrod; blue with lupines and larkspur; to red with Indian paintbrush (*Castilleia* sp.); and finally pink with fireweed, pussy paws (*Calyptridium*), and *Lessingia*. The snow plant (*Sarcodes sanguinea*) and pine drops (*Pterospora andromeda*) are common saprophytic plants of the pine forests, the former appearing like a bright red giant asparagus tip. . . . On the highest peaks are found two beautiful plants, the Sierra primrose and the sky pilot (*Polemonium eximium*). Here also cassiope, a white heather, replaces the pink one which grows at slightly lower elevations."

Only lovers of the high places on the face of the earth can feel the thrill that comes from crossing the lingering snowbanks at the summits of passes along the trail and then finding bright beds of the lovely Sierra primrose and acres of the modest cassiope clustering close to the ground around the rocks and shale of the mountainside. The streams of Yosemite are well stocked with fish, and the Waltonians may whip the remote waters of the park or fish quietly in the rivers and tributaries of the Merced Valley.

One wonders if Yosemite Valley and the High Sierra country around it might not serve as a prototype for the mythical Garden of Eden. At any rate, he who has not seen Yosemite has not yet been to Carcassonne!

SEQUOIA AND GENERAL GRANT

The Sequoia and General Grant National Parks were, of course, created primarily to preserve the Big Trees without particular consideration of the general scenic values likely to be included. In Sequoia is the famous Giant Forest, so named by John Muir and described by him as no one since has equaled. Of the long hike he made with "Brownie" the mule, down the crest of the Sierra, we have heard much. In his book on "Our National Parks," he has recounted: "Day after day, from grove to grove, canyon to canyon, I made a long, wavering way, terribly rough in some places for Brownie, but cheery for me, for Big Trees were seldom out of sight. We crossed the rugged, picturesque basins of Redwood Creek, the North Fork of the Kaweah, and Marble Fork gloriously forested, and full of beautiful cascades and falls, sheer and slanting, infinitely varied with broad curly foam fleeces and strips of embroidery in which the sunbeams revel. Thence we climbed into the noble forest on the Marble and Middle Fork Divide. After a general exploration of the Kaweah basin, this park of the sequoia belt seemed to me the finest, and I then named it 'the Giant Forest.' It extends, a magnificent growth of giants grouped in pure temple groves, ranged in colonnades along the sides of meadows, or scattered among the other trees, from the granite headlands overlooking the hot foothills and plains of the San Joaquin back to within a few miles of the old glacier fountains at an elevation of five thousand to eighty-four hundred feet above the sea.

"When I entered the sublime wilderness the day was nearly done, the trees with rosy, glowing countenances seemed to be hushed and thoughtful, as if waiting in conscious religious dependence on the sun, and one naturally walked softly and awestricken among them. I wandered on, meeting nobler trees where all are noble, subdued in the general calm, as if in some vast hall pervaded by the deepest sanctities and solemnities that sway human souls. At sundown the trees seemed to cease their worship and breathe free. I heard the birds going home. . . . Then I took a walk up the meadow to see the trees in the pale light. They seemed still more marvelously massive and tall than by day, heaving their colossal heads into the depths of the sky, among

[152]

FURNACE CREEK INN, DEATH VALLEY

Photographs—Department of the Interior
Courtesy—Portfolio, American Planning and Civic Association

THE SUN-SCORCHED SANDS OF DEATH VALLEY

ARRIVING AT GLACIER NATIONAL PARK BY TRAIN, VISITORS MAY SOON FIND
THEMSELVES ON PICTURESQUE AND INSPIRING TRAILS

BOULDER PASS IN GLACIER NATIONAL PARK

the stars, some of which appeared to be sparkling on their branches like flowers.''

In the Giant Forest is General Sherman Tree, probably the biggest living *Sequoia gigantea* in the world, though remnants and snags in the redwood forests indicate that there have been larger trees. The bole of General Sherman is fluted symmetrically and tapers so little that it might be considered a column of perfection in some giant edifice which would rival the Parthenon. The crown shows clearly the shaping described by John Muir as characteristic of the old Big Trees. In the book on the ''Big Trees,'' by Judge Fry and Colonel White, the bark of General Sherman is described: ''Generally of a rich cinnamon brown, it has a reddish tinge that is accentuated at sunset. In places the bark is deeply fluted or furrowed up and down the tree; in spots it seems fuzzy or furry. But you will also note running the length of the tree, up to the first large branches and even higher, long streaks of bark that are shiny or silvered in comparison with areas near by. On most old Big Trees you will see these silvery streaks of bark, and they are usually a sign that centuries, perhaps a score of centuries, ago a mighty fire raged up the tree, almost devouring it. Using sequoia measures of time, centuries instead of days or weeks or years, that is *new* bark. It covers great areas of the trees that have been burned.''

But it is not General Sherman alone, or even the amount of timber which the Big Tree would yield, that makes us stand spellbound in contemplation of the age-old forces which have produced such a tree. There is an impressiveness and beauty in the redwood forests that could not be captured by any single tree. No other trees better picture the phrase ''forest aisles'' than the stately columns of the Big Trees rising straight to heaven. It is an experience to walk between these warm brown pillars, where only occasional glimpses of the sky may be discovered. The forest floor is especially beautiful. Again quoting John Muir: ''Under the huge trees up come the small plant people, putting forth fresh leaves and blossoming in such profusion that the hills and valleys would still seem gloriously rich and glad were all the grand trees away. By the side of melting snowbanks rise the crimson sarcodes, round topped and massive as the sequoias themselves, and beds of blue violets and larger yellow ones with leaves

[155]

curiously lobed; azalea and saxifrage, daisies and lilies on the mossy banks of the streams; and a little way back of them, beneath the trees and on sunny spots on the hills around the groves, wild rose and rubus, spiraea and ribes, mitella, tiarella, campanula, monardella, forget-me-not, and many of them as worthy of lore immortality as the famous Scotch daisy, wanting only a Burns to sing them home to all hearts. . . .

"Imbedded in these majestic woods there are numerous meadows, around the sides of which the Big Trees press close together in beautiful lines, showing their grandeur openly from the ground to their domed heads in the sky. . . . For every venerable lightning-stricken tree, there is one or more in the glory of prime, and for each of these, many young trees and crowds of saplings. The young trees express the grandeur of their race in a way indefinable by any words at my command. When they are five or six feet in diameter and a hundred and fifty feet high, they seem like mere baby saplings as many inches in diameter, their juvenile habit and gestures completely veiling their real size, even to those who, from long experience, are able to make fair approximation in their measurements of common trees."

The life history of these Big Tree forests runs from seedlings to giants around four thousand years old. These ancients are not lone survivors of a past age; they stand in living communities amid trees of their kind of all ages. It was to preserve incomparable groves that Sequoia National Park was created.

General Grant National Park, comprising about four square miles, preserves another extensive grove, and can be reached from Sequoia by the spectacular Generals Highway. General Grant Tree is the largest redwood in the Grant Grove, and while it is said that it would not furnish quite as much lumber as General Sherman, a tree with a forty-foot diameter at the base, which is 267 feet high (matching a twenty-seven-story skyscraper) certainly must command our admiration. General Grant, which has a beauty of form and posture all its own, has sometimes been called the Nation's Christmas tree. Certainly when snow lies in soft puffs on its branches, the surrounding forest of lesser trees furnishing a frame of white etched in on the dark green of the conifers and the darker browns, grays, and blacks of the boles, one could accept the symbol and be thankful that a beneficent Government had pledged its honor to protect these Giants.

Sequoia National Park, with the 352 square miles added in 1926, now is a park 604 miles square and contains the highest mountain peak in the continental United States—Mt. Whitney —and the southern climax of the High Sierra. Of the sixty peaks in the United States which are over 14,000 feet high, thirteen are in California and six in the Sequoia National Park. The park offers fine opportunities for pack-train trips both within and without the park. Many of the Kings Canyon pack trips start from Lodge Pole, the end of the road running north from Giant Forest, passing over J. O. Pass and on into the South Fork of the Kings. But the trip *par excellence* is the trip up Mt. Whitney, across the Kern Canyon. If the marvelously picturesque country is to be seen and enjoyed to the full, at least two weeks is needed—a most interesting and enjoyable two weeks!

Walter A. Starr, Jr., in the "Guide to the John Muir Trail and the High Sierra Region," has commented on the park: "The Sequoia National Park region includes the headwaters of the Kern and Kaweah Rivers, separated by the Great Western Divide, which extends north and south, parallel to the Sierra Crest about midway across the park. Between the Sierra Crest and this great divide the Kern flows south. On the western slope of the divide the various forks of the Kaweah take their rise and flow westward, meeting just west of the park at Three Rivers to form the main stream. Scattered over the extensive basin of the Kaweah, in the western half of the park, are twenty-two groves of giant sequoias. . . . From Foresters Pass on the northern boundary of Sequoia National Park, the Muir Trail crosses the high plateau of the Kern to the summit of Mount Whitney. The last part of the route, from Wallace Creek is along the new High Sierra Trail from Whitney to Giant Forest. . . . Foresters Pass is the highest pass on the Muir Trail. The view north, extending to the Palisades and beyond, is one of the finest views from any pass in the Sierra, and is comparable to that from Junction Pass a mile to the east. By ascending Junction Peak. . . a short distance to the East, a panorama even more remarkable is presented, for this peak occupies a strategic position at the juncture of the Sierra Crest and the Kings-Kern Divide, offering an unobstructed sweep in all directions. The view southward along the Sierra Crest includes the Whitney group of 14,000-foot peaks—the end of the grand crescendo of the Sierra."

Hardy mountaineers who desire to test their skill and command the world from the clouds may find peaks aplenty to climb. Sequoia National Park, with the highest mountain and the biggest tree, cannot fail to capture and hold the attention of the American people. There are excellent accommodations at Giant Forest Lodge and public campgrounds at Giant Forest, Lodge Pole, and Dorst Creek. The camp-sites are laid out according to modern standards and, somewhat removed from the highway, provide idyllic conditions for camping. Sequoia National Park is a place where one may penetrate the wilderness and sleep out under the sky, for in the dry season there is little or no rain.

Sequoia is open the year round, and in winter there are fine opportunities for skiing, tobogganing, and snowshoeing. In summer there is also a daily bear feed. The campfire programs are well attended throughout the summer and are educational as well as inspiring. Colonel John R. White, who served the park as superintendent from 1920 to 1939, deserves the congratulations of the American people for the increasing protection which is being given to the Big Trees and for the atmosphere of reverence which he has created in the park.

MONUMENTS

In California there are eight national monuments (including the Channel Islands), covering 2,802,300 acres, of which the largest and most unique is Death Valley, established as a monument in 1933 and now containing 1,907,720 acres. Once a death trap for the pioneers who sought to cross the sun-scorched sands, it is now a favorite tourist resort, where one can see a great desert bowl nearly 300 feet below the level of the sea, and raise one's eyes to Telescope Peak which pierces the clouds at 11,325 feet in altitude. The Park Service has called attention to the "pastel colors of the rocks, intricately carved and bare of vegetation, the browns and hazy purple masses of the distant mountains, the wide, white expanses of salt and alkali, the sweeping curves of sand dunes."

MANY GLACIER HOTEL

GLACIER
NATIONAL PARK

GOING-TO-THE-SUN CHALET

Photographs—Department of the Interior

Courtesy—Portfolio, American Planning
and Civic Association

[159]

Photograph—Department of the Interior   Courtesy—American Planning and Civic Annual

KINNERLY PEAK, FROM KINTLA LAKE,
GLACIER NATIONAL PARK

THE PIONEER WESTERN PARKS

THE MAGIC ROCKIES

The Rocky Mountain parks deserve a separate and special trip if they are to be seen and appreciated, although, of course, it is possible for those who live in the East to stop over in Glacier and Yellowstone on the way to the Northwest and in Rocky Mountain National Park on the way to California or the Southwest. However, the ideal tour would be to start at Glacier National Park on the Canadian border and then to visit Yellowstone, the Tetons, and Rocky Mountain National Park, staying long enough in each to learn something about it. One might even say that three summer vacations could well be given to Glacier, to Yellowstone and the Tetons, and to Rocky Mountain Park.

GLACIER NATIONAL PARK

Except for Yellowstone and Mt. McKinley, Glacier National Park is the largest in the system. Its 1,534 square miles in northwestern Montana include some of the most spectacular mountain crests and peaks in America, spotted with half a hundred glaciers and two hundred glistening lakes. It adjoins the Waterton Lakes Park in Canada, and the two by Presidential proclamation, authorized by Congress and the Canadian Government, form the Waterton-Glacier International Peace Park.

Glacier National Park is readily accessible by train to the eastern entrance to the park, a thousand miles west of St. Paul and a little over six hundred east of Seattle, and by airplane to nearby cities. It is by automobile that our imaginary trip will enter the park from the east, stopping first, if desired, at Glacier Park Hotel, adjacent to the railroad station, but preferably for fishermen or hikers going direct to Two Medicine Lake where, either at Two Medicine Chalet or the public camp, the setting sun may be seen across the mountain-bound lake in which the massive slopes of snow-patched Sinopah are reflected in rose, gray, and white. A boat trip across the lake may be taken to the foot of Mt. Sinopah. Almost everyone takes the easy forest path to Twin Falls. There is excellent fishing in the lake and in the streams. The evening campfires at Two Medicine, conducted by the ranger naturalists, have always been popular; they cap a day's hiking or fishing with just that relaxation which permits attention to a talk explaining or commenting on what has been seen during the day.

Trick Falls, near the highway bridge, on the Two Medicine Road, is so easily accessible that perhaps it is not given its full rating of beauty, as hikers are apt to value the beauty of scenic features by the effort exerted to reach them.

Practically everyone who goes to Glacier makes a visit to Many Glacier Hotel or to the nearby camp, by way of the dead-end access road into the east-central part of the park. The self-guided walks around Lake Josephine toward Grinnell Glacier are entertaining and easy, and even easier are the boat trips on Lake Josephine and Swiftcurrent Lakes.

In the old days, visitors drove to the head of St. Mary Lake and there took a boat to Going-to-the-Sun, one of the most beautiful and secluded spots in the park. Nothing can destroy the fine combination of snow-etched mountains and sparkling lake, but since the Going-to-the-Sun Highway skirts the lake and brings thousands of automobiles to rest on the leveled-off parking space back of the Chalet, much of the romance and wildness of this once-enchanted spot have been dissipated.

Going-to-the-Sun Highway runs from St. Mary, past Going-to-the-Sun, over Logan Pass, to skirt Lake McDonald to Belton, where the superintendent's office is located. It cannot be denied that the drive is very scenic and that it introduces the heart of the park to the automobile visitor. North and south of this highway are great areas reached only by trail.

When the weather is clear and the views are not obscured by rain and clouds, the trip up the east side of the park, partly outside the boundaries, to Waterton Lakes, is very worthwhile and brings visitors into the Canadian Rockies. Just outside the boundary on the west side of the park is a Forest Service road which gives access to many trails—one, in the extreme north-western section of the park along the Kintla Lakes to the foot of Waterton Lake. A road to the foot of Bowman Lake connects with a lakeside trail finally joining the Kintla Lake trail.

One could spend weeks and months in traveling the trails of Glacier National Park. There are many shelter cabins scattered over the park for the comfort and convenience of the hiker, in addition to the many public camps, hotels, and chalets for both hiker and motorist.

The National Park Service has called attention to the geography of Glacier: "Glacier Park has within its boundary two parallel mountain ranges. The eastern, or front range, extends from the Canadian boundary almost without a break to New Mexico. The western, or Livingston Range, rises at the head of Lake McDonald, becomes the front range beyond the international line, and runs northward to Alaska. Between these two ranges in the center of the park is a broad swell which carries the Continental Divide from one to the other. This is Flattop Mountain, whose groves of trees are open and parklike, wholly unlike the dense forests of the lowlands. . . . A trail leads from Waterton over Flattop to the tent camp, called Fifty Mountain, and to Granite Park, where a comfortable high-mountain chalet is located. Here is exposed a great mass of lava, which once welled up from the interior of the earth and spread over the region which was then the bottom of a sea. The chalets command a fine view of the majestic grouping of mountains around Logan Pass, of the noble summits of the Livingston Range, and of systems far to the south and west of the park. Extending in the near foreground are gentle slopes covered with sparse clumps of stunted vegetation. In early July open spaces are gold-carpeted with glacier lilies and bizarrely streaked with lingering snow patches. Beyond are the deep, heavy forests of Upper McDonald Valley."

From these chalets, too, there is a foot trail to the rim of the Garden Wall, where may be seen the "heavenly blue alpine columbine" together with many others, including dryads, globe flowers, and alpine fireweed.

The mere catalogue of trails and trips in Glacier Park would require pages. Since the time when the late George Bird Grinnell made his first trip to Glacier in 1885, later to be publicized in an article in *Century Magazine*, the park has been a magnet for true lovers of mountains and mountain trips. There are extensive wilderness areas in the park, far from roads of any kind, where only hardy hikers and pack trains may penetrate. Of Glacier it may well be said: "So much to see, so much to learn, so much to enjoy!"

YELLOWSTONE NATIONAL PARK

The immutables of Yellowstone are today much the same as they were in the seventies when the early exploring trips revealed the marvels of the region. Nearly forty years ago John Muir said of the Yellowstone: "It is a big, wholesome wilderness on the broad summit of the Rocky Mountains, favored with abundance of rain and snow,—a place of fountains where the greatest of the American rivers take their rise. The central portion is a densely forested and comparatively level volcanic plateau with an average elevation of about eight thousand feet above the sea, surrounded by an imposing host of mountains belonging to the subordinate Gallatin, Wind River, Teton, Absaroka, and snowy ranges. Unnumbered lakes shine in it, united by a famous band of streams that rush up out of hot lava beds, or fall from the frosty peaks in channels rocky and bare, mossy and bosky to the main rivers, singing cheerily on through every difficulty, cunningly dividing and finding their way to the two far-off seas.

"Glacier meadows and beaver meadows are outspread with charming effect along the banks of the streams, parklike expanses in the woods, and innumerable small gardens in rocky recesses of the mountains, some of them containing more petals than leaves, while the whole wilderness is enlivened with happy animals.

"Beside the treasures common to most mountain regions that are wild and blessed with a kind climate, the park is full of exciting wonders. The wildest geysers in the world, in bright, triumphant bands, are dancing and singing in it amid thousands of boiling springs, beautiful and awful, their basins arrayed in gorgeous colors like gigantic flowers; and hot paint-pots, mud springs, mud volcanoes, mush and broth caldrons whose contents are of every color and consistency, plash and heave and roar in bewildering abundance. In the adjacent mountains, beneath the living trees the edges of petrified forests are exposed to view, like specimens on the shelves of a museum, standing on ledges tier above tier where they grew, solemnly silent in rigid crystalline beauty after swaying in the winds thousands of centuries ago, opening marvelous views back into the years and climates and life of the past. Here, too, are hills of sparkling crystals, hills of sulphur, hills of glass, hills of cinders and ashes,

THE SIERRA CLUB VISITS GRINNELL LAKE

GLACIER NATIONAL PARK

BOWMAN LAKE

Photographs—Charles S. Webber   Courtesy—Sierra Club Bulletin

MOUNTAIN GOATS IN GLACIER NATIONAL PARK

mountains of every style of architecture, icy or forested, mountains covered with honey-bloom sweet as Hymettus, mountains boiled soft like potatoes and colored like a sunset sky."

All these wonders are there today. Yellowstone Lake still reflects the woods and mountains and sky. The two magnificent falls of the Grand Canyon of the Yellowstone still splash the waters of the river over the highly colored stones which gave name to the lake and river. Moran's pictures are as truly photographic today as when they were painted.

Yellowstone has four principal entrances which connect with a double-loop road. The drives in themselves are charming and interesting. With "Haynes Guide" and "Trailside Notes for the Motorist and Hiker," covering Mammoth to Old Faithful and Fishing Bridge Museum to Mammoth, one can drive to all the principal points of interest and see understandingly the sights of Yellowstone. There are 328 miles of roads in the 3,437 square miles of the park, and 920 miles of trails. The road mileage has not been increased in the last thirty years, but old dirt roads have been improved with hard surface and sometimes relocated in the interests of safety. One could hardly imagine a more fascinating game than to make leisurely trips around Yellowstone to examine the 3,000 geysers and hot springs at different times of day. There are guided trips from all centers both for automobiles and on foot. There are campfire programs at many places in the park. There are a number of most illuminating museums. And Yellowstone has a bear show in which the grizzly gentry come out to feed, and which attracts a great deal of attention. There are miles of good fishing, hiking, and riding.

The season at Yellowstone is short, for in winter the park lies under a deep mantle of snow and the temperatures reach incredibly low levels. There are hotels, lodges, and public camps at Mammoth Hot Springs, Old Faithful, the Lake, and the Canyon. In spite of the large number of visitors accommodated in the popular centers, amounting at the height of the season, with park and hotel staffs, to veritable towns, it is possible to see the marvels of the park without *feeling* overcome with the crowds. And there is still much wilderness in the park which it is hoped will never be invaded with roads and hotels and lodges. Every citizen of the United States may be thankful for Yellowstone.

THE GRAND TETON NATIONAL PARK

Those same Grand Tetons which were landmarks to the pioneers who crossed the continent in the early days, now rear their craggy crests in a spectacular jagged silhouette against the sky. For many years efforts were made to enlarge Yellowstone National Park to include the Tetons, historic Jackson Hole, and the Absarokas. But, as in most other projects to increase the national parks, the resistance on the part of those who desired to make use of the resources has been very great. It was not until 1929 that a twenty-seven-mile strip, from three to nine miles wide, was created a national park. This took in the eastern slopes of the entire range of Tetons from their ragged crests to the string of crystal lakes which gird them at the base of the steep slopes. It is well recognized by park-minded conservationists that every area worthy of being a national park should have a sufficiently wide protective rim to preserve the character of its scenery. It was soon apparent to close observers that the uncontrolled areas adjoining the park were becoming a menace to its use as a park. Along the county road, on private property in Jackson Hole, there grew up the most unsightly structures, and many of these were put to noisy uses totally incompatible with the enjoyment of a national park. Mr. John D. Rockefeller, Jr., observed this when he made a visit to the Grand Teton National Park, and he purchased some 40,000 acres of private property which, with available public domain and some national-forest land, it has been proposed to add to the Teton Park as a permanent protection, but so far selfish local interests have prevented action by Congress to accept the gift and make the transfers. The Jackson Hole country which would thus be added to the park has an interesting history of its own. In the thirties and forties many famous pioneers were identified with Jackson Hole—Captain Bonneville, Father De Smet, Rev. Samuel Parker, Jedediah Smith, Jim Bridger, Kit Carson, David Jackson, Captain William Sublette, Joe Meek, and others. There has been a sprinkling of dude ranches in and around Jackson Hole of recent years, and some of these are still operated on land which Mr. Rockefeller purchased.

One complication which no way has been found to remove is that Jackson Lake, once a part of the crystal string of gems,

FISHING BRIDGE MUSEUM, YELLOWSTONE NATIONAL PARK

YELLOWSTONE FALLS

Photographs—Department of the Interior
Courtesy—Portfolio, American Planning and Civic Association

Photograph—Beckett Howorth   Courtesy—Appalachia

THE GRAND TETON

[170]

THE GRAND TETONS, WITH JACKSON HOLE FOREGROUND WHICH JOHN D. ROCKEFELLER, JR.
HAS PURCHASED TO GIVE TO THE FEDERAL GOVERNMENT, TO BE ADDED TO
THE GRAND TETON NATIONAL PARK

TEEWINOT AND JACKSON HOLE, FROM THE GRAND TETON

Photograph—Department of the Interior   Courtesy—Portfolio, American Planning and Civic Association

DREAM LAKE, ROCKY MOUNTAIN NATIONAL PARK

was terribly damaged some years ago by what is now believed to have been an unjustified reclamation project. The level of the lake was raised without even the precaution of taking out the dead timber, so that those who had loved the lake in early days came back to see the tragedy of its ruin. In recent years, CCC crews have cleared out the dead timber, but the dam and the ugly changes in the level of the lake still mar the scenery of the park. Since there are other storage sites lower down which could give to Idaho the same and more water, it is devoutly to be hoped that a way may be found to redeem the lake.

The Grand Tetons offer excellent mountain-climbing opportunities. The trails are used by both hikers and horsemen, for Jackson Hole is still a center for western saddle horses. There is an excellent museum, and the campfire lectures on the geology of the region are attended by those who come from a wide radius. When the protective additions are made, the Grand Teton National Park will become one of the finest of the national parks.

ROCKY MOUNTAIN NATIONAL PARK

The Colorado Rockies have long ranked high in the affections of the American people. There are some of the highest and finest peaks in the entire range in the Rocky Mountain Park. Longs Peak, the tallest, reaches 14,255 feet. The Trail Ridge Road, which crosses the Continental Divide, connects the town of Estes Park on the east side of the park with Grand Lake on the west side, and gives to the motorist some of the finest mountain views in America. According to the national park bulletin, a distinguishing feature of the park is its "profusion of precipice-walled canyons lying between lofty mountains." We are told that "Ice-cold streams wander from lake to lake, watering wild flowers of luxuriance and beauty. The entire park is a garden of wild flowers. . . . There are few wilder and lovelier spots . . . than Loch Vale, 3,000 feet sheer below Taylor Peak. Adjoining it lies Glacier Gorge on the precipitous western slope of Longs Peak and enclosing a group of small lakes. These, with lesser gorges cradling Bear Lake, picturesque Dream Lake, beautiful Fern Lake, and exquisite Odessa Lake, and still others yet

[173]

unnamed, constitute the wild gardens of the Rocky Mountain National Park, lying in the angle north of Longs Peak; while in the angle south lies a little-known wilderness of lakes and gorges called Wild Basin."

And yet Rocky Mountain National Park, which has so much to make it one of the great parks of the system, has been a sort of stepchild from the beginning. The boundaries were drawn far too closely when it was created in 1915. Rocky Mountain was one of the parks to which the Reclamation Service was given free entry. There was a diversion ditch in the north end of the park which it was legal to extend, and extended it was a few years ago, so that all who ride over the Trail Ridge Road see now the long gash scar of this unsightly intrusion. Grand Lake, which once was the largest and most picturesque body of water in the region, was not included in the park, and although under authorization of Congress, purchase of some of the lands along its border has been progressing, private occupation has quite transformed its once wild beauty. There are many private holdings well within its boundaries, so that it is utterly impossible to give protection to great areas which are scenically a part of the park. And then, to cap the long history of misfortunes which have been visited on it, Congress authorized in 1938 the building of a water-diversion tunnel under the park which will affect the surroundings of Grand Lake, will involve a ditch in an authorized addition to the park, and introduce power lines and plants along the picturesque Thompson-River approach to the park. Technically, if the assurance of the Reclamation Service that no air shafts will have to be sunk inside of the park can be realized, there will be no entry into the existing park; but no one who is familiar with the surroundings can escape the conviction that areas which should have been included in the park will be injured. There is an extensive region south of the park where are some fine peaks, glaciers, and lakes which might well be added to the present boundaries.

There are five public campgrounds in the park and many hotels, lodges, and camps on private lands in or near it. It is to be hoped that the private holdings in the Rocky Mountain Park will soon be acquired and that old injuries will be allowed to heal wherever possible.

THE PIONEER WESTERN PARKS

It seems logical to include the trips to the over-seas national parks under the section on western parks, as most of those who visit Alaska and Hawaii sail from western ports.

MT. MCKINLEY

Regular steamers ply between Seattle and Alaska ports, giving passengers one of the most picturesque coastwise ocean trips imaginable. Once arrived in Alaska, there is a rail trip of 348 miles from Seward to McKinley Park Station. According to the national park bulletin, the trip to the park from Seward "takes the passenger past beautiful Lake Kenai, Moose Pass, Spencer Glacier, and Turnagain Arm, which boasts the second highest tide in the world. It also offers the unique experience of crossing the Continental Divide at its lowest point in North America, where it reaches 2,337 feet elevation. The first view of Mt. McKinley is had from Talkeetna, but the majestic peak is sighted from various other points along the railroad."

Next to Yellowstone, Mt. McKinley is the largest of our national parks and in it lies the highest of North American mountains, its great white expanse at the highest point reaching 20,300 feet. Its sculpturing is in simple broad planes of shining white ice and snow which cover the mighty mountain two-thirds of the way down from its summit, which is 17,000 feet above the plateau on the north and west. Mt. Foraker, near by, is 17,000 feet high; other peaks are somewhat lower but impressive because of the distance above the "take-off." Both McKinley and Foraker have been climbed in recent years.

The Alaska glaciers offer a fine opportunity for study, and both for the scientist and the layman the wildlife of the park is fascinating. Caribou, moose, Toklat grizzly bears, Alaska mountain sheep, wolves, wolverines, coyotes, Alaska red fox, hoary marmots, lynx, beaver, martens and minks, land otters, Mackenzie snowshoe rabbits, Alaska conies, ground squirrels, short-billed gulls, the coy Alaska willow ptarmigan, and surf-birds are all found.

Within the park there are eighty miles of graveled motor roads, and there are excellent saddle-horse trails which lead to the regions about the base of Mt. McKinley and to other points of interest. Unless one is an experienced mountain climber and a part of an organized expedition, the best way to see Mt. McKinley is from the air. Hotel and tent camps are available.

Those who covet wilderness may certainly find it in Mt. McKinley National Park. The trip to Alaska, the visit to the park, with side trips to Glacier Bay National Monument of over a million acres, reached from Juneau by boat, and Katmai National Monument of two and a half million acres, reached by sailing vessel from Kodiak, is guaranteed to satisfy hunger for the back country.

HAWAII

Honolulu, the capital of the Territory of Hawaii, is reached in a four-and-a-half- to six-day ocean voyage from San Francisco or Los Angeles. Honolulu is also a port of call of steamers from the Orient, Australia, and Vancouver, B. C. The Hawaii National Park is in two sections, one including the active craters of Mauna Loa and Kilauea, covering 219 square miles of the Island of Hawaii, where the Port of Hilo is reached by Inter-Island steamers or Inter-Island airplanes from Honolulu. The other section covers the dormant crater of Haleakala on the Island of Maui.

The contrast between glacier-bound Alaska, with its national park open during a short summer season, and the Hawaiian Islands, lying just south of the Tropic of Cancer, with their everlasting summer and lush tropical verdure, is very great.

Kilauea, perhaps older than the much higher Mauna Loa, creates the impression of being a crater in the side of the larger mountain. From Hilo there is an excellent highway to the Volcano House, on the northeast rim overlooking the entire crater of Kilauea, roughly four miles in diameter. The trail from the Volcano House across this expanse of purgatorial desolation, cut by many steam cracks from which hot vapor pours forth, is an introduction to the deep pit of Halemaumau, about half a mile in diameter. Sometimes this pit is sunken a thousand feet or more and sometimes the molten lava boils up to its very surface, a lake of living fire. At night, then, the steam and heat

Photograph—Department of the Interior   Courtesy—Portfolio, American Planning and Civic Association

BIGHORNS IN ROCKY MOUNTAIN NATIONAL PARK

[177]

THE JOY OF A PACK-TRAIN TRIP

Photograph—Department of the Interior   ELEVATION 20,300 FEET   Courtesy—Sierra Club Bulletin

MT. McKINLEY, THE HIGHEST PEAK
IN NORTH AMERICA

Photograph—K. Maehara   Courtesy—Portfolio, American Planning and Civic Association

THE 1924 KILAUEA ERUPTION
IN HAWAII NATIONAL PARK

take on a fiery aspect. In some of the great eruptions, as in 1934, "without much preliminary warning, molten lava again returned to the fire pit in Kilauea. This eruption in its early stages was one of the most spectacular on record. Highly charged with gas released from the tremendous pressure, the frothy lava burst through a crack 700 feet long, halfway up the western wall of the crater, cascading in rivers of fire 425 feet to the floor below. The force of the lava cracked open the old floor left by the 1931–32 eruption across its northern and northwest end, and along the foot of the western wall dense clouds of sulphur fumes poured out, as the fiery fountains shot the liquid lava high into the air. As in the previous eruption, blocks of light pumice thrown out from the vents were whirled upward by the heat currents and gales of wind and deposited in shattered fragments over the land for more than a mile to leeward. In a few days the crater had been filled with new lava to a depth of 70 feet, and instead of the countless frothy fountains of the initial outbreak the activity centered in a lake of fire with from 5 to 10 fountains throwing jets of lava from 50 to 200 feet above the lake."

There are thirty-nine miles of highway within the Kilauea area. There are also trails which make possible a three- or four-day riding or hiking trip to the summit crater of Mauna Loa, the round trip covering about fifty miles. Mauna Loa rises to a height of 13,680 feet above the floor of the surrounding Pacific Ocean. The writer once traveled from Honolulu to see a vast flow from Mauna Loa, which came thirty miles, to the edge of the ocean. The flow was about half a mile wide, and by the time it reached the strand along the sea, it was moving very slowly. At night, as the steamer approached, a glow could be seen in the sky, and at intervals the living trees, overtaken by the great glowing embers, would burst into flames. It was necessary to walk across a stretch of "aa"—hard, flinty cinders which resulted from thin, hot molten lava.

When those who had traveled from Honolulu to see the great spectacle came close to the face of the flow, it presented at times a gray, ashy and cinder effect, like a great banked furnace. At first the movement was not perceptible, but soon it was seen that every little while the clinkers would stir, and, as though some great giant were poking the fire, great embers as large as a house would break away from the mass, split open to show a red-hot surface, and then gradually gray over again like a dying fire. It was uncanny to see koa and other trees with bright green leaves pushed by the inexorable coals, shrivel and die in the course of a very few minutes, and as the fire grew hotter, finally burst into flames and disappear altogether.

There have been eruptions from Mauna Loa many times. According to the bulletin of the National Park Service: "Following a rather violent earthquake which occurred at 1:11 a.m., November 21, 1935, and was felt generally over the entire island of Hawaii, and on Maui and Oaho as well, Mauna Loa erupted at 7:35 p.m. in its northern summit crater. . . . The flow of lava. . . was notable in that it produced both the aa and pahoehoe types of lava. The activity continued until January 2, 1936, when forward motion of the flow ceased at a point near the headwaters of the Wailuku River, about 18 miles from the city of Hilo. . . . On December 27 a squadron of United States Army planes dropped 6 tons of TNT near the point of emergence of the lava stream." The flow almost immediately slowed down.

One of the always surprising manifestations comes from the many steam cracks which emit hot vapor in the green-covered areas. The drives and trails traverse the most charming tropical forests, their floors covered with dense forests of tree ferns. The trees, flowers, and fruits comprise many not familiar to those who live in temperate zones.

The stop-over on Maui or the special trip to Haleakala brings to view a mountain a little over 10,000 feet high, once much higher, but with a great crater 7½ miles long by 3 miles wide, with walls over 1,000 feet high. Within these colored walls "lies a superb spectacle. Covering the floor are giant red, black, and orange cinder cones which, though hundreds of feet high, are dwarfed by the immensity of their surroundings."

Thus, both the extinct and the active volcanoes are great sights. And the by-product of the Hawaiian scene, with the tropical life of plants, animals, and people, and the contact with the old Hawaiian traditions, is an added lure which draws many tourists from the mainland to this island territory.

THE OLD SOUTHWEST

GRAND CANYON

OUR journey in the Old Southwest will begin at Grand Canyon, reached easily by rail and highway from east and west. It is quite sure that the reactions of those who stand today on the South Rim and look at the great spectacle are far different from the emotions of that little band of Spanish soldiers who, led by Don Lopez de Cardenas in 1540, met with such keen disappointment when they realized that no gold was to be found there—only a view!

In 1896, when John Muir visited the Canyon, he wrote in his journal: "At 6:15 p. m. I ran up to the verge of the Canyon and had my first memorable and overwhelming view in the light and shade of the setting sun. It is the most tremendous expression of erosion and the most ornate and complicated I ever saw. Man seeks the finest marbles for sculptures; Nature takes cinders, ashes, sediments, and makes all divine in fineness of beauty—turrets, towers, pyramids, battlemented castles, rising in glowing beauty from the depths of this canyon of canyons noiselessly hewn from the smooth mass of the featureless plateau." He thought the storm "dimmed. . . with the silken brush of the rain" the wondrous structure. Later he wrote: "It seems a gigantic statement, for even Nature to make, all in one mighty stone word. Wildness so Godful, cosmic, primeval, bestows a new sense of earth's beauty and size. . . . But the colors, the living, rejoicing colors, chanting, morning and evening, in chorus to heaven! Whose brush or pencil, however lovingly inspired, can give us these?"

The first Government exploration party to go into the region was under the leadership of Lieutenant Ives of the War Department, who in 1858 traveled by steamboat up the Colorado River to Black Canyon, in which Boulder Dam is now located. In 1869–71, Major J. W. Powell traveled with rowboats down the Colorado River. His studies gave the reading world the first scientific descriptions of the geological formation of the canyon walls.

The workaday explanation of the beauty of the Grand Canyon lies in erosion. The Colorado River contributed its share, working away many an eon, and the winds and the rain and the plant life joined in to produce a picture such as can be seen nowhere else in the world. Of course there was a long geological history before this last chapter. The Archean Age is represented by the crystalline schists, gneisses, and granites at the bottom of the Canyon. Summarizing the scientific account presented in that charming book on the "Grand Canyon Country," by M. R. Tillotson, so many years superintendent of the park, and Frank J. Taylor, it is recorded that the surface of these rocks, after they had been subjected to such great heat and internal pressure that many were in nearly vertical positions, which later eroded to a plain, was submerged with the water and sediments of the Algonkian era. After the deposits came to be some 12,000 feet in thickness, there was an extensive uplifting of the earth's crust, tilting the rocks above the surface of the ocean in which they were laid. After erosion had produced a rolling plain there came a second submergence, and the Cambrian Age had been reached. The succeeding geological ages left little writing to read, but in the early Carboniferous Age there was a third submergence, during which was deposited the calcium carbonate now represented by the 500 vertical feet of red-wall limestone of the Mississippian Age. Then came the Permian Age which left some of the most primitive reptilian tracks, and the Coconino sandstones. Then followed the fourth and long-continued submergence, and from this we have the Kaibab limestone, the topmost stratum of the Canyon walls, though it is estimated that there was once a deposit of 6,000 or 7,000 feet on top of the limestone. This particular stone page may be read at Cedar Mountain, two miles from Desert View. In the Vermillion Cliffs and in Zion and Bryce, complete successions of these and younger formations may be seen. The erosion which removed this overlay required many millions of years. And then the Colorado River flowed into the scene, and with its burden of sediment and loose gravel as cutting tools, it has hewn for us this great Grand Canyon.

The National Park overlooks the Canyon. From the South Rim, which is some 7,000 feet in altitude, there are hundreds of marvelous lookouts along the fifty miles of rim drives. This part of the park is open the year round. Excellent accommodations may be had at El Tovar, built in 1904, at Bright Angel Lodge

THE GRAND CANYON OF THE COLORADO

Photographs—Department of the Interior

Courtesy—Portfolio, American Planning and Civic Association

EL TOVAR HOTEL, GRAND CANYON

BRIGHT ANGEL LODGE ON SOUTH RIM OF GRAND CANYON

Photographs—Department of the Interior   Courtesy—Portfolio, American Planning and Civic Association

LUXURIOUS CABINS ON NORTH RIM OF GRAND CANYON

Photograph—Department of the Interior

Courtesy—Portfolio, American Planning and Civic Association

THE GREAT WHITE THRONE, ZION NATIONAL PARK

Photograph—Department of the Interior   Courtesy—Portfolio, American Planning and Civic Association

BRYCE CANYON NATIONAL PARK

and cabins, rebuilt in recent years, and at the public camp in the pleasant forest.

The Grand Canyon opens up an entirely new world. Every visitor should read the Tillotson and Taylor book on the ground. The Park Service issues two interesting Guide Leaflets, which should be in the hands of everyone who takes the Desert View Drive and the West Rim Drive. These, with the regular park bulletin, and such other books as may be selected from the bibliography, add greatly to the understanding of the Canyon. There is an observation station at Yavapai Point, where there is a magnificent view of the Canyon. From the parapet, powerful glasses are trained on some of the most interesting points. Pertinent exhibits in the interior room have been arranged to present an illustrated account of the geological history.

The mule trips on the trails down into the floor of the Canyon are always exciting. Horace M. Albright, in the foreword to the Tillotson and Taylor book, remarked: "I have always felt sorry for the traveler so rushed that he can see the Grand Canyon only from the rim. The descent into the great gorge is one of the real adventures of a lifetime. It is only by such a trip that one may know the Grand Canyon intimately or may appreciate the tremendous scope of this outstanding example of erosion."

The entire population of the Canyon gathers every afternoon to see the Hopi dances in front of Hopi House, built across the road from El Tovar for the display of Hopi arts and crafts. The Navajos make their displays outside of hogans typical of those inhabited by their tribe.

From the South Rim one may fly across the Canyon to the North Rim, one may pack across on the trail, or one may drive by Desert View, across the Navajo Bridge, past the Vermillion Cliffs, and then through the lovely Kaibab Forest to the headquarters on the north side of the Canyon. The Grand Canyon Lodge and the campground offer facilities for living and observation 8,000 feet above the sea, enjoyable only in summer, for here the snow blankets the Canyon all winter.

For breath-taking beauty, for geological demonstration, for contact with surviving local Indians, and for trail trips and motor drives of unparalleled and absorbing interest, the Grand Canyon of the Colorado leads in its class!

ZION AND BRYCE NATIONAL PARKS

From the North Rim of the Grand Canyon, a drive of some 125 miles by way of the spectacularly beautiful Zion-Mt. Carmel Highway brings the traveler to Zion Canyon. This approach reveals through the windows of the highway tunnels the first fine views of the highly colored cliffs flanking the valley.

According to the Park Service bulletin: "A 'Yosemite Valley done in oils' comes close to a description of the principal feature of Zion National Park. This gorgeous valley has about the same dimensions as the famous Yosemite Valley. Extraordinary as are the sandstone forms, the color is what most amazes. The deep red of the Vermillion Cliff is the prevailing tint. Two-thirds of the way up, these marvelous walls and temples are painted gorgeous reds; then, above the reds, they rise in startling white. Sometimes the white is surmounted by a cap of vivid red, remains of another red stratum which once overlay all. The Vermillion Cliff rests upon 350 feet of even a more insistent red, relieved by mauve and purple shale. That in turn rests upon a hundred feet of other variegated strata. Through these successive layers of sands and shales and limestones, the Virgin River has cut its amazing valley. The entrance is between two gigantic stone masses of complicated architectural proportions which are named the West Temple and The Watchman."

But the most impressive of all the remarkable mountains of rock is the Great White Throne which rises sheer from the valley floor to display an ethereal white crown surmounting its royal red base. There is something unreal about this huge red and white stone. It seems not to be made of the same material we are accustomed to find forming the earth's surface.

There are twenty miles of road in the park, introducing visitors to the heart of the Canyon. The trails—some twenty-five miles of them—permit those who desire, to walk far up the valley in company with a ranger naturalist or alone, and to explore a number of the high flanking cliffs.

From Zion one may retrace one's way for a short distance over the Zion-Mt. Carmel Highway and then turn north for Bryce. The Grand Canyon is much more stupendous in size and in the heaviness with which the color is laid on. Bryce, being smaller and easier to bring into the perspective of vision, is more like a delicate miniature, with beautiful but thinner colors. The Grand Canyon seems to be done in oils, Bryce in water colors.

There seems little of remarkable interest as one arrives at the headquarters building. But when one walks to the edge of the abyss, there lies Bryce, like a complicated carved cameo, done in shades of white, pink, and deep rose-reds, or, as the Indians said, "red rocks standing like men in a bowl-shaped canyon."

The trail down into the floor of the Canyon is an easy one, either on foot or on horseback. Cut off from all familiar forms of vegetation, surrounded by architectural masses, with fretted ornamentation almost Byzantine in its elaborate sculpturing, one could imagine here a deserted city of the long-distant past.

Many visitors leave Bryce to drive to Cedar City by a route which permits a detour to Cedar Breaks National Monument, another brilliant splash of color. The highway to Cedar City drops down through a rugged canyon by the side of rushing waters and is in itself well worth the trip.

Not very far from Zion and Bryce lies the Escalante, described by Merel Sager as "200 miles of countless, fantastic, weird monuments and pinnacles, slowly yielding to the relentless forces of wind and water." Cut by "the mighty Colorado, mysterious, treacherous, forbidding, carving its meandering way through red sandstone canyons, so rugged that they have thus far successfully defied east and west commutation of human kind in the whole of southeastern Utah," the area is a proposed national monument.

BIG BEND

Big Bend National Park, lying on the border between Texas and Mexico, was authorized to become a national park when the lands shall have been purchased by private and state funds and turned over to the United States Government, free of cost.

Herbert Maier has described the region: "The Big Bend country of Texas is that triangular portion in the southwestern part of the State inclosed by the big bend of the Rio Grande. The romance of the border frontier still lingers in this last wilderness of Texas. No railroad traverses it. Its few roads are largely makeshift, or improvised wagon trails, serving its few ranches and mining

[191]

claims. The Chisos Mountains range from low, semi-desert slopes to high, wooded canyons and peaks. Between the 3,000- and 8,000-foot elevations are found the Lower and Upper Sonoran Zones, the Transition, and an indication of the Canadian Zone." Then there is the Rio Grande, which "in its tortuous course, cuts through three steep-walled limestone canyons, about 2,000 feet in depth . . . and meanders over the river plains between."

CARLSBAD CAVERNS

In the southeastern part of New Mexico, easily accessible from Texas cities and from the nearby town of Carlsbad, are the most wonderful caverns yet discovered. If they are not colorful canyons, they are certainly colorful caverns. They are so large that it takes hours merely to walk through the principal chambers open to the public. Since the caverns could not be seen in the dark, and since torches could not illumine the distant ceilings, the caverns are equipped with an elaborate system of electric lighting. The extent of the caverns no one yet knows. According to the Park Service bulletin, there are now three main levels, 750 feet, 900 feet, and 1,320 feet underground. It is only to the higher level that visitors are conducted through the seven miles of corridors and chambers. Carlsbad is much visited.

The sculpturing of Carlsbad is as elaborate as that of Bryce or Cedar Breaks, and though not as brilliant, there are yet very lovely colors to be found in the caverns, as in the "Veiled Statue" in the Green Lake Room, or in the gleaming onyx of the walls of the King's Palace. These fanciful names but reflect the sumptuous effect of these great underground chambers.

Geologically, "this (Carlsbad) limestone was formed originally in a shallow inland extension of the ocean some 200 million years ago—in the Permian period, which followed the time of greatest coal forming throughout the world. After this period the area was dry land, but it may have been resubmerged and covered by sediments at a later period.

"The uplifting and folding movements that formed the Rocky Mountains also raised the Carlsbad area above sea level. The Guadalupe Mountains near Carlsbad are outliers of that great

AIR VIEW OF NEEDLES FORMATION, NORTH OF BLUE MOUNTAINS

PROPOSED ESCALANTE NATIONAL MONUMENT, UTAH

Photographs—George A. Grant, Department of the Interior   Courtesy—American Planning and Civic Annual

GRAND GULCH, RICH IN ARCHEOLOGY, DRAINS INTO THE SAN JUAN RIVER

Photographs—Department of the Interior

Courtesy—Portfolio, American Planning and Civic Association

THE BIG BEND COUNTRY (ON THE TEXAS-MEXICAN BOUNDARY, RIO GRANDE
RIVER) WHICH THE GOVERNMENT WILL ACCEPT AS A NATIONAL PARK

mountain system. The uplift of the region took place about the end of the 'Age of Dinosaurs' (Cretaceous period)—60 million years ago." Since that time the streams have carved their deep gorges, vast caverns have been hollowed, and within them, still later, the amazing decorative deposits were formed.

MESA VERDE

In southwestern Colorado, reached by highways from Arizona and New Mexico and by rail and highways from Colorado, lies Mesa Verde National Park. Named for the green of the junipers and piñons, it is chiefly interesting for the ruined habitations of the Indians who once dwelt there. Dr. A. E. Douglass, director of Steward Observatory, University of Arizona, has studied the tree rings in the tough surviving timbers of the cliff dwellings, and by an ingenious matching of the beams to cover the different widths of rings for different years of rain and drought, he has determined that the masonry in Mug House, the earliest, dates back to 1066, the year that William the Conqueror became king of England. Cliff Palace was built, added to, and repaired from 1073 to 1273. Balcony House dates from 1190 to 1272; Spruce Tree House, 1230–1274.

The archeologists reveal for us a fascinating picture of the past. From the great mass of pottery and utensils rescued from the permanent dwellings of the Mesa Verde, the archeologists tell us that the second agricultural Basket Makers once lived in these ruins. By skeletons which have been found, they conclude that the long-headed Basket Makers were displaced, at least in part, by the round-headed Pueblos.

Visitors who climb about over the ruins of Cliff Palace, Balcony House, Square Tower House, and many others, may have the life of the one-time inhabitants reconstructed for them by the park guides. From the Park Service bulletin we may read: "The population was composed of a number of units, possibly clans, each of which had its more or less distinct social organization, as indicated in the arrangement of the rooms. The rooms occupied by a clan were not necessarily connected, and generally neighboring rooms were distinguished from one another by their uses. Thus, each clan had a room for its men, which is called the 'kiva.' Each clan had also a number of rooms which may be styled living rooms, and other enclosures for granaries. The corn was ground into meal in another room containing the metate set in a stone bin or trough. Sometimes the rooms had fireplaces, although these were generally in the plazas or on the housetops. All these different rooms, taken together, constituted the houses that belonged to one clan. . . . From the number of these rooms it would appear that there were at least 23 social units or clans in Cliff Palace. . . .

"In addition to their ability as architects and masons, the cliff dwellers excelled in the art of pottery making and as agriculturists. Their decorated pottery—a black design on pearly white background—will compare favorably with pottery of the other cultures of the prehistoric Southwest. . . . Their decoration of cotton fabrics and ceramic work might be called beautiful, even when judged by our own standards. They fashioned axes, spear points, and rude tools of stone; they wove sandals, and made attractive basketry."

The museum at Mesa Verde is one of the most entertaining in the United States. Artifacts in it, from the ruins, permit the daily lives of the cliff dwellers to be reconstructed.

Spruce Tree House, not far from the museum, is easy of access. Dr. J. Walter Fewkes, formerly chief of the Bureau of American Ethnology, was in charge of the excavation of most of the "houses" in the park. He found Spruce Tree House to be 216 feet long by 89 at its greatest width. He counted "eight ceremonial rooms, or kivas, and 114 rooms that had been used for living, storage and other purposes." Around the corner of the cliff there was a spring which furnished water. At one end of the cave, a trail of small toeholds in the face of the cliff was used by the men as they climbed to the mesa above, where corn, beans, and squash were raised. It is thought that the hunters also used the trail as they went in search of deer and mountain sheep.

Cliff Palace is larger, being 300 feet long, located in a spacious cave with a high arch just under the rim of the mesa floor and 200 feet above the canyon below. In Cliff Palace there are more than 200 living rooms, with twenty-two kivas in the cave.

The architecture of the cliff dwellers took advantage of the hanging caves prepared for them by wind and water erosion. On the firm rock base of the floor of the cave the women of the tribe built the walls of stone, crudely at first, but in the twelfth and thirteenth centuries with considerable masonry skill, introducing towers, three and four stories, constructing the floors and ceiling with strong tough timbers and crossing them with fine small timbers.

But all of the ruins are not found in the cliffs. There is Sun Temple, with its 1,000 feet of four-foot-thick walls and its complicated floor plan. There is Far View House, built on the level mesa, with its kiva thirty-two feet in diameter.

The park buildings were all built in the so-called Santa Fé type, under the direction of Jesse L. Nusbaum, who has done so much to interpret the Mesa Verde dwellings to the public.

SOUTHWESTERN NATIONAL MONUMENTS

A map of Arizona, New Mexico, and southern Utah and Colorado, dotted with the archeological parks and monuments and other remarkable features, would defy any simple routing. Frank Pinkley, Superintendent of the Southwestern Monuments lying in these four States, has figured out that a single trip to each, returning between trips to base at Coolidge, Arizona, would reach a mileage equal to a tour around the world on the circumference of the equator—and some of it would be equally hot! The Southwestern Monuments Association has recently (1939) issued "The Guide to Southwestern National Monuments," which locates and describes the twenty-six National Monuments administered from the Coolidge headquarters office. Unless one made a business of it, it would be impossible to visit all of these monuments on one trip. But it is possible to visit many of them on east-west trips. Three of these are in southern Utah. There are the forty-odd Arches, sculptured by wind erosion of red sandstone into unbelievably hospitable gateways; the tremendous Natural Bridge spans of solid sandstone, contrived on graceful supporting arches; and Rainbow Bridge of salmon-pink sandstone with a high arch "so nearly perfect" that "it dwarfs all human architecture'' and so large that it could be arched over the Dome of the Capitol at Washington, with room to spare.

Across the Colorado-Utah line lies the Hovenweep National Monument, where are found ''groups of remarkable prehistoric towers, pueblos, and cliff dwellings,'' built with a masonry so peculiar and specialized that, after centuries of exposure to the elements, parts of the ruins are in an excellent state of preservation. Not far from Mesa Verde in southwestern Colorado, the mounds of Yucca House cover ruins of buildings which once rose fifteen to twenty feet above the foundations and which were occupied in the ''Classic Period.'' Southeast from Yucca House, across the New Mexico line, are the Aztec ruins, where there is a great E-shaped pueblo with 500 rooms and other pueblos yet uncovered.

Traveling east to west in northern New Mexico, not far from Raton, one arrives at Capulin Mountain National Monument —a ''magnificent cinder cone'' overlooking a region ''which bears manifestations of tremendous volcanic activity.''

On the road from Taos, a pueblo village occupied continuously for more than a thousand years, to Santa Fé, one may make a short detour to Bandelier National Monument, comprising Frijoles, Alamo, and other canyons. ''The National Park Service highway and developments open up only about 300 acres in Frijoles Canyon on the edge of the area in order to make accessible famous 200-room Tyuonyi and other representative ruins. Hardy hikers or riders who seek the primeval can wander through some 25,000 acres of untouched wilderness and canyon country, seeing isolated Yapashi and other ruins.'' Most of Bandelier's ruins are of the Regressive Pueblo period, after the abandonment of the great pueblos and cliff dwellings of northwestern New Mexico.

West of Bandelier is Chaco Canyon National Monument, with ''eighteen major and literally thousands of minor ruins.'' Pueblo Bonito ''is one of the most imposing and best known ruins in the Southwest. Built more than one thousand years ago, this five-story, 800-room village was constructed in the shape of a great capital 'D' at the base of a cliff.'' Through tree-ring dating, archeologists have come to believe that the Chacoan towns were in ruins shortly after 1200 A. D., probably deserted because of droughts, possibly brought on by soil erosion and deforestation.

Still farther west, across the line in Arizona, is Canyon de

Photograph—Department of the Interior   Courtesy—Portfolio, American Planning and Civic Association

CARLSBAD CAVERNS NATIONAL PARK, NEW MEXICO

THE WHITE SANDS NATIONAL MONUMENT, NEW MEXICO
—A STRANGE SHIFTING BEAUTY

Photographs—Department of the Interior

Courtesy—Portfolio, American Planning and Civic Association

THE RUINS OF PUEBLO BONITO, CHACO CANYON, NEW MEXICO

MESA VERDE
NATIONAL PARK

TWO VIEWS OF
CLIFF PALACE

Photographs—Department of the Interior
Courtesy—American Planning and
Civic Annual, and Portfolio

Photograph—Department of the Interior　　　　　　　　Courtesy—Portfolio, American Planning and Civic Association

BETATAKIN RUIN IN NAVAJO NATIONAL MONUMENT, ARIZONA

THE MIGHTY FALLEN TREES
OF THE PETRIFIED FOREST
NATIONAL MONUMENT

Photograph—Department of the Interior

Courtesy—Portfolio, American Planning
and Civic Association

CANYON DE CHELLY,
ARIZONA

Photograph—John W. Murray
Courtesy—Appalachia

Photograph—Department of the Interior   Courtesy—Portfolio, American Planning and Civic Association

A CLOSE-UP OF THE ANCIENT HABITATIONS OF
CANYON DE CHELLY, ARIZONA

MONTEZUMA CASTLE, ARIZONA—A PREHISTORIC RUIN

Artist James Russell; Photograph Rainbow Bridge-Monument Valley Expedition   Courtesy—American Forests

AIR VIEW OVER MONUMENT VALLEY IN THE LAND OF THE NAVAJO

Chelly, but these ruins are not for the motorist who desires to keep on hard-surfaced roads and see his sights from a car window. "Within the boundaries of the monument lie more than a hundred miles of canyons of de Chelly and its two tributaries. . . . In shallow open-faced caves are found habitations ranging in time from a Basket Maker storage cist, whose roof beams dated 348 A. D. (the earliest accurately dated timber in the Southwest), to cliff dwellings abandoned in the thirteenth century."

Northwest of Canyon de Chelly, and inaccessible except in favorable weather, are the three "wonderful cliff dwellings" in "indescribably colorful and wild surroundings"—Keet Seel, Betatakin, and Inscription House. On the way south one may stop at Wupatki National Monument, where there are red sandstone prehistoric pueblos, "backgrounded by black basaltic cliffs and facing a view of the Painted Desert." Here 7,000 habitation sites have been discovered. Farther south is Sunset Crater, "most recent cone among the 400 others of the San Francisco volcanic field." South of the main highway is Walnut Canyon, twenty miles long and some 400 feet deep, occupied by some 300 cliff dwellings, proved by tree ringing to date from about 900 to 1200 A. D.

Not included under the administration of this group of monuments, but one, nevertheless, which every motorist should see, is the Petrified Forest between Gallup, New Mexico, and Holbrook, Arizona. Here lies a whole forest of petrified fallen giants.

Traveling south from Walnut Canyon one may visit Montezuma Castle, the best-preserved cliff dwelling in the United States. Built high in the cave of the cliff, the building is five stories high and contains 20 rooms within the walls proper. "Montezuma Castle probably was built during Pueblo III times (the period of great Pueblo advancement), and was occupied into the Regressive Period (Pueblo IV) after the great northern Pueblo centers were abandoned. It may have been constructed in part as early as 1100 A. D. and probably was deserted by 1425 A. D."

South of this is Tonto National Monument, where the cliff dwelling is situated on a cliff recess more than 300 feet above the headquarters area. Still farther south, at Coolidge, are the Casa Grande towers in "the largest of the six villages, to form by far the best preserved and most imposing ruin in the southern or Desert Province of the Southwest" named by Padre Kino in 1694. "Built of hard caliche clay with walls four feet thick at the base, Casa Grande was a watchtower-apartment house, for from its relatively great height its dwellers could watch for enemies."

Southeast of Casa Grande, almost down to the Mexican line, are the ruins of Tumacacori, one of Padre Kino's Sonora-Arizona chain of churches which, with San Xavier, were probably planned by two Italian brothers by the name of Gaona, architects.

In southern Arizona are two national monuments to preserve the native flora—the Saguaro, near Tucson, and the Organ Pipe Cactus on the Mexican border. In the southeastern corner of Arizona, near the New Mexico line, is the Chiricahua National Monument, where "weirdly eroded volcanic formations form a Wonderland of Rocks high atop the beautifully forested Chiricahua Mountains."

Traveling eastward into New Mexico one finds the White Sands National Monument, where "glistening white gypsum and sand dunes, ten to sixty feet high, cover 500 square miles of the Tularoa Basin." North, near the center of New Mexico, in the Gran Quivira, we find the "new" church of the Spanish padres, begun in 1649, never completely finished, but still lifting its massive walls forty feet in the air. Northwest of this is El Morro, "a great buff promontory, rising 200 feet above the surrounding lava-strewn valley," resembling a huge castle or fortress. The Spaniards named it and left inscriptions on it, the earliest dated 1605 (or 1606), and the latest 1774. But the Spaniards were not the first to find the rock, with its cove and pool of water, "for high on the easily fortified mesa top are large ruins of pueblos which were built during Pueblo IV, the Regressive Pueblo Period, in the neighborhood of 1400 A. D. These peoples engraved undecipherable symbols on the rock, so El Morro's records cover more than 500 years."

In the wilderness of the Mogollon Mountains of western New Mexico are the Gila cliff dwellings, more interesting for their surroundings than for any special distinction.

These Southwestern Monuments preserve some of the most important geological, archeological, and historical evidences of the past forces and civilizations of the region. No traveler can claim to have seen the Southwest who has not visited some of them.

EAST OF THE MISSISSIPPI

THE MYSTERIOUS APPALACHIANS

THE APPALACHIAN TRAIL

PERHAPS the best introduction to the eastern mountain wilderness is The Appalachian Trail, which was first proposed by Benton MacKaye in 1921, and which has been realized since by the use of existing trails and the building and maintenance of new trails and feeders by the mountain and trail clubs along the way. "Mr. MacKaye," wrote Myron Avery in *American Forests*, "conceived the plan of a trail which, for all practical purposes, should be endless. He regarded it as the backbone of a primeval environment, a sort of retreat or refuge from a civilization which was becoming too mechanized." The trail starts at Mt. Katahdin, "a massive granite monolith in the central Maine wilderness," and runs for a distance of 2,050 miles south to Mt. Oglethorpe, in northern Georgia. Only part of Mt. Katahdin is in public ownership, but it is hoped that the entire mountain where the wilderness trail begins can be made a park, and the surrounding forests, insofar as they have been injured, allowed to revert to their previous wild condition.

The trail touches Grafton Notch, the White and Green Mountains, Mt. Greylock, Mohawk and Bear Mountains, Delaware Water Gap, and South Mountain before it reaches Shenandoah National Park.

SHENANDOAH

The Shenandoah National Park preserves the crest of the Blue Ridge Mountains, a part of the Appalachian system in Virginia between the Piedmont Plateau and the Shenandoah Valley, extending from Front Royal almost to Waynesboro, a distance of nearly a hundred miles. Though there is a Skyline Drive along most of the crest of the park, in most places the Appalachian Trail is well removed from the highway. Those who hike over the main and side trails of the Shenandoah Park are usually surprised at the feeling of remoteness and at the wilderness charm of much of the region. The Hawksbill, Old Rag, and other trails lead into rough country, and will remain among the favorite hikes of the Potomac Appalachian Trail Club. President Hoover's Rapidan Camp, which the Federal Government received by gift, is within the park.

There were different schools of thought concerning the Skyline Drive. Many of the hikers thought that the few old "horse-and-buggy" dirt access roads, unsuitable for automobiles, should never have been replaced by improved access and crest-line highways. It should be remembered, however, that at best Shenandoah Park is a narrow strip, flanked closely by inhabited valleys, so that, highway or no highway, the sense of remoteness is due to favorable topography, which provides an illusion of distance where there is no great distance. The rugged crests, the finely timbered valleys, and the plashing of waterfalls contribute to that sense of isolation, though all the time there are nearby habitations. The land belonging to the mountaineer settlers within the park has been purchased and allowed to revert to wilderness.

There are stretches of the Skyline Drive which give to the motorist some of the wilderness aspects. There are places where, from a car window, one may see in the misty distance crest on crest of mountain spurs, with no glimpse of the busy towns so near in the valleys below. At other outlooks the view includes the smoke of scores of towns, picturesque enough, as seen from the mountain tops. Many of those familiar with the principal western parks have commented enthusiastically on the great beauty of the Blue Ridge Mountains as seen from the Skyline Drive. It must be admitted that there are some lovely spots on the drive which were once much prized by hikers and which are now so near the highway that they have lost most of their charm, but The Appalachian Trail in the park is really very well located, and its users are little bothered by the highway, which, after all, gives them easy access to the forested valleys and high peaks. Considering the narrowness of the park, it is rather a miracle that both the highway and the trail interfere so little.

In the spring when the dogwood scallops with frothy white embroidery the edges of the spruce and hemlock forests, and later, when the dainty dimity pink of the laurel stitches in its rosy note of color, the Shenandoah is very lovely. Every year there are countless trips to see the beds of modest trilliums, white and pink

Photograph—Department of the Interior   Courtesy—Portfolio, American Planning and Civic Association

MT. KATAHDIN, MAINE (ABOVE) BEGINS THE APPALACHIAN TRAIL

CHIMNEY ON ARMADILLO   **GREEN SLAB**

Photographs—M. B. Howarth   Courtesy—Appalachia

Photograph—George Knox   Courtesy—Appalachia

LOOKING TOWARD HAWKSBILL IN THE SHENANDOAH
NATIONAL PARK

and painted. From the time when the trailing arbutus puts out its delicate fairy cups and the yellow lady's slipper hangs its charming blossoms on the green of the forest floor, through the weeks of the brilliant red-bud, the pink and white azaleas, the more showy rhododendrons, to the October days when the hardwood forests are painted bright red and yellow and brown in a glorious riot of color, the Shenandoah provides for thousands of those who live in nearby Atlantic seaboard cities, the peace and recreation which come from forest, mountain, and stream. As the park is becoming known, visitors come to it from all parts of the United States.

GREAT SMOKY MOUNTAINS

Ever since the days when Charles Egbert Craddock captured the imagination of the American people with her novel, "The Prophet of the Great Smoky Mountains," the curling mists of the Smokies, which look so much like rising wreaths of smoke, have cast a spell of enchantment over those who looked from the valleys of North Carolina and Tennessee into these mysterious mountains.

When the five hundred miles of the Blue Ridge Parkway are completed, one will be able to drive the length of the Shenandoah from Front Royal on through Virginia, and by a spreading fork enter the Great Smoky Mountains National Park from the east or the west, then crossing the Divide at Newfound Gap, from which a spur runs out to Clingmans Dome.

There are about seventy-five miles of The Appalachian Trail in the Great Smoky Mountains National Park, traversing Old Black, Guyot, Chapman, Laurel Top, Kephart, Clingmans Dome, Silers Bald, Thunderhead, and Gregory and Parsons Balds. In the northern part of the park the forests are dense spruce and fir, but in the southern part there are hardwood forests and many mountains bald of any forest cover. Carlos Campbell, in *American Forests*, gave an excellent account of an eight-day hike which covered the trail within the Smoky Mountains, "the roughest and highest portion of the entire Appalachian Trail." The crest of the Great Smokies for thirty-six miles in the park is more than 5,000 feet in altitude, with sixteen peaks above 6,000 feet high.

This park gives us our largest wilderness area in the East. The rugged mountain crests, the virgin spruce, the fine variety of hardwoods, and the heavy rainfall which produces a rich forest floor, give to the Smokies a tropical luxuriance not found in any other mountain region in the United States, with the possible exception of the Olympics. There are in the park 129 native tree species and twenty varieties of large shrubs. Tourists come from afar to see the rhododendrons bloom in June. On a single trip up the mountain, at different levels mountain laurel, flame azaleas, and rhododendrons may be seen in their full glory. The native flower gardens of the Smokies, though quite different from the western types, rival them in color and growth.

Six hundred miles of trout streams are in the park. There are 56 miles of high-grade roads, 25 miles of secondary roads, 165 miles of truck trails (not public), and 510 miles of horse and foot trails.

On the top of Mt. LeConte there is a lodge to which all supplies are taken on pack animals. The sunrise and sunset views from Myrtle Point and other vantage lookouts are magnificent, and well repay the 5,000-foot climb from Gatlinburg to the mountain top. Accommodations may be found outside the park at Gatlinburg, Tennessee, near the park line, and in North Carolina towns somewhat farther from the park.

WHERE LAND AND WATER MEET

One established park and three authorized projects of "waterfront" national parks lie east of the Mississippi.

ACADIA

Far north on the coast of Maine, in what was once French territory, Acadia National Park preserves the Mt. Desert Mountains, "whose ancient uplift, worn by immeasurable time and recent ice erosion, remains to form the largest rock-built island on our Atlantic coast, 'l'Isle des Monts deserts,' as Champlain named it." As early as 1855 summer visitors began to come to Mt. Desert Island, because of its beauty and cool summer climate. In 1914, 5,000 acres of the island were offered to the National Government by the Hancock County Trustees of Public

Reservations, and in 1916 President Wilson proclaimed the area to be the Sieur de Monts National Monument. In 1919, by Act of Congress, the area was included in the Lafayette National Park, and ten years later, when the park was enlarged, its name was changed to Acadia. George B. Dorr has given lands, money, and watchful oversight to Acadia, where he has served as superintendent and host for many years.

The native growth of the Acadian forest has, for the most part, escaped fires and human destruction. There are many varieties of pine and spruce, balsam firs, larches and arborvitae among the conifers, and a wide selection among the hardwoods.

But the great appeal of Acadia lies in the high, rocky cliffs and the beating surf of the Atlantic Ocean. From the mountain tops and from many vantage points along the driveway up Cadillac Mountain one may look out over the deep blue waters, with the many wooded and rocky promontories. The auto caravans, with ranger naturalists in charge, are very popular in this park, as are also the sea cruises around Frenchman Bay. In addition to the motor roads, there are some fifty miles of roads restricted to the use of saddle and driving horses, and this gives a taste of the age before the advent of automobiles. There are 150 miles of trails and footpaths—charming walks all, with many fine views. Accommodations are to be found outside the park in the various villages. The park headquarters are at Bar Harbor.

ISLE ROYALE, LAKE SUPERIOR

Lying just below the international water boundary in Lake Superior is Isle Royale, the largest island in the lake. Through Acts of Congress, dating from 1931, the Federal Government has indicated its desire to accept Isle Royale as a national park.

The picturesque rocky shore-line reminds one of Acadia National Park, and when Lake Superior rages in storm, the breaking surf completes the simile. The rolling hills and bare granite ledges are softened in the hazy summer air, and in the scrubby forests and on the shores of the numerous little lakes are found moose, coyotes, beaver, and other forest animals. In the waters are famous lake trout, whitefish, and muskellunge or pike.

Those who have been traveling by boat to this distant island for their summer vacations report that they acquire here a feeling of remoteness and peacefulness which seems to be one of the psychological tests for national-park fitness, along with other qualifications of land and water resources.

HATTERAS

On August 17, 1937, Congress authorized the acceptance of the first National Seashore, to cover historic Cape Hatteras and its lighthouse off the coast of North Carolina, covering roughly 100 square miles on the islands of Chicamacomico, Ocracoke, Bodie, Roanoke, and Collington. H. E. Weatherwax, writing in *Landscape Architecture*, makes the claim that "The North Carolina banks offer the finest type of Atlantic seacoast country. The area has never been developed, and its glistening beaches extend uninterrupted for miles. The series of barrier islands, or bars, on which the national seashore will be established were built of sand washed up from the sea and distributed by longshore currents. The foundations of the barrier were laid during the last stages of the ice age, when so much water was locked in the polar ice sheets that the level of the sea was 25 feet or more lower than at present. The beach ridge formed at that time is thought to have produced islands or shoals when the sea was raised to its present level by the melting of the ice. These were converted into the existing barrier formations by wave action."

EVERGLADES

On the southwest end of the peninsula in Florida, extending south of any other continental territory of the United States, we have the Everglades—a water-logged wilderness of twisted mangroves, penetrated by a complicated maze of water channels which may be navigated by boats. The whole region is rich in tropical bird life—blue herons, white egrets and ibises, brilliant red flamingoes, filling the air with their cloudy flights and perching on limbs of trees like so many huge blossoms. The Everglades, authorized to be accepted by the Federal Government as a gift, will one day be one of the most unique parks in the system. But haste is needed if the disastrous effects of forest fires and the predatory operations of the bird killers are to be circumvented.

[216]

IN GREAT SMOKY MOUNTAINS NATIONAL PARK

CREST OF THE
GREAT SMOKY MOUNTAINS
NATIONAL PARK

Courtesy—American Civic Annual

FALLS ON ROARING FORK CREEK—ONE OF EIGHT BETWEEN THE BLUFF
AND THE TOP OF MT. LECONTE. GREAT SMOKY MOUNTAINS NATIONAL PARK

Photograph—Thompson, Inc.   Courtesy—American Forests

Photograph—Department of the Interior

Courtesy—Portfolio, American Planning and Civic Association

RHODODENDRONS IN GREAT SMOKY MOUNTAINS NATIONAL PARK

Photograph—George Masa   Courtesy—Portfolio, American Planning and Civic Association

VIRGIN HARDWOODS
IN GREAT SMOKY MOUNTAINS NATIONAL PARK

**TRAIL ON TOP OF
CADILLAC MOUNTAIN**

Courtesy — Portfolio, American
Planning and Civic Association

ACADIA
NATIONAL PARK

THE THUNDERHOLE

Photographs—Department of
the Interior

Courtesy—Landscape Architecture

MOOSE IN ISLE ROYALE, LAKE SUPERIOR

THE SHIFTING SANDS AND WIND-BLOWN TREES
CAPE HATTERAS SEASHORE

PROPOSED EVERGLADES
NATIONAL PARK

CONGRESS HAS AUTHORIZED THE DE-
PARTMENT OF THE INTERIOR TO ACCEPT
THE FLORIDA EVERGLADES AS A
NATIONAL PARK WHEN ALL PRIVATE
LANDS HAVE BEEN ACQUIRED AND THE
REGION DONATED TO THE FEDERAL
GOVERNMENT. THE WHITE IBISES GIVE
A TROPICAL BEAUTY TO THESE
PICTURESQUE EVERGLADES

Photographs—Matlack Studio

Courtesy—Portfolio, American Planning
and Civic Association

WAKEFIELD, THE RESTORED BIRTHPLACE OF GEORGE WASHINGTON

IN COLONIAL VIRGINIA

Photographs—Department of the Interior   Courtesy—American Planning and Civic Annual

THE MOORE HOUSE AT YORKTOWN

Photograph—Virginia State Chamber of Commerce   Courtesy—Portfolio, American Planning and Civic Association

A QUIET STREET IN OLD YORKTOWN, WHERE THERE IS A
COLONIAL NATIONAL HISTORICAL PARK

Photographs—Department of the Interior   Courtesy—Portfolio, American Planning and Civic Association

JAMESTOWN ISLAND, WHERE THE EXCAVATION OF SEVENTEENTH-
CENTURY FOUNDATIONS HAS REVEALED VALUABLE EVIDENCE OF
THE LIFE OF THE EARLY SETTLERS ON THE ATLANTIC SEABOARD

[227]

IN MORRISTOWN NATIONAL HISTORICAL PARK

THE FORD MANSION SERVED AS WASHINGTON'S HEADQUARTERS DURING THE WINTER OF 1779–1780. THE HOUSE IS NOW OPEN TO THE PUBLIC.

Photographs—Department of the Interior

Courtesy—Portfolio, American Planning and Civic Association

NATIONAL HISTORICAL PARKS AND MONUMENTS

The Colonial National Historical Park, authorized by the Cramton Act of 1930, sets aside Jamestown Island, the site of the first permanent English settlement in North America; parts of the city of Williamsburg (privately owned and restored by funds furnished by Mr. John D. Rockefeller, Jr.); and Yorktown, where in 1781 the French and Americans besieged and captured the Army of Cornwallis in the last important battle of the Revolution.

No one who visits this cradle of American liberties can fail to be thrilled with the quaintness of quiet old Yorktown, where it is said there was established the first Custom House on American soil. The atmosphere of past centuries still hangs over this Virginia village, and many of the famous houses of Colonial times are still standing in gardens where the present-day paths follow the lines of the garden makers of the eighteenth century. In Yorktown there are museums to interpret the story, and many of the siege fortification features have been restored and the artillery emplacements reinstalled.

There is a charming parkway skirting the beautiful York River, which connects Yorktown and Williamsburg, where Mr. Rockefeller's restoration presents the old capital city, along lines discovered to be authentic through the study of old records. To-day one may see the heart of Williamsburg very much as it was in Colonial times. The Duke of Gloucester Street extends from the rebuilt Capitol to the College of William and Mary, with its old and new buildings. From the Old Bruton Parish Church a cross axis approaches by a parked highway the Governor's Palace, set amid an elaborate garden of English box and flowers. Along the main street are many restored homes and the rebuilt Raleigh Tavern, where so many important historic events took place. As the restorations take on the patina of age, there will live here again the scene of old Williamsburg, an atmosphere which is fostered by the Colonial costumes worn by the guides.

On Jamestown Island, which will one day be the western terminus of the Yorktown Parkway, the excavations of the eighteenth-century foundations have brought to light more than 80,000 pottery fragments, some 75,000 glass fragments, 85,000 iron and

nearly 50,000 clay-pipe fragments, which, when studied, will help us to reconstruct the daily lives of our earliest forebears on the Atlantic seaboard.

The second National Historical Park to be created was established in 1933 in New Jersey. Morristown Park preserves sites of important military encampments during the Revolution, the Ford Mansion, which served as Washington's headquarters during the crucial winter of 1779–80, other eighteenth-century houses, a museum and a collection of Washingtoniana.

Though these two parks are the only ones to be named officially National Historical Parks, there has developed a well-defined historical program in the National Park Service. From the time of its establishment in 1916, there have been included in the system areas of archeological and historical interest. From eight in 1916, these have grown to more than 100 in 1938. By the Act of August 21, 1935, Congress declared it to be a national policy to preserve historic and archeological sites of national significance for the pleasure and benefit of the people. The Secretary of the Interior was granted broad powers intended to place upon the National Park Service responsibility for leadership in a renewed nation-wide movement to conserve our remaining unprotected historic and archeological treasures. As a part of this program, the Historic American Buildings Survey was initiated by the National Park Service, and includes among its accomplishments a permanent working agreement with the Fine Arts Division of the Library of Congress and the American Institute of Architects to measure and record the irreplaceable architecture of the American past.

The American Antiquities Act of 1906, the Historic and Archeological Act of 1935, the appointment by the Secretary of the Interior of the Advisory Board of National Parks, Historic Sites, Buildings, and Monuments, of which Dr. Hermon C. Bumpus is chairman, and of the National Advisory Committee of the Historic American Buildings Survey, of which Dr. Leicester B. Holland is chairman, together with the transfer by President Franklin D. Roosevelt in 1933 of all National Monuments to the National Park Service, have conspired to develop a consistent program.

Among many National Military Parks transferred were those of Chickamauga, Missionary Ridge, and Lookout Mountain, near Chattanooga, Tennessee; six great Civil War battlefields, near

Fredericksburg in Virginia, Gettysburg in Pennsylvania, Shiloh in Tennessee, and Vicksburg in Mississippi. The Park Service is preserving also such Historical Monuments in Florida as Fort Jefferson, largest all-masonry fortification in the Western World, built in 1846 for control of the Florida Straits, which served as a military prison during the Civil War; Fort Marion, oldest fort extant in the United States, originally Castle San Marcos, constructed of coquina by the Spanish to defend their Florida possessions; and Fort Mantanzas, an early Spanish stronghold.

When the Spanish Monuments in California and the Southwest are considered with those of Florida, it may readily be seen that, through the preservation of historic sites, the entire Spanish northern frontier which extended in a long three-thousand-mile arc from California to Florida, may be visualized and studied by students of history. When the fine archeological monuments of the Southwest are considered with such monuments as Ocmulgee in Georgia, which preserves an area near Macon, "containing the most unique and important Indian mounds in the Southeast, the excavation of which has thrown new light on the pre-Columbian Indian civilization," the possibilities of extensive archeological research in the known and yet-to-be-discovered prehistoric ruins seem unlimited. Here is a treasure house of source material for the study of American history, useful for research and for demonstration.

In the East, the first National Parkways have been developed. The George Washington Memorial Parkway from Mount Vernon, through Alexandria, to the Arlington Memorial Bridge leading into Washington, and now being extended to the Great Falls of the Potomac in Virginia, was the first to be undertaken in 1930. The Blue Ridge Parkway, already mentioned as connecting Shenandoah and Great Smoky Mountains National Parks, is now under construction, and the Colonial Parkway between Williamsburg and Yorktown is already in use. The Natchez Trace Parkway, authorized in 1934 and 1938, to follow the general location of the famous old Indian Trail between Nashville and Natchez, is now being surveyed.

Probably most of the national parks will one day be connected by parkways, with sufficient rights-of-way to protect the eyes of those who drive over them from any sort of objectionable encroachment, and making the most of the natural roadside scenery.

The National Park Service fell heir in 1933 to the park system of the Federal City, which, under the name District of Columbia, was first established by Act of Congress, approved July 16, 1790, and which has been under continuous Federal control ever since. There are nearly 7,500 acres in the system, covering more than 700 areas and about 75 national statues and memorials, among which are the Washington Monument and the Lincoln Memorial in Washington and the Lee Mansion, across the Potomac River in Arlington. C. Marshall Finnan, formerly superintendent of Mesa Verde National Park, presides over the regional park system of the Nation's Capital.

The entire eastern part of the United States is marked with statues of historic significance, with battlefields, with historic sites and buildings, with cemeteries in which lie the famous dead of our early history. Those who travel by motor, with the aid of the National Park Service may seek out as many of these historic reminders of the past as they have time to cover. This is a fascinating way to study the history of the United States.

One National Monument there is, last seen by every departing ocean passenger from the port of New York, and hailed by every returning patriot, who may see in it that pledge of individual independence from government oppression which it was meant to commemorate—the Statue of Liberty, holding high the lighted torch of liberal leadership, given by the French Government to the American people as visible evidence to the world of the French alliance which helped to establish the Republic of the United States of America.

THE STATUE OF LIBERTY—A NATIONAL MONUMENT

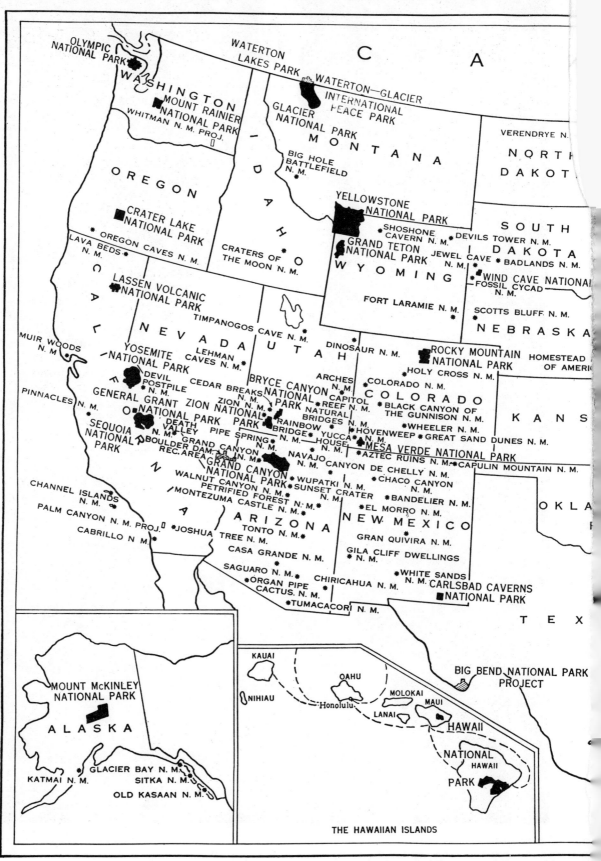

OLYMPIC NATIONAL PARK

WASHINGTON

MOUNT RAINIER NATIONAL PARK
WHITMAN N. M. PROJ.

WATERTON LAKES PARK

WATERTON—GLACIER INTERNATIONAL PEACE PARK

GLACIER NATIONAL PARK

C A

MONTANA

VERENDRYE N. M.

NORTH DAKOTA

OREGON

IDAHO

BIG HOLE BATTLEFIELD N. M.

CRATER LAKE NATIONAL PARK

OREGON CAVES N. M.

LAVA BEDS N. M.

CRATERS OF THE MOON N. M.

YELLOWSTONE NATIONAL PARK

SHOSHONE CAVERN N. M.

DEVILS TOWER N. M.

SOUTH DAKOTA

GRAND TETON NATIONAL PARK

JEWEL CAVE N. M.

BADLANDS N. M.

WYOMING

WIND CAVE NATIONAL
FOSSIL CYCAD N. M.

LASSEN VOLCANIC NATIONAL PARK

FORT LARAMIE N. M.

SCOTTS BLUFF. N. M.

NEVADA

UTAH

TIMPANOGOS CAVE N. M.

LEHMAN CAVES N. M.

DINOSAUR N. M.

NEBRASKA

MUIR WOODS N. M.

ROCKY MOUNTAIN NATIONAL PARK

HOMESTEAD OF AMERIC

HOLY CROSS N. M.

YOSEMITE NATIONAL PARK

ARCHES N. M.

COLORADO N. M.

C A L I F O R N I A

DEVIL POSTPILE N. M.

CEDAR BREAKS N. M.

BRYCE CANYON NATIONAL PARK

CAPITOL REEF N. M.

COLORADO

PINNACLES N. M.

GENERAL GRANT NATIONAL PARK

ZION NATIONAL PARK

ZION N. M.

NATURAL BRIDGES N. M.

BLACK CANYON OF THE GUNNISON N. M.

KANS

DEATH VALLEY N. M.

RAINBOW BRIDGE N. M.

YUCCA HOUSE N. M.

HOVENWEEP N. M.

WHEELER N. M.

GREAT SAND DUNES N. M.

SEQUOIA NATIONAL PARK

GRAND CANYON N. M.

PIPE SPRING N. M.

BOULDER DAM REC. AREA

GRAND CANYON NATIONAL PARK

NAVAJO N. M.

CANYON DE CHELLY N. M.

MESA VERDE NATIONAL PARK

AZTEC RUINS N. M.

CAPULIN MOUNTAIN N. M.

CHANNEL ISLANDS N. M.

WALNUT CANYON N. M.

WUPATKI N. M.

SUNSET CRATER N. M.

CHACO CANYON N. M.

PETRIFIED FOREST N. M.

BANDELIER N. M.

PALM CANYON N. M. PROJ.

MONTEZUMA CASTLE N. M.

JOSHUA TREE N. M.

TONTO N. M.

ARIZONA

EL MORRO N. M.

NEW MEXICO

OKLA

CABRILLO N. M.

CASA GRANDE N. M.

GRAN QUIVIRA N. M.

SAGUARO N. M.

ORGAN PIPE CACTUS N. M.

CHIRICAHUA N. M.

GILA CLIFF DWELLINGS N. M.

WHITE SANDS N. M.

CARLSBAD CAVERNS NATIONAL PARK

TUMACACORI N. M.

T E X

MOUNT McKINLEY NATIONAL PARK

ALASKA

KATMAI N. M.

GLACIER BAY N. M.

SITKA N. M.

OLD KASAAN N. M.

KAUAI

NIHIAU

OAHU

Honolulu

LANAI

MOLOKAI

MAUI

HAWAII

BIG BEND NATIONAL PARK PROJECT

NATIONAL

HAWAII

PARK

THE HAWAIIAN ISLANDS

NATIONAL PARK SERVICE

LEGEND

- ■ NATIONAL PARK
- ▨ NATIONAL PARK PROJECT
- ⊖ NATIONAL HISTORICAL PARK AND SITE
- ○ NATIONAL CAPITAL PARKS
- * NATIONAL MONUMENT
- ▯ NATIONAL MONUMENT PROJECT
- ▲ NATIONAL MILITARY PARK
- ● NATIONAL BATTLEFIELD SITE
- † NATIONAL CEMETERY
- ▨ MISCELLANEOUS NATIONAL MEMORIAL

AREAS AND PROJECTS

THE NATIONAL PARKS ARE THE HIKERS' PARADISE

RETROSPECT

Looking backward over our journeys in the National Parks and Monuments, we can hardly forget that great elation of spirit which crowned our views of untamed natural beauty—that mastery of ego and transcendence of self which found us high on the mountain tops. We came face to face with the mighty living glaciers which are still grinding away at their assigned task. We took to heart the thought that the stars in their courses have achieved a speed and direction which make man-made aircraft seem like silly children's toys. We marveled at the ingenuity of Nature in fashioning mountains, valleys, and streams, in husbanding forests, shrubs, and flowers, with their infinite variety of form and color. We thanked "whatever gods there be" for the birds and the beasts that we had seen, for it would be a sorry, silent world if mankind were here alone.

All that we had read of geology was illustrated with dramatic dioramas on a ten-league canvas. We felt that we had torn aside the curtain of Time and looked into the daily lives of those early Indians who lived high in the cliffs in the year 1000. We had looked upon the buildings of the Spanish padres and the scenes of the early explorers. In the East we had visited the Colonial villages where our early history was made. We had looked upon the battlefields where hard-won victories have made possible our present-day Nation. We had entered the houses where the great leaders of our country were born or lived.

When the National Park and Monument System is completed, as it will be during the next few years, the United States of America will own a rich landed estate in which may be preserved those tangible and intangible values that can never be completely enjoyed when combined with the economic exploitation of our land and water resources.

Perhaps in the soul-satisfying beauties of our national parks and other sacred regions we shall find that we can regain something of that poise of outlook and courage in action which contact with unspoiled Nature may confer on human beings, and so ensure a continuance of our civilization on the lands which were so lately conquered by our ancestors.

Let us cherish the domain we have received from the hands of Nature, and in using it for our collective enjoyment manage it wisely and damage it as little as possible. Let us study the pages of its story. Let us sense its romance. And finally, let us receive its benediction!

INDEX

INDEX

Use and Abuse
of
America's Natural Resources

An Arno Press Collection

Ayres, Quincy Claude. **Soil Erosion and Its Control.** 1936

Barger, Harold and Sam H. Schurr. **The Mining Industries, 1899–1939.** 1944

Carman, Harry J., editor. **Jesse Buel:** Agricultural Reformer. 1947

Circular from the General Land Office Showing the Manner of Proceeding to Obtain Title to Public Lands. 1899

Fernow, Bernhard E. **Economics of Forestry.** 1902

Gannett, Henry, editor. **Report of the National Conservation Commission, February 1909.** Three volumes. 1909

Giddens, Paul H. **The Birth of the Oil Industry.** 1938

Greeley, William B. **Forests and Men.** 1951

Hornaday, William T. **Wild Life Conservation in Theory and Practice.** 1914

Ise, John. **The United States Forest Policy.** 1920

Ise, John. **The United States Oil Policy.** 1928

James, Harlean. **Romance of the National Parks.** 1939

Kemper, J. P. **Rebellious River.** 1949

Kinney, J. P **The Development of Forest Law in America.** *Including,* Forest Legislation in America Prior to March 4, 1789. 1917

Larson, Agnes M. **History of the White Pine Industry in Minnesota.** 1949

Liebig, Justus, von. **The Natural Lawss of Husbandry.** 1863

Lindley, Curtis H. **A Treatise on the American Law Relating to Mines and Mineral Lands.** Two volumes. 2nd edition. 1903

Lokken, Roscoe L. **Iowa**—Public Land Disposal. 1942

McGee, W. J., editor. **Proceedings of a Conference of Governors in the White House, May 13–15, 1908.** 1909

Mead, Elwood. **Irrigation Institutions.** 1903

Moreell, Ben. **Our Nation's Water Resources**—Policies and Politics. 1956

Murphy, Blakely M., editor. **Conservation of Oil & Gas:** A Legal History, 1948. 1949

Newell, Frederick Haynes. **Water Resources:** Present and Future Uses. 1920.

Nimmo, Joseph, Jr. **Report in Regard to the Range and Ranch Cattle Business of the United States.** 1885

Nixon, Edgar B., editor. **Franklin D. Roosevelt & Conservation, 1911–1945.** Two volumes. 1957

Peffer, E. Louise. **The Closing of the Public Domain.** 1951

Preliminary Report of the Inland Waterways Commission. 60th Congress, 1st Session, Senate Document No. 325. 1908

Puter, S. A. D. & Horace Stevens. **Looters of the Public Domain.** 1908

Record, Samuel J. & Robert W. Hess. **Timbers of the New World.** 1943

Report of the Public Lands Commission, with Appendix. 58th Congress, 3d Session, Senate Document No. 189. 1905

Report of the Public Lands Commission, Created by the Act of March 3, 1879. 46th Congress, 2d Session, House of Representatives Ex. Doc. No. 46. 1880

Resources for Freedom: A Report to the President by The President's Materials Policy Commission, Volumes I and IV. 1952. Two volumes in one.

Schoolcraft, Henry R. **A View of the Lead Mines of Missouri.** 1819

Supplementary Report of the Land Planning Committee to the National Resources Board, 1935–1942

Thompson, John Giffin. **The Rise and Decline of the Wheat Growing Industry in Wisconsin** (Reprinted from *Bulletin of the University of Wisconsin,* No. 292). 1909

Timmons, John F. & William G. Murray, editors. **Land Problems and Policies.** 1950

U.S. Department of Agriculture—Forest Service. **Timber Resources for America's Future:** Forest Resource Report No. 14. 1958

U.S. Department of Agriculture—Soil Conservation Service and Forest Service. **Headwaters Control and Use.** 1937

U.S. Department of Commerce and Labor—Bureau of Corporations. **The Lumber Industry,** Parts I, II, & III. 1913/1914

U.S. Department of the Interior. **Hearings before the Secretary of the Interior on Leasing of Oil Lands.** 1906

Whitaker, J. Russell & Edward A. Ackerman. **American Resources:** Their Management and Conservation. 1951

Ronald W. Clark

The Scientific Breakthrough

The Impact of Modern Invention

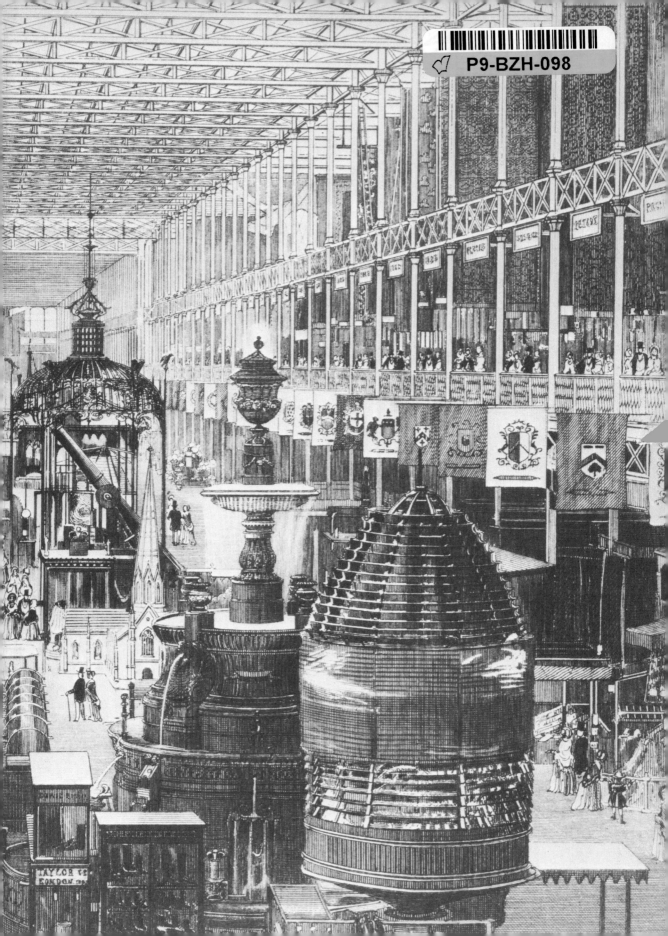

The Scientific Breakthrough

The Impact of Modern Invention

G. P. Putnam's Sons   New York

This book was designed and produced by
George Rainbird Limited,
Marble Arch House, 44 Edgware Road, London W2
for G. P. Putnam's Sons,
200 Madison Avenue, New York, N.Y. 10016

House editor: Peter Faure
Designer: Alan Bartram
Picture researcher: Patricia Vaughan
Indexer: E. F. Peeler

Color printing by W. S. Cowells Ltd, Ipswich
Text setting by Westerham Press, Westerham, Kent
Monochrome printing and binding by
Butler & Tanner Ltd, Frome, Somerset

SBN 399 11179 4
Library of Congress Catalog Card Number 73 78629

Printed in England

Endpapers Illustration:
The Great Exhibition, London, 1851

Contents

Acknowledgments

The author wishes to thank the following for help and advice, or for reading portions of the manuscript. However, all opinions expressed are his own, and any errors are his not theirs.

Brian Coe, Curator, Kodak Museum; Louis A. Jackets; C. J. Somers, Ferranti Ltd; G. H. Sturge, BBC; Mrs B. Hance, GEC–Marconi Electronics Ltd; M. Kaufman, Rubber and Plastics Processing Industry Training Board; T. Davies, Plastics Institute; K. B. Bartlett, ICI, Plastics Division; R. W. B. Truscott, UK Atomic Energy Authority; Dr D. M. Potts, International Planned Parenthood Federation; Peter Wymer, Post Office Telecommunications

List of color plates

Introduction

An invention is often a dream come true; sometimes it is a nightmare made real. In both cases it will have come to life only after certain conditions have been met. There must first be an ambition of the human race, present in varying degree over the centuries, some constant if unconscious hope which keeps an idea simmering. Thus men dreamed of flight since they first watched the birds; they hoped to unlock the power within the atomic nucleus from the moment they knew it existed; they thought of producing men like gods. But some more localized and more pressing incentive is also needed – what Dr A. P. Rowe, in charge of Britain's radar development at the Telecommunications Research Establishment during the Second World War, has called the operational requirement. In the 1950s poverty and a social conscience combined to produce the first experiments which led to the Pill; a few years earlier the urgent need to create an ultimate weapon before the enemy got it first, alone led to the massive research and development which unleashed nuclear energy.

Yet there is a third essential. When vision and contemporary need have joined up on the field, the catalyst of technology is still required. Powered flight was impossible before the petrol engine. Practical radio awaited Sir Alexander Fleming's thermionic valve, and Air Commodore Sir Frank Whittle's jet was only airborne in the wake of metals capable of withstanding the huge heats of the exhaust gases. These technological advances rested in turn on less publicized developments in many specialities, on the work of engineers and technicians who by their efforts created the *deus ex machina* who made invention possible. Below them, and never to be forgotten in any story of invention or of great scientific discovery, there were the ordinary craftsmen. Clerk Maxwell, one of the greatest theorists of all time and the father of the electromagnetic spectrum, well realized the partnership between his theories and the practical arts. 'I am happy,' he said on taking up his first Chair at Aberdeen University, 'in the knowledge of a good instrument-maker, in addition to a smith, an optician and a carpenter.'

To these requirements of vision, operational need and technological expertise, mixed in proportions that are rarely the same, there must be added luck – 'Chance, Fortune, Luck, Destiny, Fate, Providence,' which as Winston Churchill wrote of the First World War, determines whether you 'walk to the right or to the left of a particular tree, and . . . makes the difference whether you rise to command an Army Corps or are sent home crippled or paralysed for life.' Chance saved the Wrights from destruction and brought them to an appointment with history at Kittyhawk, gave the Americans rather than the Germans the harvest of nuclear fission discovered by Otto Hahn in Berlin. Chance has still to decide into whose hands will fall the possibilities and perils of genetic engineering, the techniques which in the foreseeable future may give mankind the chance of re-creating himself in tailor-made form.

The upsurge of invention of which these are the more sensational illustrations, and which marks the hundred years that began in mid-19th century, almost totally ignored frontiers. It was Lord Rutherford who used to boast that 'science is international, and long may it remain so.' The same is as true with the catalyst of technology, growing at comparable pace in most industrialized countries whatever steps are taken to conceal the growth from commercial or national rivals. Thus inventions tend to be born in different countries, in different forms, at much the same time, often in conditions of commercial or military secrecy which make the task of settling priority a nightmare search, and the problem of patenting and exploitation a rich field for lawyers. That so many of the inventions on which the world now depends began to flower out following the Great Exhibition held in London in 1851 was not chance. But neither was it the result of lonely British supremacy. Rather was it that the Great Exhibition itself reflected the belief that all was possible for all nations in the new confident morning that then seemed to be dawning. Between four and five centuries earlier the Middle Ages had been ended by the scientific revolution which creates the watershed between earlier times and our own. From it there had come in due course the Industrial Revolution. Then, with the ambition surging up within the newly-created United States, and with the long European peace that followed the Napoleonic wars, men turned in a new climate of hope to fulfil their dreams.

These dreams, made real by scientists and technologists, were to revolutionize human existence within the next hundred years with the result that life in mid-20th century is basically different from life in Victorian Britain or Lincoln's America. The advances have come in scores of fields but it is possible to study six main ways in which they have altered day-to-day existence. Photography has provided for the masses what the portrait-painter once provided only for the élite; man-made materials have enabled the many to enjoy the benefits once reserved for the few. Command of the air has effectively shrunk the planet, and control of the electromagnetic spectrum has given men power to disseminate information throughout the world in a way not previously conceivable. Use of the forces locked within the nucleus of the atom has opened up the prospect, if a distant one, of truly limitless energy; and, in a totally different field, new discoveries in biology and genetics now hold out the possibility of man being able to control the destiny of the human race. Among the welter of inventions and discoveries made since the 1850s these can be numbered as the most significant.

1 The Picture Makers

The men who came of age in the mid-19th century, as invention and technology began to lay the foundations of the contemporary world, had many ambitions they were eager to fulfil. They wished to create new sources of energy, to fly like the birds, to create for the masses the products which had so far been the prerogative of the rich.

They wished also to do something more human, something closely linked both to the human heart and human pride. They wished to keep some record of the loved one, of a family's daily occupations, or of the property that was the mark of prosperity; some record which would show not only that spirit of a person or a place which eludes all but the exceptional genius of an artist, but also the detail which means so much to those who know its significance.

Artists have benefited from this human wish since the first caveman drew figures on a wall with blackened stick or chipped an outline with primitive chisel. And, despite the urge to interpret rather than depict, to leave a portrait tinted with the artist's feelings rather than an objective record, there was through the centuries a constant demand for portraits, for landscapes, for pictorial accounts of military actions which showed events 'as they were': a demand which in the nature of things could never be fully satisfied but which called for any device which would help create a detailed picture.

To fill this operational requirement there came first the *camera obscura*, or literally darkened room, the ancestor of both the box Brownie and the elegant Hasselblad.

Just when this predecessor of the camera was first used is not clear, but there is considerable evidence that knowledge of the principles involved goes back to ancient times. In the history of photography, as in that of other inventions, it is rarely wise to use the term 'first'. Different definitions, different nuances put on the most innocent words, the genuine wish to claim honest priority and the equally genuine

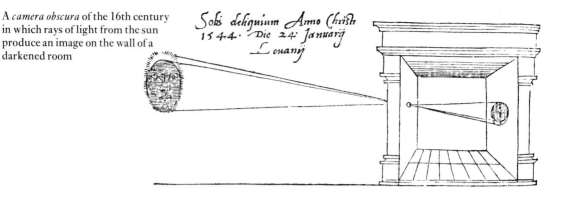

A *camera obscura* of the 16th century in which rays of light from the sun produce an image on the wall of a darkened room

wish to dismiss the holder of a rival theory or the protagonist of a rival school, can restore confusion to the most carefully sorted-out chronological story. But it is at least certain that by the 16th century the *camera obscura* is being described in detail.

The fullest account comes from Giambattista della Porta, a Neapolitan physicist who in the catholic manner of the times wrote also on physiology, gardening and arboriculture. Leonardo had already written several accounts in his notebooks, but these were not published until the end of the 18th century. Other Dutch and Italian scientists referred to the ingenious device, which appears to have been well known, but it was della Porta's description, given in his *Magia Naturalis* of 1569, which best explains how it was used by draughtsmen. The principle of the *camera obscura* is simple enough. Light-rays passing through a small hole in the side of a darkened room form an inverted image on the opposite wall of the scene outside. If a sheet of paper is held flat against this wall it will be possible to trace on it, with considerable accuracy, a replica of the scene. That was all: the uncomplicated conscription of the fact that rays of light shine in straight lines. While this fact, and the possibility of its application, had long been known, it was only in the aftermath of the scientific Renaissance that it was developed with speed. Then, in little more than a century, the *camera obscura* was transformed.

First Aniello Barbaro, a Venetian nobleman who was also a professor at the University of Padua, described in *La Pratica della Perspettiva* how the substitution of a glass lens for the pinhole would increase the brilliance of the image. 'Close all shutters and doors so that no light enters the room except through the lens,' he went on. 'Opposite hold a sheet of paper which is moved forward and back until the scene appears in the sharpest detail. There on paper you will see the scene as it really is, with distances, colours, and shadows and motions; the clouds, the water glinting and the birds flying. By holding the paper steady you can trace the whole perspective with a pen. You can shade it and delicately colour it from nature itself.'

But the addition of a lens was only the beginning. It was soon realized that if a concave mirror was added to the optical apparatus the image would be thrown rightside up instead of upside down, while a simple mirror at 45° could be used to throw the image on to a sheet of horizontal paper rather than on to the wall. By mounting the lens in a form of telescope it was possible to bring successive parts of the external scene into view, while different lenses would project different extents of the external scene.

Next, the *camera obscura* became mobile, being adapted to the sedan chair and also to the tent. It was realized that the lens could be housed in a box above a darkened area where the operator sat, and the rays directed down on to a horizontal drawing-board. The next development was construction of a lens plus darkened box with glass top, and before the end of the 18th century there was available a diverse range of small instruments that would produce on a flat surface – sometimes a ground-glass screen – an image of whatever it was pointed at.

By the start of the 19th century nature had thus been induced to provide a picture of itself. The artist producing the family portrait or the panorama of a landowner's property had at his disposal a device which helped him to pin down on paper or canvas a permanent portrait of a transient scene. But, as one artist remarked, the portraitist still had to use the pencil of man; was there no way in which he could use the pencil of nature?

So far, the line of advance was along the path of optics. By various ways man had discovered how to lead light to the surface on which he wished to draw; now, if he wished light to draw for him, it would be necessary for the light itself to affect the substance on which it fell. Thus the chemists were brought in, and were soon making possible photography as the word is understood today, a process in which two lines of improvements can be seen to run parallel. One, from the opticians, brought ever greater control over the amount and kind of light which was used; the other, from the chemists, made the utilization of that light ever more efficient and more controllable.

Man had noticed since ancient times that light changes the colour of certain substances. Many dyed fabrics fade with exposure to the sun while the human skin deepens in colour under its rays. Yet it was not until the early-18th century that the German scientist Johann Heinrich Schulze first noticed, apparently by accident, the light-sensitive characteristics of the salts of silver which form the basis of most photographic processes. Schulze filled a bottle with a mixture of chalk, silver, and nitric acid in the course of routine experiments and left the bottle near an open window. On his return he found that the mixture nearest the window had turned a deep purple while that which had not caught the rays of the sun still remained white. Repetition of the process, but with a bottle of similar material placed by a fire, brought no corresponding darkening; thus it seemed clear that the light of the sun rather than its heat was responsible. To discover whether this was so, Schulze again placed a filled bottle near the window. This time he pasted stencils of opaque paper on the outside. When the bottle was taken down and the stencils removed, their images remained in white on a darkened ground.

Schulze's work was the basis of an interesting parlour trick, but it seemed to be little more. Once the stencils had been removed their images quickly darkened, to disappear in the purple background like Prospero's insubstantial pageant, leaving not a rack behind. Nevertheless, the phenomenon was followed up, notably by the Swedish Karl Wilhelm Scheele who split sunlight up into its component colours with the aid of a spectrum and found that the different colours darkened the sensitive chemicals at different speeds.

One of the next steps forward, an abortive one, was made by Thomas Wedgwood, son of the potter Josiah, who had often seen the *camera obscura* used by artists to paint on dinner services, fired at the Etruria works, the scenery of the great country estates owned by the pottery's customers. If only the scene could be permanently imprinted on the pottery by the *camera obscura*, what an industrial breakthrough this would be!

Wedgwood's experiments were described in the *Journal of the Royal Institution* by no less a person than Sir Humphry Davy in 1802. His paper, *An account of a method of copying paintings upon glass and of making profiles by the agency of light upon nitrate of silver, with observations by H. Davy*, was an account of failure. The images cast by the *camera obscura* were not sufficiently bright to affect the sensitive material used. Furthermore, when bright enough images were created, by placing on sensitized material either bird's feathers, insect's wings, or the paintings on glass that were then the vogue, these images passed away as soon as they were exposed to normal light. No washing of the material was sufficient to remove the traces of silver salt from the parts that had not been exposed to light and these in turn merely darkened, as had the images of Schulze's stencils. Wedgwood's sun-prints could only be looked at by the dim light of a candle.

The first man to overcome this destruction of sun-prints by the light which had made them was Nicéphore Niepce of Chalon-sur-Saône, an irrepressible inventor who with his brother Claude was experimenting with sun-pictures before the end of the 18th century. At one early point in his work it looked as though Niepce would be successful in carrying Wedgwood's work a step further. Using a *camera obscura* he obtained an image on paper sensitized with silver chloride; but attempts to make the image permanent by removing the unexposed portions with acid were only partly successful and the Niepce brothers then turned to a different line. It was already known that light not only darkened certain substances but also hardened others, and the Niepces now sought a substance that would suit their particular purpose. Their aim was to use the *camera obscura* as an aid to the mechanical reproduction of engravings, and both men became familiar with a particular kind of bitumen produced when asphalt was dissolved in oil of lavender. This was resistant to etching fluids but it also hardened under exposure to light. The Niepces therefore coated a metal plate – the earliest ones being of pewter – with the bitumen. In the first experiments the plate was exposed to sunlight by placing it under an engraving whose lines held back the light, and in later ones by exposing it in a *camera obscura*. Time exposures in the latter were considerable and about eight hours were necessary to obtain the photograph

The world's first photograph, taken by Nicéphore Niepce on a pewter plate in 1826 and showing the view from Niepce's window at Gras near Chalon-sur-Saône

from the Niepces' window at Gras – the world's first success-ful permanent photograph which was discovered by Helmut and Alison Gernsheim, the historians of photography, more than a century later. After exposure, the metal plate was im-mersed in a solvent. This removed the bitumen from the parts of the plate on which no light had fallen – the shadows of the original subject – revealing the metal whose tone could then be further darkened. Where light had fallen, the equiva-lent of the highlights in the original, the light-coloured bitu-men had hardened and thus remained. Here then was the first-ever photograph, christened a 'heliograph' by Niepce, a positive rather than the negative produced today in most cameras.

Niepce's success came in the mid-1820s and the view from the window at Gras was almost certainly taken in the summer of 1826 or 1827. Earlier that year he had received the first of many letters from another key figure in the history of photo-graphy: Louis Jacques Mandé Daguerre. Daguerre was a theatrical painter who specialized in the construction of stage sets and of dioramas, popular entertainments in which huge paintings on semi-transparent material were illuminated by moving lights to give an impression of transformation scenes. He had often used the *camera obscura* and in January 1826 wrote to Niepce informing him that he, too, was trying to discover some method of producing permanent images. Niepce reacted cautiously. So, in turn, did Daguerre, not making another approach for a year. Only in December 1829 did the two men become partners and agree that they would pool their knowledge.

Niepce died four years later. Not until 1839, six years later, was the process known as the daguerreotype revealed to the world. And while the invention was bought by the French Government from Daguerre and Niepce's son jointly, it has never been clear exactly how much Daguerre and Niepce *père* each contributed to the first great breakthrough in photo-graphy. Daguerre's name lived on. It still does. And it is certainly true that he had been experimenting for some years before he sought collaboration with Niepce. Nevertheless, there is a strong presumption that the older man was the one more responsible for the new process which was formally made public in August 1839.

The daguerreotype began with a silver-plated sheet of copper. This plate was sensitized by holding it over a saucer of iodine whose vapour formed a thin layer of silver iodide on the plate's surface, and eventually gave it a rich golden colour. At this stage the plate, now in a covered holder, was placed in a

Louis Jacques Mandé Daguerre, the French theatrical painter who invented the daguerreotype process

SOCIAL STRUGGLES.

The use of a head clamp to prevent movement in early portrait photography

suitable *camera obscura* – or camera, as the box soon came to be known. Here the plate was exposed to the light. Next it was put into a developing box, at one end of which was a yellow glass window, and exposed to the fumes of a cup of heated mercury. Immediately after exposure no change could be noted in the plate; but the mercury vapour condensed on those portions of the silver iodide which had been affected by light, and the greater the intensity of light the greater the condensation. Thus an image grew on the plate and to make this permanent it was only necessary to dip the plate into a solution of common salt. The result was a one-off photograph, a unique positive which could not be copied except by re-photographing and the manufacture of a second daguerreotype. It was extremely delicate, could be damaged by fingertip contact, and had to be sealed away from the air to prevent tarnishing. Therefore the daguerreotype was usually set behind glass, which was held slightly away from the plate itself, and mounted on a plush frame. Exposures of five minutes or more were necessary, and it was customary for the heads of sitters to be held by discreetly-concealed head-clamps. However, despite these disadvantages, the daguerreotype was an immense step forward. It could reproduce textures of very great delicacy, particularly the skin of the human face, and it is not surprising that when Britain's first Census was held in 1851, more than 50 professional photographers were at work, almost all of them using the daguerreotype process.

These photographs, produced more than a century ago, have an almost uncanny way of summoning up the past. The streets of a Paris almost as remote as the Middle Ages, the lined faces of the elderly men and women who seem to have been favourites among early daguerreotype sitters, the calm beauty of the French countryside, still glow from the metal plates as though one is looking through a hole into the past. It is the faces which are most striking of all. For 'photography' – a word coined only some years later by Sir John Herschel, the British astronomer who himself pioneered many developments in the art – had achieved one of its inventors' aims. Memory of the near and the dear could now be supplemented by something more emotionally satisfying than the artist's portrait: by the daguerreotype which could bring to life flesh and blood less artistically but more reliably and more evocatively than all except the rare masterpieces from a small handful of artistic geniuses.

Yet the daguerreotype was still in one way on the far side of a wide river separating it from photography as the word is understood today. It was a one-off job. One exposure, one daguerreotype. To this extent it retained the uniqueness of the artist's portrait. It also retained the same limitation; the family portrait could be cooed over and savoured in only one place at a time.

The first man to remove the limitation was William Henry Fox Talbot, a wealthy Englishman of Lacock Abbey near Chippenham in Wiltshire. Talbot had been born here in 1800 and died in the same great house in 1877. In between he was Member of Parliament in the reformed Government of 1832; became a considerable mathematician; and was led by his interest in archaeology to decipher, for the first time, the cuneiform tablets rescued from the ruins of Nineveh. This man of many parts, so typical of the wealthy Victorians, was also the inventor of the Talbotype or calotype.

During a summer holiday in 1833 Talbot was sketching on the shores of Lake Como. 'After various fruitless attempts I laid aside the instrument and came to the conclusion that its use required a previous knowledge of drawing which unfortunately I did not possess,' he later wrote. 'I then thought of trying again a method which I had tried many years before. The method was, to take a *camera obscura* and to throw the image of the objects on a piece of paper in its focus – fairy pictures, creations of a moment, and destined as rapidly to fade away. It was during these thoughts that the idea occurred to me – how charming it would be if it were possible to cause these natural images to imprint themselves durably, and remain fixed upon the paper.' This of course was just the idea that had come to others, and some years later Talbot regretted what he called the 'very unusual dilemma' which sprang from the fact that both he and Daguerre were working, unknown to each other, along very similar lines.

Talbot was wrong. Far from being unusual, the situation in which men of imagination in different countries – or even from the same country – find themselves independently approaching a great discovery or invention or scientific advance, is very frequent. The climate of the times, the state of the art, and public demand all contribute to this embarrassing state of affairs. Darwin and Wallace separately working towards the outline of evolution; the British, the Germans and the Americans independently developing radar, and the tangled story of the proximity fuse are only three of the more obvious examples.

Talbot returned home and during the rest of the 1830s busied himself with making what he called photogenic drawings. These were on paper which had been made chemically sensitive and then 'exposed' either in the *camera*

A window of Lacock Abbey
photographed by William Henry
Fox Talbot in 1835

obscura or, in the case of objects such as leaves or lace, by merely placing the objects on the paper and exposing it to sunlight. The image could be seen on the sensitive paper and was then chemically fixed, although this fixing process was unsatisfactory and most of the original photogenic drawings have by now faded out of existence.

In the first weeks of 1839 Talbot realized that Daguerre was publishing in France the details of a process which he considered similar to his own. The result was a paper giving 'Some Account of the Art of Photogenic Drawing' which he read to the Royal Society at the end of January and a second paper on the same subject read the following month.

The fixing process in Talbot's method was particularly important for one special reason. All his pictures were reversed in tones, the blacks of real life appearing white, the whites appearing black, while those taken in the camera were also reversed from left to right. But once it had been found possible to fix the photograph so that it could be exposed to light once again without fading or disappearing, another process could be carried out. A fresh sheet of sensitized paper could be exposed with the photograph placed face downward on it; and from the original negative the positive appeared with tones correct and with image the right way round.

By 1839 there were therefore two very different photographic processes in existence. Daguerre's produced the finer results, and could be obtained by far shorter exposures, which was all-important to the portrait-photographer. Nevertheless, it still remained a once-only photograph, while from Talbot's paper negatives a large number of prints could be made.

At this stage there seems to have been an explosion of ideas. What in fact happened was that many men who had been tentatively experimenting for years were now encouraged by the success of Daguerre and of Talbot to continue with their work, to reveal ideas in which they had previously had only faint faith. From the spring of 1839 innumerable ways of making it easier to take photographs and to improve the quality of the finished product began to be published in the columns of scientific journals or discussed at scientific meetings. Of all these, two in particular were to help lay the foundations of modern photography.

The first was produced by Sir John Herschel, famous astronomer and son of an even more famous one. Herschel now, at one stroke, initiated one of the important processes in photography which has lasted, virtually unchanged, for more than 130 years. In his diaries, now held by the Science Museum in London, he describes what he did. Many years

William Henry Fox Talbot, the
wealthy Englishman whose work in
Wiltshire was contemporary with
Daguerre's across the Channel

Below Photograph on glass by Sir John Herschel of his father's telescope at Slough, taken in 1839

Right above Photograph taken about 1845 by William Henry Fox Talbot of his own photographic establishment at Reading

Right below Label advertising chemically treated paper for making 'Sun Pictures'

earlier he had found that silver salts – the salts used to sensitize photographic paper – were dissolved by hyposulphite of soda, the 'hypo' that is still linked with the photographic tasks of the amateur's bathroom. 'Tried hyposulphite of soda to arrest action of light by washing away all the chloride of silver or other silvering salt,' he wrote. 'Succeeded perfectly. Papers 12 acted on, $\frac{1}{2}$ guarded from light by covering with pasteboard, were then withdrawn from sunshine, sponged over with hypo-sulphite of soda, then well washed in pure water – dried and again exposed. The darkened half remained dark, the white half white, after an exposure, as if they had been painted on in sepia.' This is of course the treatment of modern films that are exposed, developed, and put in hypo for fixing, after which the hypo is washed away in running water and the resulting picture left as a permanent image.

During the same summer of 1839 Herschel also created history by making the first photograph on glass, a picture of the 40-foot telescope at Slough, where his father had first set up his observatory on being appointed private astronomer to George III. For the experiment, silver chloride was precipi-tated on to a circular glass plate $2\frac{1}{2}$ inches across. After two days the water was siphoned off and the plate allowed to dry. It was then sensitized, exposed in a camera or light box, and fixed with hypo, after which the back of the glass was smoked and painted black to give the picture the appearance of a positive print. But the difficulty of making the first emulsion adhere to the glass was very great and, for the time being, glass was abandoned.

Herschel's use of hypo was second in importance only to the discovery by Talbot of a process which drastically shortened exposure time. One says discovery, but application is possibly the fairer word; for the crux of the process was the use of gallic acid to develop the unseen or latent image produced by these shorter exposures, and Talbot was led on to this by the Rev. J. B. Reade, a well-known scientist who had come upon this property of gallic acid some while earlier.

The result was the calotype process, later re-christened the Talbotype, in which ordinary paper was treated first with silver nitrate and then with potassium iodide. The sensitized paper could be kept indefinitely as long as it was shielded from the light. When wanted for use it was treated with gallo-nitrate of silver and would then have to be used within a few hours. But the necessary exposure was of only about a minute, after which development and fixing produced a negative, and from this a limitless number of positives could be made by Talbot's earlier process.

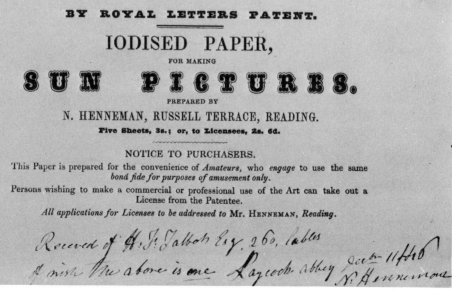

Talbot patented the process but, unlike Daguerre, allowed amateurs free use of it, as is made clear from the packets of 'Iodised Paper' sold in 1846 for making sun-pictures. A notice to purchasers warned that 'this paper is prepared for the convenience of *Amateurs* who *engage* to use the same *bona fide for the purposes of amusement only*. Persons wishing to make commercial or professional use of the Art can take out a License from the Patentee.'

Photography was therefore really born by the early 1840s and for the rest of the decade the story is one of consolidation, explanation and exploitation. But should the application of these simple chemical facts of life be patentable? And, as knowledge increased, would it be practicable to enforce patent restrictions? These were more than purely academic questions as the business of photographic portraiture got into its stride, and while Talbot in effect withdrew most of his patent rights in the early 1850s, he retained their use for commercial portraiture. By this time he had also written the first great classic of photography. In *The Pencil of Nature*, a book in which it is possible to discern a faint trace of the shadow soon to be looming over both artists and book-illustrators, he described and illustrated his early experiments. Many painters had scoffed at the very idea of the objective eye of the camera replacing the subjective eye of the artist. For long it was held that while the painter interpreted, the camera could only portray, an idea belied by the early masterpieces of such photographers as Julia Cameron and decisively refuted by the growth of creative photography during the last third of the 19th century.

In the 1850s photography saw one development even more important than Herschel's discovery that negatives and prints could be fixed by simply soaking them in hypo. This was the collodion process which used glass plates instead of the paper whose texture had been a disadvantage of the calotype. A number of early photographic workers had realized that glass would be an ideal vehicle for the sensitized solution but had failed to discover how this could be made to stick to the glass. Albumen plates prepared with the use of egg white was one solution, but the low sensitivity of these and the long exposures required severely limited their use.

Collodion is a solution of pyroxyline, a kind of gun-cotton, in a mixture of ether and alcohol. When this is poured on to a suitably cleaned glass plate it quickly dries into a thin transparent film. More than one experimenter appears to have considered using it as a basis for photography but it was only in 1851 that Frederick Archer, a sculptor who had been using

earlier photographic methods to make visual notes of his
sitters, published details of the process he had successfully
worked out. In this wet collodion process, the glass plate with
its collodion film was sensitized by dipping it into a solution of
silver nitrate. While still moist it had to be exposed in the
camera, and then developed and fixed. The one big advantage
of the process was the shortness of the exposures required;
Talbot had reduced a substantial fraction of an hour down to
minutes but Archer now reduced minutes to seconds;
nothing longer was required to produce on the glass negative
the dark blacks that were highlights in the positive prints that
could be made from it.

Speed of exposure plus the quality of the prints, far better
than that of Talbotypes, more than outweighed the fact that

Photograph by the calotype
process, 'The Ladder', taken from
William Henry Fox Talbot's
The Pencil of Nature, published in
1844

users of the wet collodion process had to have mobile laboratories. Just how great were the virtues of the process can be
judged by the fact that it was used not only by Roger Fenton in
the Crimea, but by the Bisson brothers who in 1861 took the
first photographs from the top of Mont Blanc. Twenty-five
porters were needed to carry up the several hundredweight of
equipment that included cameras, darkroom and chemicals
as well as a number of 16-inch by 20-inch glass plates fitted
into a special case. On the top of the mountain they set up the
canvas darkroom tent. Standing inside it, they poured a
layer of collodion on to a single glass plate which was then
sensitized in the silver bath. Next the plate was loaded into the
giant camera which was taken outside the tent and put in

Left Glass collodion portrait of
Scott Archer, 1855, inventor of the
wet collodion process

Above Roger Fenton's
photographic van, used to carry
his equipment in the Crimean War

The peaks and glaciers of the Mont
Blanc range photographed by
Auguste Bisson in 1861

position on its tripod. After the exposure the camera was
taken back and the glass plate first developed and then fixed –
with the aid of water obtained by melting the snow. Just two
hours had passed before the first negative was finished,
although less time seems to have been taken for a second and a
third which were exposed before the expedition moved off
from the summit.

The virtue of the process was that it allowed innumerable
prints to be made from a glass negative. However, it was also
applied in another way for production of one-off 'prints'.
These were made simply by backing the processed plate with a
piece of dark material, or even by painting it black. In such
ambrotypes, as they were called, the highlights showed up as
silver, while shadows were represented by the dark portions
of the backing seen through the unsilvered parts of the glass.

The growth of photography had numerous side-effects.
One was the increasing use by artists of the camera as a means
of preserving, for future use, the impressions or the facts that

Top Painting by David Octavius Hill, 'The General Assembly of the Free Church of Scotland, signing the Act of Separation and Deed of Demission at Tanfield, Edinburgh, May 1843'

Above Dr David Welsh, photographed by David Octavius Hill and Robert Adamson as a study for Hill's painting *(top)* in which he is shown in white rectangle

might later slip from memory. The most famous example is that of the Scottish painter, David Octavius Hill, who in 1843 was commissioned to paint a massive canvas showing the 450 delegates to the famous meeting in Edinburgh at which the Free Church of Scotland was founded. The work was not finished for more than twenty years, but it might never have been completed had not Hill invoked the help of an Edinburgh photographer and with him set up an open-air studio on Calton Hill. Here, between 1843 and 1846, Hill and his colleague Robert Adamson took more than 1,000 calotype portraits, mostly of Scottish clergymen. Other artists soon copied Hill's use of the camera – and not all of them were portraitists. Before many years were out even Edward Whymper, famous as mountaineer and almost equally famous as an illustrator of Alpine scenery, was using the camera to ensure that his facts of mountain topography were correct when he put them on paper; or, as Douglas Milner, one of today's leading mountain photographers has put it, to exercise control 'upon artistic licence or defective memory'.

This use of photographs as visual jottings was only one which developed as it became apparent that the camera could produce permanent acceptable results, and as experience began to ease the problems of handling the chemicals, and judging the exposures. Architects found that the photograph was a good method of recording their work, and less expensive than the commissioning of an artist. Fenton took his wagon-load of equipment to the Crimea, and one of his fellow-photographers, James Robertson, followed it up photographing the aftermath of the Indian Mutiny. In the American Civil War a few years later a host of adventurous men helped to provide extraordinary records of the fighting.

There were other by-products of the new photographic processes, some of which merited the word 'craze'. One was the demand for stereoscopic photographs which, looked at through a special viewing apparatus, gave an illusory three-dimensional effect. Sir Charles Wheatstone, who can claim to share with Morse the introduction of the electric telegraph, had shown as early as 1836 that if a scene were drawn from two slightly different viewpoints and the two drawings were viewed simultaneously by right and left eye, then an impression of solidity was created. Photographs using the principle were on show at the Great Exhibition of 1851 and during the next few years there was a boom in stereoscopic pictures. These were pairs, taken either simultaneously from two cameras a few inches apart or in succession from one camera which could be slid along a board to occupy either of two positions. The London Stereoscopic Company, started in 1854, sold thousands of stereo-views which could be looked at through a variety of special apparatus. Their popularity lasted for little more than a decade. Then stereoscopic photography dropped out of favour until the last years of the century, being brought back to favour once again with the rise of amateur photography.

The first stereoscope craze was followed by the rise of the *carte-de-visite*. This was the portrait-photograph usually $2\frac{1}{4}$ by $3\frac{1}{2}$ inches and first popularized in Paris. Originally intended as an alternative to the visiting card, it soon found a new use as celebrities allowed themselves to be photographed on *cartes-de-visite*, which were then sold as publicity. Collecting them became a hobby as ubiquitous as stamp or post-card collecting, and during the 1860s many millions were sold in Britain alone.

By this time the first microphotographs had been produced. Minute prints or transparencies, they could be viewed only with the aid of a magnifying glass or by projection through a lantern. Queen Victoria wore a signet ring holding five photographs of her family which could be seen through a jewel lens, while during the Siege of Paris between 1870 and 1871 messages were flown into the city by pigeons to whose legs were strapped rolls of microphotographs. On receipt, the minute negatives were displayed through a magic lantern and the messages copied out for distribution.

The extremely fine detail of microphotographs was a tribute to the wet collodion processes. Even so, this had great disadvantages. Using it for studio portraits – the bread-and-butter of the photographic business – was a very different proposition from its use on the top of Mont Blanc. The chemicals and the wet glass plates which were an intrinsic

Projection of microscopic
dispatches sent out of Paris during
the Siege of 1870

part of photography formed a strong disincentive, and during
the two decades that followed Archer's invention many
efforts were made to produce a satisfactory dry plate. A
Frenchman, J. M. Taupenot, found that if the collodion were
coated with a layer of iodized albumen, the plate could be
dried and used several weeks later. Other experimenters
devised different ways of overcoming the problem presented
by the hard surface of the dried collodion, impermeable as it
was to the liquid developer. All early efforts foundered on the
fact that dry plates were vastly slower than their wet counter-
parts, in some cases more than a hundred times as slow.

The break-through came in the 1870s with the use of
gelatine rather than collodion to hold the sensitizing chemicals.
By this time the chemical problems of photography were
under constant survey and before the end of the decade dry
plates were being made which could be successfully exposed
for about 1/25th of a second, the snapshot speed of today's
ordinary box camera.

Onward still, and onward still it runs its sticky way
And Gelatine you're bound to use if you mean to make
    things pay
Collodion – slow old fogey! – your palmy days have been
You must give place in future to the plates of Gelatine

wrote the British Journal of Photography's Almanac for 1881.

The overwhelming advantage of satisfactory dry plates was
that they could be bought instead of made. When they had
been exposed in the camera they could be taken to a specialist
for processing. Thus for the first time since Niepce and Talbot
had pointed their primitive cameras at the local view, the
photographer had become divorced from the chemist. To be
successful, a man with a camera had to know the limitations of
the materials he was using; for some years yet photographic

plates were to lack the uniformity of the mass-production line, and experience of their variations and vicissitudes still helped. But with the arrival of the practicable dry plate, which could be bought from a local shop and taken back there for development when exposed, photography was brought to the edge of the mass–market world.

Only one more development was needed to take it into that world: substitution of the heavy glass plate and its replacement by something lighter and less breakable. The first answer was celluloid, one of the early plastics, invented by Alexander Parkes as far back as 1861, and now coated with a gelatine film. This in turn was quickly replaced by successive developments pioneered by George Eastman, a New York maker of dry plates who in 1888 introduced the Kodak, a word invented by him for its ease of pronunciation in any language, and used to describe the simple camera which was to sweep the world. The new easy-to-use camera was supplied by the factory complete with a roll of film consisting of a gelatino-bromide emulsion on a holding layer of plain gelatine. This was backed by thin paper, soon replaced by a backing much thinner than celluloid. Together with the Kodak itself, the new film provided the basis of the photographic industry as it was to expand during the following century.

A photograph taken in 1888 with the first Kodak camera

The more sensitive emulsions which emerged with the ending of the wet collodion process, and the development of roll films, did more than remove the need for the photographer to be chemist as well: they enabled him to work without a tripod, to hold the camera in his hand. Roll films which occupied little space in his pocket increased his mobility when compared with that of the man forced to carry heavy glass plates. Thus most essentials of the modern photographic world had been created well before the end of the 19th century.

But it was not only the chemists who had been needed. However sensitive they were able to make their photographic plates, there were still three inevitable factors involved in taking a picture. One was the amount of light illuminating the scene to be photographed; another was the efficiency with which this light was transmitted through the lens of the camera; the third was the time during which the light was allowed to fall on the sensitive plate. All three factors were closely linked when it came to photographing moving subjects: the effect of the light on the plate was proportional to its intensity multiplied by the time during which it fell on the plate. The less the intensity, the greater the time for which the shutter would have to be kept open; but the greater this time, the greater the chance that a moving subject would be shown not clear-cut but as a blurred outline – since the image had of course moved on the plate during the fraction of a second during which the picture was being taken.

The use of a lens to concentrate light on to a flat surface had been known since the Middle Ages while methods of dealing with two of a lens' limitations – the formation of an image with coloured fringes due to chromatic aberration, and of a distorted image due to spherical aberration – had been known since the 18th century. The efficiency of such lenses in transmitting light was governed by their diameter and by the distance behind the lens at which they concentrated the light passing through them, and it was found convenient to measure this efficiency by dividing the second distance by the first – the magical 'f' number which decreases as the efficiency of the lens increases. The lenses in the first daguerreotype cameras made for sale had an effective diameter of about 1.1 inches and focused the image on a plate about $15\frac{1}{2}$ inches away, giving a working aperture, as it was called, of about f14. Little more than a year later the Hungarian mathematician Joseph Petzval had designed what is generally accepted to be the first lens produced especially for a camera, one which gave an aperture as large – and as efficient – as f3.5.

With the development of photography after 1840 it was quickly appreciated that certain photographic purposes were served best by certain types of lenses. Speed was only one of the factors involved, and a fast lens suitable for taking portraits might show distortions or aberrations when used for landscape work where a far slower lens might be preferable. Thus from mid-century the evolution of new and more sensitive emulsions, and of more convenient ways of using them, was supplemented by the manufacture of more efficient lenses, this itself being linked with the production of new kinds of glass, and new ways of processing it.

Regulating the time during which the lens allowed light to fall on to the sensitive plate was soon the task of the shutter. In the early days of long exposures, these were made simply by removing a cap or cover from the front of the lens and re-placing it after so many hours or minutes. With the reduction of exposure times first to seconds and then to fractions of a second, something more accurate was required. The answer was given by guillotine shutters, consisting of a plate containing a hole which fell past the lens; by flaps raised or lowered pneumatically; by circular plates with a hole, capable of being rotated at different speeds and therefore of letting through light for different times; and by the shutter which was made up of interleaved blades which could be spring-opened for pre-determined times. There was also the focal plane shutter in which a slit of variable width in a black blind can be made to move across the face of the film or plate.

With the refinement of the shutter there came the variable iris diaphragm, fitted in front of the lens, or sometimes between its individual components. It could be set for any of certain f-numbers, so that whether the diaphragm was opened up – letting in a lot of light and giving a small f-number – or stopped down to provide a big one, it would be possible to work out for how long the shutter should be open to affect, to any agreed extent, a film of any measured sensitivity.

Knowledge of this sensitivity became very necessary as exposures shortened. A minor error in judgment meant little with an exposure of many minutes; it could be ruinous when this was reduced to a fraction of a second. Basically the problem consisted of two halves. First the strength of light in certain specific conditions had to be determined; then it was necessary to assess how much of this light – the 'much' being governed by the size of the lens aperture and the time for which the lens was uncovered – was necessary to affect plates or films of certain speeds. The science of sensitometry, as it was called, was virtually invented by two English workers,

Ferdinand Hurter and Vero Charles Driffield in the last two decades of the 19th century. First they constructed a U-shaped capillary tube filled with a coloured liquid; one of the bulbs was painted red and thus absorbed more light than the other; this brought the liquid in the two arms to different heights and the difference gave a measure of the light-intensity falling on the bulbs. Parallel with scientific measurement of the strength of light there came into existence a large family of devices for showing how lights of differing strengths would affect photographic paper. In the most simple of these a piece of sensitized paper was exposed beneath a series of different-sized holes. From the size of the hole that gave the correct darkening of a test-sheet it was possible to work out the best exposure, and the simple next step was the construction of a calculator, or a set of tables, from which a photographer could find out the correct exposure with a film of any particular speed, under any light conditions.

Refinements of these action meters, tint meters and exposure meters and tables held the field for half a century. Only in the 1930s did they begin to be superseded by meters based on the photo-electric cell. In these the light falling on a selenium or photo-conductive cell automatically swings a pointer to a number from which, with the use of interconnected dials recording film speeds, apertures and shutter speeds, it is possible to gauge exposures for any permutation of conditions.

The last decades of the 19th century removed the worst of the exposure problems; they saw also the development of many different kinds of photography whose seeds had been sown years previously. One, directly linked with fast lenses, shutters and emulsions, was the photography not of the people and cabs of a leisurely world but of birds in flight and race-horses in action. Even before the invention of photography Sir Charles Wheatstone had shown that creation of a bright electric spark in a darkened room 'froze' a moving object as far as spectators were concerned. This principle was used as early as 1851 by Talbot who in a famous experiment in a darkened room attached a page of *The Times* to a rapidly revolving wheel. The lens-cap of his camera was removed, and the wheel lit by a bright electric spark which lasted for only 1/100,000th of a second. The light was brilliant enough, and its duration short enough, to give a sharp image of the revolving page. An alternative to the electric spark was provided from the early 1860s onwards by the intense light of burning magnesium; although its duration was far longer than that of an electric spark its major disadvantage was the cloud of thick smoke

Stereo-photograph of Sir David
Brewster taken by the light of
burning magnesium in March 1864

which accompanied it.

While electric sparks and magnesium were being used to give the intense surge of illumination required for short exposures, complementary efforts were being made to decrease the time for which shutters could be opened when bright sunlight plus a very sensitive plate made this possible. One of the first attempts to solve the problem came from Edward James Muggeridge. He was born in Kingston, Surrey, and renovated his name to Eadweard Muybridge, believing that this was the Anglo-Saxon original. He then emigrated to the United States, and as a photographer went with the official party to Alaska when the Americans bought the territory from Russia in 1868. A few years later Muybridge was hired by an ex-Governor of California to photograph his string of race-horses in action and by an arrangement of spring-released boards managed to take pictures first at 1/500th of a second, later at 1/1,000th and finally at 1/2,000th–pictures which when shown in succession are the genesis of the moving picture.

Shortly afterwards there came E. J. Marey with his photographic gun, a device in which a trigger started a circular glass plate revolving in one direction while a circular metal disc carrying a shutter-hole revolved in the opposite direction. Exposures, which clearly showed the motions of birds in flight, were made only when plate and shutter were moving

Eadweard Muybridge's photograph of the race-horse in action taken about 1887

fast, and exposures as fast as 1/25,000th of a second were finally possible.

Both Muybridge and Marey had built their equipment for specialist purposes and this was largely true of the other photographers who from the first years of the 20th century steadily widened the range of the possible. In the early 1900s Dr Lucien Bull, anxious to record the wing-beats of small insects, so arranged his apparatus that an insect emerging from a closed tube lifted a flap which set in motion a drum on which film was wound. The drum revolved at 40 revolutions a second and during each rotation a rotary interruptor fired a bright spark 54 times. Thus within one second of its emergence the insect had been photographed more than 2,000 times. Multiple lenses mounted on a rotating drum, and lenses unmasked by a rotating-disc shutter, were later used to give up to nearly 100,000 pictures a second. More recently the Kerr Cell, actuated by the momentary application of a high voltage, allowed exposures of less than one millionth of a second to be taken of Britain's first atomic explosion.

While the photography of fast-moving subjects demanded the collaboration of lens-makers, chemists and electrical experts, the lens-makers themselves, together with the glass-makers and chemists, were responsible for their own specialist progress. Lenses which distorted progressively less and which passed an increasing percentage of the available light were made throughout the second half of the 19th century, while in the 1890s J. H. Dallmeyer announced the first telephoto lens. This was an ingenious arrangement of one convex or positive lens with a concave or negative lens behind it. The effect was to give a longer focal length for any particular distance between lens and film. The size of the image was thus greatly increased so that the telephoto lens could fill a picture with the weather-vane on top of a steeple rather than the steeple itself.

High-speed photography, microphotography and tele-photography were all essentially technical advances. So were many of the methods by which photographers tried to control the final effect of light on their medium, although here it was the photographer-artist rather than artist-photographer who struggled for improvement. One interesting line of advance petered out after some decades of popularity, but not before fathering a family of methods by which prints of quite excep-tional beauty could be made. These were the various pigment processes, most of which sprang from the fact that Talbotype prints, and to a lesser extent the prints made by subsequent processes, tended to fade. Would it not be possible, it was argued, to produce an image not in silver but in a permanent pigment?

A clue to the answer had been found in 1839 by Mungo Ponton who discovered that when gelatine sensitized with potassium bichromate was exposed to light it became hard and insoluble in warm water. As early as the mid-1850s bichro-mated gelatine containing powdered carbon had been exposed under a negative and then developed in water which removed the carbon in the soluble gelatine but left the rest. The process was developed by more than one worker, but failed to bring out the half-tones from a negative. It was thus left to Sir Joseph Swan, inventor of the incandescent lamp, to patent the carbon process, in which a carbon tissue comprising a layer of bichromated gelatine on a holding paper is first exposed through a negative. The exposed surface of the tissue is then attached to transfer paper, the holding paper is soaked off in warm water and as the water attacks the unhardened gelatine the print is revealed in pigment on the transfer paper. Many variations of this original pigment process were developed during the last year of the 19th century, but Swan's carbon process was the most popular, more than 50 different kinds of transfer at one time being made by the Autotype Company which bought Swan's patents.

One of the early disappointments about photography had been its inability to portray people or scenes in colour. Niepce had confided to his brother how much he wanted to

High-speed photograph of a dragon fly in flight taken at about 1/2000 of a second by Dr Lucien Bull in the early 1900s

'fix the colours'. Daguerre and Talbot after him had written in much the same vein and throughout the second half of the 19th century there was a constant succession of photographers or would-be photographers who claimed to have found a way of solving this apparently insoluble problem. Some were optimists but some were charlatans and as late as 1891 *Chambers Encyclopaedia* could state: 'The report that the art of photographing in the colours of nature has been discovered crops up year after year with curious persistency, and may be generally traced to the work of unscrupulous persons who seek to deceive the public for their own advantage. Moreover,' it went on, 'it is difficult to see how the much-talked-of photography in colours as popularly understood can ever be achieved.' The 'as popularly understood' adds the necessary air of vagueness to the statement; but it was in general terms quite true and was to remain so until advances in technology allowed the problem to be solved many years later.

Long before the invention of photography it had been known that white light was made up of three primary colours, a fact which at first led some early practitioners to believe that the problems of colour photography might be solved without undue trouble. What they failed to appreciate – quite

Dr Lucien Bull and the spark drum camera, 1904

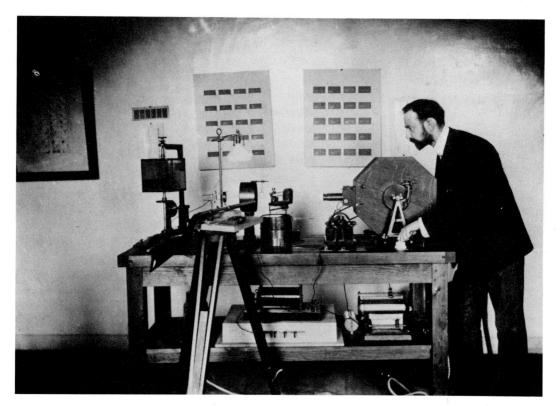

apart from the technical problems – was that the sensitive photographic plate or film responded only to some of the colours in the spectrum. Almost all early emulsions were affected only by colours in the narrow blue-violet part of the colour band: the films 'saw' the world differently from humans, a fact which explains the bare featureless white skies of many early landscapes.

The 'first colour photograph' – although hardly one 'as popularly understood' – is generally considered to have been produced by James Clerk Maxwell in 1861. Maxwell had a Scottish tartan ribbon photographed three times on three separate plates, the first time through a filter provided by a blue liquid held in a glass cell, the second time through a green filter and the third time through a red. The three resulting negatives – colour separation negatives as they were soon called – were used to make three separate lantern slides. The slides were then thrown at the same time on to a screen, that taken through the blue filter being projected with blue light, and the second and third with green and red light respectively. The resulting colour image produced by adding together the three primary colours of red, green and blue, was primitive but successful, and during the following years variations of the system were developed by a number of men. Each involved the taking of three separate photographs through different coloured filters, one of the earliest ways of doing this being with the help of a repeating back which could be fitted to an ordinary camera. Thus one-third of a photographic plate was photographed through a red filter. The process was repeated on the next third through a green filter. It was then slid along yet again, and the process repeated once more through a blue filter. An improvement was the beam-splitting colour camera, developed about the turn of the century, using two semi-reflectors set at 45° to the incoming light beam, which was reflected at the first mirror to give a red beam and at the second to give blue. Green was recorded directly. In this ingenious way one exposure could provide three separation negatives. The result of all these devices, however, still had to be projected in a darkened room or looked at through a viewing apparatus.

Attempts to overcome this disadvantage were made as early as 1869 by Louis Ducos du Hauron, who in *Les Couleurs en Photographie, Solution du Problème*, described how prints could be made by the subtractive process. Here the exposures were first made through filters complementary to the primary colours – magenta (minus green), blue-green (minus red) and yellow (minus blue). From the three negatives, prints were

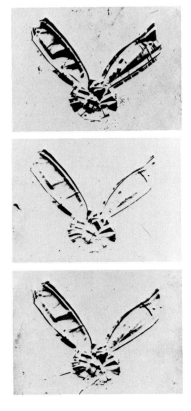

Additive colour photography. The first colour photograph was produced in 1861 for a demonstration at the Royal Institution by the physicist James Clerk Maxwell. *Above* The three negatives made by Clerk Maxwell of the tartan ribbon through three liquid filters, blue, green and red in colour (top to bottom: blue, green, red).

 1 Subject
 2 Blue filter
 3 Green filter
 4 Red filter
 5 Camera
 6 Blue filter negative
 7 Green filter negative
 8 Red filter negative
 9 Blue filter positive
10 Green filter positive
11 Red filter positive
12 Projectors
13 Positives
14 Filters
15 Screen with image
16 Clerk Maxwell's first colour photograph

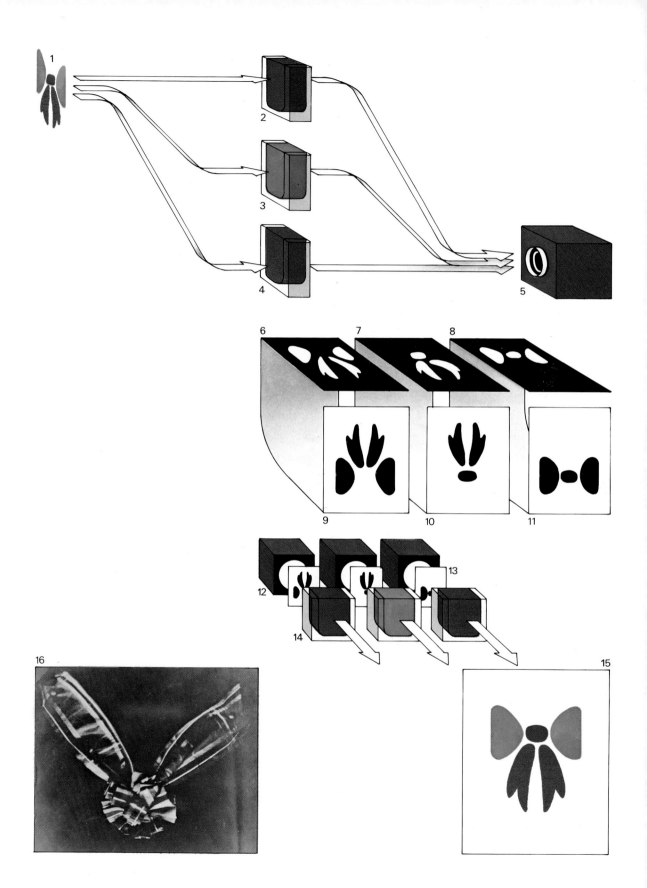

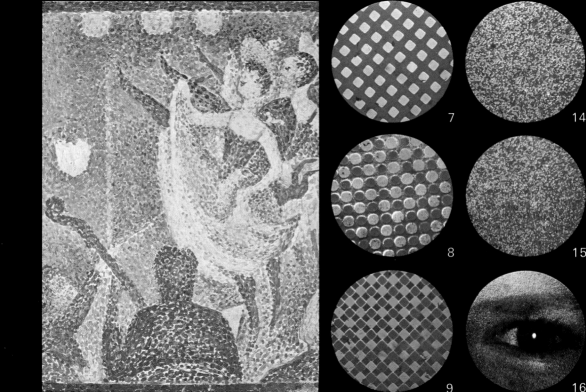

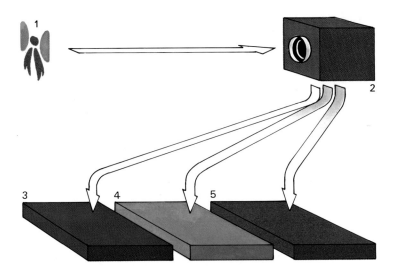

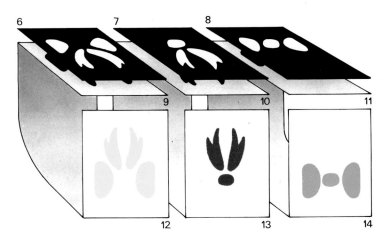

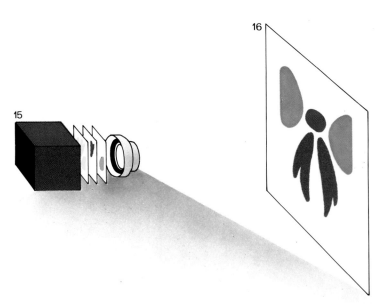

then made on to the three gelatine sheets containing carbon pigments of red, blue and yellow. When the three sheets were mounted together the result was a colour picture – a transparency if the mount was of glass and a print if the mount was of paper.

Ducos du Hauron, like other experimenters of his period, a number of whom produced roughly comparable systems, was handicapped by the response of the photographic emulsions to the colours of the spectrum, so different from those of the human eye. Not until 1873 did Hermann Vogel, a German chemist, find that if the collodion plate were bathed in a certain aniline dye, its sensitivity to green would be increased. Other experimenters went to work, gradually widening the band of the spectrum which would affect the plates. The red end was the last to succumb: only in the first years of the 20th century, following research by I. G. Farben, the German dyestuffs company, was the first plate put on the market which was sensitive to red as well.

However, it was merely one stage, although an important one, in the constant improvement of photographic emulsions throughout the last hundred years. Plates and film were soon made sensitive to infra-red rays at one end of the visible spectrum and to ultra-violet and X-rays at the other. The speed of films was pushed constantly upwards while at the same time the graininess of the emulsions – the size of the individual grains of silver which can adversely affect the print – was steadily reduced.

None of this work, which gradually brought the photographic print more into line with man's accepted view of things, did much to bring nearer the day of the genuine colour photograph. However, it did mean that a panchromatic plate sensitive to all the visible colours was available when means for utilizing it in colour photography at last appeared.

The means were a curious technological adaptation of the method used by the *pointillistes*, painters of the French Impressionist school who achieved their results by using a mass of intermingled coloured points which were merged by the human eye when viewed from the right distance. This principle was utilized by exposing a photographic plate behind a mosaic of extremely small multi-coloured filter elements. When the resulting positive was looked at through a similar screen, a colour picture was seen. The first such process, developed during the closing years of the 19th century, used a screen consisting of fine lines of the primary colours ruled some 200 to the inch on the plate. But this was superseded within a few years by the Autochrome plates which from 1907 onwards were manufactured by the Lumière brothers in France. The plates were first covered with a thin layer of extremely fine starch grains which had previously been dyed green, red or blue, and then been thoroughly mixed. Over this starch layer there was then spread a thin panchromatic emulsion. The emulsion was exposed through the starch grains, each of which acted as an individual colour filter. After development, the plate was re-exposed and re-developed, the result being a colour transparency made up of small grains of the primary colours, the colours being blended by the human eye. For some three decades Autochrome held the field despite the long exposures which its use demanded. Other processes, both additive and subtractive were put on the market, but all failed. Most were unsatisfactory, too expensive, or both.

Then, in the 1930s, the practicability of making extremely thin multi-layer films was married up to the principle of dye-coupling, discovered by Rudolf Fischer in 1912, to produce two very similar films, one made by Kodak the other by Agfa. Both incorporated a triple layer of film whose layers were sensitive to blue, green and red light respectively. After exposure the film was developed, the remaining silver bromide in each layer re-exposed, and the film then re-developed in chemicals that left dye of yellow, cyan or magenta on the three emulsions wherever the silver bromide was turned to silver. All that then remained to be done was for the silver to be bleached away to reveal a bright transparency.

Some years later the next step was taken. It was found possible to convert each of the three emulsions to an image complementing the colour which it recorded. The result was a colour negative unrecognizable by comparison with the original scene, since the negative was in complementary colours, but one from which any number of prints could be made by repeating the process with the use of the same emulsion on a white base.

All these developments had taken the photographer further and further away from the pioneers. He no longer needed to be an able laboratory technician,. competent to handle a number of chemicals; but his choice of lenses, which could offer differing extents of the picture he wished to portray, the wide variety of films from which he could take his pick, and the options offered by lightmeters which suggested how many different pictures might be conjured out of one scene, tended to make him a different kind of technician. The caricature of the photographer begirt with dangling accessories has the truth of all good caricatures. Almost as important as the

Making an instant microscope picture using the Polaroid Land Instrument camera: *Top left* attaching the universal adapter to the microscope and framing the subject. *Top right* placing the focusing tube over the universal adapter and eyepiece, and fine focusing. *Bottom left* placing the camera over the universal adapter and making the exposure. *Bottom right* peeling the finished $3\frac{1}{4}$ by $4\frac{1}{4}$ inch print from its packet after 60 seconds.

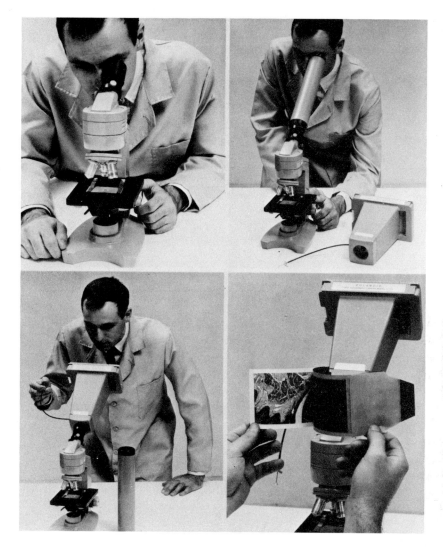

technological barrier which had tended to rise between the photographer and his subject was the long delay between the clicking of the shutter and the first sight of the result. Daguerre, developing his plate and watching the image harden up while his sitter was still on the premises, could see immediately what he had created. Even Bisson on Mont Blanc, plagued as he was by all sorts of problems, could at least set up his camera at a better view-point if his first plate showed it to be necessary. Now the most adept photographer had to wait for the result at least until he got home and it was too late for him to try again.

All this was altered with the introduction of the Polaroid-Land process, invented by Edwin H. Land in 1947 and imaginatively developed during the following years. The

Polaroid camera produces black-and-white or colour prints a few seconds after they have been taken. When Land demonstrated his new system to the Royal Photographic Society in London he said: 'In the earlier arts the artist initiates his activity by observing his subject matter and then responds, as he proceeds, to a two-fold stimulus: the original subject matter and his own growing but uncompleted work. With photography, except for those who combine a long training, high technical ability, and splendid imagination, this important kind of double stimulus – original subject and partly finished work – cannot exist. Consequently, for most people it has been of limited and sporadic interest and has not been a source of deep artistic satisfaction, and there has arisen a gulf between the majority who make snapshots as a record and as a gamble, and the minority who can reveal beauty in the medium. . . .'

The Polaroid system which bridged this gulf, responding with invention to an under-tow of public demand, utilized processing agents in jelly form, held in pods inside the camera. After a film had been exposed it was pulled slowly from the camera. During this operation the unexposed silver salts, normally dissolved and washed away by the hypo, were transferred to a receiving sheet and turned into silver by the developer. Negative and positive emerged together and the positive was peeled from the negative in daylight.

In early models of the Polaroid camera, only this one-off positive was possible, but in little more than 25 years the system has been adapted so that in addition to the positive there is also a negative from which enlargements can be made in the normal way. In addition, a multi-layer colour film has been developed with emulsions carrying yellow, cyan and magenta dyes which are diffused on to the positive as the film is withdrawn from the camera.

At first sight the Polaroid camera has a gimmick value. But it also has far more, a considerable use for architects, surveyors, scientists and many other professional men needing on-the-spot notes. It has also, a fact not commonly appreciated, restored to the artist-photographer the ability to amend and correct on the easel that became the ground-glass screen. In some ways the instant picture camera has given back to the human brain the ability to guide Talbot's 'Pencil of Nature' in a manner that is entirely new. It has also, by making instantly available as well as permanent the scenes which Wedgwood and others had hoped to record in fixed form in their early apparatus, brought photography back full-circle, technologically equipped, to the place where it can satisfy the operational demand.

2 Man Takes to the Air

At first glance, successful powered flight during the first years of the 20th century was a direct result of the petrol engine, the comparatively small package which for the first time produced enough power per pound weight to keep a heavier-than-air machine aloft. In fact, it was the outcome of something more complicated.

Men had dreamed of flight since they first watched and envied the birds, wheeling and soaring with a freedom denied to the earthbound; since earliest times the more adventurous

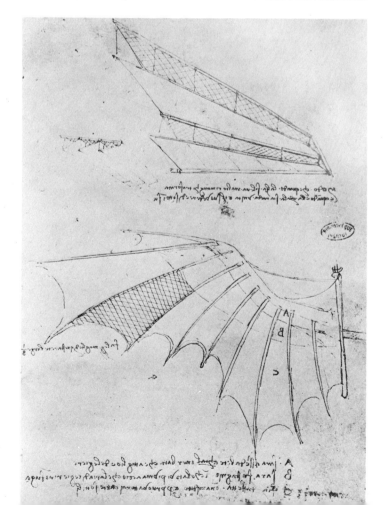

Diagram of ribbed wing, partly covered by silk, by Leonardo da Vinci, about 1486–90

had tried to make the dream come true. Icarus, building wings of feathers cemented with wax but flying so close to the sun that the wax melted, was merely one legend handed down the years and epitomizing the brave men who had leaped from high towers with contraptions strapped to their backs but failed to fly. These adventurers were paralleled by thinkers such as Roger Bacon and Leonardo da Vinci who with greater or lesser success studied the birds, started to work out the principles of flight, and thought up imaginary schemes for translating principles into practice.

The details of these would-be aeronauts are scanty in the extreme. Myth and near-myth are mixed with fantasy. Soldiers quickly grasp how aircraft can be used for bombardment. The physicist Robert Hooke provides a passing reference to the principle of the helicopter. The Swede Emanuel Swedenborg speculates on the possibility of a flying machine. Men continue to watch the birds, and a few of them make models which they hope will imitate flight. Yet there are few links between thought and experiment. In many ways they can be compared to the isolated mountaineering ascents made by a few enthusiasts in the Middle Ages, burning up brightly for only a short while before sputtering out. Not until the latter half of the 18th century does there begin one line of development which was to carry on, without break, towards manned flight more than a century later.

The line was started by the Montgolfier brothers, Joseph Michel and Jacques-Étienne. Intrigued by the idea of Joseph Priestley's 'inflammable air' – later called hydrogen – the Montgolfiers decided to use the gas to raise an airship. The plan failed. But a few years later, on 21 November 1783 the Montgolfiers were in Paris, standing in the gardens of the Royal Château de la Muette in the Bois de Boulogne, watching the inflation with hot air of their giant blue and gold balloon, 50 feet around, 85 feet high. The two men with them, a young doctor, Pilâtre de Rozier, and an infantry major, the Marquis d'Arlandes, climbed into the round passenger car held beneath the airship. A few minutes before two o'clock the ropes were cast off and the balloon, filled by hot air from a fire-grate on which a mixture of wool and straw was burning, sailed up into the Paris skies carrying the world's first aeronauts.

During the next hundred years many men followed the intrepid doctor and major. Balloon ascents in Britain and the United States soon became popular. In 1785 the English Channel was crossed and in 1804 a manned balloon reached a height of 23,000 feet. First hydrogen and then coal gas were used to give lifting power, and both provided greater control

Jean-Pierre Blanchard's balloon crossing the English Channel, 7 January 1785

Mr Blanchard accompagné de Mr Jefferies est parti de Douvres à 1 heure precise, il toucha la terre aux environs de Blanay qui est située entre Calais et Boulogne. C'est le premier qui jouit de l'honneur d'avoir franchi dans un Aerostat le Détroit qui sépare la France et l'Angleterre. Ce fut le vendredi 7 de Janvier 1785 qu'il partit traversa la mer et arriva à 3 heures sur les Côtes de la Picardie, laissant Calais à une lieue sur la gauche. Il prit terre 3 quarts d'heures après à 2 lieues et demie du rivage ou il fut reçu dans le Château de Mr d'Honnincton fils. Le même soir après souper les Voyageurs furent conduits à Calais dans une

Left Balloon contest at Hurlingham 15 July 1912

Right Pilâtre de Rozier and the Marquis d'Arlandes make the first air voyage in history beneath a hot-air balloon sent up from the Château de la Muette in the Bois de Boulogne on 21 November 1783. They travelled the five miles to Paris and landed without injury.

than the uncertainties of a fire. Meteorological records began to be taken among the clouds. Methods of releasing gas from the balloon to make it sink, or dumping ballast to make it rise, were developed. These advances took some of the dare-devil adventure out of ballooning. Ladies made ascents and during the 1800s ballooning became an almost popular sport. Thus when powered flight in heavier-than-air machines became a possibility at the beginning of the 20th century some of the psychological barriers in the competition with birds had already been broken down.

Even so, the balloon was still at the mercy of the winds. It went only where they blew, and it was to alter this state of affairs that men began to experiment with the idea of attaching power units to the lighter-than-air vehicles. Earliest on the scene was Henri Giffard who in 1852 constructed the first genuine 'airship', 'dirigible' or 'controlled balloon' as the machines were later to be variously called. Giffard powered his craft with a steam engine. He was followed, two decades on, by P. Haelin whose airship was driven by a gas engine. Ten years later there came Gaston Tissandier whose slim contrivance, more than 90 feet long, was driven through the air by a screw-propeller driven by a battery-run four-speed electric motor. And in 1896 the German Dr Wolfert used a Daimler internal combustion engine to drive his airship.

From the start it was realized that if a lighter-than-air craft was to be steered through the air, then the circular shape of the balloon would have to be abandoned. During the second half of the 19th century the airship therefore evolved into a long cylinder, the shape of the Zeppelin which was to win notoriety in the First World War and to remain the typical airship shape until the story of the craft was abruptly halted, if not finally killed, by a series of disasters during the 1920s and 1930s.

THE LONDON TO MANCHESTER FLIGHT
OVER THE LONDON & NORTH WESTERN RAILWAY

Left above An artist's impression of the 'Aerial Steam Carriage', whose designs were prepared by W. S. Henson in 1842. The model for it was unsuccessful when tested five years later.
Left below Louis Paulhan flying a Henry Farman biplane over the London and North Western Railway during the London–Manchester Air Race in April, 1910

Right The German zeppelin 'Viktoria Luise' over Kiel Harbour in 1912

Balloons and then airships carried men up into the clouds, and above them. They helped dispel the fear of the unknown which had so constantly been leaning over the shoulder of the first aeronauts. What they did not do was tell men so very much more about the principles of flight which birds used unconsciously and which men would also have to use if they were to fly as and when they wished, rather than with the by-your-leave of the winds.

A great many of these principles had in fact been discovered by one of the geniuses of the 19th century, a man whose real importance has been revealed only during the last few decades. He was Sir George Cayley, a Yorkshire baronet born in 1773 and fascinated ten years later by the story of Montgolfier's flight. Cayley's practical achievements were extraordinary. He built and flew a man-carrying glider, suggested that an internal combustion engine might be the ideal power-unit for aircraft, designed an elementary under-carriage, and used models to test his theoretical ideas.

Even more important – or at least potentially important – he appreciated the basic requirements of heavier-than-air flight. Cayley realized that before a heavier-than-air machine could become airborne it would have to be drawn or thrust forward so that there was a movement of air across an aero-foil or wing; furthermore, this would have to be of such a shape that the airflow across its upper and lower surfaces would create different pressures above and below and thereby

Sir George Cayley's man-carrying glider ('governable parachute') shown in *Mechanics Magazine*, September 1852

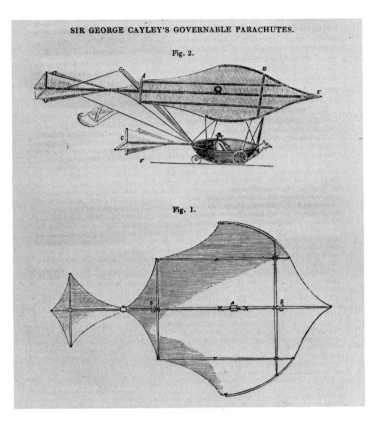

SIR GEORGE CAYLEY'S GOVERNABLE PARACHUTES.

Fig. 2.

Fig. 1.

produce 'lift', the component of the aerodynamic forces which supports an aircraft in flight. Cayley left a sketch showing a single-wing glider on which the lines of lift, thrust and drag, the last being the aircraft's resistance to movement through the air, were all marked.

During the early 1850s at least one and possibly two of Cayley's heavier-than-air gliders took people aloft, the 'lift' being created when the gliders were towed against a slight wind. The first person to be airborne in this heavier-than-air machine was a young and unidentified boy. The second was Cayley's coachman who is reported, possibly apocryphally, to have said after he landed: 'Sir George, I wish to give notice. I was hired to drive, not to fly.'

Cayley died in 1857, before his ideas for a mechanically-propelled aircraft could be tested. But they had already been taken one step further in theory by W. S. Henson – who as early as 1842 had designed an 'aerial steam carriage', a model of which failed to fly five years afterwards – and later by his colleague John Stringfellow. Henson's craft had more than one feature of aircraft to come. His main wing had the cambered profile which it was already known should produce greater lift than a flat surface, while a tail wing with horizontal

and vertical surfaces was similar to that on conventional aircraft two-thirds of a century later. Stringfellow, having built his own monoplane, then constructed a model which followed Cayley's principle of utilizing as great a wing-surface as possible, a triplane whose design did much to influence later inventors.

The model of John Stringfellow's monoplane, the predecessor of his triplane which influenced later inventors

Henson and Stringfellow, like many would-be aeronauts who succeeded them, were held back by one thing: the steam-engine, then the only means of getting power, was too heavy for the lift which it provided. This disadvantage was only overcome in 1894 when Sir Hiram Maxim used a 320-pound steam-engine to power a tethered test-rig plane with an all-up weight of about 8,000 pounds. As the lift achieved was 10,000 pounds the vital lift-to-weight ratio had been balanced in favour of flight. But Maxim's experiments were suspended. Whether or not his huge and ungainly craft would ever have become successfully airborne is very questionable. In any case the petrol engine was by this time waiting in the wings.

However, before the petrol engine took over, the initiative was to pass for a few years to the gliding enthusiasts, to the Lilienthal brothers in Germany, to Octave Chanute in the United States and to Percy Pilcher in Britain. This was as well.

Sir Hiram Maxim's steam-driven
aircraft, built in Kent in the 1890s

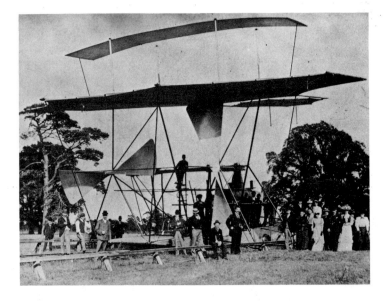

Despite the foundations which had been so well laid by
Cayley, the art or craft of aeronautics, the practical business of
keeping a craft stable in the air, was imperfectly understood
until the last decade of the 19th century. It is conceivable that
had the petrol engine been developed only a few years earlier
it might have been utilized not with the spectacular success of
the Wright brothers but in a series of disasters which would
have put back the development of flight a decade or more.
Here perhaps is one of the question-marks of history: if flight
had come too late to be given the spur or operational need
engendered by the First World War, what would its subsequent history have been?

The Lilienthals were the most important of the men who in
the closing years of the century helped to solve the practical
problems of stable flight. They came from Anklam, a small
town on the huge plain that stretches north of Berlin, only a
few miles inland from the Baltic and a staging post for the
thousands of storks who every spring would arrive from their
African homes for a long summer visit. The storks left in the
autumn, circling in scores above the roof-tops, rising higher
and higher until the whole flock would at last wheel and turn
south for Africa.

It was in studying the storks that the Lilienthal boys
learned one of their first lessons about flight. 'It was obvious,'
Gustav later wrote in describing how he and his brother had
tried to approach the birds in the meadows beyond the town,
'that it was easier to rise against the wind than with the wind,
because without some compelling cause the shy bird would
not advance towards us.'

In an effort to emulate the storks the Lilienthals built their own wings, six foot by three foot affairs which they hoped would make them airborne as they ran downhill. They failed, as they failed again a few years later in a more ambitious attempt to fly with home-made wings. Only in the 1870s, when they had started work in Berlin, Otto Lilienthal as an engineer, his brother Gustav as a small businessman, did the brothers build their first real flying machine. This had three pairs of wings; all could be moved up and down by an operator pedalling bicycle-wise. In addition, the contraption incorporated an ingenious device which enabled air to pass through the wings on the upstroke but arrested it on the down-beat. Perhaps most important of all, the Lilienthals supported their machine by rope and pulley and found that with the aid of only 40 pounds at the other end of the rope they could raise the 180-pound weight of their loaded machine by energetic pedalling. This was a scientific answer to the amount of lift required – even though it seemed to rule out any hope that man could ever fly by his own unaided efforts.

This first, and unsuccessful, phase of their efforts was ended by the Franco-Prussian War. The second, which covered the building of further wing-beating flying machines, was no more successful. One machine, whose wings were moved by spiral springs, was launched from a fourth-floor window down an inclined plane. Another had wings built in as close facsimile as could be to an actual bird's wing. 'They were moved partly by springs, partly by steam power,' Otto later wrote. 'We succeeded in making them fly freely at various speeds, but we did not succeed in establishing what we really wanted. We could not prove that forward flight saves work.'

Both men were now approaching middle age. Then they separated, Gustav emigrating to Australia and not returning to Germany until 1886. But both continued to think about flying. The permanent refusal of the born inventor to accept failure kept nagging away at them. On the ship to Australia Gustav had studied the albatross, marvelling at its skill in gliding through the rigging with only an inch or two to spare. In Germany, Otto had continued to study the storks, 'our constant models' as he called them, and had started to keep the birds as pets.

And now, as the 1890s approached, the two brothers reunited and began their decisive work. In 1889 they published what was to become one of the most important of all books on flying, *Bird-flight as the Basis of Aviation*. The titles of its chapters – *The Force Which Lifts the Bird in Flight*, *The Energy Required for Wing Motion*, and *The Wings Considered as Levers* – indicate its nature. The Lilienthals had realized one thing: that although man could not produce enough lift by beating wings with his own efforts, he could run or jump into a headwind and create enough lift on a pair of stationary wings to get him off the ground. Once in the air, he might be able to keep head-on into the wind and continue gaining height; lose it by turning out of the wind; then gain it again by turning into it once again.

Some of the first experiments with this new technique were made with a 40-pound wing of more than 100 square feet strapped to Otto's back. With this he would run along an inclined board and leap off the end into the air. 'King of the air in calm weather,' was how he described the state of the art after some hundreds of experiments.

But this was only one stage. Both men were now comparatively well-off. So much so that they were able to have a special hill built for their experiments at the Reinersdorfer Brickworks outside Berlin. Fifty feet high, the hill was crowned by the shed in which the brothers kept their wings, and by experimenting here when the wind was strong enough they found that they could become airborne for as much as 100 yards.

The next move came in 1895. In that year the Lilienthals moved out to the Rhinow Hills whose heather-broken slopes rise for 250 feet near the little town of Rathenau on the River Havel. Here improved versions of their gliders – for the early wings soon developed into something identifiable as such – did not merely become airborne. They flew 250 feet, 500 feet, eventually more than 1,000 feet. The brothers stayed in the air, under control, for as long as a quarter of a minute and when the air currents were right they were even taken up higher than their launching-point. Man was now 'flying' for the first time in the heavier-than-air machine.

Otto Lilienthal, immaculately-clad in white knicker-bockers, controlled his machines mainly by swinging his body from side to side, changing the glider's centre of gravity and, thereby, the effect on it of the headwind. This primitive method was eventually improved. There was, for instance, a form of crude elevator, to which Lilienthal was attached by a harness. By lowering his head, he could raise the elevator and cause the plane to sink. Neither was this all. 'I am now engaged in building an apparatus in which the position of the wings can be changed during flight in such a way that the balance is not affected by changing the position of the centre of gravity of the body,' he wrote in April 1896. 'In my opinion this means considerable progress, as it will increase the

One of the last flights of Otto Lilienthal, made in 1895

safety. This will probably cause me to give up the double sailing surface as it will do away with the reason for adopting it.'

By this time the Lilienthals had shown that manned flight was possible, given the movement of air across an aerofoil. So far the flyer depended entirely on the winds, but the petrol engine was now beginning to offer the chance of an aircraft being pushed or pulled through the still air – a process which would of itself generate lift since it was immaterial whether the air was moving over the aerofoil or the aerofoil was moving through the air.

Otto Lilienthal was in fact considering the addition of an engine when, in August 1896, he made his last flight. Once again, he sailed out from his launching site on the Rhinow

Hills. But when the wind dropped the glider did not, as usual, sink gradually; for some reason that was never discovered it plunged to the ground. Lilienthal died from his injuries the following day, after significant last words: 'Sacrifices must be made.'

In England Percy Pilcher, who was in correspondence with the Lilienthals, made a number of successful gliding flights, developing his machine by the addition of tail plane and undercarriage until it began to look like the early powered aircraft which were to come a decade or more later. In the latter half of the 1890s he was, like the Lilienthals, preparing to add a petrol engine. Then in 1899, having been towed off the ground by a team of horses near Market Harborough, Pilcher crashed and was killed.

Meanwhile in America Octave Chanute, a successful railway engineer, was also experimenting. Like Lilienthal, whose designs formed the basis of his early gliders, Chanute became convinced that movement of the body was no way in which to alter the aerodynamic characteristics of an aircraft; instead, he proposed wing-warping, changing the shape or camber of the wing by pulling on wires or strings. Chanute, who was in his 60s, flew only rarely but in 1896 and 1897 his colleagues made more than 1,000 successful glider flights from a launching site outside Chicago.

Thus in the final years of the century only one thing was needed for powered flight: a successful marriage between the glider and a power-pack that would produce sufficient lift for its weight. This was to be consummated by the Wright brothers, two young men from Dayton, Ohio, who as the 20th century approached prepared for their appointment with history.

Octave Chanute's 1896 glider being tested on the shore of Lake Michigan with A. M. Herring, a fellow engineer, as pilot

Wilbur Wright was born in 1867, his brother Orville four years later. They were of the pioneering American generation, ready and able to turn their hand to anything. Orville bought a printing press and started his own business while still in his teens. His brother, not to be outdone, launched his own weekly paper and the following year Orville, going still one better, started a daily paper with a third brother. Yet a third newspaper was later published by the family who shortly afterwards started the Wright Cycle Company and devised and put on the market the 'Van Cleve' bicycle, named after one of their mother's ancestors who had arrived in America two hundred years previously.

What lines this irrepressibly fecund family might have followed but for the attraction of flight no one can tell. But the catalyst came in 1896 with the death of Otto Lilienthal. News of the accident arrived on the telegraph which served the Wrights' papers. Then Wilbur, learning that Lilienthal's success had started with his study of bird-flight, took down from the shelves of his home library a copy of *Animal Mechanism*. Written by the Professor Marey whose photographic gun had first revealed the wing-movements of gulls, *Animal Mechanism* stimulated the Wrights to ask the age-old question: if a bird's body can be supported by wings, why cannot a man's?

For three years they studied all the information they could lay their hands on. Then they wrote to the Smithsonian Institute in Washington, which they found was also scientifically investigating the possibilities of flight, and were put in touch with its Secretary, Samuel Langley, whose steam-powered models were already making flights of more than three-quarters of a mile. But Langley, who can claim the first sustained powered flight with *un*manned heavier-than-air machines, was unable to scale up his work before the Wrights had leap-frogged into the lead.

The two brothers quickly saw that better control in the air should be achieved before the problem of lift-to-weight ratio was successfully tackled. Like the Lilienthals, they turned to the birds. But whereas it was storks who had given the Germans the essential clue to 'lift', it was the humble pigeon who suggested to the Wrights the form of aeronautical control which Otto Lilienthal was possibly contemplating at the time of his death. Pigeons, the two brothers noticed, would sometimes oscillate their bodies rapidly from side to side, tilting one wing up and another down, then rapidly reversing the process. 'These lateral tiltings first one way and then the other, were repeated four or five times rapidly,' Wilbur later said; 'so

The Wright brothers' no. 2 glider
at the Kill Devil Hills in 1901

rapidly, in fact, as to indicate that some other force than gravity was at work. The method of drawing in one wing or the other, as described by Chanute and Louis Mouillard, was, of course, dependent in principle on the action of gravity, but it seemed certain that these alternate tiltings of the pigeon were more rapid than gravity would cause, especially in view of the fact that we could not detect any drawing-in first of one wing and then of another.'

They concluded that pigeons exercised control by using the dynamic reactions of the air rather than by shifting the centre of gravity. At first they proposed copying this by the use of what were later called ailerons, trailing flaps on the wings which could be raised or lowered by wires. As this was found to be too mechanically difficult in the current state of the art, they investigated wing-warping, as Chanute was also investigating it.

The method was tested on a model kite and found to work.

The next step was to try it out on a man-carrying craft, an experiment which the Wrights realized would demand a strong headwind if sufficient lift were to be created. Their chosen site, picked after taking advice from the US Weather Bureau, was on the coast adjoining Kitty Hawk, an isolated fishing-village standing on a long sandy spit thrusting into the Atlantic from the mainland of North Carolina. Kitty Hawk was some 800 miles from the Wrights' home in Ohio, and their first journey took them a week during which a railway trip was followed by a steamer-voyage, followed by a small-boat trip, followed by a four-mile walk.

To the lonely testing-ground on the sandhills the brothers brought in the summer of 1900 the sections of their man-carrying glider which they then assembled on the spot. The results were satisfying if unspectacular. 'These experiments,' Wilbur later said of the flights, 'constituted the first instance in the history of the world that wings adjustable to different angles of incidence on the right and left sides had been used in attempting to control the balance of an aeroplane. We had functionally used them both when flying at the end of a rope and also in free flight.'

The following year they were back again, and this time they were visited at Kitty Hawk by Octave Chanute. They glided more than 300 feet and they made numerous alterations to the machine which was kept in a small wooden hangar. But their attempts to stabilize the craft were less successful than the previous year and they returned home disillusioned. 'When we left Kitty Hawk at the end of 1901,' Wilbur later said, 'we doubted that we would ever resume our experiments. Although we had broken the record for distance in gliding, so far as any actual figures had been published, and although Mr Chanute, who was present for part of the time, assured us that our results were better than had ever before been attained, yet when we looked at the time and money which we had expended, and considered the progress made and the distance yet to go, we considered our experiments a failure. At this time I made the prediction that men would some time fly, but that it would not be within our lifetime.'

But now luck took a hand. Or, more accurately, a chance suggestion came at the right moment of technological progress; the suggestion was made, moreover, to men who despite their apparent pessimism, still nourished that reluctance to accept defeat which is the hallmark of the pioneer down the ages.

Chanute proposed that Wilbur should lecture on his problems to the Western Society of Engineers in Chicago.

Wilbur agreed, somewhat reluctantly, but decided that he would first have to check many facts and figures. To carry out the checking he built in his Dayton workshop one of the first wind tunnels to be built in the United States, six feet long, only 16 by 16 inches in section, and equipped with various devices for holding different aerofoils in the stream of air which could be pumped through it.

In this apparatus the Wrights now tested more than 200 different kinds of aerofoil, keeping accurate results of exactly what happened.

And once the two brothers had accumulated their long columns of figures showing how different shapes reacted to different conditions, one thing became obvious: they had to test their fresh information. Thus it was back once more to Kitty Hawk, on its windswept spit of land where the US National Monument now stands.

They arrived at their former camp-site on 25 August. With them, prepared for assembly, were the parts of a biplane 32 feet from wing-tip to wing-tip. This glider – for they had not yet tackled the problem of power – had a front rudder, a vertical tail plane consisting of two parallel sections, and a wing-warping device which was operated through a harness worn by the pilot.

Throughout September and October the craft was dragged up one of three hills on the dunes – 30-foot Little Hill, 60-foot West Hill or the 100-foot Big Hill. At the top they would wait until the wind blew strongly enough. Then the brother holding down the plane would let go and the glider would sail into the wind, gaining height as it did so. More than 700 flights were successfully made. More important, the wing-warping mechanism did give better control than before.

The Wrights had, moreover, built in one major innovation before they left Kitty Hawk in the autumn. They had replaced the double tail-fin by a single fin which could be turned left or right as the wing-warping mechanism was operated. Previously, wing-warping had produced its own difficulties, but the Wrights now found that if the fin was moved as one of the wings was warped, then the result was to take the glider round left or right in a smooth turn. They had therefore not merely solved the problem of balance in the air but the riddle of how to turn away from the headwind, left or right.

These experiments of the late summer and autumn of 1902 marked a turning-point. Previously, it is clear, the brothers had looked on their flights as an adventurous hobby. Now, out of the future, they saw the beckoning shadow of man piloting himself through Tennyson's central blue. They saw also the potentials of the dream and quickly applied for a patent which covered their linking of wing-warping and rudder control.

Between the autumn of 1902 and the autumn of the following year the Wrights hoped to do two things. They had to design the right kind of propeller and they hoped to find a suitable engine to power it. Eventually, they had to design the engine as well. The propellers, two of which were fitted to the plane they took to Kitty Hawk in the autumn of 1903, were long, slim, and of a kind totally different from the marine propellers with which engineers were alone familiar. These two propellers, mounted behind a double wing and driven by two chains, one of which was crossed so that the propellers revolved in different directions, were powered by a four-cylinder petrol engine based on the single-cylinder gas engine which they had been using to pump air through their wind tunnel. The petrol was vaporized as it passed over the heated water-jacket, and the only way of controlling the engine speed was by adjusting the ignition timing, a job which obviously had to be done before take-off. Thus the engine was set 'by guess and by God' and the only change that happened later was due to pre-heating of the inlet air by the water-jacket which reduced the initial output of the engine from about 12 horse-power to about 9.

It was late in September before the Wrights arrived at Kitty Hawk, with their new machine and their 1902, un-powered, version which they assembled first and used for a number of test glides. From the start, nearly everything seems to have gone wrong. There was a 75-mph gale. Some of the shafting on the powered plane broke during ground tests and had to be replaced. It was December before the brothers were able to make the final adjustments on the powered craft and then, when they had hoped to make their first flight with it, the headwind which they still felt was necessary died away to a complete calm.

Not until 15 December was everything ready. The craft was held back on the long launching track as the engine was revved up. Then it was released. It rose for some 15 feet. Then the nose dropped – because, as the pilot Wilbur quickly realized, he had first brought the nose up too quickly and the aircraft had then developed what would now be called a stall.

Three days were needed to make the necessary repairs and it was the morning of December 17 before the brothers hauled out their machine and assembled the 60-foot wooden launching rail. There was only a week to go to Christmas Eve and with a lengthy journey back home they were greatly tempted to hold over further effort until the coming year.

Orville Wright making the first powered, sustained and controlled flight in history, on 17 December 1903

Since Wilbur had been at the controls three days previously it was Orville who now lay horizontally on the lower wing as the engine was revved up and the plane held back by a taut checkwire. Around the track which pointed straight into a 25-mph wind there were half a dozen spectators from the nearby fishing hamlet. Further off a few coastguards looked through their glasses and no doubt wondered what was to come next.

At about 10.30 Orville slipped the restraining wire and the 'Flyer' as it had been christened shot forward down the wooden rail. The aircraft had gone some 40 feet when it eased itself up from the rail and slowly rose to a height of about 10 feet. Orville kept it on course, flying into the wind at a ground speed of about 10 mph.

This first powered, sustained and controlled flight lasted a mere 12 seconds and covered about 120 feet. Then the aircraft was dragged back to the track, Wilbur lay at the controls, and the 'Flyer' made a second flight, going slightly farther this time. Both brothers made further flights that morning, the final one lasting nearly a minute and covering more than 800 feet.

Then, just about mid-day and as they and their helpers

Above Santos-Dumont flying his
14-bis in France in 1906

Below S. F. Cody in his Cody
Biplane, 1912

were discussing the next move, a sudden gust of wind turned
over the craft. Damage was not severe but it was enough to
persuade the Wrights that enough was enough; to pack up and
set out two days later for Dayton.

Nevertheless, man had flown at last under his own power
and control. The Wrights, confident now that they were on
the road to success, tried for good business reasons to make
little of the fact for the time being. But the story leaked out
and by the beginning of 1904 it was clear that the previously
impossible had been made possible.

The repercussions of Kitty Hawk were to be world-wide
but they did not come immediately. Five months after the
Wrights had been granted their patent in 1906, Alberto
Santos-Dumont, the rich and colourful Brazilian living in

Paris, made the first powered flight in Europe with his extraordinary '14-bis', an aircraft resembling a collection of box-kites strung together more by chance than design. The following year Henry Farman, artist turned car-racer turned aeronaut, began flying the first of the truly successful biplanes built by the Voisin brothers. Louis Blériot, preparing for his own appointment with history, flew the predecessor of the monoplane in which he was to cross the Channel two years later. Even so, in Europe as well as in the United States, experiments continued much as though the Wrights had not given a clear lead to the way that must be followed.

All this was dramatically changed after 1908. In that year the Wrights came to Europe and had soon flown in France, Germany and Italy. They flew for up to two and a half hours at Pau, in the French Pyrenees, and they began to train French pilots to fly the Wright aircraft that the Government was by this time buying. Later in the year Wilbur Wright flew publicly in France and his brother flew in public in the United States. In England, S. F. Cody flew at Farnborough the British Army Aeroplane No. 1, while numbers of passengers had flown for the first time in the two-seaters that the Wrights were now building.

The next year, 1909, Blériot flew the Channel, Orville Wright flew at more than 1,000 feet, and the world's first aviation meeting was held outside Rheims. Here 23 planes were airborne and Farman stayed in the air for more than three hours during which he covered more than 100 miles.

Within two years it had become clear that flying was no flash-in-the-pan development but a new method of transport with immense, if ominous, possibilities. Little time remained before the outbreak of the First World War gave its formidable impetus to the development of aircraft.

During those years, flying moved out of the experimental stage into that of the near-sporting. The planes themselves could now be flown with predictable results and the experiments lay rather in the extension of their use. The first seaplane was flown successfully, and then the first amphibian. In the United States the first take-off and landing was made from the deck of a ship. Men flew over the Alps and with the use of the first rudimentary air-to-ground radio there came the possibility of wider knowledge about the weather conditions which were now becoming an important limitation of an aircraft's use. In Britain the Short brothers built the first craft that could fly under the power of either of its two engines, the Gnome rotary power units which were themselves a considerable advance on their predecessors. In Russia Igor Sikorsky,

A Hawker Siddeley Harrier vertical take-off and landing multi-purpose combat aircraft landing on the supply ship Green Rover, moored in the Thames at Greenwich in 1971

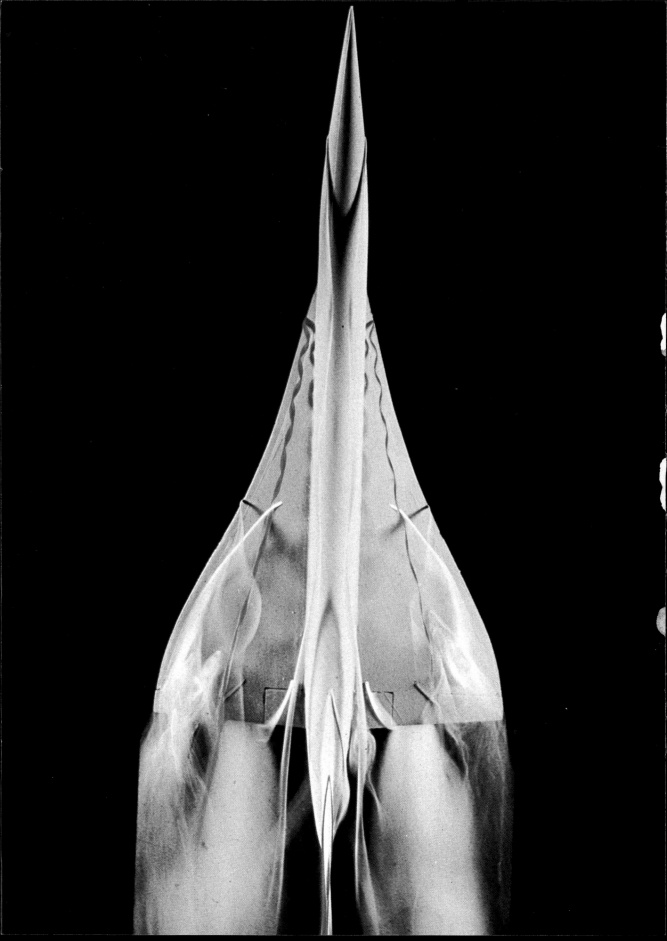

A scale-model of the Concorde undergoing a water-tunnel test in the laboratories of the French Office National d'Études et de Recherches Aérospatiales. Airflow characteristics are indicated by confetti-like streamers caused by dye released into the water.

later to become famous for his development of the helicopter, produced what was for those days a giant biplane. With a 92-foot wing-span it had the distinction of being the first aircraft with an enclosed passenger cabin.

This period also saw the world's first monocoque fuselage, an omen of things to come. So far, fuselages had consisted basically of a skeleton of longitudinal wooden members, held together at intervals with transverse braces. On to this there was then added the covering of the fuselage, usually of canvas, but it was the skeleton alone which bore the strains and stresses of load-carrying. In the monocoque fuselage – first used in the Monocoque Deperdussin which in 1912 won the Gordon Bennett Cup – the skeleton was replaced by the wooden, or later metal, shell forming a single integral unit.

Such advances had steadily made flying a practical proposition during the first decade and more of the 20th century. The World War, which broke out in the summer of 1914, decisively altered the pace of this steady progress, as the Allies and the Central Powers both desperately struggled to win the mastery of the air without which, it was already being dimly seen, victory on the ground or on the oceans would only be temporary.

The changing roles of aircraft in war did much to govern the route which progress took. In the early days planes were used largely for reconnaissance – much as balloons had been used during the siege of Paris in 1870. This demanded aircraft which could be slow but which had to be relatively stable so that the observers had time in which to notice and record what they could see on the ground. The need for stability increased as photographic reconnaissance became more general and the photographers required a more stable platform from which they could operate.

Reconnaissance aircraft were soon being shot down, by ground fire and later by enemy aircraft whose armament at first consisted of little more than revolvers and sporting rifles. Thus there grew up a demand for aircraft which could fly faster; which had a higher operational ceiling and could keep above the range of accurate ground fire; and which had the increased rates of climb which enabled them to gain, with the minimum time, the higher positions which gave the advantage in air combat. While the demand for faster and more manoeuvrable aircraft was increasing, the development of bombing from the air called for planes whose first operational requirement was the carriage of heavy loads.

These varying demands on aircraft-designers and aircraft-

The first passenger aircraft with enclosed cabin, the Sikorsky Grand, built in Russia in 1913

builders were in general met by two complementary lines of research. In Britain at the National Physical Laboratory and the Royal Aircraft Factory at Farnborough, in Germany at the aeronautical research institute at Göttingen, scientists probed the fundamentals of aerodynamics, producing more efficient wing-sections, one of the most important keys to an aircraft's efficiency, and discovering in other ways how the maximum use could be made of the power available from improved aircraft engines. Engineering research into the problem of extracting more power from less weight was the second factor which helped to give temporary advantage in the air, first to one side and then to the other.

During the war many daring experiments were made. As early as May 1916, a Bristol 'Scout' was launched from another plane in mid-air. In the United States a radio-guided flying bomb was developed which could automatically be directed on to its target. In Russia, Igor Sikorsky successfully designed the huge Ilya Mourametz bomber, powered by four engines each of 100 horse-power, carrying a bomb-load of 600 pounds, and serviced by a crew of up to 16 men who could carry out minor repairs while the giant plane was in flight.

In most of these developments, designers among the Allies

and among the Central Powers pushed ahead at much the same pace. But the Germans succeeded in gaining one major advantage for a considerable while and also in introducing a virtually new type of aircraft construction which was to have great repercussions when the war was over. The advantage came from the Fokker synchronizing gear, designed by a Dutchman and introduced by the Germans. Once aerial fighting became common it was clear that the ideal would be to have a machine-gun fitted along the main axis of an aircraft. All a pilot would then have to do would be to aim the aircraft at the enemy and press the trigger. At least, that would be the case were it not for the propeller. This seemed to rule out that type of armament for the 'tractor' plane, in which the propeller was at the front of the aircraft, and limit its use to the less efficient 'pusher' type in which the propeller was at the back. Anthony Fokker had a solution. 'The obvious thing to do was to make the propeller shoot the gun, instead of trying to shoot the bullets through the propeller,' he said. The outcome was the interruptor gear, an early crude version of which was used in a French aircraft captured by the Germans, which synchronized the firing with the swiftly-turning propeller and gave the Germans a considerable advantage until the Allies, recovering an interruptor gear from a crashed German aircraft, were able to devise something similar.

The other development pioneered by the Germans was to have a much longer-lasting effect. Thus far, a majority of aircraft conformed to a pattern. They were built largely of wood and canvas. From their central fuselage there spread a pair of wings strutted and braced with wire and wood to give them the necessary rigidity. They looked, and they were, fragile contraptions which tore and broke with little provocation. Some aircraft, such as Blériot's classic No. XI, had boasted a single wing, but they too gave the impression of being held together largely by glue and good faith.

Now the pattern was dramatically altered by the perseverance of one man, pushing against the conservative opinion of his Government. This time it was the German Government. The man was Professor Hugo Junkers, a Rhineland engineer whose successful business had brought him the money for aeronautical research. Early in 1910 Junkers had filed a patent for a 'flying wing' which would house engine, fuel, payload and crew. It was never built but five years later it provided the key to a revolutionary aircraft. This was the J1, a plane with a single cantilevered wing – a wing, that is, supported at one end only, and without any external bracing. The whole aircraft was, moreover, built entirely of metal. The initial plan had

Experimental Junkers-built iron
wing being tested at the Junkers
factory, July 1915

been to use aluminium, but when it was found impossible to
release supplies of the scarce material Junkers used sheet iron
to cover the framework of iron tubing. The 'Tin Donkey' flew
for the first time in December 1915, the predecessor of a long
line of all-metal monoplanes. Later the sheet iron gave way to
ribbed duralumin, the hallmark of the Junkers for years to
come.

The struggle to win mastery of the air during the First
World War dramatically speeded up the evolution of aircraft.
In 1914 top speeds were about 80 mph and by the end of the
war they had almost doubled. The practical ceiling for aircraft
was raised from 7,000 feet to nearly 30,000 feet. Engines that
weighed about 4 pounds per horsepower in 1914 had been
fined down to weights of less than half that by 1918, while
wing-loadings, which averaged about 4 pounds to the square
inch when war broke out had roughly doubled by 1918. In
addition the very number of men who flew during the war
years, or who were brought into direct contact with aircraft,
did much to transform flying from the rarity of pre-war days
to the near-commonplace of the 1920s. After all, there had
been only about 300 British Service aircraft in existence in
1914. When the war ended there were more than 22,000.

The main repercussions of the aeronautical advances spurred
on by the war were to be felt on civilian flying during the next
two decades. Speed, ceiling, range, carrying capacity, comfort

and safety were all increased and utilized by the civilian airlines which now sprang up. Radio began to diminish the hazards of long-distance navigation. The Atlantic was flown for the first time. Regular air services between the capitals of the world became commonplace and as commercial airports were set up on the fringes of the big cities flying began to assume the shape and the importance which it occupies today.

Even so, one of the most significant post-war pointers to the future of air power concerned the Services. It came in 1921 when, in tests off the coast of the United States, Martin bombers sank the 22,800-ton German battleship *Ostfriesland*, which had been brought there for the experiment. Although the Admirals were reluctant to admit the fact, the world's navies would no longer have the freedom of the seas unless they first gained mastery of the air – a lesson which was to be rammed home off the coast of Norway in the spring of 1940 and less than two years after that when the great battleships *Prince of Wales* and *Repulse* were sunk with ease by Japanese planes off the coast of Malaya.

The twenty years between the two World Wars witnessed the increasing threat from the bomber. It saw also the rise and fall of the airship, the civilian version of the Zeppelins which had raided London between 1914 and 1918. As early as 1919 the British R34 made a double crossing of the Atlantic, suggesting that these vast cylindrical ships of the air might well offer a new and civilized means of air travel. But the destruction of the R34 two years later, when she broke up over the city of Hull with the loss of more than 40 lives, was an omen of things to come. The Graf Zeppelin made its first passenger carrying transatlantic flight in 1928 and both Britain and Germany had ambitious plans. But in 1930 the huge British R101 crashed in France on a planned flight to Egypt and India with the loss of nearly 50 dead. It was the first of a succession of airship disasters, and work on her sister-vessel, the R100, was abandoned. Inflammable hydrogen, the gas used to lift airships, was already being replaced by the far safer helium, but the series of tragedies, culminating in the destruction of the Hindenburg as she came in to her mooring mast in New Jersey in 1937, put paid to the world's airship plans. A third of a century later it seems possible that they may be revived.

The inter-war years also saw the practical introduction of rotorcraft. As with so many other ideas, this one can be traced back to Leonardo da Vinci, whose notebooks reveal that about 1500 he had envisaged an aerial craft with rotating wings which would give it lift. More than 300 years later the British inventor W. H. Phillips devised and built an unmanned model

The Hindenburg bursting into flames on preparing to land at Lakehurst, New Jersey, 6 May 1937

aircraft whose rotary blades were propelled by wing-tip steam-driven jets. Another half century passed before two separate inventors in France, and Igor Sikorsky in Russia, began to experiment with full-scale aircraft incorporating rotors.

Such aircraft are of two kinds. There is first the autogiro in which a conventional propeller is powered by a conventional engine. But the autogiro is also equipped with freely-rotating rotors mounted above the fuselage; as the propeller pulls the plane forward through the air, the impact of air on the rotors causes them to revolve and thus provide the necessary lift to take the plane off the ground. The helicopter is a more complicated affair although today a far more practical one. Here the rotor blades are revolved by the engine which is thus used directly to provide the necessary lift. Once the helicopter is airborne forward flight is achieved by varying the incidence to the air of the rotating blades. From the earliest days, one of the main problems with the helicopter was the torque reaction effect exerted by the rotors. The fuselage tended to twist in a direction opposite to that of the rotors and was counteracted, in the earliest machines, by a small propeller fitted to the end of the fuselage and so designed that its only job was to keep the craft on an even keel.

The pioneer of the autogiro was the Spaniard Juan de la Cierva whose main aim was to provide a safeguard against the stalling of aircraft at the low forward speeds of take-off and landing. Cierva's first autogiro was demonstrated in England in 1926 and was steadily developed during the next few years. It was soon overtaken by the progress of the helicopter.

Igor Sikorsky, whose giant bomber had been built in Russia from 1915 onwards, had constructed an experimental helicopter as early as 1910. Emigrating to the United States, he developed his ideas between the wars and by 1939 had produced his first successful helicopter. In Germany the Focke-Wulf company had been doing the same, and both the Allies and the Axis powers continued during the Second World War to improve an aircraft which could use a field of cricket-pitch size for take-off and landing. Today the helicopter runs shuttle-services into city centres, evacuates mountaineers from inaccessible places, and is even used as an industrial load-carrier from which heavy pieces of machinery can be winched down on to a construction site with the minimum of trouble; and has been evolved for Services into what is in practice a new military weapon. First developed as a light gad-fly of an aircraft, it is today something very much more – the Russians have a craft with twin rotors of 240 feet span, 200 feet long and capable of lifting a 34-ton payload.

The years between the wars saw a host of technological improvements. One was the use of geodetic construction for the building of aircraft fuselages. This is a basket-work or lattice-like structure of such a design that the compression loads induced in any member are braced by tension loads in crossing members. It had been used by Barnes Wallis to contain the gas-bags of the ill-fated R100, and was later used by him in the design of two British bombers, the Vickers Wellesley – the first aircraft in the world built entirely on the geodetic principle – and the Vickers Wellington.

The aircraft propeller was also revolutionized between the wars. From the earliest days of powered flight it had been realized that to gain the maximum efficiency from an engine the propeller which it turned would need to meet the air at one angle during take-off or landing, and at another angle during

steady flight. The engineering problems involved were very great and it was only in 1924 that two British designers, Dr Hele-Shaw and T. E. Beacham, working privately but with the help of Government funds, patented a variable-pitch propeller which could be adjusted to meet flight needs. A decade later means were devised of linking engine-revolutions with propeller-pitch, thus further improving the aeronautical efficiency of aircraft.

Another technical innovation was the use of slots to raise the efficiency of the wings. A quarter of a century earlier the Wrights had found that wing-warping, which increased the camber of the wing, also increased the craft's lift as well as enabling the pilot to guide it in the air. The principle had been developed by Henry Farman who provided the trailing edges of his wings with ailerons – or little wings – consisting of flaps which could be raised or lowered independently to give lateral control. For technical reasons these flaps were of comparatively little use on biplanes and although they were fitted on the SE4 biplane which was made at the Royal Aircraft Factory at Farnborough from 1914 onwards, they were not much liked by pilots.

Like many other aeronautical innovations, the idea of slotted aerofoils, through which air passed from the lower to the upper surface when the slots were open, came to more than one man at roughly the same time. Certainly a German pilot, G. V. Lachmann, thought of the idea in 1917 while recovering in hospital after a crash brought about by a stalling aircraft. Lachmann reasoned that during level flight air would pass across the upper and lower wing surfaces without passing through the slots. When, however, the nose of the aircraft went up in the first movement of a stall, wind would begin to pass through the slots and would have a counteracting effect. In England, workers at Handley-Page came to much the same conclusion after wind-tunnel tests of aerofoils, while in Germany Hugo Junkers also conceived the idea of slotted wings. They came into use during the 1920s, finally growing into a large family of types incorporating slots which were permanently open or could be closed either manually or automatically.

This particular increase in aerodynamic theory and practice was accompanied by the development of streamlining. Today, when it is widely appreciated that the smallest excrescence on a moving object will effect its movement through the air, the aircraft of the immediate post-war years have an extraordinarily shaggy look. As two experts have written, 'until the early 1930s designers lived split lives, especially in Europe, in

Above An illustration of geodetic construction: fuselage of the Wellington bomber

Below Wing construction showing aerofoils

one of which they recognized that the reduction of drag was the simplest way of making aeroplanes more efficient, while in the other they designed airplanes which were box-like in shape, hung about with such excrescences as fixed undercarriages and festooned with bracing wires. The wires might be of stream-line section, but this was virtually the sum of the genuflection made towards streamlining.' Only in the later 1920s – partly under the influence of the British aeronautical engineer, Professor, later Sir, Melvill Jones – did designers begin to give streamlining its due importance.

Among these was R. J. Mitchell, leader in the British efforts to win the Schneider Trophy and a good deal more besides. The race had first been flown in 1913 when the French winner averaged about 45 mph. By the time that the Italian Major Bernardi won the Trophy in 1926, the speed had crept up to nearly 250 mph. This victory faced the British with a problem since the Trophy was to be won outright by the first country to gain it three times in succession or four times in all – and the Italians had already won it in 1920 and 1921.

To the rescue there came Vickers–Supermarine of Southampton, and Mitchell, their chief engineer and designer. For the 1927 contest Mitchell designed the S5 which won the race at 281.65 mph. His S6 won the next race, two years later, at 328.63 mph and a development of this, the S6b, won the following contest in 1931 at 340.08 mph, thereby gaining the Trophy outright for Britain. The importance of this triumph was to be considerable. For one of the 1931 machines had flown at more than 400 mph, a feat which induced Air Marshal Dowding, then the Air Council's Member for Research and Development, to suggest that two British manufacturers should produce prototypes of different aircraft. Each should have the highest possible performance and should be able to take off not from water, as did the Schneider Trophy float-planes, but from the small airfields then in use. From Vickers there eventually came the Spitfire, a superb example of aero-dynamic knowledge wedded to engineering skill. From Hawker's there came Sydney Camm's Hurricane.

Both the Spitfire and the Hurricane exemplified the stream-lining, made possible by ingenious design, which was excep-tional for its time but which was to become commonplace after the Second World War. As in other spheres, the demands of war – or in this case the expected demands of the expected war – were to have a drastic effect on civilian practice.

The effects of the Second World War on aviation were naturally enough comparable in many ways to those of the 1914–18 war. Planes became faster. Their operational heights

Above The Supermarine section of the British team for the 1927 Schneider Trophy with the Supermarine S5. R. J. Mitchell, the chief designer of all the Schneider Trophy aircraft and of the prototype Spitfire, is fifth from the left in the front row.
Flight-Lieutenant Webster, winner of the 1927 trophy, is standing on the aircraft.
Below A Spitfire Mk XIV

were pushed up, one result of this being that pressurized cabins, only built in the later 1930s, had become commonplace by the end of the war. New metals were produced, new methods of manufacture employed. Yet despite the importance of the technological advances which so increased the efficiency of planes and the top performances of which they were capable, all were overshadowed by two almost self-contained developments. One was the coming of radar, the latest utilization of the radio-waves of the electro-magnetic spectrum, introduced as a device to give early warning of the approach of bombers but quickly spreading into a huge range of devices which revolutionized both long-distance navigation and the problems of landing in bad weather. The second device was the jet, the new form of propulsion which has transformed civilian flying from a sometimes bumpy journey 'below the weather' to the tea-table smoothness of flying in the stratosphere.

Only towards the end of the war did aircraft begin to utilize this innovation, as revolutionary as the all-metal construction with which Junkers had changed the face of flying 30 years before. In the first half of the 1940s all aircraft were still using the same basic method of moving a plane forward through the air that had been used by the Wright brothers almost half a century earlier. An internal combustion engine was used to turn a shaft which turned a propeller. The propeller might be a 'pusher', mounted behind the engine and wings, or a 'tractor' which was mounted in front of them, but in both cases the result was the same: the aircraft was moved forward through the air and this in turn created the necessary lift to make the craft airborne.

As aircraft flew higher it became increasingly clear that this system suffered from a double built-in disadvantage. For the higher the altitude, the less dense does the air become. One result is that the propeller finds it more difficult to 'bite' and its ability to move an aircraft forward is thus affected; in addition, the efficiency of the engine itself is affected by the lack of air. This second disadvantage can be counteracted by the fitting of a supercharger, which will supply the engine with air at a pressure higher than that through which it is moving. It also means increased weight, more complexity, and more things to go wrong.

The jet engine, whose basic principle had been known even to the Ancient Greeks, consists essentially of a chamber open at the forward end. A compressor draws air into the chamber and compresses it in one or more combustion chambers into which fuel is injected. The mixture of air and fuel is ignited; it burns; it expands and, since it is prevented from moving forward, is thrust out through the rear of the chamber, passing, as it does so, through a rear turbine which drives the compressor. The result of this violent ejection of burned fuel backwards is to drive the engine forwards. The movement is in no way governed by the density of the surrounding air, being simply an illustration of Newton's law of equal and opposite reaction.

The advantages of the jet were numerous and obvious. The engine was simpler in construction than the internal combustion engine. It could use a wider variety of fuels, and it produced no vibration, while the fact that no propeller was required in itself eliminated a number of design problems.

With all these things to be said for the jet, it is natural to ask why it had not appeared sooner on the scene. The answer is the simple one of technological limitation. The temperatures of the ejected gases are very great, and it was only during the years between the wars that the manufacture of special alloys made it possible to conceive of a practical jet engine. Then, as with many other revolutionary inventions dependent on technological advance – notably radio, radar and the use of nuclear energy – the possibility of utilizing it began to be investigated independently in a number of countries.

As early as 1920 Dr A. A. Griffith of the Royal Aircraft Establishment at Farnborough had proposed that a gas turbine of the kind finally utilized in the jet-engine might turn a propeller – an idea which evolved as the turbo-prop engine after the Second World War. The following year the Frenchman Charles Guillaume patented the design of a jet-engine, although no progress appears to have been made in developing it. A new theory of turbine design from Griffith in 1926 renewed interest in the possibilities of the jet and research work continued at Farnborough, although with only slight interest from the authorities. Meanwhile, and quite independently of Farnborough, Frank Whittle, a young Flight-Lieutenant in the Royal Air Force, was working on the same problem. In 1930 he patented with money from his own pocket, his own design for what was to be the prototype of the jet engine which has today almost totally taken over in the air from the internal combustion engine.

The essential simplicity of the Whittle engine was summed up in his own words at the time. 'Reciprocating engines are exhausted. They have hundreds of parts jerking to and fro, and they cannot be made more powerful without becoming too complicated. The engine of the future must produce 2,000 hp with one moving part: a spinning turbine and compressor.'

Even so, it was not until six years later that Whittle's idea

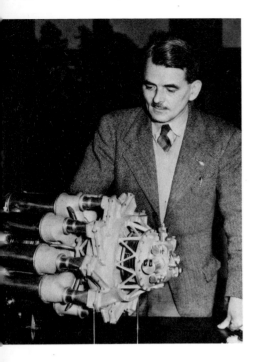

Air Commodore Sir Frank Whittle
with a model of his prototype jet
engine

began to be taken seriously by the authorities. Sir Henry
Tizard, then Chairman of the Government's Aeronautical
Research Committee, was the man who finally persuaded
Britain to pour into the necessary research the huge sums that
were needed. 'I knew it would cost a great deal of money,' he
said later; 'I knew that success was not certain; and yet I felt
that it was of great national importance to spend the money.'
As it was later written – 'to every Whittle his Tizard.'

By this time, with war only a few years away, the Germans
were also at work on the same idea. A jet-engine similar to
Whittle's was patented in 1935 by Hans von Ohain and two
years later Heinkel's began to develop it. Simultaneously a
turbo-jet programme was started by Junkers while the Italian
Caproni Company began to work on a pseudo-jet which used
a piston engine to operate a compressor.

By 1939 the British and the Germans were thus running
neck-and-neck in a race for use of an engine which with its
promise of increased speed and higher operational ceiling
might well give command of the air. The story is one of leap-
frogging records – the Germans putting the He176, powered by
a liquid fuel rocket, into the air in June 1939, following this two
months later with the He178, the world's first turbo-jet to fly.
The 178 used the Ohain engine that had first run on the test-
bench two years previously. The British followed in May 1941
with the test-flight of Whittle's jet, fitted to the experimental
Gloster E28/29. The next year the Germans put into the air
the remarkable Messerschmitt 262, powered by twin wing-
mounted jets which gave it a top speed, at 20,000 feet, of
540 mph and a service ceiling of 40,000 feet. It was followed
in 1943, by the Gloster Meteor, the production model of the
E28/29, and the British can claim to have beaten their
enemies to the post by getting the Meteor into squadron
service with the RAF before the Germans got the Me262 into
similar service with the Luftwaffe.

The jet-propelled Meteors were used effectively to combat
the German flying bombs launched against Britain during the
summer of 1944, their speed of 480 mph giving them the edge
over the robot-weapons which they shot down in numbers.
Despite this, the jet came too late to play any significant part in
the Second World War. But British jets were shipped to the
United States while the war was still on and from these were
derived the first American jet-aircraft, notably the Lockheed
Shooting Star which was used in the Korean War – where it
was completely outclassed by the MiG-15, built by the
Russians.

On parallel lines to the 'true' jet, went the development of

Griffith's idea for the turbo-prop. This, it was hoped, would claim the best from both worlds, since at lower altitudes it would have the advantages of a propeller-driven aircraft while having the smooth running characteristics of the jet. The Rolls-Royce Welland engines, the first of the 'River Class' of jet engines, named to give the idea of flow associated with jet propulsion, powered the first RAF Meteors in 1945. They were followed by the Derwent, the power unit used in the Meteors which set up new world speed records in 1945 and 1946. Next came the Trent, an adaptation of the Derwent which became in September 1945 the first airscrew gas turbine to fly. But although two Trent units were flown in a Meteor for the first time in that month, the engine was used mainly as a research engine.

The Dart, which could be run for as long as 5,000 hours – representing 1,500,000 miles – before an overhaul, was the first engine designed as a prop-jet to fly, making its initial flight in the nose of a Lancaster in October 1947. The Vickers-Viscount, fitted with four Dart engines, was the first prop-jet powered airliner.

With the aid of the jet, planes at last broke through 'the sound barrier', that concentration of air which begins to form up before a plane as it approaches the speed of sound. With the aid of the jet, passenger aircraft flying above the weather brought to the trans-world flight a new standard of comfort and safety. And with the aid of the jet supersonic planes have now been brought to the point where, for better or for worse, they seem likely to enter commercial service.

The jet, which has created its own pollution in the form of noise, is likely within the next few years to help solve the very problem it has created. This solution will probably be the aircraft designed for vertical take-off and landing, a characteristic which would confine the major noise nuisance to a small area instead of spreading it across a wide swathe of country below the conventional flight path. The idea of non-conventional take-off was developed immediately after the Second World War in a variety of aircraft which used combinations of rotating vanes, rotatable wings and propellers whose thrust could be changed at will from the horizontal to the vertical. Most were experimental aircraft and most of them, at best, produced only STOL, or short take-off and landing, rather than the ideal of vertical movement.

The break-through came in the 1950s with the use by Rolls-Royce of the turbo-jet engine in what was called the 'Flying Bedstead' – officially the Rolls-Royce TMR, or thrust-measuring rig – a device that gave man a new means of getting

airborne. Until the Rolls-Royce engineers perfected the equipment it had been possible to rise into the air either by the use of
lighter-than-air machines such as airships or balloons, or with
the help of the aerodynamic lift given by the movement of air
over a wing or aerofoil. Whittle had provided the key to a
third door more than a decade earlier when his first jet-engine,
weighing 560 pounds, had produced a thrust of 850 pounds
and during the war much effort had been concentrated on the
design and production of military aircraft which could best
utilize this new method of propulsion. During the first years
of peace, however, it was realized that once the thrust became
considerably greater than the weight of the thruster it was
theoretically possible for an engine to lift itself vertically from
the ground – and, by a cut-down of power, to land in the
same way.

The limitation was suggested by the word 'theoretically'.
Jet-engines themselves presented a large enough bag of
problems. When designers contemplated using jet-thrust not
to drive an aerofoil plus fuselage horizontally through the air
but to raise it vertically off the ground, it became evident that
there would be difficulties of control. These began to be
solved in the 'Flying Bedstead', an ungainly-looking contraption which in essence was little more than a test-bench carrying
two Nene engines. The 'Flying Bedstead' weighed 7,200
pounds but the two engines between them developed a com-

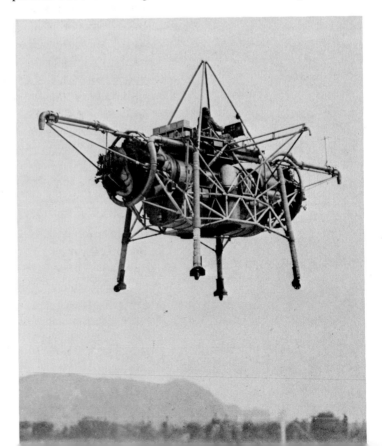

The Rolls-Royce 'Flying Bedstead',
predecessor of the vertical take-off
aircraft

bined thrust of 7,700 pounds. When both were operating all-out the three-and-a-half-ton monster rose slowly but steadily off the ground, hovering in the air above a torrent of jet-stream. Four subsidiary control jets, fore and aft, port and starboard, were used to maintain equilibrium, while by tilting the rig slightly the 'pilot' could produce forward movement.

It was clear that if a plane could be designed on this principle it would need no hard runway for take-off or landing. This would obviously have immense advantages in a commercial passenger-carrying aircraft. A Service aircraft utilizing the same principle would offer equal benefits, since the ability to land in little more than an open field – a characteristic of the first aircraft that had quickly disappeared with increasing sophistication – would give massive operational advantages. Smaller aircraft presented fewer problems of development and this fact, together with the Cold War climate of the 1950s, brought numerous kinds of VTOL Service aircraft into the air within the decade.

The simplest system was that used in the Hawker Kestrel – later developed into the Harrier – which was powered by a Bristol Siddeley Pegasus engine. The jet-stream was led out through four rotatable exhaust nozzles. With the aircraft on the ground, the nozzles pointed down and in the first moments of operation took the aircraft vertically off the ground. The jets were then slowly turned to the horizontal position to provide forward movement.

A second system, used in the Dassault-Sud Balzac among other aircraft, employed one engine, or set of engines, for vertical lift, and a separate engine or engines to give forward movement, the two groups being started up or shut down as required. A combination of both systems is also used in some designs – one set of engines is used for vertical lift, and then shut down; a second set is used first to assist the vertical take-off and then swivelled horizontally to provide forward movement.

It seems likely that during the 1970s the first VTOL passenger aircraft will come into commercial service – possibly the Breguet 941S capable of carrying 100 passengers at 400 mph; so also, in all probability, will supersonic transports flying at more than 1,400 mph. These figures suggest that on a small planet such as the earth, the lines of aeronautical advance are soon likely to be changing direction and emphasis. It is already being asked whether clipping an hour or so off the Atlantic crossing is worth either the expense or the drain on scarce men and materials that supersonic planes demand. In all the developed countries the menace of aircraft noise is increasing,

A Boeing Jumbo Jet, capable of carrying 363 passengers and more than 17 crew, at London Airport

as are the problems of siting airports to ensure that they cause minimum environmental pollution. Thus the problems that the new pioneers of flight have to solve are rather different from those of three-quarters of a century back. It is now possible to go as far, or as fast, as man in his present state of development normally needs. Pioneers will still, restless human nature being what it is, try to push back the frontiers of knowledge still further, as they are already doing by space travel. But an increasing number will be diverted to the task of producing, with existing knowledge, aircraft that serve mankind more efficiently.

3 The Magic Spectrum

While the camera was being transferred into the plain man's instant recorder of events and flight was being made an everyday affair, a totally different field of scientific endeavour was being probed and exploited for the first time. The camera was conscripted for a score of unexpected tasks, industrial as well as artistic; the jet plane brought every country on the planet within little more than a day's flight of any other; yet during the first three-quarters of the 20th century the electromagnetic spectrum helped not only to create vast new industries but to alter communication between humans more radically than they had been altered since Gutenberg set up the 42-lined pages of his Bible in movable type.

Most great scientific discoveries, as well as most inventions, can be traced back through the generations; the tracks grow steadily fainter rather than suddenly stopping so that it is easier to say that records have disappeared than that they never existed. Leonardo, sketching an armoured machine that the 20th century knows as the tank, may well have elaborated an earlier thought; the early Greek atomists, picking by chance on a theory that Dalton created with intent, were merely speculating on riddles that had entranced even earlier men. So too with the discovery and investigation of electromagnetic radiations, that huge spectrum of waves of which only a small part, covering visible light, has been known for more than a century.

Knowledge of magnetism, if not understanding of it, starts back in pre-history. From Thales, who was traditionally the first man to note that some rocks attracted iron, through Petrus Peregrinus who devised the pivoted compass needle, the line leads to William Gilbert who in the first Elizabeth's day brought the study of magnetism into the era of numerical experiment – and is remembered for his efforts in the 'gilberts' of magneto-motive force. Gilbert not only refuted such superstitions as that garlic destroys magnetism, but discovered the 'dip' of the magnet. He also put forward the idea that the needle did not point to the heavens but to the magnetic poles of the earth which he saw as a single giant spherical magnet. Almost as significantly, Gilbert discovered that a variety of gems, as well as amber, attracted light objects when rubbed, and christened them 'electrics' after the Greek word for amber.

For long after Gilbert's day, knowledge of electric phenomena advanced on lines parallel to research into magnetism but unconnected with it. Only in 1819 did the Danish physicist Hans Oersted, demonstrating to a class in the University of Copenhagen, bring a compass needle close to a wire through which an electric current was passing. The needle twitched, then turned at right-angles to the current. When he reversed the current, the needle swung round south to north, still at right-angles to the current but pointing in the opposite direction.

André-Marie Ampère, Georg Ohm and Charles Augustin de Coulomb are three of the men who in the first third of the 19th century began to disentangle the links between electricity and magnetism. Then, in 1831, Michael Faraday showed that the movement of a magnet relative to a coil of wire outside it produced an electrical current in the wire – thus presenting evidence for his belief that the phenomena of electricity and magnetism could best be considered in terms of fields, or areas of space over which their forces were exercised. With the links between electricity and magnetism increasingly recognized, the stage was set for Maxwell.

James Clerk Maxwell was the Edinburgh physicist and mathematician who in less than two decades used Faraday's experiments to furnish equations linking the two sorts of

Michael Faraday lecturing at the Royal Institution in December 1855

phenomena, boldly claimed that light itself consisted of electro-magnetic waves, and forecast the future discovery of invisible waves of the same sort. These were in fact the radio waves of Heinrich Hertz, first revealed in his laboratory 25 years after Maxwell had died of cancer at the age of 48.

Maxwell's revolutionary theory was finally described in *A Dynamical Theory of the Electromagnetic Field*. The paper declared that neither electricity nor magnetism existed in isolation and gave a simple set of equations which linked their various phenomena. The nub of the theory was that oscillation of an electric charge produced an electro-magnetic field which spread outwards at a constant speed from its source. Maxwell's equations showed this speed to be roughly 186,300 miles per second. This was approximately the speed of light, a fact which Maxwell felt was unlikely to be a coincidence. Thus light, he concluded, must itself be a form of electro-magnetic radiation, an idea which on the face of it settled a scientific argument that had been raging for years.

Since Newton's day, theories of the nature of light had fallen into one of two groups: those which descended from the Greek belief that it was composed of minute grains in rapid movement, a theory that with some reservation was supported by Newton himself; and the newer idea put forward by Christiaan Huygens which considered light as waves propagated through an all-pervasive ether much as ripples are transmitted through a shaking jelly. The Frenchman Augustin Fresnel had experimentally done much to support the wave-theory. Now came Maxwell, boldly claiming that all light, whether from a candle, a fire, the sun or one of the new electric lamps, was electro-magnetic radiation.

Maxwell predicted the existence of other electro-magnetic waves also travelling through space with the velocity of light, and acceptance of what was still a theory hung largely on their discovery. This came in 1887 from Heinrich Hertz in Karlsruhe. Hertz used an electrical circuit that built up a charge first in one then in another of two metal balls, the charge jumping the gap between them each time it had built up sufficiently. According to Maxwell, each oscillation should start off an electro-magnetic wave. To detect it, Hertz set up a simple wire-loop with a gap in it. The apparatus worked. The sparks in the first piece of apparatus were matched by smaller sparks in the second, the waves that had been started by the oscillating apparatus creating a complementary but smaller current in the receiver.

Thus were created the world's first man-made radio waves. Experiments quickly followed which showed that they were

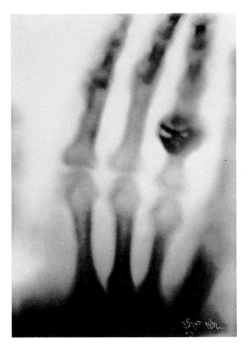

X-ray of a hand taken by
W. C. Roentgen

radiated at the speed of light, and could be reflected and refracted in the same way. All this was further support, if it were still needed, for Maxwell's conception of a whole spectrum of radiations of which visible light formed only a small part. Further evidence came a few years later when Wilhelm Roentgen produced from a high voltage discharge in an evacuated tube a new type of radiation which he called X-rays. Still more evidence came early in the 1900s when radio-active materials were found to be emitting gamma rays. Thus the existence of large segments of the electro-magnetic spectrum was known before its exploitation by inventors and technologists began in earnest at the turn of the century.

In many ways, electro-magnetic waves can be likened to waves on a pond, even though they spread in three rather than in two dimensions. They can, in particular, be described in terms of wavelength and frequency, the first being the distance between the crests of successive waves and the second being the number of cycles of the wave motion in any particular time. The huge differences in these wavelengths and frequencies are among their most curious characteristics. Thus at one end of the spectrum there are the gamma rays, with only 10^{-12} to 10^{-10} centimetres between crests, created from 10^{20} to 10^{22} times per second. At the other end there are the radio waves, up to 10^6 centimetres in length and produced 10^3 times per second. Thus the range runs, in simple terms, from gamma rays only trillionths of an inch long to radio waves up to thousands of feet. In between, increasing in wavelength from the gamma rays, there are X-rays; ultra-violet waves which play an important part in fluorescence; visible light, increasing in length from the blue to the red; the infra-red – below the red – or invisible heat rays; and finally the radio waves, which fill a big sector of the spectrum ranging from the EHF or extremely high-frequency radiations to the longer VLF or very low frequency, a contrast emphasizing the fact that high frequencies are matched by short wavelengths.

The great potentials of Hertz's experiments, which finally put the existence of the electro-magnetic spectrum beyond doubt, were appreciated only slowly; and before wire-less transmission was exploited the scientific world was startled by announcement of a new radiation that had obviously immense possibilities.

It came from Wilhelm Roentgen in the Bavarian city of Würzburg, where he was head of the university's department of physics. Roentgen was experimenting with the luminescence produced in certain chemicals by the use of a cathode ray tube, a device in which an electric discharge takes place in a partial vacuum. On 5 November 1895, Roentgen darkened his laboratory to observe results better and turned on the tube, still enclosed in black cardboard. What he saw to his surprise was that although the tube was still covered, a sheet of nearby paper coated with barium platinocyanide was glowing. When he turned off the current the glow ceased; when he switched on, the glow returned. Taking the paper into the next room he found that when the tube was switched on it continued to glow even there.

Roentgen's astonishment comes up through the sober scientific words of the report he wrote after testing the powers of the new rays. 'Paper is very transparent,' he said; 'behind a bound book of about one thousand pages I saw the fluorescent screen light up brightly, the printer's ink offering scarcely a noticeable hindrance. In the same way the fluorescence appeared behind a double pack of cards; a single card held between the apparatus and the screen being almost unnoticeable to the eye. A single sheet of tinfoil is also scarcely perceptible, it is only after several layers have been placed over one another that their shadow is distinctly seen on the screen. Thick blocks of wood are also transparent, pine boards 2 or 3 centimetres thick absorbing only slightly. A plate of aluminium about 15 millimetres thick, though it enfeebled the action seriously, did not cause the fluorescence to disappear entirely. Sheets of hard rubber several centimetres thick still permit the rays to pass through them.'

More important were the different extents to which the rays penetrated human flesh and bone. Roentgen was quick to see the immense medical value of the discovery and his anxiety to announce it was equalled by the need to have as many facts as possible verified. Only on 28 December, after seven weeks of constant experiment, did he finally submit his first paper on the new phenomenon to the Würzburg Physical Medical Society. News of its contents quickly reached Berlin and Vienna, then other European capitals, and by the evening of 23 January, when he lectured to a packed auditorium in the university, he was famous.

One point that Roentgen had already confirmed was that the new rays affected photographic film, and his lecture concluded with an impressive demonstration. Would Professor Albert von Kolliker, the university anatomist, care to have his hand photographed? The professor stepped up, and placed his hand on the sensitized film before the tube was switched on. Shortly afterwards, Roentgen held up the developed film which clearly showed the bones, the soft tissues of the hand, and the firm image of a metal ring on the professor's third finger.

Kolliker then proposed that the new phenomena should not be called X-rays, as Roentgen had so far called them, but Roentgen rays. But much of the world was unable to deal easily with the 'oe' of the German name and by the turn of the century it was X-rays whose fame had become firmly established. Roentgen himself did not apply for the use of the 'von' granted to him by the Prince of Bavaria in honour of his achievement and he did not attempt to make a penny from his discovery. 'According to the good tradition of the German University professors,' he said, 'I am of the opinion that their discoveries and inventions belong to humanity, and that they should not in any way be hampered by patents, licences or contracts nor should they be controlled by any one group.'

The use of X-rays as an aid to medical diagnosis quickly swept the world. Location of bullets in a soldier's leg, of objects swallowed by children, were among the first and most obvious applications. Later, as the nature of X-rays came to be better known and understood, it was found possible to photograph with them tumours inside the human body that could not otherwise be located, to record with their help the metabolism of the human body, and to use them in numerous other ways as a new medical tool.

Some time passed before that tool was properly understood. But eventually it was realized that X-rays were produced when the electrons forming the stream of electricity from the cathode in the tube were suddenly stopped by contact with the metal of the anode. When this happened, the electrons gave up some of their energy in X-rays much as a bullet stopped by a wall will give up its energy in the form of infra-red rays recognized as heat. It was found that when the voltage applied to the tube was increased the resulting X-rays had greater penetrating power; further experiments showed also that the greater the penetrating power of the rays the greater their frequency.

While the medical applications of Roentgen's new rays were being investigated and exploited, Heinrich Hertz's discovery in Karlsruhe was not going unnoticed. His rays had been electrically produced, they travelled at the speed of light, which for most practical purposes meant that they spread instantaneously, and they created a complementary current at a distance, without the aid of any linking wires. These facts naturally titillated the men who were already using electricity to transmit messages with the aid of wires.

As far back as 1844 Samuel Morse had used his eponymous code to send the words 'What hath God wrought?' along a 10-mile telegraph line between Baltimore and Washington. As far back as 1876 Alexander Graham Bell had patented a device in which sound-wave vibrations were turned into a fluctuating electric current which was sent along a wire before being converted back into sound waves. Now Hertz's discovery seemed to offer immense new possibilities: the transmission of messages across estuaries and channels, from ship to shore, and in dozens of other situations where the laying of a cable would be either impracticable or impossible.

First, however, a multitude of questions had to be answered. How far could these mysterious waves be made to travel? How could they be increased in strength so that they were easily detectable? How could it be certain that radiations of one wavelength would not become mixed with those of another? And even if it were possible to send the dots and dashes of the Morse system, would it ever be possible to superimpose the human voice on wireless waves in the same way that it had been successfully superimposed by Bell on an electric current?

All these questions pointed towards tremendous commercial possibilities in a booming world crying out for better communications. The result was that throughout the 1890s and the first years of the 20th century scientists in countries as distant as the United States and Germany, Russia and Britain, struggled to solve them. The basic tools of knowledge with which they worked – Maxwell's equations and the papers of Hertz and the others who had followed in Maxwell's footsteps – were available to all. The technologies available to workers in the laboratories of Washington and Cambridge, St Petersburg and Berlin, were roughly comparable. Thus it is not surprising that the record of inventions that helped transform radio from a dream to a practicality is one of competing priorities, of claim and counter-claim, usually put forward in good faith but making it unwise to give more than a measure of credit to any one man. An exception can fairly be made of Guglielmo Marconi, driving forward through the difficulties with the single-mindedness of genius.

One of the first advances was an increase in the sensitivity of the detector for picking up the wireless waves. This came with the development of a device known as the coherer. The Frenchman Édouard Branly had already noted that when a spark from an electric machine or from an induction coil was created near an exhausted glass tube in which metal filings were packed between silver electrodes, then the conductivity of the filings suddenly increased by as much as a thousand-fold. In the 1890s Sir Oliver Lodge showed that the device also responded to wireless waves and by connecting it to a circuit incorporating a bell or a Morse instrument he was able to record the arrival of wireless waves by bell or by buzz. The

Sir Oliver Lodge in his laboratory
at Liverpool in 1892

improvement in reception was again increased when the
Russian scientist Alexander Popov heightened the sensitivity
of the receiving device by attaching the Branly-Lodge coherer –
so called because at the moment of reception all the finely
divided metal filings cohered together – to a long metallic rod
called an aerial.

It is at this stage that Marconi enters the story. Heinrich
Hertz died on 1 January 1894 and some months later the young
Marconi, just 20 and holidaying at the Oropa Sanctuary in the
mountains above Biella, read Hertz's obituary notice in an
Italian electrical journal. It was written by Augusto Righi, the
Italian physicist whose experiments on the reflection of
Hertzian waves had helped to show their electro-magnetic
nature, and whose lectures Marconi had attended in Bologna.
Marconi, fired with the idea of applying the new waves to
communication, returned home for long uninterrupted
months of experiment. Having read everything available he got
to work, improved Branly's coherer, utilized an 'aerial' for
reception, and then found that if he used another aerial for
transmission this increased the range at which the wireless
waves could be detected. In the hills around his home at
Pontecchio, 11 miles from Bologna, he was soon receiving
signals sent from two miles away and had confirmed the enormously important fact that they could be received 'from the

other side of the hill'. Then, anxious to serve Italy, the young Marconi wrote to the Italian Minister of Posts and Telegraphs in Rome. In the manner of Governments, Rome was uninterested. Marconi, thinking of ship-to-shore communication, turned to the leading maritime nation. In the first months of 1896 he arrived in England.

The record of Marconi's early years in England is one of almost continuing success and of the gradual improvement of wireless transmission and reception by a multitude of small details. These did not take the idea beyond the reception, at a distance and without intervening wires, of a signal which could be produced by switching an electric current on or off. But this on-off signal allowed the transmission of messages by means of the Morse code; Marconi's determined improvement of range was, moreover, matched by his vigorous and imaginative demonstration of what his new system meant in practical terms.

He was first encouraged by a far-seeing General Post Office, whose engineering chief, William Preece, was himself a pioneer of telegraphy. His first demonstration between the GPO building in St Martin's-le-Grand and the Savings Bank Department 300 yards away was followed by experiments on Salisbury Plain. Here, before Army and Navy officers, he sent signals first 2 miles and then nearly 5. Early in 1897 the demonstrations were repeated from South Wales across the Bristol Channel to Brean Down in Somerset, $8\frac{1}{2}$ miles away.

At this point Marconi formed his own Wireless Telegraph & Signal Company, soon re-formed as Marconi's Wireless Telegraph Co. Ltd which set up a permanent transmitting station near the Needles on the western end of the Isle of Wight. From the 15-foot high mast near the Needles Marconi kept in constant touch with a receiving station on the mainland near Bournemouth, about $14\frac{1}{2}$ miles away – and, more significantly, with vessels passing up the packed shipping lanes of the Solent which had been equipped with his receiving apparatus. By this means passengers on board were able to receive messages, in good weather or foul, some time before docking at Southampton.

Using a 65-foot transmitting aerial on a steam tug, Marconi sent the world's first radio sports news, relaying details of the Kingstown Regatta in southern Ireland to a mainland receiving mast. He helped to keep the Queen at Osborne in touch with the Prince of Wales, cruising off the Isle of Wight in the Royal Yacht. And on 27 March 1899 Marconi in Wimereux, near Boulogne, sent the first of a stream of signals across the English Channel to Dover.

Post Office officials examining Marconi's apparatus used to communicate by wireless eight miles across the Bristol Channel in 1897. The upper two pieces are a Righi spark gap (*left*) and an induction coil; *below* a Morse inker and relays

By the start of the new century Marconi's first works at Chelmsford, in the south-east of England, was making in quantity the 10-inch induction coils for transmission of wireless waves and the coherers for reception, equipment already in use by the British, German and Italian navies and by a number of commercial shipping companies. And by now he had found a method of controlling oscillation frequency, which meant that transmission and reception could be made on a predetermined wavelength. This increased the efficiency of reception and made it possible to rule out chance interference by other broadcasts.

Hertz's wonderful waves had by this time been received more than 50 miles from their transmission point; it seemed as though Hertz and Maxwell had been right in their assumptions that such waves, once produced, went on indefinitely. Marconi was determined to find out if this were so. By 1901 he had set up a transmission station at Poldhu, Cornwall, on the western tip of southern Britain, and what was in his mind must have been clear to all from the moment that the tall radio towers began to rise on the coast: transmission across the Atlantic.

There was still one thing that seemed to rule out wireless messages to America. This was simply the curvature of the earth. For it was known that light travels in straight lines and it was equally certain, furthermore, that radio waves did the same. But the curve of the earth raises a giant 150-mile hump of ocean between Britain and America, and a straight line extended across the Atlantic would end up hundreds of miles above the US coast, a position where no receiver had ever been.

Marconi in the room at Signal Hill, Newfoundland, with the instruments with which he received the first trans-Atlantic wireless signals on 12 December 1901

Despite the head-shakings of those who knew better, Marconi pressed on with his preparations.

After more than one set-back, and the destruction of the aerials at his first reception site on Cape Cod, Massachusetts, all was ready. Marconi had found a new site above the port of St John's in Newfoundland and here he prepared his equipment early in December. At Poldhu, more than 2,000 miles away in Cornwall, the pre-arranged letter S in morse was tapped out automatically.

'It was shortly after mid-day (local time) on 12 December 1901 that I placed a single ear-phone to my ear and started listening,' Marconi later wrote. 'The receiver on the table before me was very crude – a few coils and condensers and a coherer, no valves, no amplifier, not even a crystal. I was at last on the point of putting the correctness of all my beliefs to the test. The experiment had involved risking at least £50,000 to achieve a result which had been declared impossible by some of the principal mathematicians of the time.'

Suddenly he heard the sharp click of the 'tapper' as it struck the coherer.

'Unmistakably, the three sharp clicks corresponding to three dots sounded in my ear; but I would not be satisfied without corroboration. "Can you hear anything, Mr Kemp?" I said, handing the telephone to my assistant. Kemp heard the same thing as I.'

The 'impossible' had in fact been achieved with the help of the as yet undiscovered ionosphere, the envelope of ionized particles surrounding the earth like the skin surrounding the flesh of an orange. Only a year after Marconi's epoch-making trans-Atlantic experiment the first of the layers making up the ionosphere was discovered by Oliver Heaviside and A. E. Kennelly who showed that wireless waves would not shoot off into space but would be reflected back and forth between the ionosphere and the earth's surface.

The repercussions of Marconi's success were immediate – and not all of them were pleasant. More than a dozen telegraph cables were already in operation across the Atlantic, and radio communication was obviously a threat to the companies which owned them. Considerable efforts were therefore made to throw doubt on the success of Marconi's work. However, the opposition was fighting a losing battle and Marconi now went on from one triumph to another. First he showed that shore to ship transmission was possible at a range of more than 2,000 miles. Then he replaced the coherer with a magnetic detector which was not so vulnerable as the coherer to the rollings of a ship at sea. A 'Marconigram' service which regularly supplied news to ocean liners came next and, soon afterwards, the first impressive demonstration of how radio could bring vital help to a sinking ship. Then, in 1905, reception of signals was made immeasurably easier by Marconi's discovery that a horizontally bent aerial would send out waves most strongly in one specific direction.

So far, however, Marconi – and the many others who were by this time following him – was still creating radio-waves by the unaided spark method used decades earlier by Hertz. The powers which he could draw upon were vastly greater but basically the system was just as inefficient. And, far more important, it was still only possible to transmit and receive wireless waves in bursts; short and long bursts could be distinguished with the result that the dots and dashes of the Morse code could be utilized to send information. But this was still a long way from the time when 'nation shall speak peace unto nation'.

During the first decade of the 20th century two main lines of invention began to transform the primitive wireless of the dot-dash era to those of the contemporary world. The first, and potentially the most important, came from John Fleming, the man who can without qualification be called the inventor of the wireless valve. Fleming found that when a current was passed through the heated filament of a lamp bulb then negative charges – but *only* negative ones – would stream from the filament on to a cold plate inside the bulb. This characteristic, it was quickly realized, could be used to turn the oscillations of the radio-waves hitting an aerial into a continuous current, a more useful transformation than could be provided by the coherer, by the magnetic detector or by the crystal detector which had by this time become a further alternative.

But although the valve quickly became a more valuable detector of radio-waves, it was to be given an even greater importance by Lee de Forest, an American radio expert who was eventually to have more than 300 patents to his name. The most famous was his development of Fleming's two-element diode valve into the triode. The third element was a grid interposed between the heated filament and the cold plate. The importance of this was that the charge placed on the grid controlled a stream of electrons passing from the filament to the plate; more significantly, variation of a very weak potential on the grid produced an electron flow that was similar but very much stronger. In other words, the triode valve could be used to amplify a weak current into a strong one. Furthermore it was discovered, some years after the first triodes were produced, that they could also be used for the generation of currents.

It was the valve which mainly helped to make possible as a practical reality the broadcasting of human speech and of music. Priority is unclear, but certainly Reginald Fessenden, a Canadian-American physicist, was one of the first to conceive the idea of using a continuous stream of radio-waves as a carrier on which a pattern of sound-waves could be imposed. Graham Bell had already shown that the fluctuations of a sound wave could be turned into a correspondingly fluctuating electric current and turned back into speech at the end of a wire. Was the same thing possible without the wire? Fessenden answered this question in the early 1900s. He did it by producing a continuous stream of waves, all of the same length and thus of the same frequency. But before transmission the stream of waves was modulated by an electric current that fluctuated according to the rising and falling of a human voice. Thus the wave-pattern transmitted was that of the carrier-wave modulated in a way that corresponded to the irregularities of a sound wave. At the receiving station, the fluctuating current corresponded, just as it would had it been sent by wire, with the original human voice and was almost as easily transformed back into sound waves. Fessenden's early broadcasts were later repeated by de Forest with his new triode and in 1910 he broadcast the voice of Caruso, an event which did almost as much for the future of radio as the inception of Marconigrams.

The fact that the sound of Caruso's extraordinary voice could be brought into the living-rooms of men and women miles away from the concert hall was technically unimportant but psychologically significant. The risings and fallings of the human voice had been sent without wires almost a decade earlier. But now, all at once, the potentialities of the radio portions of the electro-magnetic spectrum became evident. Not only voices without wires but music without wires! From 1910 until the present day progress in broadcasting has been made up largely of technical advances which have added refinements to this existing possibility. More powerful transmitters have vastly increased the area within which their transmissions can be picked up. Methods have been discovered of eliminating the crackling interference of atmospherics, the natural electrical signals of the universe. Perhaps most important of all, the aural quality of radio reception has been immensely improved.

This development sprang not only from improved equipment but from increased knowledge of how radio-waves are transmitted through the atmosphere and reflected back from the various layers of the ionosphere. The knowledge began to accumulate in the 1920s after radio, which like most other technical developments had benefited from the spur of the First World War, was launched on a commercial basis in Britain, the United States and a number of European countries. During this decade, which witnessed the first important steps to transmit without wires not only sound but also vision, research into the ionosphere was carried out primarily to improve radio reception; but it also paved the way for radar, after radio and television the most important of all techniques for using electro-magnetic waves. The story has a unique interest, partly because of the leap-frogging developments made in different countries and laboratories, partly because of the decisive part which radar was to play in the Second World War.

As early as 1887 Hertz had shown that radio-waves were reflected by metallic objects. But the power of his primitive equipment was small, the reflecting surfaces were only a few feet away, the reflections were recorded only with difficulty, and neither Hertz nor his immediate successors regarded the phenomenon as much more than an interesting fact of nature to be duly recorded and filed away. In 1904 the German physicist Christian Holsmeyer was granted a patent for an anti-collision device for use at sea which depended on the use of radio echoes, but it was not until 1922 that Marconi, accepting the Medal of Honour of the American Institute of Radio Engineers, openly speculated along the lines that the pioneers of radar were to follow.

'In some of my tests', he said, 'I have noticed the effects of reflection and deflection of these [electric] waves by metallic objects miles away. It seems to me that it should be possible to design apparatus by means of which a ship could radiate or project a divergent beam of these rays in any desired direction, which rays, if coming across a metallic object such as another steamer or ship, would be reflected back to a receiver screened from the local transmitter on the sending ship and thereby immediately reveal the presence and bearing of ships, even though these ships be unprovided with any kind of radio.'

Left Christian Holsmeyer's device of 1904 for preventing collisions at sea by the use of radio echoes

Right Dame Nellie Melba, the famous Australian prima donna, broadcasting from the Marconi works in Chelmsford on 15 June 1920 – the first advertised programme of broadcast entertainment

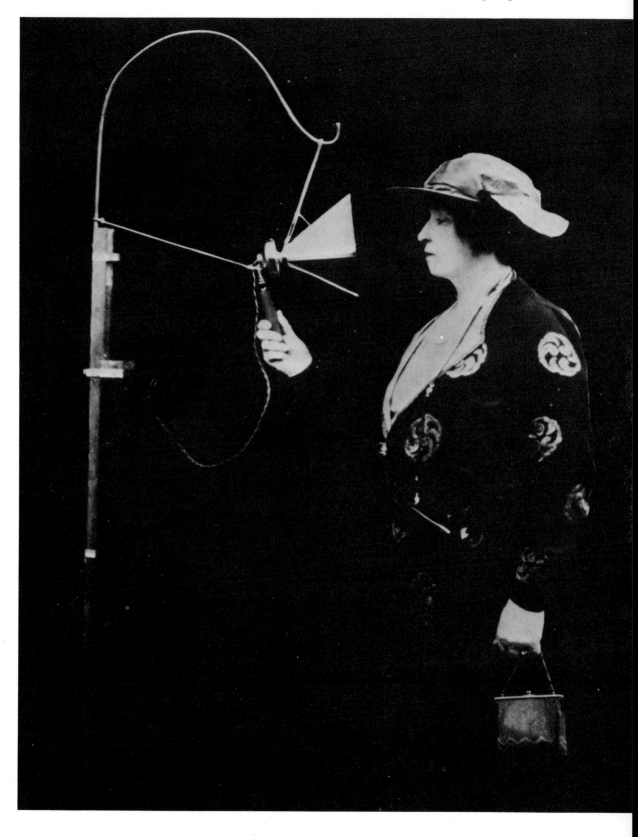

The idea of a ship, or for that matter a plane, sending out radiations and receiving back echoes, lay many steps ahead in the history of radar. But Marconi's statement is typical of the way in which men were thinking; during the next few years more than one scientist and inventor proposed that radio reflections might be conscripted to locate objects. In 1923 and 1936 Heinrich Lowy of Vienna filed two patents for 'measuring the distance of electrically-conductive bodies', one being a form of radar altimeter. In the United States one inventor lodged a patent for a form of radar signalling system, while A. H. Taylor and L. C. Young suggested that the interruption of radio-waves could reveal enemy vessels 'irrespective of fog, darkness or smoke-screen'. In Britain two workers at the Admiralty Signal School, Portsmouth, filed a secret patent as early as 1928 for what was later to be called 'a complete patent for radar'. At the Army Signal Establishment a few years afterwards two scientists devised a system for recording reflected radio pulses. But neither the Army which still believed the cavalry to be Queen of the battlefield, nor the Navy which still pinned its faith on the battleship, was interested in new-fangled detection devices, and two great opportunities were lost.

Many of these plans, patents and ideas were only in the laboratory or drawing-board stage and at first glance it is easy to understand the sceptical view of the Services. However, by the 1930s one man had in fact shown the practicality of using radio reflections. He was Edward Appleton, a Cambridge physicist who in 1924 had discovered the height of the ionosphere, the layer of ionized particles which envelopes the earth. Appleton had used a receiver to pick up radio transmissions sent out a known distance away. Some of the received waves came along the straight path from transmitter to receiver and some came a longer route by travelling up to the ionosphere whence they were reflected down to the receiver, thus covering two sides of a triangle instead of one. Appleton arranged for the wavelength on which the signals were transmitted to be varied and when the difference in length of the two routes travelled was a whole number of wavelengths these would combine to produce a loud signal; when the difference was equal to an odd number of half wavelengths the signals would tend to cancel one another out. A simple equation which used the mean wavelength, the small change in wavelength, and the number of 'fadings', enabled the difference in length of the two routes to be easily worked out; and this gave the height of the point of reflection, or in other words the height of the ionosphere.

This was Appleton's first way of doing the trick. But soon afterwards he repeated the experiment using the system of pulse transmission which had been devised in the United States. Short sharp bursts of radio energy were sent out and reflected back from the ionosphere whose height was then discovered by recording the time taken for the journey up to the ionosphere and back again.

It was still all rather esoteric viewed in practical terms. But a further, and key, step was taken by Appleton in 1932 when he led a party to Northern Norway to make observations during the International Polar Year. His main work was concentrated on discovering how thunderstorms affected the ionosphere. However, as far as the future of radar was concerned the important thing was that he recorded radio reflections on the cathode ray equipment with which he – and others – had long been experimenting. Earlier, reflections had been used to make a photographic record with the aid of a galvanometer. Now something very different was achieved, for the incoming pulses were utilized to affect the steady horizontal line on a cathode-ray tube. Each time a pulse arrived there was a small 'blip' on the line, and the position of the 'blip' gave an indication of the distance away of the reflecting layer.

At this point it is useful to summarize exactly what had been achieved. Appleton checking his thunderstorms – and the workers in the Admiralty and Army Signals Establishments who had produced their own versions of embryonic radar – had been adapting the old trick of the sailor caught in thick fog off a rocky coast. The sailor shouts or whistles and by noting the interval before he hears an echo is able to work out his distance from the cliffs of the coast. The forerunners of radar were using the same technique; but they were using radio-waves which travel a million times faster than the sound-waves of the sailor's voice and they were using a reflecting layer about which comparatively little was yet known. What they had done was to show that there lay to hand a new scientific tool which could be turned to good effect under certain conditions, by skilled operators, for limited purposes. But even this had little resemblance to a practicable weapon. It is not as surprising as it seems at first that the birth of radar itself still hung fire. As with so many inventions, what was needed was the operational requirement.

In Britain this necessary spur was administered by the Air Defence Exercises of 1934. At that time early warning devices consisted only of acoustic shields, designed to magnify the hum of approaching planes (and pointing, incidentally towards France) and the exercises underlined that for all practical purposes London was defenceless – 'the greatest target in the world, a kind of tremendous fat cow, a valuable fat cow tied up to attract the beasts of prey' as Churchill described it. An Air Ministry Committee – the famous Tizard Committee – was set up to decide what should be done, and before it met the chief scientific adviser to the Air Ministry, H. E. Wimperis, decided once more to investigate the 'Death Ray', that device which rose as a spectre at regular intervals. To make quite sure that the Death Ray was an impossibility, Wimperis sought the help of Robert Watson-Watt, then Superintendent of the Government's Radio Research Station.

The next few steps are well known. Watson-Watt ruled out a Death Ray. But simple computations worked out by his assistant, A. F. Wilkins, suggested that broadcasts at the powers then practicable might produce detectable reflections from the kind of aircraft then flying – a case of theory confirming what had already been noted. Post Office engineers had recorded a few years earlier that passing aircraft caused a fluttering of their radio signals while Appleton himself had noted more than once how planes flying over his laboratory had interrupted his work. Now, however, something else was envisaged.

On the morning of 26 February 1935 a Heyford heavy bomber, a biplane with a top speed of 131 mph, flew over Daventry, passing through the transmissions from the town's BBC station. On the ground a small group including Watson-Watt, Wilkins and A. P. Rowe, an Air Ministry observer, watched a green blob on a cathode-ray tube expand and shrink. The range at which the reflection could be picked up on the screen was only 10 miles. But it justified Watson-Watt's exuberant words: 'Britain has become an island once more.'

In this early stage of development it was merely planned that a series of radio towers should be set up round the coast to transmit overlapping spheres of radio-waves. Planes approaching the coast would reflect the waves and these reflections would be picked up by stations which would thus be given advance warning of enemy raiders. Although the distance of the approaching planes could be calculated from the position of the blob on the radar screen, nothing more could at first be learned from it. But during the following months the equipment was refined and improved to show first direction and then height. Finally it was possible to tell from the green blob on the screen whether the radar echoes were being produced from one plane, from a few or from many. And before the outbreak of war British planes had been fitted with a simple device which enabled the radar watchers round the coast to

One of the radar towers which formed part of Britain's early warning system when war broke out in 1939

tell immediately whether echoes were coming from friend or from foe. All these developments were built into the series of radar stations which by the outbreak of war ringed Britain. They not only gave advance warning of enemy aircraft but by indicating the size of individual formations enabled Fighter Command to husband its severely-stretched resources during the Battle of Britain.

German shipping at Oslo seen with the help of the radar device H_2S. The coastal area can be compared quite easily with a map of the same area. No echoes are received from the water, but the presence and location of shipping is indicated by quite strong 'echoes' or 'blips'.

The Germans also developed radar along very similar lines, and in the early days their equipment was often as good as the British and sometimes better. Their failure sprang primarily from lack of liaison between the Luftwaffe and the scientists – and from a misplaced German confidence that scientific aids were not needed for victory.

As soon as the vital importance of radar in the war was appreciated, development went ahead in Britain, in Germany, and in the United States where American defence scientists were in the autumn of 1940 told of the British work by members of the Tizard Mission.

One of the first and most important steps forward was the production of the cavity magnetron valve. Its value stems from the fact that as shorter and shorter wavelengths are used, so does the potential operational usefulness of radar increase. The original experiments had been carried out with 5,000-centimetre waves and by the autumn of 1939 wavelengths down to 50 centimetres were being discussed. There seemed, however, to be one insuperable limitation. For as the wavelengths grew shorter so did it become more and more difficult to provide them with sufficient power. It was not, it appeared, possible to solve one half of the problem without correspondingly increasing the other half, and the indissolubility with which the two halves were linked looked like a permanent limiting factor to those who were developing radar.

The problem was solved in Birmingham by Professor J. T. Randall and Dr H. A. Boot. Together, they developed the magnetron, a valve devised some years earlier and utilizing a magnetic field to produce its effects, into something radically better. Their cavity magnetron had, as its name implies, a number of long cavities machined in a solid block of copper. The electrons from the cathode were carried round in a magnetic field past a number of oscillatory circuits in these cavities which became sources of very short waves. When the first valve was tested in February 1940 the wave lengths were found to be shorter than 10 centimetres, while 400 watts was being generated, a power much greater than anything previously produced in this way.

Short waves were an essential of many other applications of radar which came into operational use as the war went on. A centimetric radar set on the Dover cliffs in the summer of 1941 detected ships 45 miles away. Large vessels could be seen leaving the enemy-held port of Boulogne in all weathers, while even the small German E-boats could be tracked more than 17 miles away. Very soon, British radar had 'closed' the narrows of the English Channel.

Before the end of the war the reflections of radio-waves were not only enabling gunners to 'see' invisible targets but were giving their missiles a new order of deadliness. This was provided by the proximity fuse, a device built in to the head of a shell and incorporating a radio transmitter and receiver. The waves sent out were reflected back from the object aimed at; when the receiver indicated that the target was a certain pre-arranged distance away the shell was automatically exploded, thus ensuring the maximum damage.

There were many other ways in which the principles of radar were exploited, particularly by those who fought the war in the air. Airborne radar sets were built and with their help pilots were able at night to 'home' on to enemy planes. Two important navigational aids known as 'Gee' and 'Oboe', were developed and enabled radar transmitters on the ground in England to guide pilots accurately to positions directly above targets in Germany. More important still was H_2S. This was not a navigational aid but a system which gave the pilot a picture of the ground over which he was flying. It was achieved by utilizing the fact that short radio-waves give a different kind of reflection when they are thrown back by open country, by water, or by built-up areas, of particular use in the war against

Inside Bawdsey Research Station, operational from early 1936

Germany since so many of the main targets were close to large areas of water – Hamburg being on the Elbe estuary, Berlin almost surrounded by big lakes, and various other cities easily identifiable by the shapes built up by the pattern of radar reflections.

These wartime uses of radar paved the way for the numerous post-war navigational and blind-landing systems without which the growth of the world's air routes during the last quarter-century would have been impossible. Today the multiple applications of radar allow planes to take off in safety in quick succession from busy airports, enable a pilot to check his position on a journey across the world, and then pick up a radar-landing device which will lead him down onto the run-way in the worst weather.

The last quarter-century's growth of commercial flying which has so changed the business and the holiday patterns of the world would have been impossible without the guiding hand of radar, itself the direct outcome of the frantic need to win the war in the air. By contrast television, that other technical marvel of the electro-magnetic spectrum which

makes the post-war world so different from the pre-war, has
grown up despite the hiatus of the war years during which
research was pressed ahead on devices of more direct Service
significance.

It is the use of electro-magnetic waves to transmit pictures
which has made contemporary television possible, but the idea
of sending images from one place to another by electrical
means goes back not only beyond the birth of radio but
beyond even the discovery of electro-magnetic waves. In fact
Morse had been sending messages by wire only a few years
when various ingenious ways of using electricity to send
pictures were being proposed. Most of them depended for
their practicability on the light-sensitivity of selenium, the
rare element first isolated by Jöns Berzelius in the early years
of the 19th century. One form of the element, the so-called
'metallic' selenium, was being used in the early 1870s by
Joseph May, at a cable station off the coast of Ireland. May
noted that unexpected variations in the readings of his
instruments were caused by the effect of light on the selenium;
for some inexplicable reason, he found, light changed the
electrical resistance of the material. More important, it
seemed clear that the variation in resistance was proportional
to the intensity of the light. Thus light itself could be made to
create an electrical signal.

A decade after this discovery of what was to be one of the
essentials of television, the German engineer Paul Nipkow
patented his scanning disc, a device which used another
principle basic to television: persistence of vision, the
characteristic of the human eye which presents to the brain as
one moving image the multiple static, and slightly different,
images of the cinema film. Nipkow made use of this by
piercing in a disc a series of small holes arranged in a spiral. If
the disc were rotated between a light source and an object the
whole of that object would be scanned by light through the
holes after one revolution of the disc. The darker and the
lighter portions of the object would reflect different amounts of
light and if these reflections were thrown on to a succession of
selenium cells, the cells could be used to send a series of
electrical impulses along a wire. At the receiving end the impulses could be used to produce signals corresponding to the
brightness of the individual parts of the object lit up at the
transmitting end of the line. If the signals – the turning on, for
instance, of individual lights in a mosaic of lights – were
viewed through a second Nipkow disc, then the eye would
briefly receive a series of transitory images corresponding to
the parts of the object being scanned. If the wheel were

Karl Jansky pointing in 1933 to the position on a chart where radio noises from space were first heard. While trying to pinpoint the source of noise interfering with the radiotelephone service, Jansky detected a peculiar hissing sound coming from the area of the Milky Way, later identified as radio signals generated by the natural processes in stars and galaxies. His work resulted in the new science of radio astronomy, in which the heavens are studied by listening to radio waves rather than by looking through an optical telescope.

revolved fast enough the eye would transmit these parts to the brain as a single image.

The basic idea of activating in succession the individual items in a mosaic of photo-electric cells was first conceived for use by means of the electric telegraph. However, even 'wired vision' as it might have been called, was ruled out for practical purposes by two things. One was that the process of scanning the mosaic of photo-electric elements by mechanical means was too slow; the separate images did not follow one another fast enough and the result was not a composite picture that could be properly recognized. The other was that while mosaics of separate elements could produce rough patterns, much as the lighting-up of separate bulbs in a mosaic of bulbs can produce numbers or letters in a display sign, the elements were neither small enough nor numerous enough to represent acceptably the infinitely numerous lights and shades of everyday scenes.

With the birth of radio, and the ability to send electrical signals through space by the use of a carrier wave, much that was possible by wire became possible by wireless. Before this, however, the key to television as it is known today had been provided by the cathode-ray tube, which was steadily improved. John Fleming discovered that the stream of electrons pouring down the length of a cathode tube could be focused by an encircling electrical current on to a target at the end of the tube – a target which if coated with a flourescent material would be made to glow at the spot hit by the focused electron stream. Subsequently it was found that an external magnetic field could be made to deflect the electron stream so that it hit any desired part of the target.

At this point, the major essentials of modern television had already been produced in embryo, although few men realized the fact. One who did so was Archibald Campbell Swinton, an electrical engineer who had already impinged on history at two points, by producing the first X-ray photograph in Britain in 1896 and by giving Marconi his vital letter of introduction to William Preece of the Post Office in the early years of the 20th century. In 1908 Campbell Swinton wrote an extraordinary letter to *Nature*, the British scientific journal. Describing what was called 'distant electric vision', he outlined a system strikingly similar to that used in television today. The transmitter incorporated a screen painted with fluorescent material on to which a scene was focused much as it would be focused on a photographic film in a camera. The screen, glowing with a fluorescent image, was scanned by a cathode-ray tube in the same way that the human eye scans the type on the written page, moving from left to right along a succession of horizontal lines which followed one another in succession down the page. The stream of electrons in the scanning tube, passing across the light and dark portions of the fluorescent image, was used to trigger off a series of electrical impulses which corresponded to the light and dark of the image. These impulses, transmitted to a cathode tube in the receiver, were in turn to trigger off a stream of electrons which, as it was scanned across a screen similar to that in the transmitter, produced on this screen a fluorescent image whose light and dark portions matched those of the original. The replica was made up of a succession of images, glowing as the electron beam continuously swept across the target from left to right, returned to the left a little lower down and continued the process until the whole screen had been scanned, when it returned to the top of the screen and began to repeat the process. The action was so quick that the human eye retained the first of the images until the scanning process had covered the whole screen and begun again, thus providing the brain with an unflickering picture analogous to that produced on the cinema screen.

At least, that was the idea behind Campbell Swinton's plan. But in the early years of the century neither methods of sufficiently amplifying the signals nor of moving the scanning beam across the target screen were developed far enough to make practical television possible. Better amplification came first, and the first television transmissions were made with the help of mechanical scanning systems based either on Nipkow's wheel or on mirror-drums whose mirrors created a succession of overlapping reflections of a subject as the drum was revolved.

During the 1920s and 1930s these systems were extensively experimented with both in the United States and in Britain. As early as 1923 a scanning disc system was used to send a picture of President Harding from Washington to Philadelphia; four years later the Bell Telephone Laboratories

Research apparatus used in the development of television. The scientist on the left is observing the image re-created through the rotating disc. The scanning disc at the other end of the shaft intervenes between an illuminated transparency and the photo-electric cell, housed in the box visible beyond the driving shaft

supported experiments which enabled pictures to be sent by radio from New York to Washington; and in 1928 a radio station in Schenectady began half-hour transmissions that were probably the world's first, even if they were only experimental. But these transmissions gave only 24 lines per picture and although other experimenters were getting 50 lines this still produced far too coarse-grained a picture to be acceptable.

The same was at first true of the system introduced in England by John Logie Baird, a Scot who is important in the story of television not so much for his technical innovations as for his introduction of television to the general public. Baird, an inveterate inventor responsible not only for a television system but for a chemically treated damp-proofed sock and a new method of jam-manufacture, started work on his apparatus in 1922. He was poor, and the state of his finances is indicated by the components of his first television transmitter which used a form of Nipkow disc and was assembled on a washstand. 'The base of his motor was a tea-chest, a biscuit tin housed the projection lamp, scanning discs were cut from cardboard, and fourpenny cycle lenses were used,' it has been written. 'Scrapwood, darning needles, string and sealing-wax held the apparatus together.'

John Logie Baird's early television apparatus dated about 1925

Baird developed his device for three years and in 1926 was able to demonstrate it before some 50 members of the Royal Institution in London. He used a revolving mirror drum which in conjunction with a spotlight projector scanned the subject being televised with a concentrated spot of light. The spot was picked up by a mosaic of photocells whose output made up the initial currents transmitted. Baird's picture had a definition of only 30 lines, his scanner covered the subject area only five times a second, and the picture itself was only two inches high and an inch and a half wide. Despite the primitive character of the picture, Baird pressed on, and by 1929 was able to persuade the British Broadcasting Corporation to start a regular series of television transmissions, the second in the world. They were something more than the purely experimental transmissions which had been started the previous year in the United States. Baird's Televisor, as he called his receiving apparatus, was now capable of producing $12\frac{1}{2}$ pictures a second and was put on public sale and within three years thousands of the British public had, for instance, seen the Derby televised from the race-course at Epsom in 1931.

However much Baird and his colleagues improved their apparatus, they were handicapped by the comparative slowness of the mechanical scanning device. Something dramatically better than this became possible during the 1930s as there emerged various practicable methods of using an improved cathode-ray tube to replace mechanical scanning. The key figure in this development was Vladimir Zworykin, a Russian electrical engineer who settled in the United States after the Revolution. In 1928 Zworykin patented the idea of using a cathode tube to scan a television screen, and during the next decade developed what he called the iconoscope, the first practical television camera.

By the early 1930s a number of companies were pressing forward with research in Britain. Baird was experimenting with 120-line transmissions, Cossors were finding what could be done with 180-line pictures, while EMI and Scophony Ltd were other firms in the field. By 1936, when the BBC began regular transmissions from Alexandra Palace in North London, two systems were used on alternate weeks – a Baird System by this time giving 240 lines, with 25 pictures a second, and a Marconi-EMI System giving 25 405-line pictures per second. The arrangements continued for only a few months, after which the Marconi-EMI system alone was used. The impact of television during these years immediately preceding the war should not be over-estimated; nevertheless, some 10,000 sets for picking up the 405-line services were sold in Britain between 1936 and 1939.

The outbreak of the Second World War put a temporary stop to anything not directly connected with the Services but the development of electronic techniques during the next six years, particularly for such war-winning devices as radar, brought forth the tools which soon turned the television images of the late 1930s into the pictures of today.

Most contemporary systems use hundreds of lines per picture (405 and 625 in Britain, 525 in the United States, 625 in Europe) and in Britain they provide 25 complete pictures per second, with interlaced scanning giving double that number of frames. Twenty-five pictures per second is not, of itself, good enough to eliminate flickering, a problem which is overcome by the ingenious interlacing method. In this, lines 1, 3, 5, 7 and so on are scanned first, followed by lines 2, 4, 6, 8 etc. This is done at twice the normal speed, thus producing two fields of $202\frac{1}{2}$ lines each on the 405 system, which are merged to produce 25 complete pictures every second, thus eliminating flicker.

Operation of most systems is basically the same. With the use of one typical camera tube an image is focused on to a light-sensitive screen in the camera. The dark parts of the screen retain all their electrons but the parts hit by light from the image lose some of them. When the beam of electrons in the scanning tube hits a dark part of the screen, already full of electrons, it is reflected back to a collecting plate and sends out a pulse. When the beam hits a light part of the screen, which has given off some of its electrons, the beam is absorbed and fails to return to the collecting plate. Thus a 'pulse' and a 'no pulse' signal is obtained, is transmitted by a carrier wave just as a sound signal would be transmitted, and is then reconstituted on a picture tube in the receiver.

The huge expansion of television in the post-war years was not only a demonstration of man's growing understanding of electronics and his mastery of electronic techniques. It was also a response to a demand, in many ways a fulfilment of A. P. Rowe's 'operational requirement', providing a more affluent world with time on its hands with a new kind of mass entertainment. The demand for colour soon came.

Crude systems for sending colour-pictures by wire had been proposed since the early years of the century, most of them using a prism system to break up into the primary colours the light from an object being mechanically scanned. However, a practicable colour system had to await the coming of electronic systems, and several arrived simultaneously in an attempt to satisfy the demand. Various methods are used for sending out from a camera three sets of signals, each linked to the amounts of the three primary colours present in the different parts of the image being scanned. With few exceptions, however, these signals are translated back into a coloured image by what is basically the same method. This relies for its operation on a receiving screen which is coated not with the usual photo-sensitive material responding to white light but with a pattern of red, green and blue phosphor dots, arranged in triangular units. Behind this mosaic there is stretched a shadow mask pierced by thousands of small holes. During reception three electron guns, each responding to the pattern of impulses produced by the red, the blue or the green parts of the original image, scan the screen simultaneously, each beam being so positioned that signals from the red parts of the original pass through holes behind the red phosphor dots, blue signals fall on the blue dots and green signals on the green. The signals are so fast and the dots illuminated are so

Drs William Shockley (*seated*), John Bardeen (*left*) and Walter H. Brattain, at Bell Telephone Laboratories in 1948 with the apparatus used in investigations that led to the invention of the transistor

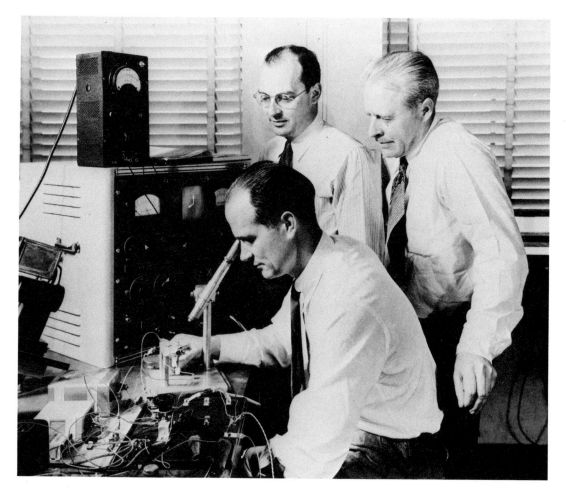

small and so closely-spaced that the eye is deceived into seeing an unflickering colour image of the original.

During the last quarter-century television – as well as radio – has been the object of extensive technological research which has steadily increased the quality of reception and the convenience of equipment. The physicists, the chemists, the metallurgists have all contributed, and television itself has become a good illustration of the way in which inventions and advances in a number of fields are closely inter-related.

Few single inventions had a greater effect than that of the transistor which from 1948 began to transform not only radio and television but a host of other equipment which depended for its working on the control of electrons. Many men contributed to its creation, and important among them was the English-American physicist William Shockley. Some years earlier Shockley and his fellow-workers in the United States had discovered that crystals of the rare metal germanium would, if they contained minute quantities of certain impurities, act like the crystals of the early radio sets: they would work as rectifiers, passing on surges of current in only one direction. They would, however, do the job far more efficiently. In 1948 Shockley discovered how to combine two slightly different sorts of crystals in such a way that they would not only act together as a rectifier but would also amplify a current. The device – soon called a transistor because it transferred current across a resistor – would do all that a radio valve would do. It had, moreover, immense advantages, since it was smaller, lighter and more rugged than a valve. In addition it would start work without any of the preparatory warming-up period that was needed with valves.

The use of transistors – whose development was speeded-up a decade later with the need for miniaturizing equipment in satellites – spread quickly throughout the radio and television industries. It also spread in other parts of the electronics industry which had been developing along parallel lines.

One spectacular example of the way in which technologists in the industry have utilized the fresh knowledge of the electron, acquired as men discovered more about the electromagnetic spectrum, is the contemporary electronic computer. Its importance springs basically from one fact: that in carrying out calculations it employs not the human hand, as in an abacus, not a physical mechanism as in a mechanical computer, but an electric current that allows information to be sent from place to place in a minute fraction of a second.

It was in the 1930s that American researchers first pointed out the similarities between the on-off states of an electric

Colour television transmission

1 Dichroic mirrors
2 Image orthicon
3 Blue signal
4 Red signal
5 Green signal
6 Early synchronizing pulses
7 Encoder
8 Synchronizing generator
9 Synchronizing pulses
10 Chrominance signal
11 Luminance signal
12 Transmitter
13 Receiving aerial
14 Receiver
15 Video panel
16 Decoding panel
17 Deflection yoke
18 Radial convergence magnet
19 Electron guns
20 Magnetic shield
21 Shadow mask
22 Phosphor dot screen with image

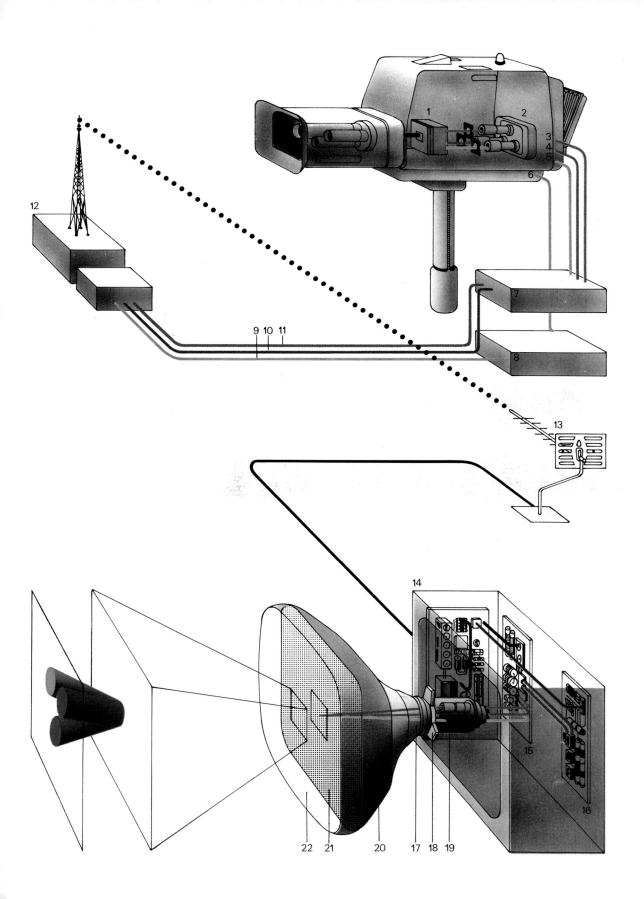

An experimental laser being used by Montague Burton, the tailors, to cut through thick piles of cloth without distorting them

circuit and the basic twin alternatives of logic. From here the next step was the combination of the binary system, in which all numbers can be expressed in a two–symbol notation, and the operations of mathematical logic. This enabled the most complicated sums and calculations to be carried out at what would previously have been unimaginable speeds.

One of the disadvantages of the new electronic computers which began to be built soon after the end of the Second World War, was their size. Thus the American machine ENIAC weighed 3 tons, and used 130 Kw – largely because it was packed with thousands of valves. It was these valves which were eliminated in later computers by transistors, the devices which, as much as any other single item, transformed the prospects for the new electronic machines which within two decades became an almost everyday feature of business and commercial life.

4 Man Makes Materials

Man's use of the electro-magnetic spectrum had one thing in common with the development of photography and the conquest of the air: it enlisted in its service a new class of artificial material which man began to make during the closing decades of the last century. These were plastics. The first may have evolved directly from research into photographic plates, the evolution of others was encouraged by the growing demands of the electrical industry, while later plastics were tailor-made by chemists specifically to treat the fabric which covered the wings of early aircraft. Invention, like peace, seems indivisible.

Since the earliest times man had not only used such naturally occurring materials as wood, stone, minerals and animal and vegetable fibres. He had also learned how to process some of them into metals such as bronze and into brittle amorphous mixtures such as glass. These materials, though literally man-made, were different in one very important way from the huge family of plastics which evolved from the pioneer work of the mid-19th century. For they were produced by men who learned, very largely by trial-and-error, how to create materials with whatever characteristics of hardness, malleability or transparency they required. They got the right end-product but they rarely knew why.

This hit-and-miss method changed as during the first half of the 19th century the science of chemistry finally burst away from the tendrils of alchemy which had continued to hold it back. But it was a gradual process; although public display of the world's first plastic articles came only at the 1862 International Exhibition in London, their story can be traced back for at least three decades. In 1832 Professor Henri Bracconat of Nancy discovered that if he poured concentrated nitric acid on to cotton or wood fibres he got a hard water-resistant film which he called xylodine. A few years later Professor Théophile Pelouze of Paris found that the same materials could be used to produce an explosive substance. However, neither Bracconat nor Pelouze thought it worthwhile to follow up their work and it was left to Christian Schönbein, a German-Swiss chemist, to take the next step a decade later. One story is that Schönbein, experimenting in his wife's kitchen, spilled some acid, mopped up the mess with a cotton apron, began to dry the apron over a stove and then saw the apron disappear with a smokeless bang. Whether or not the story has the mythological quality of Newton and the apple, Schönbein certainly arrived at Woolwich Arsenal to demonstrate the new smokeless powder that might revolutionize warfare. What he had produced was cellulose nitrate, commonly called guncotton; he had, moreover, discovered how to make it under controlled conditions. These conditions governed the characteristics of the new material, and a letter Schönbein sent to Michael Faraday at the Royal Institution in 1846 gave a hint of things to come. 'To give you some idea of what may be made out of vegetable fibre I send you a specimen of a transparent substance which I have prepared from common paper,' this

Alexander Parkes, inventor of 'Parkesine', an early plastic

went. 'This matter is capable of being shaped into all sorts of things and forms, and I have made from it a number of beautiful vessels. The first perfect one I obtain is destined to be sent to the Mistress of the Royal Institution.' There were other possibilities, and Faraday soon gave Schönbein an introduction to John Dickinson, the founder of the famous firm of paper-makers. Would not the new substance be suitable for the making of bank-notes? This was not the only idea floating through the minds of the inventive 19th-century chemists and another who was sent a specimen of Schönbein's material commented: 'The glass-like paper is indeed very beautiful, and I wish it could be obtained sufficiently thick to be used for windows.'

However, Schönbein's main concern was with the explosive potential of nitrocellulose, and its development into the world's first useful plastic was left to Alexander Parkes, a Birmingham metallurgist and one of those typical Victorians with brain never very far from a new idea and energy always on hand to exploit it. Parkes used to claim that he was first an artist and only secondly a metallurgist or chemist, a claim that sprang from his first patent which covered the 'Electro-deposition of Works of Art'. While the idea of electro-plating was not entirely new, Parkes refined it to new levels. When Queen Victoria visited his Birmingham works she was presented with electro-plated roses. When Prince Albert did so, something more extraordinary was produced: an electro-plated spider's web, every strand of which was coated with the thinnest covering of silver. Parkes was also the pioneer of the cold vulcanization of rubber, while as early as 1843 he patented a process for waterproofing fabrics with a solution of rubber in carbon disulphide, an idea later sold to a firm which founded not only an industry but a word: Charles Macintosh & Co.

Just what led Parkes into the world of nitrocellulose is not clear, but it has been suggested that Schönbein's English patent agent discussed the subject with him. Parkes was attracted to new ideas for their own sake but in this case he already had certain links with the subject. One of his earliest patents concerned improvements in the photographic uses of collodion; and collodion, it will be remembered, is a solution of cellulose nitrate in alcohol and ether. One of Parkes's ideas was to prepare a layer of collodion so thick that no glass would be necessary to support the sensitive photographic emulsion, and it is possible that this interest led him on to production of 'Parkesine'. There was also his hobby of moulding objects in sealing wax – a figurine of Napoleon made by Parkes was for years in the Birmingham Art Gallery – and this also played a part in his development of a cheap colourless material which passed through a plastic stage during its production.

From the start, Parkes had a number of problems. The cotton material, he soon discovered, had to be less heavily nitrated than if it was destined to be guncotton. Once he considered making a material in what would now be called production quantities, rather than the small one-off amounts made by Schönbein, he had the problem of raw materials. There were various qualities of cotton and only some of these fitted his purpose. There was also the question of cost. Parkes lived in that curious world between science, technology and business, but he knew that it would be useless to consider commercial possibilities until he could think in terms of practical prices.

Some of his early processes were sophisticated and ingenious, although one of them opens with an air of Mrs Beeton's 'Take six chickens'. 'I take a hundredweight of disintegrated or divided cotton waste or similar substances, and this is placed in an iron vessel called a converter,' he wrote. Nitric and sulphuric acid was then forced into the converter and after 20 or 30 minutes the resulting mass was dropped on to a perforated tray from which most of the remaining acid drained away. After another hour the cellulose nitrate was forced by hydraulic pressure into a hard cylinder. This cylinder of solid guncotton was subsequently broken up and mixed with a solvent. It was here that the real difficulties began. Many of the possible solvents were highly flammable; there seemed an infinitely large number of additives which could be used; and when Parkes found one that did the trick – camphor – he seems to have ignored its significance. What the camphor did was control or remove the contraction of the product during the later stages of its processing. But this seems to have been masked by the other ingredients and Parkes failed to recognize an essential factor in the production of what was a few years later to be registered as 'Celluloid' in the United States.

In the next stage, the guncotton was dissolved in the solvent to produce a malleable plastic mass, various resins and oils being added to give the end-product the necessary qualities of hardness or flexibility. It could then be processed into sheets, or moulded into shapes.

The versatility of this strange new material was outlined by Parkes, who noted that it could be used as an insulator on telegraph wires. 'It can be spread on textiles or other materials,' he went on. 'The layers of one colour may be spread on another and beautiful granular or marble effects may be obtained by rolling dissimilar coloured sheets together while in a slightly soft state.'

In practice, these characteristics meant two things. One, the cheap production of what the trade calls 'fancy goods', was illustrated by a display of products made from the new material at the International Exhibition of 1862. Here, in the words of the official catalogue, Parkes showed 'medallions, hollow ware, tubes, buttons, combs, knife handles, pierced and fret work, inlaid work, bookbinding, card cases, boxes, pens, penholders, etc.'. As if this were not enough, Parkesine, as it had now been christened, could be made 'hard as ivory, transparent or opaque, of any degree of flexibility, and is also waterproof; may be of the most brilliant colours, can be used in the solid, plastic or fluid state, may be worked in dies and pressure, as metals, may be cast or used as a coating to a great variety of substances'. Furthermore, it could be used to imitate tortoise-shell or wood, as well as to produce 'an endless variety of effects'. To men and women in 1862 it must have seemed that the millenium was on its way; Tennyson had been justified after all:

> Men, my brothers, men the workers, ever reaping something new:
> That which they have done but earnest of the things that they shall do.

In fact, it was a little more difficult than that. Parkes

A plaque moulded from 'Parkesine'

Below Ivoride head of Daniel Spill's own walking-stick

Below right Back of an ivoride hand-mirror made by Daniel Spill

claimed that his patented processes of making the new material reduced its cost from 130s ($16.00) a pound when he had begun experimenting to only 1s (12 cents) a pound by the 1860s. It was certainly a cheap product and during the later 1860s it was used to make, for the working classes, a whole range of imitation goods which would otherwise have been far beyond their pockets. But in fact, Parkesine was too cheap. The company which Parkes founded to exploit it had rushed too quickly into 'full-scale' production. Its raw materials, the cheapest it was possible to buy, were sometimes impure or contaminated, and from the scanty records that remain it seems that production problems were not carefully enough thought through. All this, quite apart from the maddening inflammability of Parkesine, added up to a recipe for disaster. Before 1870 the Parkesine Company was wound up.

While Parkes happily returned to the metallurgical and other fields where he was successful, the infant plastics industry was kept alive in England – but only just – by Daniel Spill, another minor inventive genius who could turn his hand to almost anything, and who had become Parkes's works manager. Spill made an improved version of Parkesine which he called xylonite. To exploit it, he founded the British Xylonite Company. His first products were coral jewelry and combs and these were followed by sheet xylonite coloured to produce imitation ivory and tortoise-shell. Next, the material was employed for the first of its 'social' uses – to make collars and cuffs which could be washed clean every night. The company had its ups and downs before eventually expanding into what was to become today's Bakelite Xylonite Ltd employing more than 10,000 people.

Spill's personal fortunes were dominated by his legal

battles with John Wesley Hyatt, an American who took over the plastics story in the United States as Parkes retired from it in Britain. Hyatt was a journeyman printer who in the 1860s settled in Albany, New York. In the spirit of the times he could turn his hand to anything that held out the prospect of great reward and he was attracted by an offer of Phelan & Collander, the local makers of billiard balls. Even a century ago, hunters were making their depredations on the big game of Africa, including the elephant whose ivory was the raw material of billiard balls. Phelan & Collander, looking ahead to the time when scarcity would send prices over the top, announced that they would pay $10,000 (£4,200) to anyone discovering a substitute.

Hyatt was one of those who set to work. Legend, which runs riot even more frequently in the history of the plastics industry than in most others, recounts that having cut his finger he sought out the collodion bottle, found it had tipped over, and that the liquid contents had turned into a rubbery mass. This mass became malleable under heat from his hand but hardened again on cooling.

He had already experimented with a number of substances and now found that vastly improved results were obtained if the artificial billiard balls were coated with collodion. Whatever the truth of the story it is clear that he now followed in Parkes's footsteps. What Hyatt realized, however, was that the addition of camphor would eliminate shrinkage during the manufacturing process; from this he went one step further, cutting out the use of a normal solvent and relying instead on the solvent power of camphor when it had been liquefied by heat. However, the necessary temperature was higher than that of the safety limit for nitro-cellulose and the danger was only overcome by dissolving the camphor in ethyl alcohol rather than heating it. There seems doubt as to whether Hyatt won the $10,000, but in 1869 he took out a US patent for the manufacture of what was trade-marked in 1872 as 'Celluloid', the name derived by his brother from cellulose.

The next step was the formation of the Hyatt Manufacturing Company, soon afterwards transformed into the Albany Billiard Ball Company. Not all billiard balls are white and to give the necessary colour to the others these were coated with the thinnest possible layer of nitro-cellulose. For technical reasons only the smallest amount of colouring matter was added – with the result that the balls were covered with a film of almost pure guncotton. 'Consequently a lighted cigar applied would at once result in a serious flame and occasionally the violent contact of the balls would produce a mild explosion

Cover of a Xylonite catalogue showing the plastic collar of the time

Interior of the Albany Billiard Ball
Co., New York, showing
production of plastic billiard balls

like a percussion guncap,' Hyatt later wrote. 'We had a letter
from a billiard saloon proprietor in Colorado, mentioning this
fact and saying that he did not care so much about it but that
instantly every man in the room pulled a gun.'

Although such troubles were eventually overcome, Hyatt
was glad of a fillip given to 'Celluloid' from a different direction.
This came from the makers of dental plates who had been
using hard rubber as their raw material. But rubber manufacturers were sending the price soaring, confident that they
could do so in the absence of a suitable alternative. But could
not 'Celluloid' do the job? Hyatt decided that it could. The
Albany Dental Company was formed and from that moment
onwards 'Celluloid' was in business in a major way.

The new material was soon being made in France and
Germany, as well as in England, despite the number of patent

cases which began to come into the courts. Even with the best will in the world – not always present – and even in the absence of the high financial stakes soon involved, law suits would probably have been numerous since it was almost inevitable that different men in different countries would arrive at similar solutions to similar technological problems. Thus one impression created by the new industry was of somewhat bitter commercial dispute. Another, which hung for decades like a millstone round its neck, was that plastics were second-best substitutes. To a limited extent this was true for some years. Ivory billiard balls were *the* thing. White linen collars were also *de rigeur* and the celluloid alternatives which could be taken off and washed at the end of the day were for long, and however strongly the makers might claim the contrary, the sign of the man who could not afford a new clean collar every day. This feeling changed but slowly – in fact only when chemists began to produce plastics virtually tailor-made to specification. Tailoring for the job in hand not only meant that the substitute was as good as the material it replaced, but that it could in some cases be produced with characteristics making it more suitable for a specific task than any naturally occurring substance.

However, the raw materials of these early plastics were not entirely synthetic since cellulose itself had natural cotton fibre as a base. The end-product came from the addition of acids or other chemicals under carefully controlled conditions, but the mere presence of natural-growing cotton rules out the word 'artificial' in its modern meaning. The same was true of two other early plastics which were first devised in practical form about the turn of the century and whose use continued in one form or another for two decades or more. These were cellulose acetate and casein.

The first attempts to produce a non-flammable celluloid by treating cellulose with something other than nitric or sulphuric acid had been made in the 1860s. None of them was successful and it was not until the 1890s that Charles Cross and Edward Bevan, who had already discovered how to turn natural cellulose into an artificial fibre called viscose, found a satisfactory way of turning the same raw material into a transparent non-flammable sheet of cellulose acetate. Patents were taken out in many countries, but despite the attraction of its non-flammability, cellulose acetate might not have survived had it not been for the outbreak of the First World War. This brought a demand for a non-flammable lacquer which could be used to paint the frames of aircraft and stiffen the fabric of wings. Here two Swiss, the Dreyfus brothers, were the pioneers. When the war ended they realized the potential of cellulose acetate as a fibre and within a remarkably short time had put on the market a fibre under the name of 'Celanese'. It was the first of the really popular rayons, a generic name later used to describe all fibres made from cellulose and viscose; a name sometimes used, more debatably, to describe all man-made fibres.

Casein is the main protein in milk, and its discovery as a raw material for a plastic leads back to the probably apocryphal story of the German chemist's cat who upset a bottle of formaldehyde in his saucer of milk. When the hardened casein in the milk was found to be water-resistant a new off-shoot of the plastics industry was born. Whatever the truth of the legend, chemists in both Europe and the United States patented processes for turning casein into a useful plastic. With their ability to take up the most delicate shades of dyes, and the ease with which they could be processed, casein-based plastics quickly led the field in a limited range of applications, notably for buttons and buckles and fancy goods.

The next steps were so important that they are sometimes described as founding the modern plastics industry. They were taken by Leo Baekeland, a modest likeable man whose orderly organization of life was in strong contrast to the absent-minded scientist of legend. Baekeland was a Belgian who emigrated to the United States where his personal interest in photography led him on to develop 'Velox' printing-out paper. In 1899, at the age of 36, he sold his photographic interests for enough money to make him independent for life. Then, typically enough for a man of such restless interests, he returned to Europe for what he called a year's refresher course in electro-chemistry.

Back again in America, Baekeland began to develop new methods of air conditioning. He improved electrolytic cells. But in the early 1900s it was another task to which he turned – one which was to bring him world-wide fame. It was the search for a man-made material which could replace shellac, the yellowish natural resin secreted by the lac insect which on account of its insulating properties was being demanded in growing quantities by the expanding electrical industry.

At the start, Baekeland's idea was to build on the earlier work of Adolf Baeyer and Werner Kleeberg. Baeyer had announced as far back as 1872 that when phenols, a class of aromatic organic compounds, reacted with the aldehydes, another class of organics, the result was a resinous sticky substance. Nearly two decades later, when formaldehyde was newly available in cheap commercial quantities and one

Women workers doping aeroplane canvas before painting in a Birmingham factory, September 1918

particular phenol was coming from the developing coal-tar industry, Kleeberg found that he could get from their reaction a malleable paste that eventually set rock-solid. But both men, as well as those who read the papers describing their work, regarded these products as commercially irrelevant if scientifically interesting. Baekeland, probably leafing back through the literature in his methodical way, believed that he could do something with them.

His first idea was to produce a sticky residue from the reaction, find a solvent that would dissolve it, and then use the solution as the shellac substitute. But few solvents seemed to work satisfactorily. Why, therefore, Baekeland asked himself, should it not be possible to produce this sticky residue itself in useful form? Once the thought occurred to him he began to investigate earlier work, and he found that previous experimenters had apparently set about the job without exercising strict control over such factors as temperature or pressure.

A number of years passed before Baekeland was satisfied. He used raw materials produced in different ways, combined in different percentages, and in varying conditions of pressure

'Old Faithful', the still in which Leo Baekeland produced his first resins

and temperature. One of the keys to his final success was a piece of apparatus which he called a Bakelizer. 'Such an apparatus', he explained, 'consists mainly of an interior chamber in which air can be pumped so as to bring its pressure to 50 or better 100 pounds per square inch. This chamber can be heated externally or internally by means of a steam packet or steam coils to temperatures as high as 160°C or considerably higher, so that the heated object during the process of Bake-lizing may remain steadily under suitable pressure which will avoid porosity or blistering of the mass.'

Baekeland worked on for five years. Not until February, 1907 did he file what became his most famous patent, the first of 119 concerning plastics, and the one which described how to make the material soon known throughout the world as Bake-lite. It was not the world's first plastic, since Parkesine was that, but it did not require any natural material such as cotton fibre and was therefore the first entirely synthetic material to be put on the market.

There were three kinds of Bakelite. The first, Bakelite A, was made when the reaction was stopped while the material was hot and liquid; it set solid on cooling but was still soluble in the right solvents. If the process were allowed to continue without cooling, then Bakelite A was turned into Bakelite B, a solid which was soft when hot but hard when cold and thus admirably suited for moulding. The third variety, Bakelite C, was made by heating Bakelite B under pressure.

The new material had all the insulating characteristics which Baekeland expected of it, but it also had something more. It was the first of the plastics which, having been moulded in the hot state and then allowed to cool, would keep its new shape even when heated again. Almost as important was the wide variety of ways in which it could be used. In 1909, the plastics industry had not even started its ramifications. Even so, the famous paper which Baekeland read that year to the American Chemical Society in New York gave a hint of things to come. Wood dipped into liquid Bakelite could be given a brilliant coat of the material which was, he claimed, superior to even the most expensive Japanese lacquer. 'But I can do better,' he went on. 'I may prepare an A, much more liquid than this one, and which has great penetrating power, and I may soak cheap porous soft wood in it, until the fibres have absorbed as much liquid as possible, then transfer the impregnated wood to the Bakelizer, and let the synthesis take place in and around the fibres of the wood. The result is a very hard wood, as hard as mahogany, or ebony of which the tensile, and more especially the crushing strength, has been considerably increased and which can stand dilute acids or steam; henceforth it is proof against dry rot. In the same way I have succeeded in impregnating cheap ordinary cardboard or pulp board and changing it into a hard resisting polished material that can be carved, turned and brought into many shapes.'

The new plastic could be compounded with sawdust and wood-pulp, colouring matter or a wide variety of materials which would help produce special substances for special jobs. 'I cannot better illustrate this than by telling you that here you have before you a grindstone made of Bakelite,' Baekeland went on, 'and on the other hand a self-lubricating bearing which has been run dry for nine hours at 1,800 revolutions per minute without objectionable heating and without injuring the quickly revolving shaft.'

It was typical of Baekeland that he should end his account by saying: 'The opened field is so vast that I look forward with the pleasures of anticipation to many more years of work in the same direction. I have preferred to forego secrecy about my work, relying solely on the strength of my patents as a protection. It will be a great pleasure to me if in doing so, I may stimulate further interest in this subject among my fellow chemists and if this may lead them to succeed in perfecting my methods or increase still further the number of useful applications of this interesting compound.'

There was, in fact, to be an almost limitless number of useful applications. Bearings that needed no lubrication was only one prospect opened up. In the electrical industry the uses of Bakelite were soon going far beyond the replacement of shellac. The Westinghouse Electrical Manufacturing Company began using it to impregnate paper sheets made for insulating material while the infant motor car industry was quickly demanding Bakelite for junction boxes, distributor heads and the multiplicity of other parts which had to be chemically resistant, electrically insulating and capable of standing up to both heat and rough treatment.

Within a few years the use of Bakelite had become world-wide. Even so, many men in many countries were developing their own plastics in the years immediately before the First World War. One of the most important was James, later Sir James, Swinburne, a pioneer both in electrical engineering and plastics. Swinburne had the bad luck to apply for a phenol-formaldehyde patent shortly – some records claim only one day – after Baekeland had done so. He nevertheless persevered with different methods and eventually succeeded in the plastics field that Baekeland had first entered. Britain of the early 1900s was still the age of brass – brass fenders, brass fire-irons and brass bed-steads. All these needed much polishing, and a coating of shellac was often put on to reduce the elbow-grease required. Swinburne succeeded in perfecting a plastic lacquer whose quality was suggested by the name of the company which he founded to make it – the Damard Lacquer Company.

In the plastics industry the First World War divided separate stages of development quite as surely as it did in other fields. In some ways the German invasion of Belgium in August 1914 ended the 19th century; similarly, the war-time advances in the plastics industry marked an end to the old hit-and-miss, trial-and-error, methods which even the most scientific of the pioneers had tended to use. Baekeland and Swinburne, and the many men who did only slightly less important research in other countries, worked to fine tolerances of temperature and pressure; nevertheless, they realized their own limitations and well knew that if one set of ingredients did not provide what they were trying to make, then a pinch of something else might well turn out to give the answer. The reason, which they would have been the first to admit, was that comparatively little was yet known about the complex chemistry of the new materials they were making. All this was changed during the next two decades.

The change was closely linked with the new kinds of raw material which began to be available as the popularity of the petrol engine helped to open up the oil wells of the world. Before the war, coal had provided both phenol and for-maldehyde. Cellulose had provided celluloid, cellulose acetate, and a variety of other synthetically made materials. With a small handful of other materials incorporated into such pro-ducts as synthetic rubbers, this was virtually the entire list of substances which went into man-made materials.

Then came petrol. Or, more accurately, then came crude oil, a mixture of hydrocarbons and other organic compounds from which it was possible to separate, by distillation, by fractionation or by other processes, a huge number of different chemicals. Most of them are based on the simple constituents of carbon and hydrogen but most are more or less complex molecules. It was the study of this complexity which did much to make possible the impressive families of plastics which began to grow during the years between the wars.

One of the first realizations was that the physical charac-teristics of plastics were closely related to the size and com-plexity of the molecules of which they are built up. Thus cellulose, the constituent of the early plastics, consists of molecules in each of which six atoms of carbon, ten of hydrogen and five of oxygen have been linked together by the complicated chemical processes taking place within the living plant, the result being a molecule more complex than most of those met with in run-of-the-mill work in laboratory or factory. With the quickening pace of organic chemistry, three things were realized. The first was that it might be possible to take chemically simple materials and then turn them, in the chemical works, into molecules as elaborate as those produced by nature. The second was that the booming petrol industry might produce, as by-products, and in comparatively large quantities, just such simple materials. The third was that it might even be possible to tailor-make artificial substances with characteristics which could be forecast in advance.

The possibilities were increased by the work of one group of specialists, the polymer chemists, notably Hermann Staudinger in Germany and Wallace Carothers in the United States. Their story, that of polymerization, the chemical union of two or more molecules of the same compound to form larger molecules, has a history that goes back at least as far as 1872 when E. Baumann reported what was in fact the polymerization of vinyl chloride into what was to be known, more than half a century later, as polyvinylchloride or PVC. An earlier attribution gives credit to Regnault in 1835. However, it is not certain that Baumann realized what he had done. Eight years later Georg Kahlbaum polymerized methylacrylate. Even so, it was not until another 30 years had passed that the first polymerization patent was taken out. This applied to isoprene, one of whose polymers forms the bulk of natural rubber. A decade afterwards in 1920, the Belgo-American chemist Julius Nieuwland found that acetylene, the colourless gas with its molecules of two carbon atoms linked to two hydrogen atoms, could be made to polymerize into a giant molecule that had some of the properties of rubber.

Shortly afterwards Hermann Staudinger began to provide scientific chapter and verse for the macromolecules, or giant molecules, of polymerization which in all cases seemed to consist of large numbers of smaller molecules linked together into long chains. In nature, the chemical reactions of plant life produced the parallel unbranched chains of glucose units which were condensed into the fibrous structure of cellulose. In synthetic plastics, heat and pressure did much the same thing.

While Staudinger was investigating this theoretical basis of polymerization, the big American Chemical Corporation, Du Pont, took one of the first steps to study the industrial

Above Dr Wallace H. Carothers, who directed the Du Pont fundamental research programme from which came Neoprene synthetic rubber

Right Manufacture of viscose, showing the consistency of the material in an early stage of manufacture

possibilities of what was still little more than a chemical curiosity. Under the leadership of Carothers, it was found that if a chlorine atom was added to the polymerizing acetylene chain at the right point, the end-product was a synthetic rubber which had a high tensile strength and better heat resistance than the natural product. This was soon to be registered as Neoprene, one of the most important early synthetic rubbers, and one which was to help save the Allies after the Malayan rubber jungles were lost to the Japanese during the Second World War.

The advances in man's theoretical knowledge of polymerization, epitomized by Staudinger, merged with the practical industrial experience typified by Carothers. With both went the rapidly expanding supply of hydrocarbons from the petroleum industry. The outcome was the foundation not only of today's plastics industry but also of the closely allied industries making synthetic rubber and synthetic fibres. The links between these three empires are strong, for with few exceptions they turn members of the same family of raw materials into high polymers, the main differences in the characteristics of their end-products being the nature of the chemical forces operating between the chains of molecules. Put in a very over-simplified form, if these forces are weak, the result is rubber; if they are stronger, the outcome is a plastic; while if the links are really strong but the molecule-chains are long and slim, the end-product is a fibre.

However, no hard dividing line can be drawn between these various groups. Thus nylon was first produced by Du Pont as a result of Carothers's work – after the expenditure of $27,000,000 (£11m) and the efforts of 230 chemists and engineers – as a substitute for the silk of silk stockings, and is still most familiar in some form of thread, whether for sewing, for bootlaces or for climbing rope. Yet nylon is also produced in bulk and turns up as a family of polymers which can be moulded or extruded into a wide variety of end-products.

The word 'nylon' is also used as a generic name for any long-chain synthetic polymeric amide which conforms to certain specifications, a fact which highlights the confusion existing about many words, names and definitions in the plastics industry. One reason for this confusion arises from the fact that a specific chemical product can be registered under more than one trade-name. Polymethyl methacrylate has been known as 'Plexiglas' on the Continent, as 'Lucite' in the United States and as 'Perspex' in Britain. Quite as bewildering is the frequent use of what are really proprietary trade-marks for a far wider range of materials. Thus the word 'perspex'

A flame boils water, but a 1/1000 of an inch thick Kapton film between them remains intact. Kapton, developed by Du Pont, is an exceptionally strong and extremely resistant film with an unusual combination of mechanical and electrical properties. It retains high tensile strength as well as flexibility, cut-through resistance and resistance to cold flow over a wide temperature range. It has been used successfully in various applications from −269°C to 440°C. The Apollo lunar module used fourteen miles of wiring insulated with Kapton and it was used in the sun shield which helped salvage the Skylab space station.

itself is sometimes employed to describe all kinds of acrylic sheet; and 'fibreglass' is incorrectly used for many sorts of materials consisting basically of fibres of glass usually less than one thousandth of an inch in diameter, woven into cloth and then impregnated with resin. 'Bakelite' is often incorrectly used to describe a whole range of phenolic plastics while the trade name 'Formica' in the same way is sometimes incorrectly used to describe laminates that are not Formica.

The huge range of contemporary plastics has come into existence partly as a result of experience gained during the Second World War, when artificial materials were made with characteristics fitting them for specific jobs; partly because of the post-war demand for the lighter, cleaner, and eventually cheaper, products which plastics seemed likely to satisfy. It is also a direct result of the chemists' questioning of nature, of their persistent desire to find out more about the ways in which atoms of the various elements are bound together to form materials that are plastic.

Further there has been a good deal of luck, a classic example being the story of polythene, whose initial discovery 'provides an unusually clear-cut instance of the unexpected results that may come from research, and of the importance of the role of chance in such work.'

In the early 1930s Imperial Chemical Industries embarked on a research programme designed to investigate chemical reactions under very high pressures. These pressures were not to be the few hundred atmospheres of previous research, but pressures up to many thousands. Such work involved expensive apparatus and the spending of very large sums which might produce some results or none. It says much for the imaginative outlook of the firm that they went ahead with this project in the depressed economic conditions of the early 1930s.

In the United States J. B. Conant, later President of Harvard and the man who was to hold a number of key roles in the American war effort between 1941 and 1945, had discovered that polymerization was greatly affected by high pressures, and this was one of the effects which ICI began to investigate. At first the results appeared to be of little significance. However, early in March 1933 an attempt was made to react ethylene with benzaldehyde, at a pressure of 1,400 atmospheres and at a temperature of 170°C. 'There was no indication from change in pressure that reaction had occurred,' wrote Michael, now Sir Michael, Perring who played a major role in the series of experiments, 'and when the pressure vessel was dismantled the benzaldehyde was recovered unchanged.

The walls of the vessel were, however, found to be coated with a thin layer of a "white, waxy solid" to quote from R. O. Gibson's notebook record of 27 March. This material was analysed and found to contain no oxygen, which confirmed the observation that the benzaldehyde, present in the vessel, had taken no part in the reaction. The solid was recognized as a hydrocarbon and, apparently, a polymer of ethylene. A similar result was obtained when ethylene alone was subjected to this pressure but the amount of product formed was always extremely small.'

The researchers next did the obvious thing. They increased the pressure. This not only caused the ethylene to decompose but in addition produced a further and sudden rise so great that joints and gauges on the apparatus were blown open. It was clear that different and more expensive equipment would be necessary before the work could be continued, and in April it was decided that it should be abandoned for the time being.

In fact it was a lapse of more than two years. Work was dropped, then resumed, very great improvements in technique were made, and when experiments started again in the autumn of 1935 far higher pressures were possible without risk. This time ethylene alone was put in the reaction vessel before the pressure was raised and a series of experiments eventually resulted in a new material which was crystalline, of high molecular weight, and apparently of the long-chain structure which Carothers had already found in nylon. More important, it had characteristics which made it of great potential use in industry – it did not melt in boiling water, it could be formed into films and threads when heated under slight pressure, it was chemically resistant, and it had outstanding insulating properties.

Production of this polymer of ethylene, first known in Britain as polythene and now officially called polyethylene, was soon got under way, but the production first in ounces and then in pounds of what had so far only been made under laboratory conditions demanded immense, and expensive, development work. Despite this, by the outbreak of war, polythene was being produced by the ton. This was as well. One of its major uses was to be in the high-frequency equipment needed for radar. Soon after the war annual production of polythene in Britain alone had reached 100,000 tons.

The war speeded up the advances of plastics technology just as it spurred on the development of radar, and from the 1950s onwards industry was offered a growing range of man-made plastic materials, some tailor-made for specific jobs.

From the comparatively simple experiments of scientists

such as Carothers and the workers at ICI a host of different complicated manufacturing processes evolved. Most of them involve one of two different kinds of polymerization. In one, addition polymerization as it is called, a simple substance known as the monomer – ethylene in the making of polythene for instance – is subjected to specific conditions, usually heat and pressure, in the presence of a catalyst. The catalyst then helps to set off or speed up the joining of the simple molecules into long-chain molecules.

In the second kind of polymerization, condensation polymerization (or more simply polycondensation), two different kinds of simple molecule, each containing two chemically reactive groups, are heated together. The reacting ends of two molecules link up to form a larger molecule and a simple by-product such as water. But this larger molecule still contains reactive end groups, and the process can continue as heating goes on, with the molecules getting longer and longer.

These products, made only on a laboratory scale a decade earlier, were after the war produced by the ton in large chemical plants whose design and erection demanded great engineering and technological expertise as well as chemical know-how. They are made in various forms. Polyvinylchloride or PVC for instance is a fine white powder. Polyethylene comes as chips or granules. Other plastics consist of viscous liquids.

Other substances are often added to this raw plastic material, the stuff of a multitude of products found in every home and office, before it goes to the fabricating side of the plastics industry. Some plastics, such as PVC, require the addition of a heat stabilizer if they are to be processed above a certain temperature. Plasticizers can be added to produce a softer end-product, and so can dyes or pigments if particular colour effects are required. A fibrous inert filler can be added to the plastic either to make the end-product tougher or to make it cheaper.

The ways in which this raw material is then made into the plastic products of contemporary life depends to a very large extent on whether it is thermosetting or thermoplastic. This basic division among plastics, of paramount industrial interest, is a very simple one. Thermosetting plastics become soft and malleable when they are heated; but once they have hardened on cooling they cannot be made plastic again. In the case of thermoplastics the process of heating to make plastic can be repeated indefinitely.

With thermosetting plastics the most common method of processing is compression moulding in which the raw material

Typical narrow tube extrusion of polythene

is compressed in a heated mould. Another is laminating, in which the plastic is squeezed under heat and pressure onto and into layers of paper or cloth. Thermoplastics, on the other hand, are more usually formed into articles by extrusion in which the thermoplastic material is fed as powder or grains into a heated barrel and then, when softened, forced along the barrel and through the hole or die which gives it the desired shape. Various kinds of moulding are used – the blow moulding technique usually used for making the plastic bottles which are steadily replacing glass; or injection moulding used to make the complicated small parts of electrical equipment. Foamed plastics, the sponge-like products also known as expanded plastics, are produced by ensuring that a gas is given off as the plastic mass hardens, thus expanding the mass as the process continues. Plastic film can be made by the calendering process used in the paper-making industry. Articles can be given a plastic covering by dipping them in a fluidized bed of powdered thermoplastic, while many finished plastic products can be machined, cut, stamped, drilled or glued as though they were of traditional wood or metal.

Plastics are no longer substitutes. In their multitudinous guises they are an accepted part of everyday life and it is difficult for an open eye not to see them: in the office as the plastic telephone hand-set and a score of commercial articles; in the home the curtains of artificial fibre, on the river the plastic fishing-line and on the mountain the nylon climbing rope. The man with poor sight may well view life through plastic spectacles.

The qualities of lightness and durability are not the only ones which give such materials the advantage in an increasingly large number of fields. Another lies in the fact that they are biologically inert; specifically, they do not provide food for insects. Thus clothes made of plastics do not suffer from attack by moth; neither, in a different field, do the plastic jackets of books or the synthetic resins which for many applications have replaced vegetable and animal glues. Moreover these advantages, which spring directly from man's chemical control of his available materials, may very well be only the beginning. Molecules are made up of atoms. Atoms are also susceptible to human manipulation, and it has recently been found that man-made materials themselves can be further changed if subjected to the processes offered by the nuclear revolution of the last quarter-century.

5 The Nuclear Revolution

The conscription of the electro-magnetic spectrum to produce radio, television and radar in less than a century is a prime example of scientific discoveries being exploited by inventors for purposes which have radically changed the world. Only more important is the release, taming and use of atomic – or more correctly, nuclear – energy, a development whose principal stages have been carried through in only half a century but which represents man's most revolutionary step forward since the taming of fire. The story is a classic example of the way in which knowledge is first gained by scientists and then used by engineers, technologists and inventors. There has been the slow piecing together by men from many nations of different bits of the jig-saw puzzle; there has been the outside impetus – in this case war and threat of war – so often needed to interest non-scientists in what had been a purely academic affair; and there has been a long technological struggle, still continuing, during which pure science, applied science and engineering have all helped to create the hardware which fresh knowledge about the physical world has made possible.

The idea of nuclear energy – the energy locked within the nucleus of the atom – is intimately bound up with man's beliefs about the structure of matter. These beliefs hardened into recognizable form, as did so many others, as long ago as the days of ancient Greece. About 420 BC Democritus first asserted that matter was not continuous but was made up of indivisible and ever-lasting bits which he called 'atoms', or particles which could not be divided. The theory enabled him to explain the difference between various substances on the grounds that denser materials had their particles packed more closely together. A century later, Aristotle led an opposing school which asserted that all matter was composed, in varying proportions, of four constituents: solid earth, liquid water, gaseous air, and the element fire which successfully defied definition.

For some 2,000 years there seemed little chance of deciding between these two basic ideas. But for much of the period Aristotle's views held the field, while the alchemists unsuccessfully tried to turn base metals into gold by juggling with the proportions of their alleged constituents. Only with the birth of 'modern' science in the 18th century, with the growth of chemical theory and the chance of using controlled experiment to prove or disprove theory, did a rudimentary atomic belief again come to the fore, a belief which it was hoped would explain the mass of new facts by this time being brought forward by the chemists.

Newton, Robert Boyle, Antoine Lavoisier and Joseph Proust who had speculated that two elements could combine only in the ratio of whole numbers – 6:1 for instance but never 5.9:1 or 6.1:1 – were all men whose work led back towards Democritus's particulate theory of matter. It was left to the English chemist John Dalton, colour-blind and poor, to pull these separate strings together and to tie them into the atomic theory from which the nuclear revolution eventually emerged. Dalton outlined his ideas in 1803 and five years later gave them in full in his *New System of Chemical Philosophy*. The first tenet of his system was that the elements of matter – Dalton named 20 of them – consisted of invisible and indivisible particles for which he used Democritus's name of atoms. The atoms of any one element were always of the same weight, but the atoms making up different elements were of different weights. Furthermore, when atoms of different elements combined to form molecules of a compound, they always combined in fixed and simple ratios. As for the atom itself, Dalton saw this as a solid sphere – the hard billiard-ball of matter whose existence was accepted with little questioning for almost a hundred years.

Not until the last decade of the 19th century was doubt thrown on this simple and cosy idea of the atom. As early as 1875 Sir William Crookes had shown that when a cathode, or negative electrode, was placed under strong electric potential within a vacuum tube, there came from it an emission of what he christened cathode rays. At first the rays were thought to be merely a form of electro-magnetic radiation, although Crookes finally put them down to streams of electrically-charged particles, an idea which was met with extreme reserve by most other scientists. However, only two decades later J. J. Thomson, working in the Cavendish Laboratory at Cambridge, proved Crookes's point: cathode rays were in fact streams of negatively charged particles, now christened electrons. Yet these particles could have come from nowhere other than the

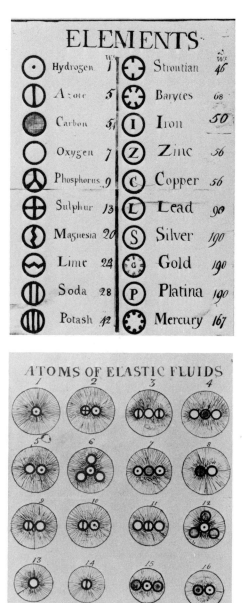

Top John Dalton's list of elements

Bottom Reproduction of lecture diagram prepared by John Dalton between 1806 and 1809 to illustrate his early conception of composition and relative sizes of atoms of gases and liquids

Sir J. J. Thomson with early
equipment in the Cavendish
Laboratory, Cambridge

metallic cathode – even though Thomson went on to show
that their mass was but a very small fraction, roughly 1/1837th,
of the lightest known atom, hydrogen. In one set of experiments he had thus destroyed the idea of the 'billiard-ball
atom'.

In Paris meanwhile, Henri Becquerel was also casting doubt
on the indivisibility of the atom after finding photographic
plates fogged by streams of particles thrown out by the rare
metal uranium. Marie Curie soon afterwards did the same
with her experiments on radium. Together, they made
scientists re-think their ideas about the basic structure of
matter.

Thomson had his own theory. For him the 'billiard-ball
atom' was replaced by the 'raisin-cake atom'. This was still
solid; but in Thomson's view it was a sphere of positively
charged matter, studded with just enough negatively charged
electrons – the raisins in the cake – to neutralize the positive
charge. This theory, which held the stage at the start of the
20th century, was soon to be demolished by the most brilliant

of all Thomson's pupils, Ernest Rutherford, the man perhaps most correctly known as the 'father of the nuclear age'.

Rutherford, studying the radioactive substances already noted by Becquerel and Curie, concluded first that the rays given off by such substances were of various kinds. There were the alpha rays, soon discovered to be streams of positively charged particles – in fact the nuclei, or central cores, of helium atoms; beta rays which were streams of electrons; and the gamma rays which were in fact electro-magnetic waves of very short wave-length.

It was with the first of these, the alpha rays, that in 1908 in the University of Manchester – after a short but fruitful spell in McGill University, Montreal – Rutherford began the experiments which yielded the vital clues to what the atom was really like. The crucial stage came with the 'firing' of alpha particles at a sheet of gold foil. The foil was only one fifty-thousandth of an inch thick, but it consisted of no less than 2,000 layers of atoms. The results were startling and almost contradictory. Most of the alpha particles passed straight through the foil, completely undiverted by any of the 2,000 layers, and impinged on the photographic plate behind them. To Rutherford this could mean only one thing: if the particles could pass through 2,000 layers of gold atoms and not be deflected by them, then atoms must be made up largely of empty space.

But this conclusion, staggering as it was, explained only part of the experiment's results. For while most of the alpha particles passed through the gold leaf without giving any sign of its existence, a few did completely the reverse: they were not only deflected by the foil, but deflected very sharply indeed, some of them even bouncing back from it. As Rutherford said afterwards, it was as though a big shell had been bounced back by a sheet of tissue paper. The experiment, repeated time after time, showed the same result and only one conclusion could be drawn: that somewhere in the atom there was an area of strong positive charge which, since like charges repel, brusquely repelled the positive alpha particle.

The picture that emerged was, with some modifications, that still seen today. At the centre of the atom, and forming its nucleus, there are one or more positively charged particles or protons. Circling them at a relatively immense distance are the negatively charged electrons, one for each proton under normal conditions. The numbers of protons and electrons in each atom, different for each element, range from one in the hydrogen atom to 92 in the atom of uranium – and 94 in the extremely rare plutonium 244 only discovered in 1971 – and the chemical characteristics of each element are entirely the result of these differing numbers of charged particles. To make this picture more up-to-date it is necessary to jump ahead to 1932 when the British physicist, James, later Sir James, Chadwick proved the existence of a third type of particle. This was the uncharged neutron, one or more neutrons being present in the nuclei of all atoms except those of normal hydrogen.

Rutherford's conception of the atom as a miniature solar system with negatively charged electrons forever orbiting a positively charged nucleus presented physicists with a number of problems. They were solved before the First World War by the Danish physicist Niels Bohr and by the end of the war the idea of the Rutherford-Bohr atom was firmly established.

Up to this point, research into the structure of matter appeared to have only theoretical importance, even though it was by now known that immense amounts of energy were locked up inside the atom. The existence of this energy became clear when it was established that the weight of the atomic nucleus was different from the separate weights of its component protons and neutrons added together. If it were thus possible to break up a nucleus into nuclear fragments that weighed less there would be a loss of mass. This in itself was

Right Lord Rutherford (*left*) and Niels Bohr with Lady Rutherford (*left*) and Mrs Niels Bohr photographed in the Rutherfords' garden about 1930

Far right Dr E. T. S. Walton (*left*) and Dr (later Sir John) Cockcroft (*right*) with Lord Rutherford after the first artificial transmutation of the atom

interesting but no more. What made it important was the size
of the energy release given by Einstein's famous equation of
1905 – $E = mc^2$, which in the shorthand of science gives the
amount of energy released when a mass of m grams is completely converted into energy. Now the difference in mass
which might be possible in nuclear transformations would no
doubt be very small. But Einstein's equation showed that the
energy involved consisted of the mass multiplied by c^2 – where
c is the velocity of light in centimetres per second. Little
mathematical expertise was required to show that a very small
amount of mass was equal to a relatively huge amount of energy.

On the face of it, the first step towards making use of this
nuclear energy appeared to have been taken by Rutherford
himself in 1919. Shortly before becoming Director of the
Cavendish Laboratory in Cambridge he used the particles
thrown out by radium to bombard a quantity of nitrogen. Very
occasionally one of the particles would penetrate a nitrogen
nucleus and transform it into the nucleus of an oxygen atom.
Thus Rutherford had succeeded in carrying out the alchemist's
dream of turning one element into another.

But what about the energy released? This was certainly
greater than that of the alpha 'bullet'. But only about one

bullet in every million hit its target; the rest of them passed through the relatively large spaces which existed between the targets and their encircling electrons. Thus more energy had to be put into the nuclear stockpot than could be obtained from it.

This was still true 13 years later when two of Rutherford's workers in the Cavendish, the young John Cockcroft who was later to become head of Britain's first nuclear research station at Harwell, and C. T. Walton, succeeded in 'splitting the atom' as it was then called, by different and more sophisticated means. Whereas Rutherford used naturally radio-active radium to provide the bullets, Cockcroft and Walton used streams of hydrogen protons which they speeded-up by the use of high voltages to bombard small specimens of lithium, a light silvery-white metal. The result, in the almost throw-away words of their statement in *Nature*, was that, 'the lithium isotope of mass seven occasionally captures a proton and the resulting nucleus of mass eight breaks into two alpha-particles, each of mass four and each with an energy of about eight million electron volts.' But although the number of 'hits' was much greater than those in Rutherford's experiments of 1919, and although the phrase 'eight million electron volts' was enough to send shudders through the uninformed, the energy released in the experiment was still only a small frac-tion of that put into it.

The analogy between putting more energy into the nuclear stockpot than could be taken from it still held after Cockcroft and Walton's historic experiment. In fact Rutherford, naturally cautious and anxious not to encourage the wilder speculations, used an address at a meeting of the British Association to describe as 'moonshine' any hope of using atomic energy. Even so, the visionaries could hardly be held in check. As far back as 1903 Rutherford had made in a letter to Sir William Dampier what his correspondent had later called a 'playful suggestion that, could a proper detonator be found, it was just conceivable that a wave of atomic disintegration might be started through matter, which would indeed make this old world vanish in smoke.' In 1921 the Austrian physicist Hans Thirring had written after Rutherford's initial experi-ment that 'it takes one's breath away to think of what might happen in a town, if the dormant energy of a single brick were to be set free, say in the form of an explosion. It would suffice to raze a city with a million inhabitants to the ground.'

Less pessimistic dreamers forecast how a great liner might cross the Atlantic on the energy from a pound of nuclear fuel. More significantly there had taken place in London only a

few days before Cockcroft and Walton's experiment, the first performance of *Wings over Europe*, a play which like Wells's *The World Set Free* raised the spectre of nuclear weapons. 'The destiny of man', wrote Desmond McCarthy, 'has slipped (we are all aware of it) from the hands of politicians into the hands of scientists, who know not what they do, but pass responsibility for results on to those whose sense of proportion and knowledge are inadequate to the situations created by science.'

Frédéric and Irène Joliot-Curie in their Paris laboratory

McCarthy was before his time, but only by a year or two. By 1934 the next experiments leading mankind into the nuclear age had been made – although their significance had been missed. By 1934 a refugee Hungarian physicist had lodged with the British Admiralty a patent for a nuclear chain reaction of a type to be used in the first nuclear weapons. And by the spring of 1939, with world war only a few months away, Great Britain, France and Germany were mobilizing their physicists to discover whether it would be possible to make a nuclear weapon of gigantic power.

The events of those five years – in their results, possibly the most momentous five years that science has ever known –

follow one another in almost chain-reaction fashion. Early in 1934 Irène Curie, daughter of Madame Curie, and her husband Frédéric Joliot, discovered in Paris that by bombarding certain normally stable nuclei with alpha particles, these nuclei could be made radioactive. In England Leo Szilard, a Hungarian physicist who had studied under Einstein in Berlin a decade earlier and who has rightly been called the *éminence grise* of nuclear physics, had meanwhile been considering Rutherford's 'moonshine' statement. 'It suddenly occurred to me,' he later wrote, 'that if we could find an element which is split by neutrons and which would emit *two* neutrons when it absorbed one neutron, such an element, if assembled in sufficiently large mass, could sustain a nuclear chain reaction.' This was in the summer of 1933. Then, in the spring of 1934, came the announcement of the Curies' work. 'I suddenly saw,' Szilard said, 'that tools were at hand to explore the possibility of such a chain reaction.'

The reasoning was clear. In the earlier experiments by Rutherford, Walton and Cockcroft – and by others who had followed them – the initial nuclear transformation had been, as it were, a one-off operation. After it had taken place another million or so bullets had to be fired before a further hit was made on the target. What Szilard now foresaw was that if a neutron could be made to create a nuclear transformation and at the same time to release two neutrons these in turn might create two more transformations which in turn would create four; and so on. Furthermore, if these events took place quickly enough, the result could be an explosion which would make the energy-release of normal chemical explosions look puny by comparison. Within a year Szilard had filed with the British Admiralty a patent, sealed secret as it is called, since it was his conviction 'that if a nuclear chain reaction can be made to work, it can be used to set up violent explosions.'

In Rome, the Italian physicist Enrico Fermi had meanwhile been following up the Curies' work, finding that first one and then another element could be activated by bombardment with neutrons. Most of his results were explicable in terms of contemporary knowledge; particles were 'chipped away' from the nucleus and new elements were created. But in some cases, particularly that of uranium, the heaviest of the elements, with 92 protons and about 140 neutrons jostling together within its nucleus, there seemed to be some mystery. It was not altogether surprising. The material with which these early experimenters were dealing consisted of micro-quantities whose accurate identification by chemical test was itself something of a triumph. Fermi published his results. But he left it to others to

Lise Meitner and Otto Hahn in the laboratory of the Kaiser Wilhelm Institute in Berlin, 1925

discover exactly what happened when a uranium nucleus was hit.

Among these others were Otto Hahn, Lise Meitner and Fritz Strassman of the Kaiser Wilhelm in Berlin. And it is with them, as the nuclear story gathers pace and world war approaches, that the extraordinary ironies of the tale become apparent. Enrico Fermi and Leo Szilard were merely two of the nuclear physicists who played key parts in the tale – and were forced to play them not in Europe but in the United States, where they had finally sought refuge. And now, in March 1938, the work in the Kaiser Wilhelm was grotesquely disrupted by the German invasion of Austria. For Lise Meitner was Austrian; she was also a Jewess, and the German absorption of her country thus brought her under threat of the concentration camp. She moved first to Holland, then to Sweden. The work in the Kaiser Wilhelm had to continue without her.

In this gaunt ugly building, soon to be laid in ruins by

British bombers, Hahn and Strassman went on with their experiments. They, like Fermi, bombarded uranium. The substance which they found in minute traces after the bombardment had all the chemical characteristics of barium, a silvery-white soft metal. What is more, Hahn the chemist could soon show beyond all reasonable doubt that it was in fact barium. But the nucleus of a barium atom contained only 56 protons; that left 36 protons of the 92 in the uranium nucleus – 36 protons, the number which it was known were contained in the nucleus of an atom of the inert gas krypton. If this process had occurred it was something very different from chipping away at the nucleus. Hahn himself was not quite sure what he had done and when he settled down in his laboratory on 21 December 1938 to write his report he described his results only as 'at variance with all previous experiences in nuclear physics.'

Before his report appeared in *Naturwissenschaften* on 6 January 1939 it had reached Lise Meitner in Sweden, for what was more natural than that Hahn should send it to his former collaborator? In Sweden Lise Meitner discussed it with her nephew Otto Frisch, a worker in Niels Bohr's Copenhagen research laboratory who was spending Christmas with his aunt. Walking in the snow-covered Swedish woods, they realized what Hahn had done.

'It took her a little while to make me listen,' Frisch has said, 'but . . . very gradually we realized that the breaking-up of a uranium nucleus into two almost equal parts was a process so different from the emission of a helium nucleus that it had to be pictured in quite a different way. The picture is not that of a particle breaking through a potential barrier, but rather the gradual deformation of the original uranium nucleus, its elongation, formation of a waist, and finally separation of the two halves. The striking similarity of that picture with the process of fission by which bacteria multiply caused us to use the phrase "nuclear fission" in our first publication.'

The news that Hahn had split the uranium nucleus in two was taken across the Atlantic by Niels Bohr who was fortuitously due to speak to the Fifth Washington Conference in January 1939. Events then moved quickly. Within a few days the Berlin experiments had been repeated in the Carnegie Institution of Washington, the Johns Hopkins University and the University of California. Frisch had already repeated them in Copenhagen. Similar work was carried out in Warsaw by a brilliant young Polish worker, Joseph Rotblat. The Leningrad Physico-Technical Institute announced a similar success in April, while in Paris a strong team of physicists working in the

Collège de France quickly answered one of the questions raised by the newly discovered fission process.

That process was dramatic enough. 'The picture,' as Frisch put it, 'was that of two fairly large nuclei flying apart with an energy of nearly two hundred million electron volts, more than ten times the energy involved in any other nuclear reaction.' So far so good. But this brief spark of nuclear fire had of itself little practical significance. The important thing was whether the spark could be kept alight. From the first it seemed that there was a good chance. For the two new nuclei were created 'in a strongly deformed and hence excited state' to quote Frisch. Thus they might expel one or more neutrons as they were created. But it was the impact of a neutron which had created the fission in the first place. Therefore, further neutrons could be directed to create further fissions – the chain-reaction which Szilard had envisaged four years earlier.

All now seemed to rest on the answer to the simple question: 'Did the nuclear fission of uranium create "spare" neutrons?' The French team in the Collège de France came up with the answer in February 1939 – and considered it so important that the paper containing it was rushed to Le Bourget airport so that it could appear in the earliest possible edition of *Nature*.

The answer was that nuclear fission did indeed produce spare neutrons. Thus it seemed plausible that under certain conditions it would be possible to detonate an explosion immensely more powerful than any caused by merely chemical reactions.

At this point, the European countries being sucked down towards the whirlpool of war began to act. The German physicist Paul Hartman wrote to the German War Office suggesting that nuclear weapons should be investigated, and shortly afterwards two groups in the Third Reich began work on 'the uranium problem'. In Britain, research on a nuclear weapon was brought under the surveillance of Sir Henry Tizard and with the support of the Committee of Imperial Defence Tizard tried to obtain control over the world's stock of uranium, a relatively uncomplicated matter since virtually the only important source lay in the Belgian Congo where it was mined by the Belgian Union Minière. And in Paris the Collège de France team was authorized to obtain another raw material then thought essential to the manufacture of nuclear weapons – the 'heavy water' produced exclusively by the Norsk Hydro Company at Rjukan in central Norway.

The apparent need for heavy water – a substance whose molecules contain oxygen and a rare variety of hydrogen called deuterium – underlines the fact that in the summer of

1939 immense practical difficulties still seemed likely to rule out the utilization of nuclear energy, for peaceful or for warlike purposes, even though a chain reaction in uranium was now seen to be theoretically possible. It was in this summer that Einstein signed the famous letter written by Leo Szilard, now a refugee in the United States, urging President Roosevelt to investigate the possibilities of nuclear weapons. But Einstein, like a majority of other leading physicists, was very doubtful whether such weapons could ever be built.

To appreciate the practical difficulties, it is necessary to ask why, since uranium is apparently 'fissile', the uranium stocks of the world did not blow themselves apart as they came into existence. The first answer is that the metal is found not in its pure form but as an ore from which it has to be separated. The second answer was supplied by Niels Bohr in the spring of 1939. Bohr put forward a theory – later found to be correct – based on the fact that uranium consists of a number of different kinds of atom each of which has a different number of neutrons locked inside the nucleus together with the 92 protons. Bohr suggested that it was only the uranium 235, whose atoms had 92 protons and 143 neutrons in each nucleus which was readily fissile. But these atoms formed only about 0.7 per cent of natural uranium, or roughly seven in every thousand. If any of the other 993 uranium nuclei in each 1,000 were hit by a neutron bullet, the chances of its being split were very remote; it would be far more likely to absorb the neutron, setting off a process of nuclear rearrangement which was interesting but which would not help to keep a nuclear fire alight.

Thus the first problem would be one of separating uranium 235 from the other kinds. The size of this problem, which for some time seemed to rule out any chance of using nuclear energy and which was eventually to demand the utmost ingenuity in invention from the chemical and the engineering industries, rested on the basic characteristics of isotopes, as the differing atoms of the same elements are called. The different isotopes of uranium – and of other elements – have the same number of protons in their nuclei but different numbers of neutrons. But, as with the various isotopes of other elements, the chemical characteristics of uranium 235 are identical with those of uranium 238. So are the physical characteristics with the sole exception of those determined by atomic mass. Thus for all the normal chemical processes which might be used to separate them they are as alike as two peas in a pod or two grains of sand on the sea-shore. In the summer of 1939 the practical chances of separating them in more than micro-quantities looked extremely remote.

But this was only one of the problems. Even if some way of separating the fissile from the non-fissile nuclei could be found there was a further awkward fact to be considered. It was soon apparent that two and a half neutrons were released on average by each fission. But even if these were released in a mass of uranium 235 not each of them would necessarily produce further fissions. Some would merely pass through the empty spaces, comparatively immense, which exist between the uranium nuclei and then escape from the lump of uranium before hitting a target. Others would almost certainly be absorbed by impurities which it was realized would remain in the uranium 235 however much care was taken in its processing.

It is at this stage of the argument that the heavy water comes in. It was known that the neutrons released in fission moved at a speed of about 10,000 miles a second; but it was also known that if they could be slowed-down the chance of their causing further fissions would be greatly increased. What was needed was a moderator – some substance which would not itself absorb neutrons but would certainly reduce their speed. According to calculations, heavy water would be a good moderator; so would graphite, a form of carbon; and so too would beryllium – all of these being light elements with only a small number of protons in their nuclei.

Even so, a uranium block of a certain minimum size would be needed for the nuclear fire to be self-sustaining. This was the 'critical size' and in this stage of nuclear research there was very great doubt as to what the size was. In addition there was the important matter of just *how* the fire would burn. In one set of circumstances the burning of the whole mass would take place in a minute fraction of a second, thus causing a nuclear explosion of immense proportions. But it seemed possible that in different, but perhaps inevitable, conditions most of the explosive force would be dissipated.

But before either of these contingencies could be taken further scientists had to discover more about the whole process of nuclear fission. They had to estimate, within fairly close tolerances, what the critical mass of uranium would be. And they then had to decide how they could separate the chemically identical isotopes of uranium – not on a laboratory scale where a few micro-milligrams had been separated with the greatest difficulty but as an industrial process which might have to produce hundredweights.

This was the situation in nuclear research when Germany invaded Poland on 1 September 1939. It appeared to offer a very faint hope of a vastly more powerful weapon, and an only slightly less faint hope of a new source of industrial power. What it certainly did present were problems, theoretical, industrial and financial, which would not have been tackled for years, or more probably for decades, had not the possession of nuclear weapons held out a hope of victory. Nuclear fission had been discovered in Berlin. Neither Britain, nor later the United States, could afford to let the Germans get the ultimate weapon first.

The story of the world's first atomic bombs is too familiar to be told in detail here. But there are some supremely important twists and turns to the tale that are hardly known and need underlining.

The first took place in February 1940 when Otto Frisch, who had by this time arrived in Britain, worked out with Rudolf, now Sir Rudolf, Peierls, what the critical mass of uranium was really likely to be. Sir James Chadwick, the discoverer of the neutron, was already at work on the nuclear problem in Liverpool University with Joseph Rotblat, who had been caught in England by the outbreak of war. Sir George Thomson, son of the J. J. Thomson who half a century earlier had helped to lay the foundations for the nuclear age, was already at work in Imperial College, London, and a handful of scientists elsewhere in Britain were investigating other aspects of the problem. Yet if any single act can be singled out as carrying the world across the watershed towards the nuclear age it is that of Frisch and Peierls in Birmingham, sitting down and working out, almost on the back of an envelope as it were, how big the critical mass of uranium would be.

Few men alive knew more about nuclear fission than Frisch and Peierls. Even so, their initial calculations, in the late summer of 1939, suggested a figure of tons. Only after an immense amount of work had been carried out in the university were they able to refine their calculations – and to discover in February 1940 that the figure was not measured in tons at all. 'In fact,' Peierls has stated, 'our first calculation gave a critical mass of less than one pound.'

This single calculation, whose result was later shown to be of the right order of magnitude, transformed 'the uranium problem' as it was known. Separating even a pound of uranium 235 was an undertaking of almost staggering dimensions but it was different from separating many tons. Filling an egg-cup with sand, grain by grain, might be a formidable task; but it was manageable compared with the fantasy of filling the Albert Hall.

Frisch and Peierls' discovery led directly to a committee

under George Thomson which in the summer of 1941 issued a crucial document, the Maud Report which firmly stated 'that the scheme for a uranium bomb is practicable and likely to lead to decisive results in the war.'

Four of the British team which joined the Americans working on nuclear weapons during the last war. *From left to right :* Dr (later Lord) Penney, Dr Frisch, Professor (later Sir Rudolf) Peierls and Professor (later Sir John) Cockcroft

This report was to have an immensely important effect on events in the United States, a country then still at peace. Here Einstein's letter to Roosevelt had led to the setting-up of a Committee under Dr Lyman J. Briggs, director of the US Bureau of Standards, and to work by the National Academy of Science. But none of this had given much encouragement to Dr Vannevar Bush or Dr James Conant, the two Americans in charge of the country's defence research.

But the whole scene was changed by the Maud Report which was shown to the Americans without delay. '[It] gave Bush and Conant what they had been looking for,' says the official history of the subsequent US nuclear effort; 'a promise that there was a reasonable chance for something militarily useful during the war in progress. The British did more than promise; they outlined a concrete programme. None of the recommendations Briggs had made and neither of the two National Academy reports had done as much.' Within a matter of days Professor Harold Urey, the discoverer of heavy water, and Professor G. B. Pegram were on their way to Britain. Within weeks the first steps had been taken to set up what eventually became the Manhattan Project which, under

General Groves (*second from left*),
head of the American 'Manhattan
Project' which produced the
world's first nuclear weapons, with
Sir James Chadwick (*left*) and
American scientists Dr Richard
Tolman and Dr H. D. Smyth

command of General Leslie Groves, produced the world's
first nuclear weapons.

Scores of technological riddles still had to be solved when
the Americans decided – a few hours before the Japanese
struck at Pearl Harbor – that they must try to make the
world's first nuclear weapons. So had a mass of scientific
questions. Only microscopic quantities of fissile material had
so far been produced and many of its characteristics were not
known, let alone understood. The whole subject of fission
still lay on the extreme edge of scientific knowledge, and it was
appreciated that before a bomb could be built that frontier of
knowledge would have to be pushed forward an immense
distance into the unknown. Only two things were clear. The
materials would be more dangerous than any which scientists
or industry had yet handled. And the effort demanded would
involve more men, more money, and more scientific expertise
than any other project which had ever been tackled, in the
United States or elsewhere.

During the first months of 1942, three major question-
marks hung over the enterprise which, it was realized in
Washington, was in many ways an immense gamble. First of
all, could a nuclear chain reaction really be created? In theory
this was now possible, but even the men who said so admitted

that the imponderables were immense and that what had seemed possible in theory might be impossible in practice. Secondly, in view of what seemed to be the wildly immense industrial problems involved, could enough fissile material be produced? Thirdly, if it were possible to make enough material, would it be possible to bring this together in such a way that the resulting critical mass would explode? For theory had suggested early on that if two lumps of fissile uranium, each less than the critical mass but together forming more than it, were united too slowly then the result might be a bomb which, in the words of the physicists' lingering doubt, might 'swell up rather than explode'.

The first of these problems was put in the hands of Fermi and under his direction there was built in Chicago during 1942 the world's first nuclear reactor. It was obviously not meant to explode, and the uranium used in it was the natural metal in which the fissile uranium 235 was effectively swamped by the vastly larger amount of uranium 238. The neutrons released by the fissions that did take place were slowed down by a moderator consisting of graphite, a form of carbon, and calculations showed that under the right conditions these sloweddown neutrons would create further fissions numerous enough to keep the nuclear fire burning. If this were so, the device would not only give practical proof of the physicists' figures; it would also, it was calculated, manufacture [its own] quantities of what was correctly believed to be a second fissile material. This was plutonium, an element not found in nature until 1971, but one which would, it was estimated, result from the nuclear reactions which would go on inside a successful reactor.

Fermi's reactor – or 'pile' as it was at first called since the graphite consisted of blocks which were piled up one on another – gave a foretaste of the industrial problems to come. Only a few grams of pure uranium metal had previously been refined in the United States but more than six tons were needed for Chicago. The graphite had to be of clinical purity, and had to be processed into about 40,000 separate blocks, each of which had to be finished to the strictest engineering tolerances. There were also the control rods. These were made of the metal cadmium, which was known to be a good absorber of neutrons. As the reactor was assembled from November 1942 onwards into an agglomeration of uranium and graphite, some 25 feet across, the cadmium strips were built into it, thus effectively preventing the chain reaction from starting.

On 2 December 1942 the cadmium strips began to be raised up by the complex machinery built around the reactor. Instru-

The world's first nuclear pile
consisting of graphite blocks and
uranium metal under construction
in Chicago in 1942

ments built into the reactor continuously recorded the intensity of the neutron-flow inside. And between 3 and 4 o'clock in the afternoon the needles on the instruments passed the all-important mark. Inside the reactor the nuclear fire was burning steadily. High officials in the Manhattan Project were given the news by an historic telegram which merely said: 'The Italian navigator has entered the new world.' Something quite as momentous as Columbus's landfall had in fact taken place.

The success of the Chicago reactor showed that a second fissile material, plutonium, was available but the reactor itself, built largely as a demonstration unit, had no cooling system, could be operated at only a low level, and could not therefore be used to make plutonium in practicable quantities. Even had it been able to do so, the whole reactor would have had to be dismantled to get it out. However, the Americans could now hope to produce their nuclear fuel in one of four ways.

First, it would be possible to make special plutonium-producing reactors – and the huge industrial complexes soon to be built at Oak Ridge and Hanford, costing millions of dollars and employing tens of thousands of men, were to make this element.

In addition to the production of plutonium, an immense industrial gamble whose success long hung in the balance, there was the separation of uranium 235 from its super-abundant uranium 238. This appeared to offer the three other

ways of producing a nuclear explosive. But the amounts of fissile uranium known to be needed were some hundred million times more than those that had been produced in the laboratory, and each of the different ways of separating the chemically identical atoms on an industrial scale involved its own appalling difficulties. One was gaseous diffusion which had been experimented with in England before the British effort was moved to the United States and Canada in 1943. The method rests on the fact that if a gas containing two isotopes is diffused through a porous barrier, the molecules of the lighter isotope will diffuse more quickly; thus the gas on the far side of the barrier will contain slightly more light molecules than are in the gas which has not gone through the barrier.

The difficulties were numerous. For various reasons the only practicable gas was uranium hexafluoride, or 'hex', a compound of uranium and fluorine which is solid at room temperature but is easily vaporized; but 'hex' was one of the most difficult gases that had ever been handled, extremely corrosive, extremely reactive, and of an intractability that brought tears to the eyes of engineers faced with building equipment to handle it. In addition, to provide an end-product rich enough in the rare uranium 235 the dangerous gas would have to be passed not through a few dozen barriers, not through a few hundred but through many thousands. Thus the gaseous dif-

A painting by Gary Sheahan showing the moment when the world's first nuclear pile went critical. Enrico Fermi stands next to the instrument rack near the balcony rail, slide-rule in hand, computing the rise in the neutron count inside the layers of graphite interspersed with uranium.

The U.S. Atomic Energy Commission's Oak Ridge Gaseous Diffusion Plant for the production of enriched uranium. Today the plant, built in 1943, produces enriched uranium for nuclear power plants in many parts of the world.

fusion plant eventually built at Oak Ridge contained hundreds of acres of diffusion barriers, spread across more than 50 acres of factory floor and connected by many hundreds of miles of piping – the whole unit, with its hundreds of joints and valves being built to a precision, and welded with a care which would previously have been unthinkable.

The second way of separating the fissile uranium from the rest was by the electro-magnetic method, a scaled-up version of the laboratory method which utilizes the fact that different isotopes in a stream of ions are deflected differently by electric and magnetic fields. But the magnets required are 100 feet in length, the electric supplies involved are enormous and the process demands the most exacting kind of high vacuum equipment.

The third method was a thermal-diffusion technique in which 'hex' was circulated between two concentric pipes, the inner being steam-heated and the outer water-cooled, a process which caused the uranium 235 isotope to concentrate near the inner pipe. Simple by comparison with the other methods, thermal-diffusion demanded such immense quantities of steam – and therefore of coal – that it was eventually considered impracticable.

Any of these means of producing a nuclear explosive would in normal times have been considered an almost reckless gamble, so small did the chances of success seem and so great were the demands on scarce men, materials and money. But so menacing did the threat of a German nuclear weapon appear that the Americans went ahead, simultaneously, with the production of plutonium and of uranium by all three possible ways. The outcome was that partially enriched uranium from the gas-diffusion and thermal-diffusion plants was fed into the electro-magnetic plant in June 1945. Within a month, enough bomb-quality uranium had been produced to make one weapon. And by this time the plutonium production plant had produced enough fissile material for another two.

Meanwhile other groups of scientists under Robert Oppenheimer had been solving the problem of how to bring the two halves of a critical mass together with sufficient speed. In the uranium bomb, dropped on Hiroshima on 6 August 1945 this was accomplished by firing one half of the sub-critical mass down a squat barrel at the target of a second sub-critical mass. In the plutonium bomb, as tested in the Nevada desert in July 1945, and as dropped on Nagasaki a few days after the Hiroshima bomb, the characteristics of plutonium fission ruled this out and made necessary an 'implosion' device in which a hollow core of less than critical mass was compressed into a critical mass by the explosion of encircling TNT charges.

The destruction of Hiroshima and Nagasaki revolutionized warfare and international relations. There had, of course, been few scientific secrets about the bomb, since the basic facts of fission had been published before war broke out, and the laws of nature were known to operate in the same way both sides of the Atlantic and both sides of the Iron Curtain. Only in the purely technological field were there industrial secrets which governed the ease, speed and cost with which 'the bomb' could be built, and it was no surprise to most nuclear physicists that Russia, followed by Britain, France and eventually China, exploded their own nuclear weapons.

Abandonment among civilized nations of the conventions which had previously protected civilians is not necessarily the most important outcome of the release of nuclear energy, although it is the most obvious and spectacular. Even so, two developments along the road from Hiroshima must be noted.

Test rig in the Allmänna Svenska
Elektriska laboratories for
electro-hydraulically operated
control rods of their boiling-water
reactor at Vasterås, Sweden

One is the hydrogen bomb in which the intense heat created
by the fission of a critical mass of uranium is used to fuse the
hydrogen nuclei in a surrounding layer of hydrogenous
materials into helium nuclei. Fission breaks apart the heaviest
nuclei, but fusion transforms the lightest. The energy released
by the second nuclear transformation is the greater, and the
explosive power of the hydrogen bomb is some 1,000 times
that of the first atomic bombs, a single one being more than
capable of completely destroying the largest city in the world.
At the other end of the weaponry scale has come the production of ever smaller atomic weapons and it is now claimed,
though with dubious credibility, that they could be used in a
tactical role on the battlefield without necessarily leading to
the use of strategic nuclear weapons.

While the new threat has within the last generation transformed diplomacy, the balance of power, and the credibility of
war as a plausible method for a nation to get its own way, the
release of nuclear energy has had immensely important
results in other fields. The most obvious of these is the
possibility that within the foreseeable future man may have
access to limitless power, first from electricity stations based
on reactors using nuclear fission, then on breeder reactors
which can actually create more fuel than they use, and finally
by nuclear fusion in which power would be obtained from the
nuclear reactions induced in the hydrogen from sea-water.

At the heart of all such power-producing schemes is the
nuclear reactor, the descendant of Fermi's 'pile' in Chicago,
and these reactors are also the starting-points for the production of radioactive materials which for the last two decades
have been playing ever-more important roles in industry, agriculture and medicine.

The scores of nuclear reactors which have been built during
the last generation, a great diversified family, have usually
been tailor-made for some specific task: for research and training purposes, for the production of fissile weapons material or
of radioactive materials for peaceful purposes, for the propulsion of surface ships or submarines; or, more usually, for the
production of power. Such reactors can be classified as either
heterogeneous, where the fuel and the moderator are separated
from one another in a carefully calculated geometrical
pattern, or as homogeneous where the fuel and the moderator
are mixed to provide a uniform medium through which the
fission-born neutrons will pass. Another classification, and
one more generally adopted in the nuclear industry, is based on
the kind of moderator used or on the kind of coolant which
carries off the fission-created heat; thus there are graphite-

moderated reactors and heavy-water reactors, boiling-water reactors and gas-cooled reactors.

As far as the production of power is concerned, all these reactors work in roughly the same basic way. The burning of the atomic fuel, whose intensity is governed by the insertion or withdrawal of control rods which absorb the fission-created neutrons, heats a gas or a liquid which is continuously passed round the central core of the reactor – much as a household immersion heater raises the temperature of water before this is drawn out of the taps. The gas or liquid heated by the nuclear fire is then used to produce steam; the steam operates a turbine and this in turn operates a generator which in turn produces electricity.

The method seems convoluted, and it is true that there are losses in efficiency at each stage of the operation. Even so, the energy released by nuclear transformations is so much greater than that in chemical reactions, that a single gram of uranium can in a nuclear reactor produce as much power as two tons of oil.

The problems in creating this power are very great. Vast quantities of water are needed for cooling, whatever kind of reactor is used, and as a result nuclear power stations tend to be sited on the coast, on wide estuaries, or on large inland lakes. Despite the safety precautions enforced where fissile material is present – precautions which in fact give the nuclear industry an enviable safety record – commonsense plus public opinion demands that large centres of population shall be avoided and this, taken with the previous requirement, lays the nuclear industry open to attack by the conservationists. Capital costs of a nuclear power station are much greater than those of oil-fired or coal-fired stations, and it is only recently that the costs of generating electricity at them have fallen below those of conventionally produced power.

There are also immense engineering problems, indicated by some typical facts and figures from British stations. Thus a reactor alone can weigh up to 50,000 tons, while the pressure vessel in which it is encased, and the necessary shielding, can bring the weight to 200,000 tons. The thousands of tons of concrete for the foundations must be laid to an accuracy of a hundredth of an inch. The 100,000 graphite blocks in one typical reactor had each to be made to the strictest engineering tolerances before being vacuum-cleaned, sealed in transparent bags and taken to the site. In another the fuel consisted of 42,445 uranium rods 19 inches long and 1.1 inches in diameter, each machined to within a few thousandths of an inch before being loaded into more than 3,000 channels in

the graphite core. Special steels, new methods of welding, and fresh ways of inspecting and handling at long range the dangerously radioactive by-products of fission have all had to be developed before nuclear power has become a possibility.

For the immediate future there is the power station which creates more fuel than it uses, typified by a prototype built at Dounreay on the north coast of Scotland. Here the nuclear core is only 3 feet long and $4\frac{1}{2}$ feet in diameter, providing enough electricity for a town the size of Brighton. Its fuel is plutonium obtained as a by-product from the operation of the earlier type nuclear power stations. Surrounding this is a 'blanket' of natural uranium. Not all the neutrons released in the core create the further fissions which produce the heat – carried away in this case by liquid sodium. Some of them travel on until they hit the natural uranium of the 'blanket'. What happens then depends largely on the speed at which they are travelling; but a percentage of the neutrons will hit the nuclei of U238 atoms in the natural uranium and convert these into nuclei of plutonium. Thus it is possible to look forward to a future in which not only the rare uranium 235 but most of the atoms of natural uranium will eventually be

The U.K. Atomic Energy Authority's prototype fast reactor at Dounreay on the north coast of Scotland, which produces considerable amounts of electricity for the North of Scotland Hydro-Electricity Board energy-producers – the seven fissile atoms in each 1,000 being used in the earlier type nuclear power stations and most of the remaining 993 being converted into fissile plutonium and used in reactors of this later design.

There is also the possibility of thermo-nuclear power, the taming of the fusion process utilized in the hydrogen bomb. But this is still no more than a gleam on the distant horizon and before it becomes a practicability the mini-reactor is likely to become almost commonplace. The first nuclear-powered submarine, the US Nautilus, was launched as long ago as 1954 and the first nuclear-powered cargo vessel, the US Savannah, in 1959, the year in which the Russians launched a nuclear ice-breaker. Germany and Japan are other countries which have used small compact reactors for their ships. The Americans have developed under the SNAP (System for Nuclear Auxiliary Power) scheme, a whole series of miniature reactors, some of them as small as 14 by 13 by 18 inches, while the Russians have built a 'pocket power station' which can produce one megawatt for two years from a few hundred pounds of fuel – compared with the 4,000 tons of oil needed for a diesel engine.

All these increasingly small and increasingly versatile power-producers are straight developments of 'the boiler', as the peaceful possibility of fission was described three decades ago. But even the explosive force of the bomb is being adapted for peaceful purposes, and while the use of nuclear explosives for engineering is still in an early stage of development some experts believe that many projects which would be impractical or economically ruinous if planned with conventional explosives will be possible with nuclear charges.

The quantities of material which have to be moved in the building of canals, tunnels, dams and underground reservoirs are usually immense. But experiments which began as far back as 1961, when the American Operation Plowshare got under way, show that the back of the work can probably be broken by the underground explosion of nuclear charges. As in a nuclear weapon, the key lies in the immense amount of energy that can be released from a device which is comparatively small, comparatively light and, when weighed against the cost of moving mountains by chemical explosives, comparatively cheap.

Yet further application of the same technique lies in the nuclear mining of minerals, petro-chemicals and natural gas. In this an underground nuclear explosion loosens the geological holding layers and both speeds up the extraction of what is being mined and reduces the cost of the operation.

Preparation of radio-pharmaceutical compounds labelled with mercury-197 in a standard shielded cell in the laboratories of the Radiochemical Centre Ltd, Amersham, Bucks

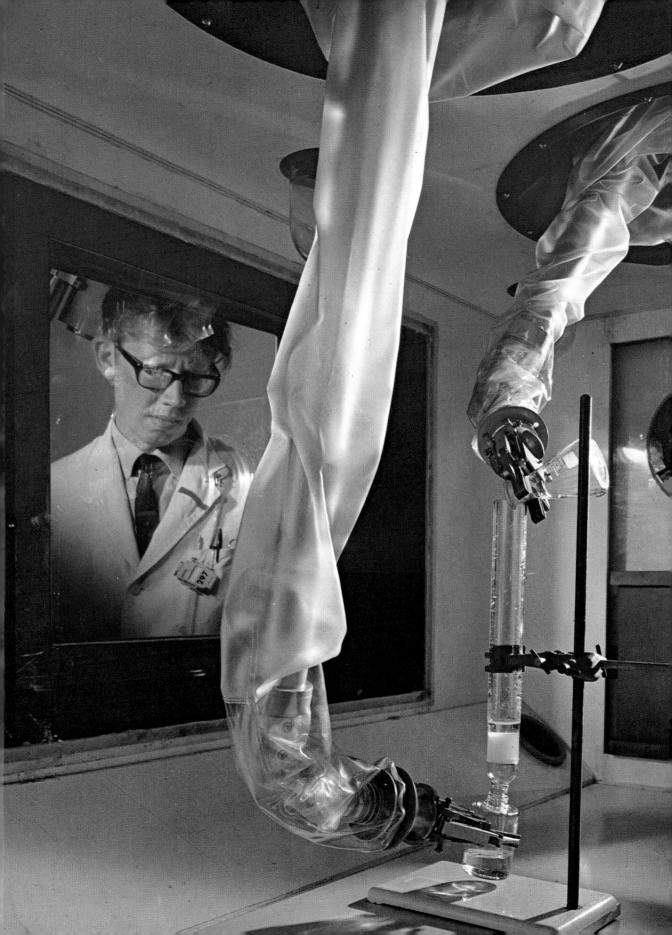

Left The head of a reactor vessel being lowered into place on top of Sweden's Oskarshamn I boiling-water reactor

Right above The nuclear-powered U.S. Nautilus entering New York Harbor, 25 August 1958, after making a trans-polar voyage under the Arctic ice cap

Right below The launching in Leningrad of the 16,000-ton ice-breaker Lenin, the world's first nuclear-powered surface vessel

The radioisotope thermoelectric generator (*foreground*) left on the moon by American astronauts in February 1971

These and similar engineering uses of nuclear explosions suffer from the same handicap that has made the development of nuclear power more difficult, more dangerous and more expensive than it would otherwise have been: the need to deal effectively with the radioactive by-products of a chain reaction. The process does not only involve the breaking in two of heavy nuclei and the release of neutrons. This is merely the start of a long series of events. The sudden release of energy is the fact important to the success of the bomb or the boiler; but it is merely the beginning of a string of nuclear reactions which create a new family of radioactive substances. Their number, and their dangers, depend on a large number of variables, and while some radioactive materials are for practical purposes harmless, it is true to say that from the earliest days of the nuclear revolution the problem of dealing with the rest has caused a perpetual headache.

In the early years of the century it was found that X-rays produced by naturally radioactive materials could not only kill the malignant growths of cancer but could also cause damage or death if used without proper caution. In the early 1920s it was found that radium, painted on watch-faces to provide night-time luminescence, was accumulating in the bodies of workers who had licked it off their paint-brushes, and that its continuing radiation was affecting them. Further information accumulated during the last three decades has shown that the by-products of nuclear fission can not only cause illness or death but can also bring about mutations in the genetic material of living cells. Thus they can affect the characteristics handed down from one generation to the next, whether the cells are of fruit-flies or rabbits, of butterflies or humans.

The best-known radioactive by-product of nuclear fission is of course 'fall-out', the deposit of radioactive substances which descends on the earth from the atmosphere after the explosion of a nuclear weapon. In the nuclear reactor designed to produce controlled power, the radioactive substances are retained in the body of the reactor behind some form of bio-logical shield – one part of a complex series of safety measures incorporated in the design of all reactors. However, radio-activity is retained in the reactor, not destroyed there. Some of it will continue for thousands of years and the disposal of radioactive nuclear waste is one of the constant, and naturally growing, problems of the industry. Nuclear fission has given men the possibility of limitless power; it has also given them the problem of disposing of lethal waste.

Not all radioactive by-products can be pushed to the debit side of the nuclear account. Many of them are made use of by the growing battery of radioactive devices which during the last two decades have revolutionized whole areas of medicine, industry and agriculture. Thus radioactive strontium, pro-cessed from the spent fuel of nuclear reactors, lies at the heart of a new family of thermo-electric generators which power marine navigation lights, unmanned weather stations and aircraft beacons. The word 'spent' is comparative and the heat from the continuing decay of the radioactive strontium is enough to generate electricity in an assembly of thermo-couples. Outputs from a few milliwatts to several tens of watts can be obtained and the equipment will go on producing it, unattended, for more than a decade.

But it is not only 'unwanted' radioactive material that comes from reactors today. While the destruction of Hiroshima and Nagasaki was the apocalyptic sign that man had released nuclear energy, and the utilization of nuclear power was the sign that he could tame it, the production of many hundreds of

Measuring the uptake of iodine-131 hippurate in the kidneys at Edinburgh Royal Infirmary. The patient has been given an intravenous dose of iodine-131 in a form which concentrates it in her kidneys. The two scintillation counters measure the build-up of activity and two graphs, one for each kidney, produced on the recorder above the patient's head, show the concentration of iodine-131 and its excretion.

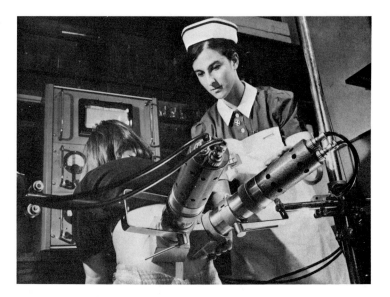

radioactive isotopes shows that he can fashion with the help of nuclear reactions a large number of new and almost unimaginably sensitive tools. This third result of the nuclear revolution is far less spectacular than the other two, and far less well-known or understood; yet it would be a rash man who claimed that in its long-term and all-pervasive influence it might not eventually be just as important.

Until the Curies began to make minute quantities of radioactive material in their Paris laboratory in the 1930s, radium was in practice the only radioactive material available. It had been used by doctors since the start of the century, and with some success, to 'burn out' growths in the human body. But radium had one great disadvantage, quite apart from its cost: the speed and other characteristics with which it disintegrated could not be controlled. Thus for the medical profession it served as a single tool with useful but somewhat restricted possibilities – much as if a carpenter had one single saw for his work instead of a range of them on which he could draw at will.

The release and control of nuclear energy altered all that. For from 1939 onwards it became increasingly clear that radioactive isotopes of many elements could be made by inserting samples of non-radioactive elements in a reactor core and there irradiating them. More important, it was possible to select the 'raw materials', and to treat them, so that the irradiated material gave off radiations of a kind and of an intensity which had previously been selected. The scope provided by this new technique can be judged from some simple figures: by the mid-1960s, one British centre alone was offering 150 radio-isotopes available in more than 1,000 chemical compounds and in more than 600 kinds of radiation appliance – a total of more than 2,000 items.

These materials could be virtually tailor-made. At first the tendency was to concentrate on their medical uses, a continuation and extension of pre-war methods. But just how such techniques could be refined by the post-war materials available is illustrated by one typical example from Sweden. Here rays from a number of different radioactive sources of the correctly selected intensity were directed on a growth in a patient's brain. Where the radiations passed individually through different parts of the skull, they had no effect; where they met, their combined effect killed off the growth.

However, it was not only in this way that medicine found a new tool in the radio-isotopes that first research stations and then commercial nuclear reactors began to produce. The radioactive material was chemically identical with the non-radioactive variety – even though it could be identified at a distance, without seeing it or touching it, simply by picking up on an instrument such as a Geiger counter the radiations which the radioactive version was constantly giving off.

As one example from many, this meant that doctors soon had a new diagnostic tool with which they could discover the metabolic processes of the human body. Metabolism transforms some substances very slowly. Only about 100 microgrammes of iodine passes through the average body each day and to trace its progress was out of the question until the advent of radio-isotopes; then it was possible to add a small amount of harmless radioactive iodine to the non-radioactive intake. How the body dealt with it could then be discovered with comparative ease. Such was the case with many other substances utilized by the body, so that during the 1950s and 1960s it became increasingly easy for a doctor to find out what portion of a patient's body was failing to change properly the various materials that it would have metabolized if healthy.

The medical uses of radioactive materials had to some extent been foreshadowed before the war. But a completely new use which followed the manufacture of tailor-made isotopes in the first post-war reactors was in agriculture. Here a common problem is to find out what growing crops do with different fertilizers. Until the mid-1940s this was virtually impossible; but when a small amount of radioactive material is incorporated in a fertilizer, its progress through the living body of a plant can be followed in detail. In exactly the same way the course of normal 'food and drink' can be traced through plants merely by ensuring that a small percentage of this is radioactive.

Also entirely new was the adaptation of radio-isotopes to industry in the post-war world. The point where an underground water-pipe leaks can be detected by adding a radio-isotope to the water and following the course of the pipe, above ground, with a Geiger counter. It is possible to incorporate small amounts of radioactive 'tracers' in the rubber of motor car tyres and then work out, by the disappearance of these from the tyres, just how much wear and tear is caused by differing conditions. When a radio-isotope is incorporated in metal piston rings, the amount of this later found in the engine oil indicates how quickly the rings wear under certain conditions. Radioactive ground glass has been used to trace the movement of mud in the Thames Estuary, and the movement of radioactive pebbles has revealed the currents which cause coast erosion. Radioactive materials released in the streams of an area picked for a new reservoir have provided an estimate of seepage from the site.

A different use for radio-isotopes in industry is in measuring-instruments which can indicate the thickness of a metal sheet or the density of a liquid. Here the radioactive source is placed on one side of the material and a detecting instrument on the other, the amount of radiation reaching the instrument showing the thickness of the material between. The same technique can be used to check whether packets on a production line are properly filled.

Another by-product of the nuclear revolution, quite important even though little noted in the shadow of nuclear weapons and nuclear power, is the new ability to sterilize materials by radioactivity which can inhibit or kill both the individual cells of living bodies or complete organisms such as bacteria.

One application is the irradiation of potatoes which are thus prevented from sprouting while in storage, and mobile units on which boxes of potatoes are carried through a 20-ton lead-lined drum and irradiated by radioactive cobalt, have been found successful in Canada. In the United States at least one factory is treating sea-food a ton at a time by the same process, and plans have been made for a similar plant in Germany. Soft fruit, fish, and tins of food have also been 'sterilized' in this way but so far no satisfactory method has been found of preventing changes in flavour. However, comparatively little is even now known about the biological and chemical problems involved; within a few decades, nuclear systems producing much of the world's power may well be helping the food industry.

Already the extraordinary effects of irradiation are being

applied in a host of unexpected one-off applications. In Australia it has been used to ensure that no anthrax bacilli exist on the goat-hair that goes into carpets. In Britain, medical syringes, scalpels and similar instruments are sterilized in large numbers by irradiation. New methods of pest-control have been introduced by the sterilization of insects, while the genetic changes induced by irradiation have been used to produce new varieties of flowers.

All these are comparatively little-known items on the credit side of the nuclear ledger. Perhaps most revealing is the number of them which impinge, directly or indirectly on the biological processes of living things, plants and potatoes as well as human beings. For if the nuclear revolution is now in full swing, the biological revolution, man's increasing ability to condition and control the life-cycles of many species, including his own, is only just beginning. In the long run it may well equal in importance the fresh control that man is beginning to exercise over inanimate materials.

Potatoes in the Brookhaven National Laboratory, Upton, New York. That shown top left was stored normally. The rest were subjected to various doses of gamma rays and the illustration shows how greater doses increasingly inhibited sprouting.

6 The Challenge of the Future

The nuclear revolution which took place between 1938 and the early 1950s after four decades of preparation by the world's scientists, may well alter the prospects for the human race more far-reachingly than any other development since man's taming of fire and his first deliberate sowing of crops. This is still the popular theory, and it is strengthened by the steadily increasing battery of uses to which radio-isotopes are being put, a process now affecting almost every aspect of life. Yet it seems possible, perhaps even probable, that the biological revolution which is already under way, may be even more important: it is, after all, giving man for the first time in history, a measure of control over his own biological future.

This revolution is perhaps more concerned with 'pure' science than those which have given man command of the air and the ability to produce raw materials to his own specification. It has possibly depended more on the intellect of man and less on purely technological advance than the steps which have enabled engineers to exploit the knowledge of the physicists and produce nuclear power. However, the work of the biologists in the age of the electron-microscope and irradiation is clasped tightly to the bosom of technology; and the discovery in mid-century of 'the double helix', the helical structure of deoxyribonucleic acid which is the molecular vehicle for heredity, demanded a unique merging of data and techniques from chemistry, physics and biology.

It is possible to trace back man's enquiring interest in heredity to the beginnings of the recorded past. 'Like begets like' is a saying which springs out of the mists of prehistory, an observation which throughout the generations men noticed was true of all living things, insects and animals as well as plants and men. Various hypotheses were put forward to account for it, as well as for the equally common fact that offspring could apparently show the characteristics of male parent, female parent, or both. However, as recently as a century ago Darwin himself was able to write: 'The laws governing inheritance are for the most part unknown. No one can say why the same peculiarity in different individuals of the same species, or in different species, is sometimes inherited and sometimes not so; why the child often reverts in certain characteristics to its grand-father or grand-mother or more remote ancestor.'

The vital clue to this tantalizing riddle which had intrigued man since he had first stood up on two feet out of four had in fact already been offered by Gregor Mendel when Darwin wrote these words. Mendel was an obscure Austrian priest whose story illuminates the truth that fact is stranger than fiction. Having failed three times to pass scholastic examinations which would have given him greater opportunities, he was forced to teach in the local school at Brunn – today Brno in Czechoslovakia. But he lived in the Abbey of St Thomas. And in the abbey garden he combined his interests in mathematics and botany by carrying out botanical research. This research consisted of breeding and cross-breeding pea-plants having characteristics which could be easily identified. First he used tall varieties and short varieties. When these were crossed he found that all the hybrids were tall; but when the hybrids were in turn crossed among themselves they produced 'offspring' one-quarter of which were dwarf and three-quarters of which were tall. The dwarfs, cross-bred in turn, all produced dwarfs. But when the talls were cross-bred about a third of them produced true-breeding talls, while two-thirds produced non-true-breeding talls. He next carried out comparable experiments with two varieties producing red and white flowers respectively. The results were comparable, with white and red substituted for dwarf and tall.

Mendel's conclusions were three-fold. It appeared that characteristics such as tallness or dwarfness, redness or whiteness, must be transmitted in some way from one generation to the next without dilution. It appeared that the transmission-mechanism must involve each parent-plant to an equal degree. And it appeared that some characteristics, such as tallness or redness, were dominant; but that the contrasting characteristic, dwarfness or whiteness, while recessive, did not disappear but could show itself in subsequent generations if not linked with the dominant characteristic.

Mendel carefully wrote up his experiments and sent his account to Karl Nageli, a Swiss botanist who was appalled by the mathematics of the paper, had little sympathy for an unknown amateur, and gave the Austrian little encouragement. Only years later, in 1866, did Mendel publish the first of two

Gregor Mendel, the Austrian priest whose work laid the foundations of genetics

papers on his work, in the obscure *Transactions of the Brunn Natural History Society*. Then, appointed Abbot, occupied with administrative duties, and becoming too corpulent to continue properly with his gardening, he slid back into an obscurity that was not to be broken for three decades.

In 1900, by one of the chances of science, Mendel's work was discovered. Moreover it was discovered, quite independently, by three men: Hugo de Vries in Holland, Carl Correns in Germany and Erich von Tschermak in Austria. All worked in the after-glow of Darwin and all sought to explain the question that Darwin had left unanswered; how was it possible for individuals to vary in the way that they did?

All three men, searching over the literature after they had reached tentative theories, came across Mendel's papers and all, to their lasting credit, gave prominence to their predecessor and put forward their own ideas mainly as confirmation. De Vries, however, was able to make an important addition to what was soon known as Mendelism. Some years earlier he had collected a number of primrose plants that had been introduced to the Netherlands from America. In breeding these he found that on purely random occasions the plants would produce a 'sport', a variety differing in some main essential not only from its immediate ancestors but from any ancestor that could be traced. For some while there had been no obvious explanation. With the re-discovery of Mendel, however, it was possible to conclude that there was a sudden change, or mutation, in the mechanism of heredity. This, it was later found, was what actually took place.

Some details of the hereditary mechanism had been discovered more than a decade earlier even though their significance had not been appreciated. As with most scientific discoveries, the credit belonged not to one man, or to one team, but to a series of workers advancing upon the successes of their predecessors. Important among them were Walther Flemming, a German anatomist, and Edouard van Beneden, a Belgian cytologist. Between them, they helped to establish the existence of minute thread-like structures in the nuclei of living cells. Soon afterwards these structures were named chromosomes or coloured bodies, since they took up the colour with which cells were stained.

Early in the 20th century the work by cytologists, or cell-specialists, became united with the more theoretical work of those studying the mystery of heredity from the more theoretical angle. It became increasingly clear that inheritance was in some way dependent on the chromosomes. All living things were found to contain chromosomes, all the members of any particular species having the same number – from one to more than 100. A fertilized cell at first contains double the number of original chromosomes but after division, is left with the original number, half coming from the fertilizing cell and half from the fertilized.

This picture was increasingly seen to give a very simplified picture of the truth as, throughout the first decade of the century, scientists began to realize that inheritance was, as suspected, governed by the chromosomes. Among the most important of the men to give detail to the broad outline was T. H. Morgan, the American whose 'fly-room' at Columbia University became world-famous. Morgan in effect introduced a new tool of research in the form of the *Drosophila* fruit-fly. This insect could be bred in huge numbers without trouble, a fresh generation could be produced in a matter of days, while for the researcher it had the great advantage of having only four pairs of chromosomes, thus considerably simplifying his work.

Morgan discovered that the *Drosophila* was subject to mutations, showing that at least this part of the mechanism of inheritance was the same for the insect as for the plant-world. Together with other evidence, his discovery began to make it more and more clear that heredity in men was governed by chromosomes as surely as heredity in insects or plants.

However, it was here that one problem immediately loomed. Man was known to have only about two dozen pairs of chromosomes – for years 24 was thought to be the correct figure, now it is known to be 23. But if the multitudinous characteristics of the human race were to be accounted for, then a large number of these variables must exist as separate, discrete factors on each chromosome. A clue to the truth of this was presented by William Bateson, the English biologist who in the early years of the 20th century showed that some characteristics appeared to be inherited not independently but together, a pointer to the fact that they might be due to different factors on the same chromosome. Bateson's deduction led to the suggestion that the name for the discrete factor of heredity should be 'gene' from the Greek 'to give birth to', and that the study of heredity should be called genetics. It also led to much complicated work in Morgan's fly-room which eventually demonstrated that while specific factors on a chromosome were often inherited together, this was not always so. The explanation was 'crossing-over', a process in which portions of pairs of chromosomes were sometimes switched. This in turn led to the first 'mapping' of

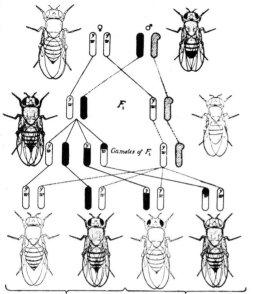

Non-cross-overs 98.5%   Cross-overs 1.5%

Diagram to illustrate crossing over in a cross between a female fruit-fly with white eyes and yellow wings and a male with red eyes and grey wings. The blocks represent the chromosomes in which the two characters are linked and the genes are represented by the letters y and w. In this case crossing over between the genes has taken place in 1.5 per cent of the offspring, giving flies with red eyes and yellow wings and white eyes and grey wings respectively, instead of the normal linkage in the parents. (After Morgan)

a chromosome. For by studying how often two linked 'genes' became unlinked it was possible to estimate the gap between them on the chromosome; and, eventually, to decide what part of what chromosome was responsible for what inherited characteristic.

To a greater and greater degree this work involved complicated mathematics, a fact which drew into genetics the man who after the First World War succeeded in making the first map of a human chromosome. He was J. B. S. Haldane who marked the position on one particular chromosome of the genes causing colour-blindness, severe light-sensitivity of the skin, night-blindness, a particular skin disease, and two varieties of eye peculiarity.

Haldane's work on human genetics was only one piece of research from many which during the years between the wars helped increase man's understanding of the mechanisms governing not only the colour of a child's hair and eyes, and a multitude of other features, but also his or her susceptibility to certain diseases of which the best-known are probably haemophilia, Huntington's chorea and phenylketonuria.

In this field of human genetics research was carried forward over areas where facts were more than usually difficult to obtain, and more than usually contentious when they were obtained, the scientific data often being at the mercy of non-scientific interpretation. It was possible to question the respective importance of nature (or genetic inheritance) compared with nurture (in other words, upbringing) in such hotly disputed matters as intelligence. It was possible to ask whether living organisms could, as claimed by the Russian Trofin D. Lysenko, pass on not only characteristics which they had inherited but those which they had acquired, a proposition with fearsome political overtones. The answers to such dynamite-filled questions were rarely without sociological or political bias.

What had become clear by this time was that inheritance in all living things – flowers and insects, the lowest mammals as well as *homo sapiens*, was governed by particulate units, formed together to make long thread-like chromosomes, which duplicated themselves during the process of fertilization. And, despite the effects of random mutation, they did in general pass on inherited characteristics to follow certain laws which might be so complex that their details were difficult to unravel, but which were nevertheless statistical laws.

What was still in question at the start of the Second World War was the chemical composition of the material which acted as the mechanism of heredity, and also the way in which it transmitted the multitudinous characteristics of any one species.

The geneticists had at least something to go on. It had been known for some while that both proteins and nucleic acids were present in chromosomes and it was deduced that one of these groups of substances was in some way responsible for a genetic code. Until the early 1940s it was generally believed that the proteins were involved; then, however, it was found that one of the nucleic acids appeared to double its quantity between successive cell divisions and was reduced by half when a cell divides. This bore too great a resemblance to the replication of chromosomes to be coincidence; from this time on, attention was concentrated on the nucleic acids.

They had first been investigated by Albrecht Kossel during the last two decades of the 19th century and were known to consist of very large molecules which fell into one of two groups. Sugar was present in both groups; but in one it was a sugar called ribose which consisted of five atoms of carbon, ten of hydrogen and five of oxygen, while in the second group the sugar was of a different sort, containing only four atoms of oxygen and known from this as deoxyribose. These different varieties of sugar thus helped to christen the ribonucleic acids known as RNA and the deoxyribonucleic acids known as DNA.

After the war the general chemistry of the nucleic acids was worked out, notably by Alexander (later Lord) Todd. It was found that DNA contained, as well as the sugar, a phosphoric acid and four nucleotide bases – adenine, guanine, cytosine and thymine. They were, it was to be discovered, vital elements in the transmission of heredity.

During the years that followed the war, improvements were made in many of the 'tools' of research which could be used by geneticists. Among them was the use of X-rays to help discover how the atoms of complicated molecules were arranged. Earlier in the century Max von Laue and the famous father-and-son team of the Braggs (Sir William H. and his son Sir Lawrence) had shown that X-rays were diffracted by the regular spacing of atoms in a crystal, and that from the way in which this took place it was possible to discover the positioning of the atoms inside the crystal.

Maurice Wilkins, a young New Zealander who had been a member of the British team which had gone to the United States during the war to work on the atomic bomb project, was among the first to conscript X-ray crystallography in the search of the genetic code. Like many other physicists, Wilkins had turned away from nuclear work after the war; he

An X-ray diffraction photograph of
DNA in sodium salt

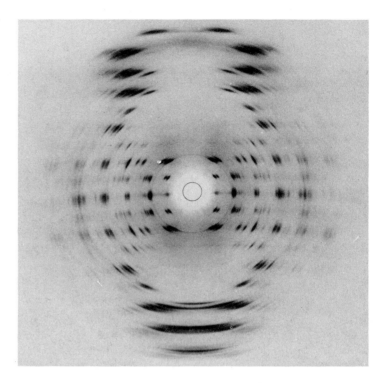

had been intrigued by a book on the riddle of life written by
Erwin Schrödinger, one of the founders of wave mechanics
in the years between the two World Wars, and had thus been
attracted to biology.

Wilkins typified a large number of physicists who after the
war were together instrumental in founding the new science of
molecular biology which utilized both physics and chemistry
to help answer the riddles of biology. Prominent among them
was Max Perutz, the specialist in the X-ray diffraction of
proteins who was, under Lawrence Bragg, to run the molecular
biology section of the Cavendish Laboratory.

However, one of the next steps forward – a phrase that is
something of a generalization since by the end of the 1940s
very many scientists were attacking the problem of the genetic
code from different angles – was made by a straight biochemist.
He was Erwin Chargraff who modified the new technique of
paper chromatography for the task. This method had been
used to discover details of the amino acids making up certain
proteins, and Chargraff now adapted it to determine the
amount of each of the bases in the nucleic acids. The results
were both intriguing and puzzling. For it was found that the
amount of adenine was always roughly equal to the amount of
thymine, and that the amount of guanine was always roughly
equal to the amount of cytosine. This was not all, for it was also

discovered that the amount of A plus T, in relation to the
amount of G plus C, while always the same in any one
organism was different from one organism to the next, the
proportion being different in men from that in cattle, and that
in other organisms being different again.

Dr James Watson (*left*) and
Dr Francis Crick with their model
showing the structure of
deoxyribonucleic acid, whose
molecular structure they discovered
and announced in 1953

By the early 1950s a good deal of information had thus been
collected over the years. The constituents of DNA were known
but the riddle that remained was how these atomic constituents were arranged. How were the very large number of
atoms making up the DNA molecules, which in turn helped
to make up a chromosome, connected together?

The men who answered this riddle were the English biochemist Francis Crick and the American James Watson, two
men who by worrying away at the problem eventually produced a theoretical answer whose correctness was to be amply
confirmed by a decade of investigation and research.

Using Chargraff's chemical data, and the physical information yielded by Wilkins's X-ray pictures, Crick and Watson
produced the double helix, a model of how the component
parts of DNA were put together. Once described as 'a rope
ladder wound up a spiral', the model was that of a DNA
molecule in which each of the two helices was made up of the
sugar-phosphate backbone which Todd had already shown to
exist. The bases extended inwards from the backbones

towards the centre of the model. Crick and Watson assumed that an adenine base from one backbone always 'stretched out' as it were, towards a thymine base from the other backbone; and that a guanine base from one always reached out towards a cytosine base from the other.

The model of the molecule did two things, quite apart from fitting all the available chemical and physical information. It accounted for the fact that the amounts of thymine and adenine, and of guanine and cytosine, were always the same. And, of yet greater importance, it allowed biologists to see, for the first time, how the replication of chromosomes took place. For it could well be imagined that in this process the two helices unwound, each then serving as a model for a complementary helix. A 'free' adenine would select a 'free' thymine, and a 'free' guanine would find a 'free' cytosine. Thus the first No. 1 helix would produce a complementary No. 2 and the first No. 2 would produce a complementary No. 1.

This postulated structure also made it possible to understand the variety of the genetic information passed on from one generation to the next by what at first looked like the beguilingly simple method of a single chemical. For just as the dot, dash and gap of the Morse code can be used to build up any number of letters and words, so the four 'letters' of the genetic alphabet, the A, T, G, and C of the bases, could be differently arranged in strings to make up an almost infinitely large number of different units of inheritance.

Knowledge of the more detailed mechanism of inheritance has increased immensely since Crick and Watson 'cracked the code of life' as it has been called. With this increase there has come speculation about 'genetic engineering', the ability to discover what chemical composition governs what specific inherited factors; and, from that, to make human beings to required specifications. It is difficult to rule out any future possibilities although most serious geneticists do not visualize the prospect within the foreseeable future, and many of them regard such speculations as nonsense. The most reasoned judgment is that any practicable development along these lines will require immensely more knowledge, and immensely more technique, than is available at the present moment and that it will come, if it comes at all, many decades in the future.

This is not, of course, to suggest that the problems and dangers should not be considered today. Already, in the United States, Robert Sinsheimer, chairman of the California Institute of Technology's biology department, has proposed

Eight radiation–induced mutants of the African Violet surrounding a normal specimen (centre of middle row)

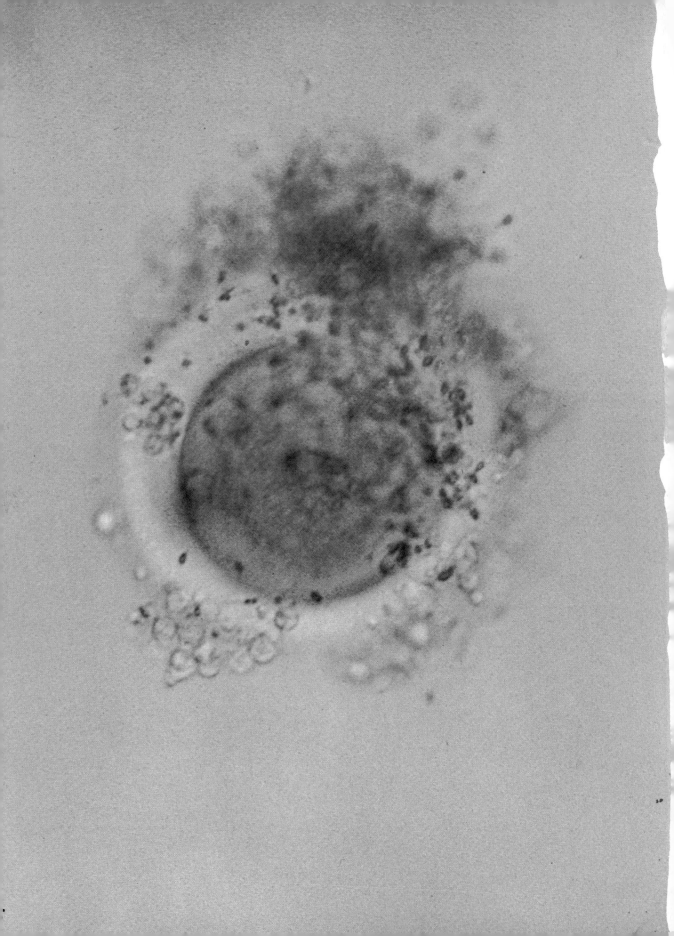

that only an international authority for human genetic research can furnish a safeguard against abuse. This, perhaps based on the unadopted Baruch Plan for regulating nuclear energy, would obviate an international 'genetics race' by ensuring that the results of significant research in the field were made available to all.

If a scheme of this kind were started its effects might well radiate outwards so that other aspects of biological and medical research began to be considered on an international rather than a national basis, a process already happening in the fields of nuclear energy and of space research.

At this point the biologists become intimately connected with the nuclear physicists. For it has now long been confirmed that the random transformation of genes known as mutation is speeded up when living matter is subjected to the radiation created by nuclear fission. So far, relatively little is known about the process of radiation-induced mutation. But just as it has already been used to breed new kinds of grain and of flowers, so may it be used in the future to breed 'tailor-made' humans. Such ideas are still the stuff of science-fiction – as much so as were the chances of using atomic energy when in 1933 Lord Rutherford described them as 'moonshine'.

The prospect of making humans to specification, dream or nightmare, is only one of many biological speculations which have been offered during the last quarter-century. Researchers have discovered more about the way in which the mind itself responds to purely physical, in particular chemical, treatment of the body. It has been found possible to cure by chemical treatment some forms of mental illness. New means of identifying genetic abnormality, and of forecasting its consequences, have suggested ways of identifying potential criminals. Thus biochemists have shown how human behaviour, both 'good' and 'bad', has a definite chemical base and may thus be susceptible to chemical control.

At this point the geneticists and the biochemists, the doctors and the mental specialists, step out into fields where their actions become inextricably entwined in ethical and moral arguments. Even so, the problem of where scientific advance *should* lead rather than of where it *can* lead, pales into insignificance beside another which is in some ways complementary to the understanding of genetic inheritance.

The breeding of 'tailor-made' humans, the control of potential criminals by chemical means, even the medical refinements which during the last few years have made it possible in exceptional circumstances to continue human life deeply into the penumbra existence where life merges almost

The follicle of the human ovary exposed to human spermatozoa in human blood serum. The outer material of the egg, the zona pellucida, can be seen breaking away from the nucleus. The spermatozoa appear as little black dots and can be seen trying to penetrate the egg.

imperceptibly into death, are never likely to affect more than a comparatively small number of the population. The Pill, the chemical contraceptive whose immense potential repercussions on human life are only now beginning to be realized, affects the masses of the world.

The desire to prevent childbirth at will is as old as the human race, and in primitive societies there have long existed beliefs that conception could be avoided if infusions of certain plants or herbs were drunk. These beliefs were based not on knowledge of the way in which such preventatives worked but on observations carried out over generations and handed down from mother to daughter. Indeed, the details of conception and birth, the chemical mechanisms which actually control what seemed to be a purely chance affair, continued to remain a mystery until the early years of this century.

Yet as far back as the 17th century biologists had begun to collect the information which a later generation would put to use in the development of the Pill. Thus in the 1660s Regner de Graaf of Delft gave the first reliable description of the *corpus luteum*, the yellow area formed in the mammalian ovary after the release of an egg in the process of ovulation.

More than 200 years passed before the significance of the *corpus* in conception began to be discussed at the end of the 19th century. It is notable that the sudden furore of interest – which, had technical expertise been available, might have brought the Pill to the 1900s rather than to the 1950s – came as physics was being shaken by its own revolutionary ideas. In fact the 10 years beginning in 1895 significantly paved the way for the mid-20th century in the air, in atomic research, the use of electro-magnetic spectrum and the production of man-made materials. It would be a rash man who claimed that any of these were potentially more important than the control over its own reproduction towards which the human race was now at last beginning to grope.

The first renewal of interest in the *corpus luteum* came in 1895 from Johannes Sobotta, an anatomist of the German city of Würzburg. Shortly afterwards John Beard, lecturer in Comparative Embryology in the University of Edinburgh, published a paper on *The span of gestation and the cause of birth*. Here, Beard put forward the idea that in the higher mammals the release of eggs during pregnancy was stopped by some mechanism that researchers should now try to understand, an idea which was taken up within a few years by Auguste Prénant, a Professor of Histology in the University of Nancy. Prénant took the thoughts of his predecessors one firm step onwards. The cessation of egg-release during pregnancy was, he suggested, the direct result of some substance or substances secreted by the *corpus luteum*; it was now up to researchers to find out what these substances were and how they did their job.

All this, it should be stressed, was still of a very theoretical nature. It was, moreover, concerned primarily with experimental animals. At this stage no one appears to have considered seriously the possibility of their research ending in a chemical contraceptive for humans. Yet a pointer to the future had already been given. Freud had written in the closing years of the 19th century: 'It would be one of the greatest triumphs of mankind, one of the most appreciable liberations of natural constraint, if one could achieve the elevation of the responsible act of procreation to an arbitrary and planned one and unbind it from its entanglement with the necessary satisfaction of a natural desire.'

During the first years of the 20th century, more than one worker in the United States and in Europe began to accumulate experimental evidence which supported the idea that, when mammals became pregnant, the very process of pregnancy started the production of an anti-ovulatory substance. But it was left to the physiologist Ludwig Haberlandt to provide really convincing proof. In 1921 Haberlandt found that the transplantation of pregnant rabbit and rat ovaries into non-pregnant animals induced sterility. More important, he found that the same results could be obtained by feeding or injecting ovarian extracts from the pregnant animals. Haberlandt went on to coin the phrase 'hormonal sterilization' since he believed that the substances which had the contraceptive effect were hormones produced by the mammalian endocrine glands. He also, rather daringly, suggested that doctors might try to use this method of contraception on humans. But in the 1920s there were no takers in the medical profession.

The caution was natural enough in the climate of the times. Birth control of any sort was still a barely mentioned subject, and in 1921 Marie Stopes had astounded the world by opening the first birth-control clinic in Britain. Even when the subject was raised, moreover, the birth-control devices discussed were little more than technological improvements on those used by the more educated members of earlier generations. The prospect opened up by Haberlandt and other workers in the same field was something radically different: a fundamental alteration in the functioning of the female body through hormonal activities of which very little was so far known.

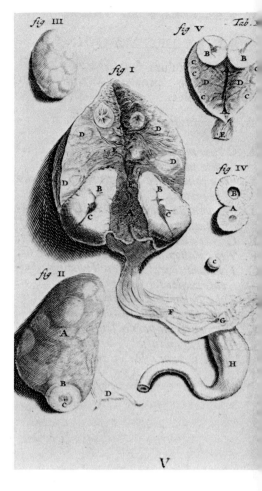

The reproductive organs of a cow from *Regner de Graaf: Opera Omnia* by Janus Leoniceus, 1677

Dr Margaret Sanger and her
sister, Ethel Byrne, in a U.S.
courtroom in 1916 during
Ethel Byrne's trial on the charge of
distributing obscene literature and
selling contraceptive devices.
In 1951 Dr Sanger arranged,
through the International Planned
Parenthood Federation, for the
first grant which started
Dr Pincus and others on their
fundamental investigation into
oral contraceptives.

For these reasons much of the research that went on during
the 1920s in universities throughout the world, and in the
laboratories of many pharmaceutical companies, has a slight
air of unreality. On the face of it, the work had few links with
humans and fewer still with human conception. If there was
any chance of the end-product being a chemical which could
bring about the temporary sterilization of humans, the fact
was scarcely mentioned.

The possibility was brought much nearer in 1929 when two
research workers, Allen and Corner, succeeded in isolating
a crystalline hormone from the *corpus lutea* of sows. Their
success, although they were not aware of the fact at the time,
was to be one of the key steps towards the Pill in its contemporary form. In 1929, any chance of the hormone being
available for more than research use seemed to be ruled out by
the difficulty, and therefore the expense, of making it. The
remains of many thousands of sows had to be obtained from
the slaughterhouses before even a few milligrams of the

One of Dr Marie Stopes's mobile clinics in the early 1920s

hormone could be manufactured. Years later, when it was found that it could be used to suppress ovulation in humans it still appeared to be impracticable for contraceptive purposes since a daily dose of no less than 300 milligrams was necessary. The structural formula of the substance was determined soon afterwards. It was found to consist of carbon, hydrogen and oxygen atoms linked together in rings to form a 'flat' molecule. Five years after Allen and Corner's discovery, the hormone was produced from an inert steroid of known composition, a success which threw a completely fresh light on its possible use.

By this time a number of other female hormones had been isolated, both in Europe and the United States, and it was becoming evident that some of them at least would be used medically. It was essential that biochemists throughout the world should agree to some measure of standardization and in 1935 a conference was called in London. The necessity for this is underlined by the fact that the same hormone was being isolated in the United States under the name of theelin, was being produced in Germany as progynon, in France as folliculin and as oestrin in England – an echo of the various names given to identical man-made plastics. So far, Allen and Corner's product had no name, although Allen had suggested progesterone without much enthusiasm. It was tried out by the British biochemist Sir Alan Parkes at a pre-conference party and met with success. 'The name progesterone may thus be said to have been born, if not conceived, in a place of refreshment near the Imperial Hotel in Russell Square where Willard Allen was staying,' Parkes later wrote.

Yet both progesterone and the other female hormones were still being considered almost exclusively as potential remedies for gynaecological disorders. Three barriers still barred the way to their contraceptive use. The first was the persisting difficulty of making them in industrial quantities rather than

Roots of *cabeza de negro*, the plant
that made the birth-control pill
possible, are chopped from the
ground by a labourer in the
Mexican jungle.

in the comparatively minute amounts required for specialized
medical use. The second was the psychological barrier which
still inhibited any serious suggestion that women might be
allowed to decide for themselves whether or not to conceive
and to implement their decision simply by making use of a
chemical. Until these two barriers had been removed it was
impossible to tackle the third; this was the disadvantage imposed by the fact that to be effective most of the newly
synthesized drugs had to be injected rather than taken
orally, a disadvantage which could be overcome only, if at all,
by large-scale and expensive experiments which pre-supposed
the acceptability of oral contraceptives.

The first of these barriers was removed by one of the most
colourful characters in the entire story of the Pill. He was
Professor Russell Marker, a Pennsylvania chemist who in 1940
turned his thoughts and energies to the problem of synthe-
sizing progesterone in quantity. The traditional stories of
folk-remedies to prevent conception had continued as a
shadowy background to all the work of the biochemists, and in
1941 biologists working for the US Bureau of Plant Industry
found evidence which confirmed at least one of them. For years
infusions of the herb *Lithospermum ruderale* had been used as a
contraceptive by Nevada Indians; tests with mice now
showed that something in the herb did indeed decrease
fertility.

Marker thought along similar lines but placed his faith in the
Mexican wild yam which he garnered in quantities in the
jungles of Veracruz. Finding American drug firms dis-
interested in his activities, he set up his own laboratory in
rented premises in Mexico City. Within three years he had
not only found how to synthesize progesterone from the
Mexican plant; he had also, and with comparatively primitive
equipment, made four pounds of progesterone – in an age
when it was normally considered in milligram quantities.
Legend claims that he then walked into a small pharmaceutical
firm in Mexico City, asked if they were interested in making
synthetic progesterone, and dumped down on the desk two
jars containing nearly £50,000 (approx. $125,000) worth of the
hormone.

Whether or not fiction has embroidered fact in this case,
one thing is certain: Marker's work removed one of the
barriers to production of a contraceptive pill. From the mid-
1940s onwards, progesterone could be produced with only
little more difficulty than the other female hormones known to
affect conception in a variety of so far not totally understood
ways.

Dr Gregor Pincus whose pioneer
research helped to make the use of
the pill a practical birth-control
method

The next step came in 1950. In fact it was two steps in one
since a definite decision to search for a revolutionary new
kind of contraceptive was immediately followed up by a
major experimental programme designed to find out whether
hormones could be made to do the trick. Chance seems to have
played its part, bringing to a major birth-control centre in
New York Dr Gregor Pincus, research head of the Foundation
for Experimental Biology in Shrewsbury, Mass. Pincus had
been giving progesterone orally to numbers of rats and
rabbits as part of an independent research programme not
directly connected with birth-control. In New York it was
emphasized to him that what was really required was a pill
which could be taken regularly and which would stop ovulation over a period of time. No ovulation meant no free egg to
be fertilized, and thus no conception. If a child was wanted,
stopping the pill allowed ovulation to start again.

Five years research was needed before Pincus produced a
pill, based on synthetic progesterone, which was orally
acceptable and appeared to work. Only after that, in 1956, did
he and two colleagues start the classic series of experiments
which transformed the pill, with its small 'p' of a laboratory
experiment, into the Pill which within a decade was being used
by millions of women throughout the world.

For his tests Pincus chose the West Indies, where over-
population was a major problem. One trial took place in
Port-au-Prince, Haiti: two others in Puerto Rico – one in
an agricultural area and one in the towns. Over a period of
many months, each of the housewives taking part in the test
was given 20 pills a month. The results were impressive: a
reduction in pregnancies of 96 per cent. The final paragraph of
Pincus's report noted that the data obtained 'would appear to
demonstrate the finding of a highly effective oral contraceptive, usable in several different localities in the West Indies. It
appears to be safe for use over a considerable number of
months, has no deleterious effects on the reproductive tract nor
on general health. Normal menstrual cycles occur regularly
in the subjects taking the medication. Attendant on its use are
certain side-reactions which appear to be in large measure
psychogenic, and which minimize with continued use.'

The contraceptive pill Enovid was made in 1956 by G. D.
Searle, the Chicago firm for whom Pincus worked as a consul-
tant. The firm was the only one which dared to market such a
product, and the climate of the times is indicated by the fact
that when the US Food and Drug Administration approved it
the following year it did so for treatment of menstrual difficulties and not as a contraceptive. But by 1960, when the

Giving a three-month injection of the contraceptive hormone, Depo Provera, in Thailand, 1972. Depo Provera has been approved for use as an injectable contraceptive in many countries although it is not available as such in the United Kingdom. An application for its use as a contraceptive is under consideration in the United States

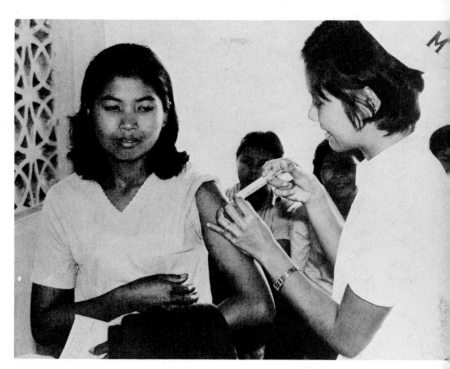

Administration openly acknowledged its contraceptive use, roughly 500,000 American women were already using it.

During the decade that followed the Puerto Rico experiment, both the Pill and public reaction to it underwent a transformation. The first effect was to encourage manufacturers other than Searle into making their own contraceptive pills. With the increased use that followed, there began to be built up a large mass of clinical experience; this in turn enabled the chemical make-up of the Pill to be so altered that it was more effective even though its side-effects were minimized. Side-effects have not been entirely removed. However, few unbiased observers who study the figures of the last sixteen years will deny that their dangers are considerably less than those of unwanted pregnancies.

One other fear has been removed by experience. In the nature of things, the greatest human and social benefits of a virtually fool-proof method of contraception would obviously spring from its use in under-developed countries, where education is minimal. Would women in such places use the Pill effectively? The answer has been 'yes' and is typified by one report from Ceylon: 'About 8–10 per cent never attended school,' says an account describing one group attending a contraception centre, 'but lack of education has not been a problem either in understanding the method or maintaining the record showing regular medication. One of the uneducated women of "low income" group said she will never forget to take her pill just as she will never forget to take her dinner, and accordingly to her "a pill a day after dinner, till the bottle is finished", is simple enough instruction for regular medication.' However, it is estimated that less than a tenth of Pill-users live in the developing countries. In some such countries the Pill is not part of the national family planning programme; when, moreover, it is only available on prescription it is in effect denied to most women, particularly those in rural areas where the doctor to patient ratio may be as high as 1:100,000.

There is no doubt about the sincerity of those who justify on ethical grounds a non-interventionist attitude towards over-population and an acceptance of the unhappiness brought by unwanted children. But the battle, determined though it may be, is a rear-guard one. With the easy availability of the Pill, the birthrate has begun to fall as dramatically in Catholic countries as in most others, and there can be little doubt about its gradual acceptance throughout the world. However, an important reason for the fall, at least in Latin-America, is believed to be an increase in illegal abortion.

But what comes next? One possibility is the injection of a hormone which would remain effective for three months, or perhaps for six. It is known that such injections have been used on many tens of thousands of women, although their use is not allowed in the United States by the F.D.A. or in Britain by the UK Committee of Safety on Drugs, as their toxic hazards have not yet been evaluated. It seems feasible, moreover, that research along these lines may be overtaken by something different. With the Pill, as with so many other 'inventions', advance in one field is aided by advance in another. In this case it is the plastics industry. At the end of the 1960s a young chemical engineer working for the Dow Corning Corporation mentioned to a doctor of the Population Council in New York's Rockefeller Center, that a new artificial rubber known as Silastic was being developed. One of its characteristics was that if certain substances were put in a Silastic capsule, they would diffuse out through the rubber over a very long period and, quite as important, at a constant rate. Would it not be possible, it was argued, for a capsule containing the chemicals of the Pill to be implanted under the skin in such a way that the diffusing chemicals would give contraceptive protection for five, ten or even fifteen years? The answer is not yet certain. But experiments made with female rabbits and monkeys have suggested that such capsules would not only work efficiently but could be removed at will and would produce no after-effects. Thus within the forseeable future control of conception will have been turned from a problem into a free choice unhindered even by the comparatively small inconveniences of today. Post-coital hormone preparations are also interesting, but will have little impact unless they are freely available throughout the world.

The next step, enabling a couple to ensure that a child will be of the chosen sex, has often been forecast, and more than one method of doing the trick has been proposed and investigated. So far, all have failed. But the problems of reproduction are being tackled on so many different fronts, the tools for research are increasing so quickly, that it would not be surprising if a way of handing this potentially disastrous choice to the human race suddenly appeared.

Yet not too pessimistic a view should be taken. The inventions and discoveries of the last hundred years which have been described and discussed are not only those which have in general had the greatest effect on human life – the reason why they have been chosen from among an immense number of candidates; in addition, each has posed its own threat and its own warnings of doom and disaster. In the case of photography it was perhaps nothing more than a fear that the art of painting might be driven from the face of the earth by the 'mechanism' of the camera – a phrase used by those unaware that in proper hands the camera could be an artist's instrument as readily as a paintbrush. The conquest of the air produced its warnings of the wrath to come, yet despite the undoubted menace of environmental pollution it seems likely that by the time manned flight celebrates its centenary the advantages will more than outweigh the disadvantages. Utilization of the electro-magnetic spectrum has produced its own challenges, particularly those provided by the threat of instant communication and its manipulation by small numbers of determined men. In their own way, synthetic materials were for long thought to be second-class products which might eventually drive out first-class natural materials – a threat whose lack of justification is only now beginning to be fully appreciated. Threats from the nuclear revolution need no stressing, although here, too, it looks as though mankind may already be turning the dangerous corner, so that the threat of nuclear extinction will become no more fearsome than the Darwinian threat of links with the apes that so terrified many Victorians.

There remains the genetic challenge presented by man's growing ability to control his own reproduction. It is a challenge which will probably be met as successfully as the others. It had better be.

Illustration acknowledgments

Note
Pictures credited Science
Museum are from the
Science Museum, London.
The diagrams on pages 41, 44,
and 121 are by Howard Dyke.
For assistance in preparation
of the diagrams we are
grateful to Kodak Ltd (41, 44)
and Thorn Consumer
Electronics Ltd (121).
Jacket: *Front* Telefunken.
Spine Daily Telegraph Colour
Library. *Back, above*
Science Museum; *below*
Courtaulds Ltd.
Endpapers: Mary Evans
Picture Library.

13 From *De radio astronomico et
geometrico liber*, 1545, by
Reiner Gemma Frisius.
Gernsheim Collection
16 Gernsheim Collection
17 Science Museum
18 From *John Leech's Pictures of
Life and Character, from the
Collection of 'Mr Punch'*,
1842–6
20 Science Museum
21 Science Museum
22 Science Museum
23 *Both* Science Museum
25 Science Museum
26 Science Museum
27 Science Museum
28 Gernsheim Collection
29 *Above* Scottish National
Portrait Gallery, by courtesy
of the Free Church of
Scotland College. Photo:
Tom Scott
Below National Galleries of
Scotland
31 Science Museum

32 Science Museum
36 Kodak Museum
37 From *The Horse, Vol. 8*,
1905–8, by Joan Wortley Axe
38 Science Museum
39 Science Museum
40 Kodak Museum
41 Photograph of tartan ribbon
Cavendish Laboratory,
Cambridge
42 Kodak Museum
43 Kodak Museum
44 Study for Le Chahut,
Courtauld Institute Galleries,
London
47 Polaroid (U.K.) Ltd
49 Institut de France, Paris
51 Courtesy Sotheby & Co.,
London
52 *Left* Radio Times Hulton
Picture Library
Right Bibliothèque Nationale,
Paris. Photo: Giraudon
54 *Above* Royal Aeronautical
Society. Photo: Derrick Witty
Below Science Museum.
Photo: Derrick Witty
55 Flight International
56 Science Museum
57 Science Museum
58 Vickers Ltd
61 Science Museum
62 Library of Congress
64 Science Museum
68 Science Museum
69 *Above* Popperfoto
Below Sport and General Press
Agency Ltd
70 Hawker Siddeley Aviation Ltd
73 Office National d'Études et de
Recherches Aérospatiales
74 Courtesy John Taylor
76 Imperial War Museum
78 United Press International

80 *Above* Vickers Ltd
Below Flight International
83 *Above* Vickers Ltd
Below Vickers Ltd
86 United Press International
88 Rolls-Royce (1971) Ltd
90 Camera Press
92 Royal Institution, London.
Photo: R. B. Fleming
94 Deutsches Museum, Munich
98 Science Museum
99 The Marconi Company Ltd
100 The Marconi Company Ltd
104 *Left* Deutsches Museum,
Munich
105 *Right* The Marconi Company
Ltd
108 Imperial War Museum
109 Imperial War Museum
111 The Royal Radar
Establishment, Malvern
113 Bell Telephone Laboratories,
New Jersey
115 Bell Telephone Laboratories,
New Jersey
116 Science Museum
119 Bell Telephone Laboratories,
New Jersey
123 Daily Telegraph Colour
Library
125 Science Museum
127 Science Museum
128 *Both* Ideal Home Magazine
Photos: Clifford Jones
129 The Plastics Institute, London
130 The Albany Billiard Ball Co.,
New York
133 Imperial War Museum
134 Bakelite Xylonite Ltd
138 *Above* Du Pont Company
(U.K.) Ltd
Right Courtaulds Ltd
141 E. I. du Pont de Nemours &
Co.

Index